Globalizing Race

FLASHPOINTS

The FlashPoints series is devoted to books that consider literature beyond strictly national and disciplinary frameworks, and that are distinguished both by their historical grounding and by their theoretical and conceptual strength. Our books engage theory without losing touch with history and work historically without falling into uncritical positivism. FlashPoints aims for a broad audience within the humanities and the social sciences concerned with moments of cultural emergence and transformation. In a Benjaminian mode, FlashPoints is interested in how literature contributes to forming new constellations of culture and history and in how such formations function critically and politically in the present. Series titles are available online at http://escholarship.org/uc/flashpoints.

A complete list of titles begins on page 369.

Globalizing Race

Antisemitism and Empire in French and European Culture

Dorian Bell

NORTHWESTERN UNIVERSITY PRESS | EVANSTON, ILLINOIS

the modern language initiative

THIS BOOK IS MADE POSSIBLE BY A COLLABORATIVE GRANT FROM THE ANDREW W. MELLON FOUNDATION.

Northwestern University Press
www.nupress.northwestern.edu

Printed in the United States of America

10 9 8 7 6 5 4 3 2 1

Library of Congress Cataloging-in-Publication Data

Names: Bell, Dorian, author.
Title: Globalizing race : anti-Semitism and empire in French and European culture / Dorian Bell.
Other titles: FlashPoints (Evanston, Ill.)
Description: Evanston, Illinois : Northwestern University Press, 2018. | Series: FlashPoints
Identifiers: LCCN 2017022776 | ISBN 9780810136892 (cloth : alk. paper) | ISBN 9780810136885 (pbk. : alk. paper) | ISBN 9780810136908 (e-book)
Subjects: LCSH: Antisemitism—France—History—19th century. | Antisemitism—France—History—20th century. | Antisemitism—Political aspects—France. | France—Ethnic relations.
Classification: LCC DS146.F8 B35 2018 | DDC 305.8924044--dc23
LC record available at https://lccn.loc.gov/2017022776

For my parents, David and Martine

Contents

Globalizing Race

Introduction

Between Relationality and Scalarity

Over a tense week and a half in March 2012, three related gun attacks in the southern French cities of Toulouse and Montauban killed seven people. Among the dead were four Jews: a religious studies teacher, his two young sons, and an eight-year-old girl, all shot near the gates of the Jewish Ozar Hatorah day school in Toulouse. The three others were French paratroopers of North African descent; a fourth paratrooper who was injured but survived was Guadeloupian. As the world looked on in alarm, and with the mysterious killer or killers still at large, speculation mounted that neo-Nazis were to blame. Reports circulated that the dead paratroopers belonged to a regiment from which three other soldiers had been dismissed in 2008 when a photograph surfaced of them giving a Nazi salute in front of a swastika-adorned flag.[1] Here, it seemed, might be a disturbing eruption of an eternal European xenophobia stoked of late by social and economic unrest.

The truth proved different. When French authorities caught up to the gunman, Mohammed Merah—a twenty-three-year-old French and Algerian citizen raised in Toulouse—it became clear that Merah had, in fact, singled out Jews for attack. But of course he was no neo-Nazi. In communications with the press and police before and during the extended stand-off at his apartment that resulted in his death, Merah claimed ties to Al-Qaeda and called the shootings a retaliation against the enemies of Islam. The paratroopers, he boasted, were shot for their participation in NATO's war against the Taliban in Afghanistan. That they were Muslims and soldiers of color seems to have been incidental. That the Ozar Hatorah school victims were Jewish, however, was very much the point. These Merah executed in reprisal for, as he put it to police, "all the children who are killed" by Israeli forces. By killing French Jews, he was killing "the same Jews who kill . . . my little brothers and sisters in Palestine."[2]

Merah's rampage raised a familiar tandem of specters. The first is the historical brand of antisemitism evoked by the photograph of three shaven-headed young men pledging allegiance to Hitler. Early eyewitnesses described the gunman as tattooed, scarred, and heavyset, terms better suited to the jackbooted race warrior easily summoned up by the collective European consciousness than to the slight and unmarked Merah.[3] This shared continental anxiety helps account for how, even before the killer had been apprehended and his motives ascertained, French president Nicolas Sarkozy could opine that the antisemitic nature of the crime was "obvious."[4] In post-Holocaust Europe, every murder of a Jew is understandably suspect.

The Merah case, however, confirmed that the same is true of postcolonial Europe. In his conflation of every Jew, everywhere with the state of Israel, and in his affinity for a militant Islam preoccupied with existential Jewish evil, Merah incarnates what some have called the "new antisemitism": namely, an antisemitism that takes Israel and Zionism as its bêtes noires and that substitutes the discredited nineteenth-century-era notion of the Jew as cosmic racial other with the more contemporarily palatable notion of the Jewish state as cosmic political foe.[5] The oft-cited mainspring of the new antisemitism is an ongoing Israeli-Palestinian conflict responsible for engendering anti-Israeli passions and an attendant antisemitism among certain constituencies, like Muslims, sympathetic to the Palestinian cause. In France, whose population counts the most Muslims and Jews of any European country, and where Muslim immigrants live alongside Sephardic Jews likewise arrived from former African colonies, these tensions raised by the Israeli-Palestinian conflict are especially and uniquely permeated by the postcolonial fact.

Vexed though such questions obviously remain, it would seem uncontroversial enough to conclude from current circumstances that the histories of antisemitism and empire are entwined. A premise of this book, however, is that to do so is at once justified and risky. Justified, because French antisemitism and imperialism indeed co-evolved, I will argue, in important ways dating to the late nineteenth-century era of racial classification, hierarchization, and domination from which they both emerged as modern ideologies. Risky, because the postwar, postcolonial context within which antisemitism and empire are so often considered in tandem has a tendency immediately to foreshorten our perspective on their longer shared history—one that, furthermore, produced reflexive assumptions framing European debates about race and difference now. Some of those same assumptions threaten to distort our understanding of how antisemitism and empire shaped each other from the outset. So if this is primarily a book about the first few decades of the shared modern history in question, it is also a book about how antisemitic (and anti-antisemitic) narratives forged in the crucible of empire survive in contemporary approaches both to Europe's postwar, postcolonial condition and to its imperial, antisemitic past. The analytical note I mean to sound remains no less urgent for being cautious. In May 2014 a French national of Algerian descent opened fire on and killed two Israelis, one Frenchwoman, and one Belgian at the Jewish Museum of Belgium in Brussels. Some of the pro-Palestinian rallies in France over Israel's July 2014 Gaza Strip offensive devolved into attacks on Jewish synagogues and shops. And the January 2015 shooting at the Parisian headquarters of the satirical weekly newspaper *Charlie Hebdo*, which riveted the world's attention on yet another fundamentalist Islamic attack in France, was followed two days later by the murder of four Jewish hostages at the Hypercacher kosher market on the outskirts of Paris. Such events, and the reactions to them, are defining what it means to be European in the twenty-first century.

In what manner does the interaction between antisemitism and empire over a century ago still subtly inflect analyses of these and related phenomena? My answers roughly separate into two motifs that recur throughout the book and that I use now to organize this introduction. The first has to do with how the very lenses through which postcolonial antisemitism is often examined—from basic historical suppositions to sophisticated theoretical frameworks—are themselves sometimes tinged with nineteenth-century discourses about Jews and empire. The results are nontrivial. Seeking to dispel the notion of an intrinsic Muslim antisemitism, for instance, those in France who historicize that antisemitism into a product of colonial domination sometimes inadvertently echo colonial-era constructs about internecine hatred between North African Muslims and Jews. Such constructs persist in the abiding fiction of what I call the Crémieux myth, a phenomenon I will want briefly to take up below for what it reveals about the ongoing pertinence and stakes of the nineteenth-century discourses documented in the book.

Consider as well the seminal reflection on the relationship between antisemitism and empire offered by Hannah Arendt in *The Origins of Totalitarianism* (1951). Critics have charged that Arendt herself did not prove entirely immune to the imperialist (or even antisemitic) prejudices she so forcefully dissected. But as I suggest in Chapter 1, for Arendt to have linked imperialism and antisemitism in the first place is itself an artifact of sorts, since her analytic frame constitutes an implicit rejoinder—and so remains structurally indebted—to the nineteenth-century topos of the colonially conspiring Jew. I propose something similar when in Chapter 4 I trace Max Horkheimer and Theodor Adorno's indebtedness, for the detailed theory of antisemitism developed in their *Dialectic of Enlightenment* (1947), to a nineteenth-century degeneration theory so notoriously wielded against Jews and the colonized alike.

This is not to throw the baby out with the bathwater; Arendt, it will become clear, still furnishes important guideposts, as do her contemporaries in the Frankfurt School. Nor can I ignore my own potential entanglement in past discourses. I have tried to avoid doing something like what I believe Arendt did when, in pointedly attributing the rise of modern European antisemitism to the Jews' absence from imperial expansion, she let old narratives about the Jews' complicity in empire dictate the terms of her argument. That is to say, she assumed a relationship between antisemitism and imperialism based at least in part on previous antisemitic notions about the Jews' role in the European imperial project. I would be committing a second-order version of this error simply to assume, necessarily working as I am in Arendt's shadow, a historical relationship between the two phenomena based solely on her example. If, then, I am arguing that the rise of empire shaped the rise of modern antisemitism—a central claim of the book—it is not just because Arendt suggested the possibility, or just because political antisemites once had spurious things to say about Jewish colonial involvement. It is, rather, because a careful examination of nineteenth-century French antisemitic newspapers, novels, tracts, poems, and related ephemera convinced me that modern antisemitism simply would have developed differently had its purveyors not honed their arguments against the rapidly expanding backdrop of empire.

Crucially, the proposition I am advancing at once exceeds and contains the associated notion of a co-constitutive relationship between antisemitism and colonial racism. Such a relationship appeared especially poignant after World War II, when observers from Arendt to Aimé Césaire and W. E. B. Du Bois concluded that the European racism practiced in Africa and elsewhere had contributed to antisemitism's exterminationist turn on the continent. European antisemitism has, conversely, also been cited as a continental precursor to and model for racism directed outward against imperial subalterns overseas. I will elaborate on these two symmetrical ideas momentarily. Let me only pair them now, to denote the basic conceptual and methodological assumption toward which they point, under the heading of what David Theo Goldberg calls "racial relationality."[6] By this he means to convey how racializing and racist discourses and practices everywhere draw on, reinforce, and otherwise interact with each other across space and time. It is instructive, I think, that of the handful of theorists Goldberg credits for having first conceptualized race in these relational terms, so many—Arendt, Du Bois, Frantz Fanon, Albert Memmi, Jean-Paul Sartre—came to their relational outlook at least in part by considering together the fate of Europe's Jews and of racialized subalterns elsewhere. Positing connectivities between antisemitism and colonial racism thus furnished a key starting point, even *the* starting point, for the relational method.

That this first analytical step grew, as Michael Rothberg reminds us, out of the conjuncture between genocidal war in Europe and the first great stirrings of decolonization remains of vital importance.[7] To consider racisms mutually and relationally constitutive is to expand the basic insight offered by Césaire, Fanon, and other architects of decolonization when they identified in the Holocaust not only a homologue of colonial racism but also its result. Reconsiderations of antisemitism have, in turn, become central to the ever-widening relational conversation about how different racisms previously circulated and acted on one another between metropole and colony. New scholarship reveals thorough enough colonial-era convergences, for example, between negative German representations of black Africans and Jews to warrant describing racism in the colonies as having "realized for 'natives' much of what contemporary racial anti-Semites envisioned for Jews back in Germany."[8] Where for Arendt and others German racism emerged sufficiently envenomed and programmatic from the colonial encounter to engender the Holocaust, this latest wrinkle in the Arendtian "continuity thesis" suggests that the bureaucratic framework for colonial racism was already profoundly anticipated in, and arguably even shaped by, unsuccessful attacks on German Jewish rights of the kind formalized by the 1880 Antisemites' Petition.[9] Black Africans, goes the thinking, received a treatment planned by Germans for Jews, who in turn would go on to be treated like Africans.

Yet in mapping the circulations produced as racisms have flowed, combined, and recombined across geographies and histories, we must also take care not always to read the outcome—the infliction on one racialized population of logics and technologies devised against or in relation to another—back into the initial stages of the circulatory process. Here I arrive at the second motif promised above. The first, recall, is that antisemitism and empire's historical intertwinement has naturalized certain distorting optics through which we contemplate their shared present-day legacy. The second is that their spectacular eventual conjoining in the Holocaust has the retroactive effect of making them seem only ever to have interacted as manifestations of racism. Commentators sometimes warn against taking the Holocaust as an endpoint and so granting previous antisemitism too teleological a historical consistency.[10] One might similarly locate in Holocaust teleology a reason why, as I began suggesting earlier, a racial relationality conceptualized from a postwar, postcolonial perspective risks seeing nothing else in the co-evolution of antisemitism and empire than "one racism chasing another" toward a final genocidal destination.[11] Better in addition to remember, with Étienne Balibar, that antisemitism and "colonial racism . . . have a joint descent which reacts back upon our analysis of their earlier forms."[12] In other words, we cannot assume a conceptually steady relationship between the two phenomena over time, even if we understand some relationship to have long existed. Rather, we must allow for the more disjunctive possibility that one moment of the relationship can be influenced, however unexpectedly, by a potentially very different such moment at a different historical point.

Balibar gives as an example the present-day dynamic between antisemitism and a current European xenophobia descended in part from colonial racism. That dynamic is inflected by the closeness of the relationship, in Nazism, between antisemitism and colonial racism, though not in a way similarly conjoining antisemitism and racism now. In fact, argues Balibar, it is the very closeness of the association between Nazi racism and antisemitism that today's xenophobes use as an "alibi" against accusations of racism, since one's prejudice would ostensibly need to rise to genocidally antisemitic proportions to qualify as properly racist. And while such a move also appears to uncouple xenophobia from antisemitism, he concludes, it actually attaches them anew, insofar as antisemitism now almost necessarily co-occurs with racist xenophobia as "the metaphorical expression" of the unavowed racist's unconfessed "desire for extermination."[13] I would add, however, that for Balibar even to frame the foregoing relationship in terms of colonial racism is to reinforce the ex post facto effect I described above, whereby the self-evidently racist nature of empire and antisemitism immediately forecloses other perspectives from which to approach their long co-constitution. Those perspectives matter too. If I will be at pains, therefore, to consider the history of antisemitism within the context of imperial expansion more generally, rather than in exclusive relation to colonial racism, it is because the nature itself of empire interrelated with antisemitism in ways not always at first completely reducible to their shared quality as racist systems.

European antisemites certainly often gravitated toward empire for what the racialized subalterns there could furnish them discursively, something I consider in Chapter 2 by examining how nineteenth-century French political antisemitism capitalized on France's colonization of indigenous North African Jews. Yet as I offer in Chapter 4, antisemites were also influenced by empire when they looked abroad for solutions to metaphysical problems seemingly intractable within the metropole alone. Here empire served primarily to furnish a space and scale apart. Rather than functioning solely, then, as a neutrally given context in which Europe's Jewish others might be brought into racial relation with its other others, empire also constituted a feature—and even constructed result—of what I want to call *racial scalarity*: namely, the tendency of racializing logics to change scales in an effort to resolve contradictions internal to the logics themselves. David Harvey has written of the "spatial fix" attempted when capitalism's interior conflicts and crises drove it necessarily, imperially afield in the search for new markets.[14] So, too, I will be arguing, did metropolitan antisemites seek spatial fixes abroad when mounting ideological inconsistencies left them grasping for answers at home.

I borrow here from the rich tradition in Marxist and critical geography of contemplating space as something produced rather than given, constructed instead of natural. That I do so using the idiom of scale has to do with the role of modern antisemitism in making it possible to toggle between the governing fictions of nation and empire, something I will return to below. Suffice it now to say that I mean to augment, not supplant, the relational approach to race. Sophisticated recent work by Jonathan Boyarin, Gil Anidjar, and others has made it more possible and necessary than ever to understand the "Jewish question" as a set of discourses historically intent on relating Jewish difference to, and often triangulating it across, other shifting sites of difference—Muslims, for instance, or American Indians—about which Europeans likewise obsessed.[15] But one must not be tempted into assuming that the resulting relationalities always found Europeans using the more locally familiar category of Jewishness "as a means of explicating," in Tudor Parfitt's words, those "unknown or little-known peoples of wildly differing characteristics" encountered elsewhere.[16] Neither is it any longer viable to conceive space only as an absolute container detached from and predating the grids of relation developing within. Destabilizing uncertainties introduced by representations of Jewishness at home could also shift European gazes elsewhere to begin with. Put another way, racial scalarity sometimes enabled the conditions under which racial relationality subsequently obtained. Or more concisely yet: it was as possible for race to produce space as for space to mediate race. Claire Jean Kim's suggestion in her pioneering essay on racial triangulation that "racialization processes are mutually constitutive of one another" across "more than one scale at a time" should therefore not just be taken as an encouragement to examine, as I think she means, how race and racism move relationally among existing scales. It also invites us to pose the question of how race has subtended the development of scale itself.[17]

By posing that question now, I intend at a broad level to use what Edward Soja has called the "spatial turn" in social theory to complicate, nuance, and refine how theories of race think the relational method.[18] More specifically, the effort finds me joining the colonial turn in approaches to antisemitism. Only relatively recently have scholars begun paying concerted attention to the material and ideological causeways between European antisemitism and imperialism. Much of the work has occurred in German studies, where Arendt's continuity thesis continues to reverberate in renewed efforts to demonstrate how German colonialism shaped and reflected antisemitism before and during the Holocaust.[19] From the moment we agree, however, with Ivan Kalmar and Derek Penslar that "it is worth considering if the development of what became known as 'imperialism' . . . was in some ways linked with the growing agitation against Jews," our attention must also necessarily turn to France, where in the late nineteenth century the rise of modern antisemitism and empire proved especially concomitant.[20] France's rapid-fire imperial expansions into Tunisia, Tonkin, and Madagascar in the 1880s inaugurated a period of near-constant warfare during which repeated French military expeditions fought protracted battles around the world, exacting an incalculable human toll on peoples from Africa to the Far East. Against this unprecedented backdrop of global warfare, French antisemites in the metropole began agitating for an equally unprecedented war against Jewry. Édouard Drumont's 1886 *La France juive* (*Jewish France*), a best seller, launched antisemitism in France as a bonafide ideological and political movement. Complete with its own newspapers, journalists, political organizations, candidates, and street-level enforcers, the movement stirred antisemitic hatred for a decade and a half. That hatred erupted most forcefully in the Dreyfus Affair, during whose 1898 high point dozens of violent antisemitic riots broke out across France.[21] The same year, France's near-war with Britain over Egypt brought imperial passions to a boil and definitively rallied French sentiment for empire.[22] France's late century "antisemitic moment," as it has been called, thus overlapped with the fevered dawn of high imperialism.[23] Yet to date, limited scholarship exists on metropolitan French antisemites' nineteenth-century articulation of the imperial question with the Jewish question. Though signs indicate that this might be changing, a significant road remains ahead, one down which I hope to make some progress in this book.[24]

It is in France, wrote Arendt, that the antisemitism sweeping across Europe in the second half of the nineteenth century reached its "climax."[25] And it is in France that a twenty-first-century recrudescence of antisemitic attacks has taken particularly unnerving form. I want to pause briefly now to revisit these contemporary events, for two reasons. One is to illustrate right away the previously suggested persistence of misleading optics inherited from the past. The other is to begin thinking in different ways about the historical interconnection of racial relationality with racial scalarity. Muslim antisemitism lends itself obviously enough to the racialization of Muslims in terms of what they are understood to think about Jews. Less obvious is the longer antisemitic history of this relationality, which will become clear in the next section. And less obvious still is how, as I suggest further on, the present-day relationality was also prepared long ago by a racial scalarity pitting anti-antisemites against antisemitic foils.

ANTISEMITISM "OLD" AND "NEW": THE FRENCH CASE RECONSIDERED

In recent years French intellectuals like Alain Finkielkraut and Pierre-André Taguieff have not only popularized the idea of a new antisemitism but also proposed that the new antisemitism represents the "Islamization" of anti-Jewish hatred.[26] The center of European Islam, France offers a continental foothold to frustrations and prejudices inflamed in the global Muslim community by Palestinian suffering. And after North African Jewry's exodus in the era of decolonization and Arab-Israeli warfare, Maghrebi Muslims and Jews now coexist mainly on French soil. The stage appears set by history for the Middle Eastern dispute to find a demographic echo in the West.

Or at least, this seems the case if one accepts the media-driven impression of a convergence in the new French antisemitism between two imports: that of an ideological Islamic antisemitism forged abroad and that of a historical animus between Muslims and Jews in what once comprised French North Africa. Merah, a French Algerian radicalized during trips to Afghanistan and Pakistan, would appear situated at just such an intersection between the global ripple effects of the Israeli-Palestinian conflict and the vicissitudes of France's colonial legacy. A July 2012 investigation into antisemitism in the center-left *Nouvel Observateur*, the highest-circulation French newsmagazine, juxtaposes a lead article about "the new antisemitism" exemplified by Merah with a companion piece about the putative history of Muslims and Jews as *frères ennemis* ("enemy brothers") that locates in France's nineteenth-century colonization of Algeria a "first shock" in the otherwise relatively historically stable relations between North African Muslims and Jews.[27] The intimation is clear: with the two communities reunited in France, and with radical Islam stoking a Muslim antisemitism first incited in the colonial era, the North African shock has come home to roost.

Let us examine where the *Nouvel Observateur*'s mainstream report falls in the current French polemic about antisemitism and where that polemic itself stands. Befitting its moderate editorial tone, the magazine stakes out a middle ground between ratifying the existence of a new antisemitism and heeding the rejoinder by some that the new antisemitism—so often imputed, explicitly or implicitly, to French Muslims—loses some of its "newness" when considered in the historical context of colonial domination. If, as Nicolas Weill has cautioned, the increased focus on Muslim antisemitism too blithely "exteriorizes" the problem by uncoupling it from France's homegrown antisemitic tradition, the ascription to Muslim antisemitism of colonial origins reinteriorizes that antisemitism within a larger framework of European culpability.[28] But that culpability remains debated. Is the new antisemitism partially symptomatic of the Republic's failure to integrate its postcolonial African and Muslim minorities, a failure whose reversal would presumably curb antisemitism among the disenfranchised by easing the "legitimate frustration" caused by socioeconomic marginalization?[29] Or does this attitude amount, as Taguieff would have it, to the "pious sociologization" of an antisemitism whose Islamic underpinnings require direct and forceful confrontation?[30]

These approaches, roughly consonant with left-leaning and right-leaning orthodoxies, differ in their respective biases. One side considers antisemitism the handmaiden of structural inequality; the other emphasizes the new antisemitism's association with a radical Islam alien to French republican values. Yet the two nevertheless share an underlying premise. Irrespective of their ideological orientation, commentators reliably assume that today's young, antisemitic Muslims have inherited antagonisms from the past. In France, this past is a colonial past. Thus can Taguieff claim that in outbursts by French Muslim avatars of the new antisemitism, Algeria's war of independence—fueled as it was by Islamic nationalism—is being "replayed on French soil."[31] Thus, too, from a perspective friendlier to Muslims, can the sociologist Nacira Guénif-Souilamas identify in contemporary Muslim antisemitism repercussions dating to the 1870 Crémieux decree, which collectively naturalized all Algerian Jews (but not Muslims) and "maybe . . . made daily interactions [between Algerian Muslims and Jews] worse, since it may have been difficult for Muslim natives to understand how this proximate subaltern had become the equal of the colonist."[32]

Such invocations of colonial discord in relation to present-day Muslim antisemitism work to varying ends. Locating a distant source of the new antisemitism in the Crémieux decree traces responsibility for modern Muslim anti-Jewish resentment to French intervention. Accustomed to regarding their Jewish countrymen as a protected but inferior class of non-Muslims (*dhimmi*) tolerated under Islamic law, Algerian Muslims suffered, under this interpretation, a collective and lasting trauma when the colonial power suddenly elevated Algeria's 35,000 Jews above the second-class status accorded Muslims under the colonial *indigénat* legal code. The implication is that the new antisemitism is as much a French creation as a Muslim one, at least in France. But the Crémieux decree has also been referenced to underscore the ostensibly foreign, "colonial" nature of a Muslim antisemitism extrinsic to France because fashioned in another time and place. The sociologist and philosopher Shmuel Trigano, for instance, pointedly contrasts the antisemitism of an only recently decolonized French Muslim population with Algerian Jews' longstanding, nineteenth-century embrace of French citizenship, the better to situate that antisemitism outside a historical republican march toward progress.[33]

Whatever the intent—to identify in Muslim antisemitism a by-product of French domination or to exteriorize the problem into something profoundly un-French—analyses like these hypothesize an antisemitism bequeathed to France's Muslims by their subaltern past. Muslim antisemitism thus becomes an effect of colonial history, a nucleus of prejudice snowballing through time as the geopolitical fortunes of Muslims and Jews have evolved. Lost in the conversation, however, is the opposite possibility: namely, that the way we understand colonial history is itself sometimes the effect of past antisemitism.

Here again, the Crémieux decree represents a signal event. The *Nouvel Observateur* story solemnly relates that the decree provoked a definitive "rupture" between Jews and Muslims in Algeria, and in a sense this is true.[34] Though historians have recently downplayed the overnight effects of collective naturalization on Algerian Jews, arguing that it codified and accelerated a French acculturation already decades underway, the decree certainly marks a watershed in the turn of North African Jewry toward the West and away from Islam.[35] But within the presumed telos of ever-increasing enmity between *frères ennemis*, the rhetoric of rupture also echoes an old commonplace about the decree's noxious influence on Muslim-Jewish relations. Threatened and angered by the enfranchisement of 35,000 indigenous Algerian Jews, Algerian colonists quickly blamed the Crémieux decree for the 1871 Muslim tribal insurrection that erupted across Algeria after the Second Empire's 1870 collapse during the Franco-Prussian War. Joining them were French officers upset with France's new republican government for imposing civil administration on a colony over which the military had previously enjoyed free reign. Together, these colonial malcontents insisted that tribal Muslim leaders, incensed at their newfound legal subordination to Jews and dismayed that their contributions against the Prussians had gone unrewarded, were left no other honorable choice than to rebel.[36]

The narrative proved seductive to French antisemites busy launching the popular and political antisemitic movement that roiled France in the 1880s and 1890s. Drumont, the movement's patron saint, dedicated one of the six sections in his 1886 antisemitic broadside *La France juive* to denouncing the Crémieux decree. Calling the decree a perfidious attempt by French Jews to bolster their numbers at the country's expense, Drumont celebrated the "noble and loyal" Kabyle leader Mohammed el-Haj el-Mokrani for dying as a "hero" at the helm of the 1871 rebellion, and abrogation of the decree would become a favorite antisemitic rallying cry in France and Algeria for years to come.[37]

Historians have since discredited the thesis that the Crémieux decree sparked the 1871 insurrection. The uprising's leaders almost never included the naturalization of Algerian Jews among their complaints, and Muslims do not seem to have envied their Jewish neighbors' newfound citizenship. A number of other motives—including the opportunity presented by France's wartime disarray and tribal frustration with the new civilian administration—better explain the timing of the revolt.[38] Yet the Crémieux myth of Muslim resentment against Jews, so convenient to the antisemitic agitators who propagated it, still retains currency.[39] One imagines that this is in part because it provides flexible fodder in the culture wars over contemporary French Muslim antisemitism. Those eager to exteriorize the new antisemitism can invoke the decree, and the wedge it supposedly drove between Jewish citizens and Muslim subalterns, to cast Muslims in the alien role of antimoderns historically at odds with the Republic. Those more inclined to seek explanations for Muslim antisemitism in social inequity can, for their part, cite the decree as an early wound inflicted by the Republic on its Muslim charges.

So understood, the tenacity of the Crémieux myth suggests the extent to which debates about the new antisemitism paradoxically reproduce terms established long ago by antisemites themselves. As much of a given as friction between Muslim and Jewish *frères ennemis* may now appear in France, especially after mass Sephardi emigrations from North Africa in the 1950s and 1960s, the cultural seeds for thinking that intimate hostility were sown by late nineteenth-century racial ideologues intent on making Algerian Muslims' imagined uprising against Jews a model for antisemitic convulsions on the continent. This is not to rule out that contemporary Muslim antisemitism has nineteenth-century colonial antecedents, or twentieth-century ones for that matter. But it behooves us to consider such antecedents from the perspective of what Ian Hacking, borrowing a term from Foucault, calls historical ontology—that is, an appreciation for how social phenomena are constituted over time by a complex, reciprocal interaction between actual behaviors and the categories of thought simultaneously naming those behaviors into existence.[40] Just as the traditional relegation of Jews by Islam to subordinate *dhimmi* status anchored the Crémieux myth of Muslim anti-Jewish hatred in some semblance of social reality, continued references to that alleged hatred have worked, in the other direction, to produce it for real.[41] Consider Mokrani's brother and successor Bou Mezrag, who recalled submitting the Crémieux decree to his peers as grounds for rebellion after receiving anonymous letters from antisemitic European colonists warning him against Jewish designs.[42] Or fast-forward to the possibility, advanced by Guénif-Souilamas in a 2004 editorial, that certain young French Muslims today exhibit antisemitism precisely because it is expected of them, and that doing so equates to a consciously self-destructive "performance" of their predestined social role.[43]

Interdependent at any given moment, Muslim antisemitism and its construction also act on each other from across historical time. Students of contemporary Muslim antisemitism have proposed that, in lashing out against Jews, Muslims are sometimes targeting a fellow minority perceived to have more successfully integrated into French society.[44] This choice of Jews by French Muslims as a totem for their postcolonial disaffection retroactively legitimizes the Crémieux myth of Muslim envy and frustration over Algerian Jews' 1870 enfranchisement by the colonizing power. The same myth, in turn, reinforces an a priori tendency among certain observers to read into current Muslim antisemitism the envious disappointment of the spurned. It is easy, from French commentators' generally hegemonic republican perspective, to situate Muslim antisemitism within a narrative of troubled but gradual Muslim assimilation to the Republic, much as it is easy to imagine Muslim antisemitism as a sort of cultural content similarly passed down through time. It is comparatively difficult, though, to appreciate how alongside such apparently tangible contents subsist habits of mind for thinking those contents, habits of mind that are likewise descended from the colonial past and that, subtly but surely, impose categories inherited from the old antisemitism on today's understanding of the new.

Finkielkraut, remarking on a 2003 conference about antisemitism titled "Old Demons, New Debates," ironizes that a better title might have been "New Demons, Old Frameworks."[45] His point is that traditional ways of approaching antisemitism are grievously unsuited to what antisemitism has become. And yet, so far at least, there is something traditional still in the new analytic framework emerging to describe the new antisemitism. Skeptics of the idea wonder if the attribution of novelty unfairly stigmatizes the actors held responsible, in particular Muslims.[46] A subtler question is this: Will resilient narratives linking France's Jewish and Muslim others, narratives bound up in an antisemitic and colonial past, make it possible now to racialize Muslims in relation to the Jews for whom they putatively harbor an intrinsic, historical, and violent hatred? The connectivities at hand serve as a sharp reminder of how relationality can simultaneously play out across multiple geographies and temporalities. French Muslims risk racialization with respect to their fellow Jewish citizens. They are potentially racialized, too, in regard not only to Muslim counterparts outside of France but also to the already relational dynamic linking those foreign populations of Muslims with equally different populations of Jews. And all of these contemporary relationalities are related along a temporal axis to what supposedly transpired, for instance, between Muslims and Jews after the Crémieux decree or after its revocation by Vichy in 1940.[47] Old demons do linger—just not always only where we have come to expect.

RACIAL SCALARITY

The great and painful irony here hardly needs underscoring. How is it that accounts of Muslim antisemitic unrest peddled by antisemites in the late nineteenth century are now taken for granted by those campaigning fervently *against* antisemitism? One can certainly point, as a matter of relationality, to the protean robustness of racializations that survive transmission across even the most divergent contexts to take root, adapt, and flourish anew. But as I argued above, it is also sometimes necessary to think in terms of racial scalarity to understand the conditions under which relationality occurs and spreads. In Chapter 5 I will be proposing that, already in the nineteenth century, conflicts internal to the metropole were generating the conditions of possibility for the notion of subaltern antisemitism to go from a tool developed by nationalist antisemites to a device wielded from contrasting perspectives like republicanism or Europeanism. The conceptual terrain on which the shift occurred was scale: representing antisemites as reactionaries blinkered by their resolutely nationalist outlook, their ideological opponents endeavored to show how, at the scale of empire, the Jewish question diminished in importance. But thereafter, I argue, would the structure be increasingly in place for the colonized to assume the intolerant role played by antisemites at the scale of the metropole. The same trope of Muslim antisemitism could now for instance function, within a different set of ideological parameters entirely, to legitimize a "civilizing" republican universalism against which French antisemites had previously understood Muslims rightfully to rebel.

I look ahead to this example as a way of introducing two key preliminary points, one brief and one longer. The first, more historical point is that the interrelation between French antisemitism and imperialism did not just function in one direction to shape the modern antisemitic narrative against Jews. As should be clear now, antisemitic topoi carved from the material of empire also acted in the other direction to influence the trajectory of imperialism itself, up to and including that imperialism's current postcolonial legacy. This is another of the basic conclusions I want to draw in the book.

The second, more conceptual point is that the aggressive nationalism so closely correlated with modern antisemitism offers a useful point of entry into understanding how scale mattered critically to debates about race in the era of imperial expansion and consolidation. Earlier I described racial scalarity as reminiscent of the "spatial fix" effected when capital streamed outward from Europe in necessary response to contradictions rending it from the inside. But the spatial fix, in this sense, only occurred as European capital expanded into a finite, planetary-bound amount of absolute geographic space—or, to use Harvey's formulation, as it continued to be possible for capital to be "attracted to some open frontier."[48] Once no real frontiers were left, something the geographer Neil Smith dates to the European powers' partitioning of Africa in the 1880s, capital turned from acquiring raw, absolute space to producing differential spaces within a single consolidated world system.[49] And the new spatial logic, Smith has influentially argued, entailed the production of scale. The crises to which capital had sought a spatial fix involved sending underemployed labor and overaccumulated capital to new spaces abroad, transforming them into new markets and centers of production. Imperial consolidation imposed a different kind of tension. Capital's newfound geographic mobility made it possible to universalize wage labor and value, and so to equalize profit, like never before. Yet at the same time, offers Smith, capital still needed attaching to specific locations—with their local labor forces, resources, and infrastructures—in order for commodity production actually to occur. The resulting tension between fixity and mobility, production and circulation, found its resolution in the elaboration of scale. So, for example, did the nation develop in part as a scalar economic construct designed to protect commodity production fixed around local cultural identities (like French ones) from competition with or disruption by similar agglomerations elsewhere in the capitalist world system. Meanwhile, the global scale emerged as a continuing means by which, when production in agglomerations like these yielded destabilizing overaccumulation, capital might still circulate from one place to another in search of equilibrium.[50]

I limit myself here to two scales, the national and the global, because these are the two levels at which antisemitism came predominantly to figure itself in the nineteenth century. The typical neo-Marxist way of explaining modern antisemitism—as an alibi for capital—tends to highlight antisemites' alignment with the national against the international. Bourgeois capitalism's mystified antisemitism scapegoats the Jew for a threateningly "cosmopolitan," speculative capital falsely dichotomized from local industrial production, in the process sparing bourgeois factory owners their workers' ire.[51] Such a theory of antisemitism naturally predicts an accompanying nationalist jingoism, and the antisemites I will be considering were, indeed, expounders of racist nationalism. But what critical geography allows one more expansively to conceptualize is that, however nationalist or even anti-imperialist their predilections, these same antisemites might nonetheless have been drawn discursively (and occasionally physically) to imperial matters by contradictions inherent in their metropolitan ideology. Insofar as they conceived imperial space as that which lay beyond the national sphere, they could seek there a spatial fix otherwise impossible within the hermetic confines of the nation. Think of this as a first-order version of racial scalarity, whereby contradictions untenable at one scale (the national) radiate outward toward attempted resolution at another (the imperial or global). Such a heuristic implies a straightforward causal direction to the process: just as the Marxist idea of the spatial fix identifies in empire's global scale something produced by tensions intrinsic to a metropolitan capitalism compelled to expand, so here does racial scalarity assume intrinsic, a priori contradictions in metropolitan racial thought requiring subsequent resolution at a global scale.

Sometimes the analogy holds well. In Chapter 4, for example, I read Ernest Renan's infamous 1871 paean to colonialism as a scalar remedy for the contradictory national results produced by his theory of a Germanic racial superiority common to all Frenchmen. Complicating the parallel, however, is that the racial thought about which I will have the most to say—modern antisemitism—*already presupposed* the global scale to which its practitioners sometimes turned for ideological resolution. However specious the conflation of Jewishness with international capital, it presumed, accurately, that a world system existed. In such a system, Smith tells us, space became something to differentiate internally and relatively within a single, all-encompassing global frame rather than to incorporate absolutely through expansion.[52] Henceforth might nationalists privilege in the nation not only a space apart from other nations but also a scale at which to retreat from a leveling world scale setting all manner of disparate spaces into increasing and threatening relation. In other words, the nation was being constructed into a scalar bulwark against the global, and not just a benchmark beyond and against which to imagine the global scale itself.

Henceforth, too, emerged a constitutive tension within the nationalist antisemitism blighting Europe at century's end. In its modern racializing guise, the new ideological formation echoed the system it critiqued: after all, did not the Jews' supposed racial interchangeability require, to think it, something like the principle of liquid equivalence that unsettled so many about the finance capital Jews were taken to control? Nationalist antisemitism was therefore as wedded to the universalizing scale and liquefying mobility of the race principle as to the comforting particularity and fixity of the nation. And if, following our critical geographic perspective, capitalism developed scalar mechanisms to manage the competing imperatives of fixity and mobility, then so too, for similar reasons, did nationalist antisemitism require scalar negotiations not always reducible to a first-order spatial fix. Rather than emanating simply from the metropole, a tension emanated now from the dialectic between the national scale antisemites affirmed and the global scale their outlook increasingly presumed, required, and reinforced—because of their globalizing racialism, yes, but also because imperial spatial fixes by definition worked themselves to produce the global scale of empire.

Under these circumstances, any attempted spatial fix by antisemites only seemed further to knot the dialectical relation between national and global-imperial scales. This is what I mean in Chapter 4 when I conclude that the fin-de-siècle project to escape, in empire, a "Jewish" degeneration figured at the national scale succeeded less in solving the supposed metropolitan problem than engendering a permanent, looping imbrication between scales prefiguring fascism. This is what I mean as well to register in my title, *Globalizing Race.* Whatever empire's global scale offered antisemites in the way of spatial fixes beyond expanding imperial frontiers, it also undercut as the capitalist world system's eventual consolidation internalized those frontiers into the network of shifting interior boundaries across which a more complex racial scalarity would take hold. Race, then, did not just become globalized when European race-thinking drove and accompanied imperial penetration into the farthest reaches of the world, or when modern antisemitism's theory of global Jewish conspiracy helped make race into an apparent planetary principle. Rather, race became most thoroughly global as a tool—perhaps the chief tool—for constructing and negotiating scale in the era of late imperial capital. And if antisemitism was only one among the racisms devised by the West, it was also, for reasons I will give shortly, most historically and organically suited to the scalar task at hand.

FROM MARX TO FANON (AND BACK)

Some reflection is in order about how materialist I intend to be. I began by analogizing the spatial fix to what transpired when, looking toward empire, modern antisemites labored to resolve intrinsic tensions in their developing ideology. Then I complicated the analogy with a few more elements. A first is that, with the late nineteenth-century imperial consolidation of the capitalist world system, the era of the external spatial fix gave way to the era of scalar negotiation. Another is that modern antisemitism was implicated in that consolidating world system even as it continued to seek spatial fixes to its internal difficulties. So I am proceeding in two ongoing, occasionally intersecting modes, one more analogical and one more materialist. The analogical mode, while drawing on the spatial fix as a conceptual model, does not presume that the contradictions to which modern antisemitism sought external, imperial resolutions were necessarily always material in nature. Some of the contradictions I will examine most closely—the paradoxes of nineteenth-century deterministic thinking, for instance—have more to do with the history of ideas than the history of capital.

Likewise will my treatment of scale sometimes depart from the materialist bases on which scale was so productively reevaluated a generation ago. After foundational Marxist work in the 1980s by Smith and others demonstrating how capital "produces" scale to manage its inherent crises, subsequent decades have found geographers using a more neutral vocabulary of constructedness to think about how "non-capital-centric" struggles and tensions might shape and reshape scale.[53] This is the vein in which, for instance, I will consider the scalar stakes of the anti-antisemitic reaction to antisemitism.

Indeed, the flexibility of the various available spatial and scalar heuristics is such that in Chapter 3 I turn to the implications for nationalism, rather than antisemitism, of an imperial spatial fix undertaken to resolve temporal quandaries facing a new late-century strain of reactionary French nationalism. Yet alongside the insights provided by the analogical mode of analysis I have been describing, I want to maintain a more concretely materialist appreciation for modern antisemitism's relation to capital. To suggest, as I did above, that antisemites covertly reproduced the economic processes they overtly blamed on the Jews is intentionally to offer a variation on the Marxist understanding of antisemitism as what Sartre called "a mythical, bourgeois representation of the class struggle": namely, a bourgeois diversionary tactic designed to palliate class frustrations while leaving the nature of the capitalist system unchanged.[54] This is not, I hasten to add, to advance a single, materialist explanation for modern antisemitism, which it should be clear I consider a multifactorial phenomenon. But by adducing a material dimension to modern antisemitism, while simultaneously reading that antisemitism's emergence against capital's modern production and negotiation of scale, I am also offering more than analogy. For if antisemites similarly found themselves negotiating between the scales of nation and empire, each inhering in the other, it is at least in part as a superstructural manifestation of—and reciprocal contribution to—material developments in the base driving scalar reorganizations across the entire world system.

Here one can begin reframing the perennial complications facing Marxist glosses of the relationship between antisemitism and colonial racism. Fanon, among the first to interrogate that relationship, brings into relief the promise and pitfalls of materialism for doing so. Writing *Peau noire, masques blancs* (*Black Skin, White Masks*) (1952) as decolonization movements stirred in the wake of world war, Fanon drew inspiration for his account of anti-Black racism from Sartre's rumination on antisemitism a few years earlier in *Réflexions sur la question juive* (*Anti-Semite and Jew*) (1946). The revolutionary's indebtedness to the philosopher defies easy summary, and the economic threads of Fanon's analysis rarely stand out from the largely psychoanalytical and phenomenological fabric of the book. Still, it is possible to find him engaging with Sartre's most classically Marxist explanation of antisemitism as a petit bourgeois *ressentiment* harnessed by bourgeois capitalists. Fanon offers the following quote from *Réflexions sur la question juive*:

> Thus I would call antisemitism a poor man's snobbery. And it would appear that the rich for the most part *exploit* this passion for their own uses rather than abandon themselves to it—they have better things to do. It is propagated mainly among middle classes, because they possess neither land nor house nor castle.[55]

Fanon then likens the effect to that produced when South Africa's "poor Whites," in their hatred and domination of Blacks, misrecognize their own status as a "white proletariat."[56] He is less sanguine than Sartre about the class pervasiveness of racial hatred. Declaring that "we find scarcely any antisemitism among workers," Sartre had echoed Friedrich Engels's unwillingness, in his own explanation of antisemitism as the embittered reaction by déclassé "medieval, declining strata" against capitalist modernity, to consider racist scapegoating a proletarian disease.[57] Nonetheless, Fanon replicates the basic principle at work of a diversionary racism favorable to the ruling elite.

Fanon's South African parallel lays an impressive foundation for appreciating the nuances of what Immanuel Wallerstein has called capitalism's "'ethnicization' of the work force," an ethnicization capable not only of rationalizing cheap labor and slavery but also of placating some workers with myths about their racial superiority over others.[58] Yet the parallel runs as well into a difficulty transposing Sartre's contention, quoted by Fanon from the same passage, that the poor man (or more specifically, for Sartre, the petit bourgeois) treats "the Jew as an inferior and pernicious being" in order to claim his place among "the elite."[59] For what lends itself in the poor man's antisemitism to exploitation by the rich capitalist, what really makes the Jew inferior *and* pernicious, is that despite his perceived inferiority he is still understood to pull the strings of capital. In both instances the system mollifies disgruntled social strata by encouraging their self-ethnicization relative to a demonized foil: in Europe the Jew, in Africa the Black. But the foils themselves are ethnicized along different lines. "Regarding the Jew, we think of money and its derivatives," writes Fanon, whereas "regarding the black man, we think of sex"; and while "the black man represents the biological danger," the Jew represents "the intellectual danger."[60]

Fanon's binaries map onto the epidermal distinction he seeks to preserve: that the Jew, unlike the black man, "can pass undetected" in white society.[61] The binaries also work tacitly, though, against a different kind of schematic tendency emanating from what makes Sartre's Marxist assessment transposable to the colonial context. In Sartre's ascription of "Manichaeism" to the antisemite, Fanon locates the unit of comparison for appreciating how the Jew and Black function similarly under the structural economic conditions common to both the European and colonial example.[62] "Both of us stand for evil," writes Fanon of the Jew and the Black, and hence both conveniently distract the propertyless classes from real injustice.[63] But something troubles the reasoning. To approach antisemitism from Sartre's Marxist perspective is to adopt a certain understanding of how Jews are racialized in ways the bourgeoisie can exploit—that is, as Manichean others distracting capitalism's losers from their fate by giving them an enemy over whom to feel superior. Sartre insists less on the Jews' racialization as capital personified. And critically, the choice makes his analysis more portable among contexts. Thus can Fanon's brief economic analysis make Jews and Blacks occupy the same structural position, without having to account for why Jews are taken to incarnate capital and Blacks are not. It matters only that they each provide a bottom rung in the social hierarchy, above which others might be content to situate themselves. The specificity of the two racializations, however, then risks disappearing, schematized as they have been into fairly interchangeable results of a same basic dynamic. So Fanon, unwilling to reduce one to the other, reinserts particularity into his argument. Antisemitism and "negrophobia" share a form but diverge in content; no antisemite, for instance, "would ever think of castrating a Jew," since it is Jewish intellect that threatens antisemites most.[64]

In short, Fanon's comparison of antisemitism and colonial racism circles back around toward precisely the element—the association by antisemites of Jews with capital, power, and cunning—whose relative downplaying by Sartre facilitated the comparison initially. The move can certainly be read as resistance on Fanon's part to the universalizing, Sartrian theory of generalized racism that he has otherwise embraced. What results, as Bryan Cheyette puts it, are two "incommensurable narratives" in *Peau noire* regarding Jews: one that aligns them with the black experience, and one that locates them back on the European side of the black-white divide.[65] Of special interest to me here, though, is that at times both narratives can nevertheless be said to share a materialist perspective (if one fairly concealed, again, behind the more psychologizing and phenomenological perspectives Fanon tends to prefer). Sartre's Marxism furnishes Fanon a basis for equating the two racisms' respective economic functions in Europe and South Africa. But Fanon's reassertion of specificities distinguishing antisemitism from anti-Black racism significantly complicates the parallel, since it becomes difficult to explain why the Jews' diversionary inferiorization would proceed according to the trope of superior intelligence. Note, however, the materialist tenor of the element reintroduced by Fanon into Sartre's generalizable schema. For what is Fanon's insistence on antisemitism's association of the Jew with money, if not an implicit reflection on the importance to the Jew's diversionary usefulness that he provide an effigy for capital's safely simulated destruction by proletarian or petit bourgeois dupes?

In *Peau noire*, then, there quietly circulate two materialist frameworks for contemplating antisemitism. One productively treats antisemitism in its homology with other, similarly racializing structures of economic mystification and oppression around the globe. The other returns more narrowly, and perfectly legitimately, to the Jew's specific privileging as an alibi for capital. Yet each seems to undercut the other. We have here in a nutshell the historical quandary dogging materialist approaches to antisemitism. Abstract modern antisemitism from its association of the Jews with capital, and it becomes possible to draw potent connections with other racisms influenced by capital's insidiously ethnicizing effects. Focus on antisemitism's capitalist particularities, however, and the connections blur and dim.[66] What is more, even the connections uncovered by the abstracted, global model reveal only structural homologies linked by a common racio-economic cause. Under such conceptual circumstances, it becomes difficult to envision, let alone describe, more direct connectivities between anti-Jewish and anti-Black racializations. No materialist context remains for theorizing how the antisemitic topos of metropolitan Jewish wealth might, for example, have worked in tandem with notions about Jewish colonial primitivity, notions themselves interwoven with representations of blackness; after all, even to start with the figure of Jewish wealth would be to erode, in the way indicated above, the diversionary hypothesis according to which Fanon groups European antisemitism and South African racism together in common racio-economic terms.

Little wonder, perhaps, that Shu-Mei Shih's field-defining 2008 statement on "comparative racialization," which takes *Peau noire* as an ur-text for thinking racializations in a way designed to bring "submerged or displaced relationalities into view," makes no mention of Fanon's extended comparison between antisemitism and anti-Black racism. Instead she foregrounds Fanon's psychoanalytic development of *comparaison* ("comparison") as the relational mode in which the black man, and in particular the Antillean, is constantly induced by the ideology of whiteness to compare himself contemptuously with other black men.[67] Still, we might usefully recuperate the glancing, bipartite materialism of Fanon's views on antisemitism as a point of departure for resolving the Marxist quandary outlined so far, and thus for excavating submerged racial relationalities from a different kind of Fanonian perspective. Doing so means asserting, with Fanon, that one of modern antisemitism's abiding specificities—the narrative of Jewish financial and political power—requires consideration alongside the narrative of Jewish inferiority easier to reconcile with inferiorizing representations of imperial subalterns. But doing so without reaching Fanon's unspoken impasse between specificity and generality also requires reconciling the dual imperatives, in modern antisemitism, to label the Jew at once superior and inferior. Not that these two characterizations are inherently mutually exclusive: Sartre is right, I think, when he declares about the Jews' purported intelligence that the nationalist antisemite can "disdain it in all tranquility," since the antisemite's self-satisfied supposed communion with the nation means "he does not *need* intelligence."[68] Nevertheless, to disdain the Jew for his intelligence is a different proposition from disdaining colonized Blacks for their primitive potency. The "Jewish peril" is not really "replaced," as Fanon puts it, "by the fear of the black man's sexual power."[69] The first mostly imperils the nation from the top down, secretly pulling the levers of elite economic and political power; while if the second threatens the nation at all, it does so from the bottom up—demographically and genitally—by threatening a more individualized white masculinity. Even Fanon remarks that "it's because the Jews commandeer a country that they are dangerous," something not traditionally imputed to the black man.[70]

And yet, reassessed from the standpoint of racial scalarity, it is precisely the pivot of the nation around which the myths of Jewish intelligence and world power take their place in a larger, flexible racializing logic as capable of conflating Jewishness and blackness as distinguishing between them. Against the "abstract intelligence of the Semite" ostensibly required to manipulate the circulating, endlessly fungible instruments of finance capital, Sartre's antisemite opposes a model of property rooted in hereditary ownership.[71] Sartre reads this phenomenon, like Engels, as a rejection of large-scale capitalism by petit bourgeois "functionaries, office workers, small businessmen, who possess nothing."[72] But one might alternately locate in it the racial corollary—and supporting apparatus—of a national scale securing the local fixity necessary for commodity production in a globalized world system of otherwise accelerating labor and capital flows. Founded on cultural and ethnic unity, and codified in the nineteenth-century division of the globe into stable national units, such a scale benefited from modern antisemitism's exclusionary claim to national cohesion at the Jew's expense. For antisemitism, however, to have proven so indissociable from European nationalisms hints as well at the ongoing emergence and importance of the global scale with whose circulating, equalizing effects national fixities and differentiations struck a dialectical balance. Had nationalisms only been concerned to delimit one nation from another, French jingoism might, for instance, only ever have taken the form of Anglophobia or Germanophobia. Yet the colonizing nations' growing dependence on the increasingly interconnected world system into which their empires implicated them made it necessary to find racializable others useful not only for shoring up an imagined national homogeneity but also for negotiating between national and global scales. And as I will argue in Chapter 2, it was the Jews who fit the bill. Avatars of an internationalized capital, they represented the global scale against which to construct and defend the national scale. Racializable, though, into non-European, non-white others, they simultaneously furnished a more palatable mechanism for negotiating the comparably unfamiliar alterity—Arab, Black, and so forth—suffusing the global scale with which the nation necessarily remained bound up.

That Jews, then, were understood to circulate conspiratorially between metropole and imperial periphery was not just a symptom of anticapitalist or anti-imperial reaction. It was also a way of managing the new global principle of equivalence to which parochial nationalists subscribed despite themselves. Even the notion of rooted French territorial integrity, for example, accommodated a logic of substitution and exchange once colonial North Africa was deemed acceptable compensation for provinces lost to the Germans back home. Antisemitism facilitated this delicate ideological operation, possible as it was to translate, on the Jew's very body, imperial phenomena back into national terms whenever the global threatened excessively to swallow the local. Thus might the same Jew, we will see, be made usefully (and bizarrely) to remain a German enemy of the nation on the continent even while he stood in for a more racialized imperial subaltern in Africa.

In their presumed racial liminality—classified somewhere between Occident and Orient, Europe and Africa, white and black—Jews perhaps offered a suitably elastic device for mediating between domestic and imperial varieties of difference. But it is also not merely as a sort of template or blueprint for otherness that Europe's Jewish "first others" helped Europeans navigate the more radical difference with which empire brought them into permanent, intimately structural association. It is as a privileged figure of scalarity, too. In the West's historical attitude toward Jews, there had always lingered an anxious trace of the circumstances surrounding the Church's origins and self-definition. Christianity represented something of a demographic scalar reversal: originally a Judaic sect, the religion had grown to envelop the Jews who once contained it. And theologically speaking, the Church doctrine of supersessionism concerned no less scalar a question than how God's new, Christian chosen people intended, like the Jews before them, to maintain the particularity of their chosenness while laboring for the universal salvation of all mankind.

Centuries of subsequent legal discrimination having relegated the Jews to commercial endeavors, Jewishness offered a ready-made emblem of capital as feudalism gave way in Europe to the modern economic order. Yet the choice of Jews as economic scapegoat owes its specificity, I think, to more than their real or imagined association with money. For the Jews likewise offered a ready-made metaphor for capital's growing dialecticization of the local and global. The myth of an occult, conspiring Jewish world power took special hold in the modern era because it emerged reinforced by both sides of the Enlightenment divide. Secular Enlightenment thinkers like Voltaire, seeking in Greco-Roman reason an alternative to Christian orthodoxy, had manifested what Arthur Hertzberg calls a "classicizing anti-Semitism" by seeing in the Jews what the Romans had: a resentful, enslaved, particularist people refusing "to eat at the same table with other men" and plotting against those around them.[73] The Christian reaction, worried in the meantime that Enlightenment reason and economic modernity threatened the Church's pretension to universality, perceived these as a bold new scalar plot on the part of an old enemy—the Jews—to avenge its erstwhile spiritual supersession with a contemporary material supersession of the Church's earthly influence. Combining both tendencies as the nineteenth century wore on, the idea of a Jewish world power therefore came to represent conspiratorial Jewish finance as the double effect of both an intransigent, local, particularist resistance to non-Jewish surroundings *and* a global network binding individual Jewries cooperatively together. What better figure than this to express (or defer onto, or contain) the similar requirement by capital that it fix itself locally and particularistically even as it continued to circulate at the global scale?[74]

HISTORY, CONTEXT, SPECIFICITY

As racial relationality requires, to understand fully its conditions of emergence, an appreciation of racial scalarity, so racial scalarity demands an awareness of the historical relationship between race and scale. Appending the modifier "racial" to scalarity means recognizing the role played by scalar realities and fictions in processes of racialization. But it also means becoming aware of the historical importance of racializing representations to the Western scalar imaginary. I have chosen here to focus on antisemitism at least in part because of the specific power of anti-Jewish representations, some dating to the early days of Christianity and before, for explaining scalar reactions to and complicities with capital's latter-day production of scale. In this sense, I understand modern antisemitism to have drawn from an extant archive of Western tropes regarding Jews. I am, however, largely following a "contextualist" approach—to borrow Weill's nomenclature—when I understand the contingent, historically specific, and scalar realities of capital and empire to have activated latent possibilities in Western anti-Jewish discourse for conceiving the world along scalar lines.[75]

In the latter, contextualist sense, I approach antisemitism less as a proto-racist cultural content transferable or adaptable to Europe's other others (though this certainly was also the case) than as part of the larger modern framework facilitating the transferability or adaptability of various racializing logics. So the well-trodden question of whether antisemitism is a racism is poorly posed, at least in its zero-sum form, since both answers are equally legitimate. Antisemitism retains a specificity distinguishing it from other racisms not because it predates their essential modernity, as Léon Poliakov vigorously maintains, or even because it takes a specific object.[76] Rather, it stands apart for having played a uniquely scalar and catalytic role in the globalization of race, all while itself remaining simultaneously and firmly inscribed—for the very same reason—in the larger history of European racist thought.

It befits us as well to stay contextually minded about the fact that the categories through which we contemplate scale today are themselves not so easily isolable from their racialized histories. Given how indebted the recent theoretical ferment around the construction of space and scale remains to Marx, I will have something to say in the last chapter about the significance of the Jews to his own scalar imaginary. As important, however, as it is to decolonize the critical geographic terms I have deployed so far, a more exhaustive treatment of the matter must wait for another day. For the most part I will be concerned here to decolonize, and sometimes repurpose, some of the more established modes of thinking about antisemitism and empire. That task starts with Arendt, by way of whom I want to begin sketching the trajectory of the book and its chapters.

Chapter 1 ("The Labor of Superfluity: Hannah Arendt, Empire, and the Jews") undertakes a reevaluation of the connections that Arendt develops in *The Origins of Totalitarianism* between imperial expansion and the rise of modern antisemitism. The chapter approaches Arendt in ways both recuperative and critical. I argue that the voluminous recent scholarly literature on Arendt's celebrated "boomerang thesis," so called because she understood European colonial racism to have come boomeranging back to the continent as antisemitic fascism, has tended to obscure an important other facet of her thinking about antisemitism and empire. In what I dub her "displacement thesis," Arendt also advances the highly original notion that modern antisemitism took hold in Europe when an influx of bourgeois imperial capital into government-backed enterprises abroad displaced European Jews from their traditional role as financiers to the state. Perceived now as superfluous, Jewish wealth could be more easily labeled parasitic.

Though I suggest in the chapter that Arendt was wrong, and that if anything empire made Jews seem *more* entangled in government affairs, I am nevertheless interested to recuperate the displacement thesis as a key tool. For one, it provides essential context for understanding the role of the boomerang thesis in her political philosophy. Arguing that the displacement thesis itself displaces onto Jews a creeping, unacknowledged superfluity haunting Arendt's concepts of the state and Europe, I conclude that her representation of the boomeranging interrelation between Africa and the continent is in turn designed to draw this troubling superfluity away from the Jews. Arendt's preoccupation with Jewish superfluity also owes much, as previously indicated, to her implicit debunking of nineteenth-century accusations about colonially conspiring Jews. All the same, the displacement thesis offers a way forward from the usual, linear approach—reinforced by the dominant influence of Arendt's own boomerang thesis—that sets European antisemitism into direct relation with the colonial racism of which it is understood to be either a cause or consequence. Attuned more holistically to the overall imperial circumstances (economic, political, etc.) framing antisemitic discourse in Europe, this forgotten side of *Origins* presents an alternative methodological point of departure for thinking, as I want to, empire as a space and scale to which modern antisemitism turned for resolutions to its ideological contradictions.

If Chapter 1 reads Arendt's theory of antisemitism in part as a reaction to the idea of Jewish colonial conspiracy, Chapter 2 ("Colonial Conspiracies: Racializing Jews in the Era of Empire") charts the idea's nineteenth-century emergence. The chapter takes up a series of colonial developments, like the Crémieux decree and the financial scandal surrounding the 1881 invasion of Tunisia, that indelibly associated Jews with empire in the French consciousness. These events, I argue, helped shape modern, political antisemitism by furnishing the growing narrative about Jewish global conspiracy with evocative contemporary tales—some anchored in truth, most imagined—of cooperation between metropolitan and North African Jewries. Noting the biologizing tone characteristic of such newly concrete warnings about a Jewish political and demographic threat, I also describe how the trope of Jewish colonial malfeasance functioned along racializing lines to construct a "primitive" Jewish essence supposedly discernible in the colonies and attributable to Jews everywhere.

As I previously began explaining, however, the constructed Jewish imperial menace constituted more than just an easy nationalist device or knee-jerk rejection of French embroilments overseas. Importantly, too, it furnished a mechanism for rendering the complex otherness of the imperial world system into national terms, while stealthily crafting an imaginary according to which the national scale might still be conceived to function alongside—rather than simply against—the global scale with which it necessarily remained interrelated. Novels were particularly effective at making the Jewish colonial conspirator function in this overdetermined way. The conspiratorial plot shares a certain historical continuity with the nineteenth-century novelistic plot, which so often revolved around some central machination or intrigue. The very notion of conspiracy, in other words, authorized one of the central structuring principles of modern literary narrative, making the novel especially fertile ground for the ideological work accomplished by modern antisemitism. Reading French novels both canonical and forgotten, I trace the emergence of the Jewish literary antagonist as the device par excellence for representing a protagonist's unwitting participation in the global economic system, then recasting this anxiously registered participation along more tolerable lines: those of a conspiracy whose secret might remain discoverable, and those of a metropolitan racial conflict less threatening than that encountered in the imperial periphery.

Literature provided a vehicle as well for late-century elaborations of a uniquely radical conservatism that, in Chapter 3 ("Men on Horseback [1]: The Marquis de Morès, Nationalism, and Imperial Space-Time"), I associate with some of the most notorious antisemites in fin-de-siècle France. Shifting the focus from antisemitism proper to other key cultural and ideological currents with which it intersected, the chapter considers how, for a certain brand of late-century French reactionary, imperial expansion dovetailed with new ways of thinking time and the nation. Exemplary in this respect was the Marquis de Morès, the virulently antisemitic agitator who in 1896 died attempting single-handedly to dislodge England from Egypt and tilt the African balance of imperial power in France's favor. Morès's political peers treated his Saharan demise like the death of a martyred knight who, as if brought to life from chivalric romances of old, had graced a decadent present with remnants of a glorious past. But to Morès' admirer Maurice Barrès—architect of the French reactionary nationalism coalescing during the Dreyfus Affair—such literary mourning signaled a more complicated temporal possibility. The Marquis offered no mere continuity, for Barrès, between the nation past and present, though this was certainly part of his appeal. Rather, Morès seemed to incarnate a continuity between different *kinds* of time altogether: the smooth, linear time of modernity and progress, and the more disjunctive "messianic" time, as it has been called, of Christian chivalry and salvation.

Rarely have these two temporalities been deemed compatible. From Walter Benjamin to Benedict Anderson to Jacques Derrida, critics generally understand messianic time to have given way historically to linear time, even as they sometimes oppose the messianic (or some reconceptualization thereof) against the violences committed in the name of temporal progress. Either way, the assumption remains of a fundamental contrast between messianism's discontinuities, with its causality-confounding jolts of prophecy and fulfillment, and linear time's gradual succession of apparently incremental advancements. Yet to Barrès—and indeed, I suggest, to many in the fin de siècle—things were not so binary. Might not one look, they wondered, toward the future for radical (that is to say novel) improvements in societal organization, while simultaneously embracing a conservative nostalgia for past national grandeurs supposedly missing from a degraded present? But how, then, to consider the past as at once a series of stages necessarily eclipsed on the way to progress, and a repository of ideals with which to remain messianically bound despite the march forward of linear time? The search for answers motivated nationalist efforts by Morès, Barrès, and others at recuperating an erstwhile French chivalry in the space of empire, while remaining under the self-consciously modern auspices of imperial progress. Attempts like these at a spatial fix, I conclude, complicate the usual postcolonial representations of European imperial space-time as concerned only with transforming various subalterns into superseded relics.

Space and time likewise figured prominently in an ideological conundrum marking late-century antisemitism, to which I shift back in Chapter 4 ("Men on Horseback [2]: Melchior de Vogüé, Imperial Regeneration, and the Dialectic of Determinism"). Nationalist French antisemites by and large subscribed to the thesis of social decline, a decadentist narrative given particular momentum in France after the 1870 military collapse against the Germans. The difficulty arose when the ambient intellectual tendencies often marshaled to conceptualize the decline—positivism, empiricism, determinism—were blamed by reactionaries for the decline itself. Such was the nature of these reactionaries' ideological confusion, though, that they sometimes continued embracing the same scientistic tendencies as a way of shoring up their idealism's self-professed modernity. The problem was especially acute for antisemites, since the more they resorted to pseudoscientific degeneration theory in their condemnations of a supposed Jewish decadence, the more they reproduced a deterministic positivism about which many of them otherwise felt deeply ambivalent.

Looking for a way out of such contradictions, antisemites increasingly turned to empire. The antisemitic novelist and politician Melchior de Vogüé, theorist of a decadent metropole's regeneration by the imperial project, is emblematic in this regard. So, for instance, did Vogüé seek spatial solutions to the apparent contradiction that time might deterministically impel the same organism, including the nation, toward both life and death. Cleaving and spatializing determinism into two variants—one salubrious, Aryan, and imperial, the other insalubrious, Jewish, and metropolitan—Vogüé believed he had made the dictates of reason serve the moral imperatives of conservative reaction. But what he best demonstrated, I argue, is that antisemitism and empire were emerging reinforced as the twin, logically intertwined symptoms of a long-simmering metaphysical tension. Broadening my discussion to consider French theories of race and empire developed since the middle of the century by Renan, Arthur de Gobineau, and others, I trace the unforeseen consequences occasioned by an increasingly common intellectual reliance on the temporal, deterministic notion of intergenerational inheritance. A notion itself handed down from previous generations, in particular as developed by August Comte in the nineteenth century and Henri de Boulainvilliers in the eighteenth, this unsteady temporal variable encouraged various spatial remedies. Among these were antisemitism and empire, as well as the fantastical fin-de-siècle regenerative scheme that combined them. Yet so too, now, did the latter system spin in its own, even more dangerous ideological circles. Drawing on the work of Max Horkheimer and Theodor Adorno to rethink anxious nineteenth-century presumptions about the reversibility between space and time (though ones from which Horkheimer and Adorno themselves, I note, were not entirely removed), the chapter concludes by examining how this reversibility in turn deepened a dialectical interpenetration between national and imperial scales redolent of twentieth-century fascist disasters to come.

But scale, of course, was never just the domain of conservative nationalists like Vogüé. Chapter 5 ("Bigger Pictures: Anti-Antisemitism and the Politics of Scale") ends the book by radiating out from France to consider the supranational, utopic imperialism of the nineteenth-century French novelist Émile Zola alongside a number of nineteenth-, twentieth-, and twenty-first-century European intellectual frameworks—including, especially, Nietzsche's but also those of Marx and others—likewise concerned to think beyond the nation. What these had in common, I argue, at least in the century of their inception, was the idea that nationalism, antisemitism, and related provincialisms sweeping Europe were rooted in scalar falsities and blind spots. To maintain this was not simply to accuse, say, nationalist antisemites of failing to appreciate the existence of a global scale; after all, those same antisemites were claiming, with their increasingly detailed accounts of world Jewish conspiracy, to uncover and explain just such a thing. Rather, it was to contest their grasp of scalar interrelation. Hence, for example, could Nietzsche ridicule German antisemites for unwittingly participating, precisely as strident nationalists and Christians, in the "real" global conspiracy: an ongoing infection of the world by Judeo-Christian values.

However idiosyncratic Nietzsche's allegation, such a tactic reflects the extent to which, as the material processes of capital and empire produced scale, various social actors engaged in heated ideological conflicts determining how scale would be perceived, understood, and constructed—often for a long time to come. Contemplating the profoundly scalar stakes of the conflict erupting in the nineteenth century over the Jewish question, while returning to the contemporary events with which this introduction began, the chapter maps the intellectual history of a European anti-antisemitism whose complicated influence can still be felt today. I argue that the current French and European preoccupation with Muslim antisemitism not only indexes tensions in the "new" Europe understood to have emerged from the mid-twentieth-century ashes of war and decolonization but also harks back to an older mode of figuring the European colonial periphery. That mode emerged when explicit foes of antisemitism like Zola and Nietzsche turned toward empire for solutions to reactionary parochialisms on the continent and to instabilities in their own philosophical systems. Henceforth, I demonstrate, would Muslim colonial subalterns increasingly be constructed into antisemites, paving the way for their postcolonial European descendants to play the "fascist" role in a postwar European dramaturgy of anti-Nazi vigilance. This is how the sins of the colonizer became the sins of the colonized. And this is why, more now than ever, the stories contained here have become important to tell.

CHAPTER 1

The Labor of Superfluity

Hannah Arendt, Empire, and the Jews

The enduring unorthodoxy of *The Origins of Totalitarianism*, Hannah Arendt's doleful 1951 postmortem chronicling Europe's descent into the abyss, is reflected in some of the criticisms leveled against it. Throughout *Origins*, Arendt makes a complicated, idiosyncratic case for the interrelation between modern antisemitism and imperialism. She has since been accused of having herself maintained insufficient discursive distance from both. Writing in the *Times Literary Supplement* in 2009, the historian Bernard Wasserstein denounced Arendt for internalizing the various antisemitic and Nazi authorities she cites.[1] A number of critics have also recently sided against Arendt in the ongoing debate over whether her depiction of black Africans in *Origins* partakes of the imperialist perspective she otherwise condemns.[2] I will return to these two critiques below; for now, let me note only the extent to which they never overlap, as if Arendt were exempt from her own fundamental insight concerning the historical co-constitution of attitudes toward Jews and empire. But might she not have been? Arendt's novel association of Jewish and imperial histories, it would seem, still holds the power to surprise.

My goals in this chapter are threefold. The first is to demonstrate that Arendt's frequently contentious claims about Jews and empire do, in fact, have everything to do with each other, though not always in the ways that Arendt herself is at pains to elaborate. I read Arendt *contra* Arendt to examine how her analyses symptomatize, illuminate, and reconfigure an older tradition of linking Jews and empire. It is conceivable enough that Arendt's impressions of Africans might recall bygone imperialist constructions more than we would like. It is even imaginable that, in citing the antisemites she abhorred, she could have affirmed aspects of their thought. Far less immediately intuitable, however, is the possibility that, as I will be arguing, Arendt's very interest in Africa owes something to what antisemites once argued about European Jews—or the possibility that, conversely, her sometimes jarring portraits of Jews intersect with how antisemites once felt about Africa. To properly appreciate Arendt's insights about the evolution of European racism, we must better recognize how her own analyses are not entirely unencumbered by the interwoven histories of antisemitism and empire she documents.

My second goal is to show that Arendt's partial embedment in discourses dating to the nineteenth century represents more than just epistemic inertia. For if Arendt is drawn to thinking Europe and Africa together, it is also to defuse, or at least attempt to defuse, a tension immanent to her political philosophy. This tension threatens to unsettle the deep, binary narrative that structures so much of Arendt's analysis in *Origins*: the losing battle between the modern state and the various modes of rampant "superfluity" that overwhelmed it. Arendt locates the sources of superfluity elsewhere than in the state, diverting superfluity instead to the account of various phenomena, like capital and imperialism, which she understands to have infected the state from without. Yet as I want to propose, Arendt's theoretical and historical frames also inadvertently suggest the state's own inherent tendency to generate the dreaded superfluity from within. I will be locating the aporetic heart of this tendency in Arendt's later distinction between the categories of labor and work, which rejoins a fissure in her political thought already evident in *Origins*. The fissure snakes through the theme of superfluity that suffuses *Origins* and of which Arendt makes the Jewish experience a privileged signifier. The gesture has helped earn Arendt accusations of insensitivity toward the Jewish people. But it is ultimately better understood, I conclude, as an anxious tactic on her part for exorcising a constitutive paradox from her notion of the state.

My third and final goal is to reevaluate Arendt's contribution to thinking racial relationality. Her boomerang thesis on the link between colonial racism and fascist antisemitism counts among the earliest, best-known, and most ambitious attempts to conceive the ever-shifting grid of relations through which, as Étienne Balibar describes it, every racialization inflects every other across a "historical system of complementary exclusions and dominations which are mutually interconnected."[3] The devil, of course, is in the details, something made plain by even the most cursory glance at the robust debate—on which I will have more to say—surrounding the actual routes followed back to the continent by racist logics and technologies refined in colonial Africa. One difficulty stems from the fact that distant portions of the racializing grid might resonate together, but in ways dispersed along so many intervening pathways that the nature and mechanisms of the resonance escape us. The task at hand, now and throughout this book, is to acknowledge the heterogeneity of these diffuse trajectories across which racializations interact, take hold, and evolve. An overlooked aspect of that heterogeneity is scalarity, which I have been arguing became particularly salient when modern antisemitism made Jews the linchpin around which to negotiate the nation's place in a world system, as well as when empire provided antisemites and others a scale at which to address contradictions difficult to manage in exclusively metropolitan terms. Though such scalarity was often profoundly racializing, in that it shaped the development of modern antisemitism, it was not inherently relational, since here scalarity involved a variety of contingent imperial circumstances irreducible to imperial racism alone. As I have also been arguing, however, scalarity provided a condition of possibility for relationality to take hold. And what we will see makes *Origins* worth revisiting on this relational front is, precisely, Arendt's willingness to entertain a historical connection between modern antisemitism and empire *not* predicated on imperial racism.

The complexity of *Origins* is that it models the recognition of a contingent such connection, even as it pursues more straightforwardly linear and genealogical explanations for how racisms are related. I begin with the latter. Arendt considers various nineteenth-century racisms to have descended from a common European "race-thinking" invented during the Enlightenment and refined in the nineteenth century by thinkers like Arthur de Gobineau. When combined with changing political exigencies, Arendt contends, this race-thinking lent itself to various manifestations of focused, ideological racism. So, for instance, did imperial racism serve the requirements of overseas expansion, or antisemitism serve the requirements of political reactions on the continent. European racisms might have functioned differently and targeted different groups, but they all proceeded from shared discursive ground.

This genealogical demonstration by Arendt carries an unspoken and overlooked corollary critical to the rest of *Origins*: a mutual intelligibility between racisms that, owing to their common discursive source, made it easy for them to reinforce each other. In what has come to be called the boomerang thesis, Arendt famously suggests that a bureaucratically administered racism honed in the nineteenth- and early twentieth-century imperial periphery produced "boomerang effects" on the European continent—including the Nazi disaster that forced her to leave Germany for France in 1933, then France for the United States in 1941 as she fled the horror that eventually claimed six million of her fellow Jews. Searching, as she wrote *Origins* in the late 1940s, to explain the totalitarian tragedy that had engulfed Europe, Arendt seized among other factors on the Scramble for Africa and the role she felt it had played in unleashing the hitherto latent potential for race-thinking to destroy the European body politic. If various continental and imperial racisms shared a common origin in race-thinking, then it was natural enough that they should easily interrelate, like the separated branches of a river joining again with torrential force.[4]

Arendt's genealogical, metonymic narrative of a European racialism fastening sequentially onto one victim after another dovetails with *Origins*' dominant metaphor and conceit of "superfluity." Arendt postulates a new category of superfluous man jarred loose by the nineteenth-century dislocations of capital and empire, a category as emergent in the superfluous European masses consigned to the imperial periphery as in the colonized masses relegated by racism to the margins of human endeavor. All of this reaches its culminating expression in the absolute superfluity of the concentration camp victim, rendered infinitely expendable because, as Arendt puts it, he has been banished "from the human world altogether" (*OT*, 444). Surging forth from Europe, then gaining potency in Africa before returning to the continent with a vengeance, superfluity provides Arendt a conceptual pivot around which to portray the Jews as the final and arguably most quintessential victims of empire.

What this lasting boomerang imagery has tended to obscure is that, for Arendt, European Jews were not just the final repository of the superfluity set in motion by imperialism; they were also among the very first. With the late nineteenth-century rise of empire, Arendt offers, Europe's ascendant bourgeoisie saw its first opportunity to profit from state enterprise. The resultant flow of bourgeois capital into the imperial project dislodged the Jews from their traditional, privileged role as bankers to the state. Arendt's conclusion about the outcome is profound: Jewish wealth no longer explainable as the consequence of a tangible and potentially still justifiable financial service provided to nation-states, the Jew could now be portrayed more convincingly than ever as the social parasite par excellence. Arendt, in other words, credits the rise of empire with the late nineteenth-century emergence of a modern antisemitism that, by categorizing the Jews en masse as socially superfluous, prefigured a twentieth-century totalitarian exterminationism radically intent on demonstrating the Jew's corresponding expendability.

In Arendt's account, then, empire twice renders the Jews superfluous: a first time when the bourgeois project of empire ended the longtime symbiosis between European nation-states and Jewish finance; and a second time when the concentration camps made Jews the final and most abject category of superfluous man incarnated in Africa by colonizers and the colonized. The two processes are related, with the earlier attribution to the Jews of superfluity setting the stage for a later attempt at eradication. But a fundamental difference also remains. Arendt's thesis of a bureaucratized imperial racism coming home to roost in the Holocaust groups Jews and the colonized on the receiving end of a single, if evolving, pattern of European racist domination. Her notion of a perceived Jewish superfluity in the initial wake of the Scramble for Africa, however, posits a more contingent relationship between antisemitism and empire. If the promise of overseas riches prompted bourgeois investors to displace the Jews as financiers to the state, this had little to do with imperial racism, at least as regards the Jews. The same conditions for antisemitism would presumably have arisen had the bourgeoisie found any other reason to overcome its traditional disinterest in state-backed commerce, or had the Jews themselves simply decided to withhold their capital from governments.

Next to Arendt's more readily visualizable narrative tracing a rebound onto Europe of imperial misdeeds, her comparatively abstract correlation of modern antisemitism with a diminishment of Jewish influence in the age of empire has generated far less commentary. For one thing, it confounds the genealogical reflex that conceives European Jewry as the eventual target—or, as I discussed in the Introduction, the prototypical target—of discourses and practices aimed at imperial subalterns. For another, it attends to the prehistory of the Holocaust rather than to the Holocaust itself, a peripherality compounded by the difficulty of connecting Nazi exterminationism to the modern antisemitism Arendt attributes to a Scramble for Africa in which England and France played far greater roles than Germany.[5] Yet Arendt's underexamined claim of a Jewish superfluity born first of the imperial fact, and only later reinforced by a boomeranging imperial racism, opens the methodological door to a more varied appreciation of the historical articulation between antisemitism and empire. It also offers purchase on Arendt's own subtle indebtedness to the late nineteenth- and early twentieth-century discourses this articulation produced, as well as on what I will be proposing is an even deeper blockage in her political thought.

Charting these potentialities and fault lines in *Origins* begins with recognizing the perverse symmetry implied by what, in order to distinguish it from the more celebrated boomerang thesis, I will be calling here Arendt's displacement thesis. If European Jews were displaced from state finance by the advent of empire, and if that displacement provoked the antisemitic groundswell Arendt attributes to it, then there is a grand historical irony indeed to the subsequent antisemitic ascription of unpopular imperial developments to Jewish connivance with the state. French antisemites, for example, argued with seductive specificity that France's 1881 invasion of Tunisia had been ordered by Jewish holders of Tunisian debt. A similar logic prevailed, mutatis mutandis, when at the turn of the century British antisemites charged Jewish diamond and gold interests in the South African Rand with embroiling Britain in the bloody Second Boer War (1899–1902).[6]

How could the imperial tectonic shift that for Arendt diminished Jewish state privilege convince so many that Jews had actually tightened their grip on state power? The displacement thesis accommodates this counterintuitive outcome, theoretically at least. Citing Tocqueville's contention that the French revolutionary masses most hated the aristocracy once its waning state privileges no longer seemed to justify its continued wealth—whether or not the masses had ever perceived those privileges as fair[7]—Arendt reasons that Jews similarly attracted "universal hatred" when empire ended their influence in a way that stripped their wealth of "visible function" (*OT*, 15, 4). When legitimized by their formal or quasi-formal arrangements with the state, Jews could at least command a grudging respect for their observable role in the administration of power. But once they had lost this role, all bets were off. Arendt's schema accordingly explains the late-century recrudescence and refinement of antisemitic conspiracy theories. By divesting Jews of their longstanding capacity as financiers to the state, the bourgeois-financed imperial project definitively removed the phantasmic Jew to the smoke-filled back rooms where plots were hatched and governments bought. Anything was thinkable now, even the possibility that soldiers might be sent halfway across the world to die in unwitting defense of Jewish financial interests.

There remains something a bit neatly coincidental, though, about Arendt's contention that Jews proved largely inessential to one of the very things—imperialism—that antisemites accused Jews of fomenting and manipulating. I will return to this momentarily. Note, for the time being, that Arendt herself comments little in *Origins* about the apparently paradoxical accusation by antisemites of imperial malfeasance against a European Jewry sidelined from and by the imperial project.[8] She might have mobilized her own previous argument, developed in an unfinished essay titled "Antisemitism," that bourgeois antisemitism in early nineteenth-century Germany deflected to Jewish account bourgeois financial behaviors derided by aristocrats.[9] The topos of the Jewish colonial conspirator potentially echoed that ideological legerdemain, offering a convenient screen later in the century for bourgeois involvement in the unpopular imperial adventures that roiled European public opinion in the 1880s and 1890s. Even so, Arendt uncharacteristically never seizes this opportunity to ironize at the bourgeoisie's expense. Perhaps she sought to minimize a historical discourse—antisemites' linkage of Jews and empire—at first glance so conspicuously dissonant with her thesis about a modern antisemitism emanating from, precisely, the relative unimportance of Jews to state-backed imperialism.

Perhaps, too, Arendt did not press the issue because she sensed that the displacement thesis itself rested on shaky historical ground. The most zealously imperialist of all French governments, the Third Republic (1870–1940), opened its ranks like never before to Jewish public servants. These Jewish functionaries in turn proved some of the most enthusiastic evangelists for the Republic's imperial *mission civilisatrice* ("civilizing mission").[10] Not only did French Jews thus arguably enter into a *more* visible partnership with the state during the age of empire, but they also did so at the vanguard of the official imperial project; whatever authorized status the new imperial reality may have cost French Jews at the level of state finance, it returned to them at the level of administrative and governmental relevance.[11] There is reason here to doubt Arendt's notion that empire kindled modern antisemitism by causing Jews to seem less functionally integrated with the state.

It bears asking, in fact, whether Jews were ever anywhere really displaced as financiers to the state by bourgeois investment in the imperial project. Arendt provides no evidence for this imperial decline in Jewish financial relevance to states and even dates the beginning of the decline to the first half of the nineteenth century, before the era of high empire.[12] What, then, explains her insistence on an imperial genesis to waning Jewish state privilege? My suspicion is that the displacement thesis itself doubles as a displacement, into the fabric of Arendt's argumentation, of the antisemitic outcry about Jews and empire. Granted, Arendt strategically inverts the antisemitic narrative, inherently rebutting colonial conspiracy theories by insisting on Jews' basic inconsequentiality to the imperial project. But that is exactly the point: conditioned at least as much by a rhetorical imperative as by any insight into the political economy of empire, Arendt's argument remains inscribed within parameters established the previous century by antisemites themselves. In other words, the displacement thesis less accurately describes a historical phenomenon than reflects Arendt's transposition of a historical discourse.

The complicated result—and this will be my fundamental claim about Arendt's legacy as a theorist of antisemitism—opens a productive avenue for critical and historiographic analysis even as it signals an impasse in Arendt's thought. Usefully, the displacement thesis implicitly adopts a perspective that other possible interpretive frameworks risk missing. Consider my attempt, in the following chapter, to explain antisemitic colonial conspiracy theories as a projection onto Jews of anxieties about empire. Too superficially approached, that model invites reducing modern antisemitism to a simple cognate of the racial anxiety triggered and institutionalized by the encounter with imperial subalterns. Arendt's own boomerang thesis assumes something like this, postulating as it does that the Holocaust became possible once Europeans had in Africa encountered peoples "alien beyond imagination or comprehension" who could be massacred, like the Jews after them, as less than human (*OT*, 195).

The displacement thesis points the way toward accomplishing something different. Associating the advent of modern antisemitism with a reaction not to imperial conquest as such but rather to its effects on internal state dynamics, Arendt's thesis nuances any easy conflation between imperialist and antisemitic "mind-sets" of racial superiority. After all, the initial opposition by many outspoken antisemites to late nineteenth-century European expansion overseas often found them combining the Jewish and imperial questions in ways that owed as much to the fact of empire itself as to imperialism's status as a racist enterprise. This is not to say that antisemitic discourses about empire bore no relation to the racism that helped legitimate imperial expansion; indeed, the topos of the Jewish colonial conspirator derived much of its shock value from the image of metropolitan Jews conniving with their more exotic and therefore more easily racializable indigenous Jewish counterparts in colonies like Tunisia, Algeria, and South Africa. Yet antisemitic discourses prompted by imperialism also betrayed preoccupations with everything from the impact of overseas conquests on France's prospects of revenge for the humiliating defeat of the 1870 Franco-Prussian War to stock market fluctuations attributable to events overseas. For all their remove from the actual business of conquest or from comparative racial taxonomies, these preoccupations remained no less inflected by the unique geopolitical circumstances of empire. Such circumstances furnished modern antisemitism the material for what I am calling racial scalarity: that is, representations of Jews informed by the possibility that one might move between scales, in particular the national and global-imperial ones. So, for example, as I will be arguing in Chapter 2, did modern French antisemitism enable the translation of a troubling imperial alterity into a Jewish otherness more tolerable because reconceived at the scale of the nation.

Metropolitan Jewish otherness was here fashioned into a variety of imperial otherness, then, but only because Jewishness had first provided a springboard for fashioning and representing scale. In other words, the racial relationality implicitly or explicitly posited between metropolitan Jews and imperial subalterns was made ideologically meaningful by an accompanying scalarity. Such a scalarity was contingent, in the way I mean to use the word here, because it was determined by what the whole of empire made possible to think about the Jews, rather than by a more narrowly motivated, one-to-one correspondence imagined between internal and external racial others. Arendt's displacement thesis makes analytic space for this overlooked aspect of the interrelation between antisemitism and imperialism, imagining how the late-century encounter between two great hydras of modernity produced discourses about Jews that empire—as a comprehensive political phenomenon, and not just as a racist ideology—specifically allowed to flourish. We need not agree with the content of the thesis, as I do not, for the basic gesture to remain valuable.

Historical accuracy and methodological utility aside, the displacement thesis haunts *Origins* with a troublesomely stubborn ghost: that of a bygone antisemitic narrative of Jewish colonial conspiracy for which Arendt would obviously have shown no patience but whose transposition into her arguments nonetheless structures and delimits *Origins* in important ways.[13] My intent here, I should state quite clearly, is not somehow to impute a repressed or inadvertent antisemitism to Arendt. I aim instead to demonstrate how Arendt's struggle with her indebtedness to so problematic a paradigm indexes an even more fundamental strain in her political philosophy. That strain caused Arendt to share a basic epistemic tendency—the impulse to link the Jewish and imperial questions—with narratives about Jewish colonial conspiracy. But if she did so without reproducing any attendant antisemitism, the consequences of this tendency reverberate no less uneasily in her work. Prominent among these, I will argue, is Africa's role in *Origins* as a metaphysical outlet for aporias dogging Arendt's conception of the nineteenth-century European political order, of the Jews' place within it, and of political community itself. Even as she decries Europe's imperial encounter with the Dark Continent, Arendt is herself drawn to that encounter for its seeming potential to reinvigorate politico-ontological distinctions eroded in Europe.

We will see, for example, how Arendt's assessment of imperial adventurers and black tribes in Africa works to distill and isolate a biological menace less dissociable from her ideal of European civilization than she would like. In so doing, *Origins* reprises a gesture to which antisemites once resorted when they likewise sought in empire to resolve their own vexed internal logics (see Chapters 3 and 4). If the displacement thesis possesses methodological value—and I believe it does—recuperating that value therefore requires acknowledging how, for all its critical originality, Arendt's consideration together of antisemitism and imperialism nonetheless retains certain continuities with the nineteenth century. To that end, I turn now to Arendt's dialogue in *Origins* with an antisemitic theorist of empire and to the contortions it entails.

A "PARADISE OF PARASITES"

Bernard Wasserstein's aforementioned critique of Arendt pulls no punches. Wasserstein reproves Arendt for having relied too uncritically, in *Origins*, on perspectives offered by the likes of Édouard Drumont, the godfather of French antisemitism, and Ernst Schultze, the Nazi propagandist. Included for opprobrium are Arendt's invocations of the celebrated British economist J. A. Hobson, author of the landmark 1902 anti-imperialist study *Imperialism* and a key influence on her thinking about empire. Arendt's queasy ventriloquizing of unfriendly remarks by Hobson about Jews prompts Wasserstein to recall Walter Laqueur's dry observation that Arendt "perhaps . . . had read too much antisemitic literature for her own good."[14]

A reader could indeed be forgiven for raising an eyebrow at Arendt's apparently untroubled reproduction—more on this below—of Hobson's antisemitic vituperations. But this is to miss a crucial complexity in the interaction of the philosopher with her source. Arendt scholars have debated whether, in her zeal for historical empathy and understanding, she occasionally showed too much interpretive "generosity" toward objectionable behaviors and opinions in her subjects.[15] Her engagement with Hobson, however, documents no mere empathic overreach. Neither does it simply convey uncritical acquiescence to Hobson's antisemitic sentiments, as Wasserstein would have it. Rather, Arendt's brief but significant exchanges with Hobson in *Origins* reveal a thinker grappling with her indebtedness to a certain epistemic paradigm. Arendt at first seems partially to rehearse the antisemitic canard, popularized by Hobson, that Jewish finance greased the wheels of European imperialism. She soon qualifies her stance with the now-familiar refrain that bourgeois investment rendered any Jewish imperial influence short-lived. Yet Arendt does so in a way—and the point is capital—that itself adopts the underlying structure of the antisemitic trope bequeathed by Hobson. In what follows, I want to trace the vicissitudes of Arendt's awkward maneuver, as well as begin considering what it reveals about the conceptual freight carried for Arendt by the theme of superfluity that so animates *Origins*.

Arendt's endorsement of Hobson begins straightforwardly enough. Like Lenin before her, Arendt accepts Hobson's central premise that imperialism was driven by the need of "superfluous" European capital to ceaselessly "press farther afield" in the search for new markets and investments.[16] Building on Hobson's notion, as well as on Rosa Luxemburg's related critique of imperialism as the inevitable political corollary of accumulated capital, Arendt portrays superfluity as both the engine and self-reproducing outcome of empire. Empire channeled abroad the superfluous labor and wealth generated by capitalism; it expropriated the resources of others to produce further superfluous wealth; and finally, having institutionalized the superfluity of its agents and victims, it added European Jewry to the disposable ranks of superfluous man. Driving all this for Arendt was a bourgeoisie enthralled with making "money beget money" (*OT*, 137)—an obsession that, in its imperial configuration as "expansion for expansion's sake," she felt had upended the principles of the nation-state and set Europe on the path to totalitarianism and exterminationist antisemitism (*OT*, 126).

But Arendt did not just count the Jews among the victims of a ravaging imperial superfluity. She argued as well that they helped unleash it. Arendt submits that it was "Jewish international financiers" who "opened the channels of capital export to superfluous wealth" by facilitating government investment abroad during the initial phase of imperialism in the 1870s and 1880s (*OT*, 135–36).[17] In support of her claim she cites Hobson, whose early critiques of imperialism contained choice words about the Jewish role in imperial South Africa. Endorsing Hobson as "very reliable in observation and very honest in analysis" (*OT*, 135n34), Arendt reproduces at length a passage from a 1900 article he penned whose tenor speaks for itself. Jewish financiers, Hobson reports, went to South Africa

> for money, and those who came early and made most have commonly withdrawn their persons, leaving their economic fangs in the carcass of their prey. They fastened on the Rand . . . as they are prepared to fasten upon any other spot upon the globe. (quoted in *OT*, 135n34)

Hobson considered himself an eyewitness, having traveled to South Africa in 1899 at the behest of the *Manchester Guardian*. In a passage of the article not cited by Arendt, Hobson labels Jewish financiers the "*causa causans* of the present trouble in South Africa" because they stood to gain economically from British imperial intervention.[18] Hobson's impassioned book-length denunciation of the Second Boer War, *The War in South Africa: Its Causes and Effects* (1900), likewise features Jews prominently on the "causes" side of the ledger. To the question posed by one chapter title, "For Whom Are We Fighting?" Hobson offers a familiar response: the Jewish diamond and gold magnates, who have transformed Johannesburg into "the New Jerusalem" on the helpless watch of the "slower-witted Briton."[19]

Shocking as it is, though, for Arendt blithely to recycle Hobson's tale of vampiric Jews—or, for that matter, to borrow approvingly an account by Hobson's contemporary J. A. Froude of Jewish merchants in South Africa "gathered like eagles over their prey" (quoted in *OT*, 198)—Arendt does so with calculated intent. Her praise for Hobson's "reliability" is mostly designed to demonstrate that if in *Imperialism* Hobson no longer blamed the Jews for the Second Boer War, it was because he had since correctly and honestly recognized that "their influence and role had been temporary and somewhat superficial" (*OT*, 135). Arendt means to illustrate that, despite an initial role as financial facilitators, Jews were eventually wholly supplanted in their imperial function by the bourgeoisie. Jews were "only the representatives, not the owners, of the superfluous capital," she writes (*OT*, 200). It follows that the Jews themselves were easily made superfluous by empire, something to which, as we have seen, Arendt attributes the rise of modern antisemitism.

Notice here the inversion accomplished by Arendt. Hobson at one point considered Jews responsible for the imperial developments he decried. But Arendt takes Hobson's later silence on the matter as more than just evidence that Jews had not, in fact, played a determining role in South African affairs. Rather, she exchanges the terms of the equation altogether: whereas Hobson and others blamed Jewish influence for the rise of empire, Arendt locates in the rise of empire the beginning of a perilous Jewish irrelevance. In other words, Arendt maintains the old causal link between empire and the Jewish question, even if she reverses its polarity. Arendt is in many ways writing against Hobson. She explicitly rebukes him for suggesting in *Imperialism* that the Rothschilds, the international Jewish banking clan and eternal bête noire of antisemites, pulled the strings of every European war (*OT*, 24–25). More subtly, her argument about the Jews' reluctance to translate economic influence in South Africa into political influence represents an implicit rebuttal to Hobson's own contention that Jewish businessmen had, in South Africa, made an exception to their usual disinterest in political matters (*OT*, 136).[20] Yet Arendt is also unmistakably writing *within* a long discursive tradition of linking the Jewish and imperial questions—a tradition shaped by antisemites who, beginning in the late nineteenth century, saw in the passions stirred by empire a chance to stoke hatred against Jews. This tradition supplied epistemic grounds for Arendt to think Jews and empire together. One finds it difficult to imagine that Arendt would otherwise have formulated so circumstantial an explanation for modern antisemitism as the relative nonparticipation by Jews in empire, given that the terms of her argument would seem inherently to militate against conceiving any relationship between Jews and empire in the first place. That her thesis so symmetrically inverts existing assumptions about Jews and empire only underscores her dependence on so improbable a conceptual forebear.

From this perspective, Arendt's unsettlingly approving reproduction of Hobson's antisemitic invective might be considered symptomatic, a stray artifact of her reliance on and only partial reconfiguration of an existing discourse. There is also the matter of Arendt's ever-contentious insistence on the Jewish portion of responsibility for antisemitism (more on this below), which perhaps occasioned an overeagerness to treat antisemitic sources as reliable. At least when it comes to her indulgence of Hobson's dubious remarks about Jews in South Africa, however, I would offer that the picture is rather more complex and that Arendt's micro-appropriation here of antisemitic language actually finds her trying to exorcise her macro-dependence on an antisemitic discourse about empire. By deploying familiar topoi from the antisemitic lexicon in her depiction of an imperial South Africa afflicted by gold lust, economic predation, and financial parasitism, Arendt lays the groundwork for reapportioning blame to a variety of other imperial actors—all of whom, Arendt means clearly to suggest, behaved more "Jewishly" than the Jews themselves.

Thus, for instance, does Arendt memorably dub imperial South Africa "the first paradise of parasites" (*OT*, 151) because it channeled superfluous capital and labor into the ne plus ultra of bourgeois fantasies: directly transforming money into more money by literally mining it from the earth. Arendt's inclusion of Jews among these "parasites," though only as temporary avatars and middlemen of the real (bourgeois) owners of parasitic wealth, possesses the rhetorical advantage of acknowledging rather than eliding the historical fact of Jewish involvement in the South African gold and diamond mines.[21] But Arendt also willfully plays up the "parasitism" of these Jews, the better to transfer its stigma to their bourgeois patrons—and to rehearse, by the same token, her own substitution of the bourgeois for the Jew in the old antisemitic narrative about empire that she has only partially recast.

Thus, too, does Arendt draw unlikely correspondences between Jews and the Boers of turn-of-the-century South Africa. "Like the Jews," she declares, the Boers "firmly believed in themselves as the chosen people" (*OT*, 195). And if the Boers were the most virulent in their antisemitism, it was because they identified in the Jews a competing "claim to chosenness" (*OT*, 202). Arendt's analogy foreshadows her later argument that supranational racist movements in Europe shared an affinity with, and even patterned themselves after, the "rootlessness" and "tribalness" of the Jews (*OT*, 239). It serves as well, in the manner I have been describing, to offload onto others the structural role played by Jews in the antisemitic narrative about empire that Arendt inherits and reconfigures. The Boers are like Jews for Arendt because on a certain level she requires them to function *as* Jews, something that perhaps explains why, in citing the Boers' "complete lack of literature and other intellectual achievement," she echoes a classic slur directed by antisemites at the Jewish people (*OT*, 196).

Simply put, Arendt seeks to make Jews as redundant as possible to the imperial South African economy of superfluity she theorizes. What becomes, in that case, of those superfluous to superfluity itself? Like the negative of a negative, they revert to a positive, at least in the South African context. Arendt reports that after having been displaced from their earlier speculative activities, South African Jews became an island of "normalcy and productivity" in the gold-distorted imperial economy by becoming manufacturers, shopkeepers, and members of the liberal professions. This only earned them more hatred from the Boers, Arendt adds, because they were now antithetical, in their very productivity, to the parasitic economy of superfluity predicated on the racist spoliation of labor and mineral wealth (*OT*, 205). The irony is superb, and quite intentional on Arendt's part: here is a group of non-Jews become more stereotypically "Jewish" than the Jews themselves, and hating their real Jewish neighbors for *not* engaging in predatory economic activity! With this wry series of inversions, Arendt completes her transfer away from the Jews of the "Jewish" function in the old antisemitic critique of empire whose basic conceptual armature she otherwise maintains.

Arendt's correlation of Boer antisemitism with the displacement of Jews from the financial machinery of empire recalls her larger thesis about European antisemitism, which she likewise correlates with the ultimate absence of Jews from the imperial state project. Even so, the mechanisms she invokes to explain the two correlations—suspicion of Jewish productivity in the South African case and suspicion of Jewish non-productivity in the European case—prove difficult to reconcile. The fact that Arendt's core notion about the superfluity of Jews to the project of empire survives these varied and contradictory applications bespeaks less, I think, an analytic confusion than a steady projection by Arendt in her arguments of her own tacit preoccupation: namely, the preoccupation to render the Jews superfluous to a theory of empire problematically descended from a bygone narrative of Jewish colonial conspiracy.

Origins is hence at pains, for reasons internal to its architecture, to cleave the Jew from the workings of empire. That imperative exacts a historiographic price, for instance in Arendt's inaccurate claim that the substantial population of indigenous Jews in French colonial Algeria did not "play much of a role" in French imperial politics (*OT*, 50)—counterexamples to which are beginning to multiply.[22] We can see, too, how Arendt reproduces a quasi-theological conviction from the schema she adapts. Substituting the bourgeoisie, or bourgeois capital, in the role formerly occupied by Jews in colonial conspiracy theories, Arendt merely swaps one inexorable motive force (a supposed Jewish thirst for world domination) for another (an ostensible bourgeois lust for "power for power's sake"). Both amount to the "diabolical causality" assumed, as Léon Poliakov has proposed, by antisemitism and Marxism alike in their respective elevations of Jews and the bourgeoisie into abstract, supra-individual agents of history.[23]

There is a subtler problem yet. Arendt's granting of rhetorical redundancy to the Jews—that is, her corrective marginalization of them from the theory of empire she inherits—strangely doubles and rejoins the actual condition of superfluity to which, following Arendt, Jews were dangerously condemned by imperialism. Each mode of superfluity, rhetorical and real, effectively inheres in the other: think of the displacement thesis, whose postulation of a sudden Jewish superfluity is conceivably governed more by the rhetorical necessity to dissociate Jews from the business of imperialism (and thus from Arendt's refurbished theory of empire) than by historical evidence. Two preliminary conclusions accordingly emerge. The first is that, as instantiated by the Jews, the figure of superfluity so central to *Origins*—and whose source Arendt locates in capitalist production—in fact expresses a tension intrinsic to Arendt's own logical economy. Put another way, Arendt's arguments produce the key phenomenon they purport to apprehend. The second preliminary conclusion follows from the first. Echoing the manner in which, for Arendt, empire channeled away a superfluity generated by capitalist Europe but uncontainable there, imperial spaces evidently bear a structural relationship in *Origins* to the quandary of superfluity intolerably generated by the Arendtian system itself. But what is this relationship that it should so intertwine, as *Origins* does, the Jewish and imperial questions? And how does the question of superfluity come to exert such pressure on the whole? The answers lie deep in Arendt's account of human history.

INTERSTITIAL JEWS

It appears curious at first that so thoughtful an adversary of antisemitism as Arendt could be drawn to a theory of empire such as Hobson's, one amenable to (and possibly even derived from) antisemitic suspicions that Jewish financial interests had entangled governments in imperial wars. Rosa Luxemburg's similar theory about capital's innate imperial expansionism, a theory that never implicates the Jews and whose "brilliant insight" Arendt lauds in *Origins* (*OT*, 148n45), would seem to have sufficed. Yet this does not take into account the opportunities Hobson affords Arendt. Already we have seen how Arendt locates in Hobson a tool for paring the vestigial antisemitism from an anti-imperialist tradition epitomized by Hobson himself. Significantly, she does so according to that tradition's own premise: the surplus imperialist capital that for Hobson was synonymous with international Jewry becomes, in Arendt's hands, the mechanism by which Jews were excluded from imperial finance. Arendt in this fashion reproduces Hobson's definition of imperialism as the violent solution to the problem of surplus capital, while at the same time inoculating that definition against its antisemitic heritage.

A less obvious point is that Arendt also reproduces, by the same token, Hobson's association of empire with the Jews. Arendt might simply have dismissed that association; instead she reframes it, transposing the Jews from imperial perpetrators into imperial victims. Previously I cited this transposition as evidence of the displacement thesis's indebtedness, for its impetus, to the myth of Jewish colonial conspiracy it is manifestly intended to refute. The symmetry of the transposition is itself noteworthy, however. Arendt proposes a pivotal historical relationship between European Jewry and empire, though not the one imagined by antisemites. But why propose such a relationship at all? Arendt surely savored reversing the argument by antisemites that Jews engendered imperialism into the argument that imperialism engendered antisemitism. Nevertheless, one finds it hard to accept that so fundamental a historical claim in *Origins* should serve an essentially derivative rhetorical purpose. And yet neither is there especially compelling historical evidence for the displacement thesis. What, given this, motivates Arendt's attachment to blaming the historical fate of Jews on empire?

Arendt's embrace of Hobson suggests an explanation. Arendt, it becomes increasingly clear, is drawn to Hobson not in spite of his divagations about Jews but *on account* of them. This is because Arendt's inversion of Hobson's antisemitic narrative accompanies a more wholesale movement of strategic adaptation and inversion. Just as for Hobson the Jew helps resolve the mystery of empire, so for Arendt does empire help address a difficulty concerning the

Jews—hence Arendt's reproduction of the basic Jew-empire dyad. But the difficulty addressed is not confined, as Arendt would have it, to the mystery of antisemitism. Rather, it extends to what I would argue is the constitutive problem posed by the Jews—or at least by what Arendt makes the Jews incarnate—to her fundamental political and philosophical frame. Call this Arendt's Jewish problem, a problem made visible by empire and that impels *Origins* outward as Arendt moves from European Jewry in part 1 ("Antisemitism") to the conquest of Africa in part 2 ("Imperialism").

Consider, to begin, the Jews' fraught political ontology in the story *Origins* tells. Arendt submits that emancipation produced a nineteenth-century paradox. What Jewish difference disappeared in the equality of citizenship, European states reinscribed by only emancipating Jews for what they might provide, as a group apart, to their fledgling state patrons. With its postrevolutionary, postfeudal "claim to be above all classes" (*OT*, 17), the modern nation-state had cut itself off from society: only the Jews now, in their similar detachment from the class order, proved willing to finance state affairs. The resulting civil, de jure inclusion of Jews in the national body thus institutionalized their social, de facto exclusion from it.

Empire eroded this already tenuous status of the Jews as included exclusion, displacing them from their national niche when the bourgeoisie partnered with the state in the business of imperial expansion. Allied, henceforth, with an ascendant class power, states no longer required a socially unaligned partner in the Jews. But Arendt advances a second way as well in which empire rendered moot the Jews' utility to states as an independent group. The class neutrality that won Jews state favor at the national level reinforced the international Jewish ties necessary, in the absence of class ties, for funneling sufficient resources to each emancipated Jewry's governmental protector. These international ties in turn modulated Jewish loyalties to individual states, such that even after the importance of Jewish state finance waned at the national level, Jews retained their state relevance at the European level as a "non-national" diplomatic element useful for negotiating treaties and disseminating news (*OT*, 21). Arendt credits these "good Europeans" (*OT*, 23)—the expression is Nietzsche's[24]—with having sustained a delicate European political order predicated on mutual national respect and common belonging. She understands that "comity of nations" to have dissolved, though, when the imperial directive of limitless expansion infected continental mentalities and undermined the very premise of European plurality (*OT*, 15).

Arendt's unconcealed nostalgia for the lost European comity of nations contrasts with her critique elsewhere in *Origins* of the nation-state. Arendt famously identifies a "secret conflict between state and nation" inaugurated when modern nation-states like France grounded the legitimacy of human rights in the principle of national sovereignty (*OT*, 230). This subsumption of universal justice under particular belonging caused the "perversion of the state into an instrument of the nation" by making human rights conditional on citizenship (*OT*, 231); woe to anyone who, like European Jews in the twentieth century, might find themselves stateless. But "even in its perverted form," the state remained for Arendt a legal bulwark against a nationalist ethos that, unchecked, threatened the lawlessness of imperialism (*OT*, 231). Marcel Stoetzler reasonably concludes that Arendt considered the nation-state a "*lesser* evil" than empire and "believed in a benign form of the nation-state before anti-Semitic and imperialist nationalism conquered it."[25] Likewise did Arendt mourn a European comity of nations ostensibly preferable to the imperial order that followed.

The sophistication of Arendt's narrative lies in the potential it suggests for the benign to turn malignant from within. Imperialism overtook nation-states when the "secret conflict between state and nation" tilted decisively in favor of the nation and its exclusionary, easily racializable insistence on chosenness and belonging. That secret conflict nevertheless conceals what I will be proposing is an even more secret tension vexing Arendt's theory of the nation-state and European comity. In keeping with her general political philosophy, which championed an oppositional, if cooperative, play of relations among unique political actors, Arendt understood the modern state to have usefully "counterbalance[d] the centrifugal forces constantly produced in a class-ridden society" (*OT*, 231). Preventing these centrifugal forces from rending the nation, while retaining the heterogeneity that produced them, the state imposed a tricky equilibrium. Key to that equilibrium was the state's non-alignment with the classes, establishing it as an authority common to all but beholden to none. Arendt frequently resolves this dynamic into an agonal binary, noting the "precarious balance between society and state" or the "precarious balance between nation and state" (*OT*, 56, 231). By this Arendt means to emphasize the contrast between the state as bearer of rational, abstract legality, and nation and society as bearers of various behaviors—egoistic individualism, nationalist conformism, mass consumerism—incommensurate for Arendt with true political life. But the opposition is somewhat misleading. If the modern state, following Arendt, promised a legitimate politics, it did not do so as some sort of functional, self-immanent repository of values opposable to the uglier tendencies in social existence. Rather, it did so by providing a common space, a medium if you will, that both gathered citizens together as a collectivity of equals and empowered them, by the same token, to affirm their singularity as individuals. In Arendtian terms, the state expanded the man-made "world" that "relates and separates men at the same time" in the way necessary for an authentic public realm.[26] Strictly speaking, then, the "precarious balance" that preoccupies Arendt does not reside between the state and society as much as it resides, more diffusely, among the infinite interstices across which citizens are at once related and separated in an endlessly fragile play of countervailing forces.

Arendt better captures the interstitial quality of this equilibrium in the other precarious balance she describes, the "precarious balance of power" maintaining the European comity of nations before it was destroyed by empire (*OT*, 3). She conceives the European balance of power as having functioned on the same principle of relation and separation, with nations bound together by a common ethos—mutual respect for sovereignty—that simultaneously guaranteed each nation its individual autonomy. Arendt never remarks that the relational balance among nations is also obviously interdependent with the analogously relational balance within nations. Legitimacy accrued to each state's intranational efforts at binding together disparate local elements as the state itself achieved legitimacy from participation in an international order; conversely, the international order was strengthened by the emergence of states that, by virtue of their class neutrality, enjoyed more affinity with other like states than with supranational aristocratic configurations like the Hapsburgs. But this raises a difficulty Arendt would rather avoid. At the scale of the individual nation-state, Arendt's idea of the state imparts at least some tangible, institutional form to the otherwise slippery interstitiality it implies. At the scale of the European comity of nations, however, only interstitiality remains. Nothing within the nations themselves was sufficient to regulate their interrelation with one another. It follows that the international order Arendt invokes and by extension the nations it contains and helps define require something *outside* the nation-state to function.

What is the nature, for Arendt, of this interstitial supplement to the nation-state? In a word: the Jew. Or rather, the Jew is the name Arendt gives to a necessary condition for the equilibrium she details. As financial avatars of the modern state, Jews seeded the public space that relates and separates. And as the only "good Europeans," Jews similarly facilitated a comity of nations dependent, for its precarious balance, on a non-national element at once common to and distinct from its sovereign participants. Arendt quotes approvingly from Diderot's *Encyclopédie*, whose entry for "Jew" notes that Jews "have become instruments of communication between the most distant countries" and are thus "like the cogs and nails needed in a great building in order to join and hold together all the other parts" (quoted in *OT*, 23n15). That structural liminality made Jews especially vulnerable:

> It is therefore more than accidental that the catastrophic defeats of the peoples of Europe began with the catastrophe of the Jewish people. It was particularly easy to begin the dissolution of the precarious European balance of power with the elimination of the Jews, and particularly difficult to understand that more was involved in this elimination than an unusually cruel nationalism or an ill-timed revival of old prejudices. (*OT*, 22)

The precariousness of the Jews coincided with the precariousness of the European system of nation-states they helped maintain; destroy one, and you destroyed the other. But either destruction merely culminated a basic disequilibrium introduced, Arendt suggests, by unchecked growth in one of the components of the nation-state system. So, for example, did Nazi Germany's violent expansionism deal the death blow to a comity of nations whose participants had "never dreamed of . . . annihilating their neighbors completely" (*OT*, 22). So, too, did rampant activity by a single national element, the bourgeoisie, earlier catalyze overseas imperialism at the expense of the state and the interstitial equilibrium it sustained.

Observe the deflection of emphasis here. Rather than entertain the innate precariousness of nation-states uneasily contingent, for their collective and individual existence, on something outside themselves—that is, on an interstitial supplement surrounding and pervading them—Arendt focuses instead on unnatural expansion by nation-states or their constituent elements. This cancerous proliferation in turn does away with the agents of supplementarity: thus does expansionist totalitarianism target all Jewry, or bourgeois imperialism overrun the state.

It is evidently in the logic of the Reich and of imperialist "expansion for expansion's sake," as Arendt understands them, that there in fact *be* nothing outside their limitless reach. But by locating the crisis of the nation-state system in a disequilibrium plaguing its internal elements, then attributing to that disequilibrium the demise of the interstitial balance within and among nation-states, Arendt herself erases the problem of supplementarity. Or, more accurately, she defers it. For if *Origins* is anything, it is the story of what Arendt believes similarly exceeded and yet defined the modern European order: namely, superfluity, that by-product of capital whose perniciousness she traces from Europe to Africa and back again. Following Hobson and Luxemburg, Arendt presents superfluity as the creeping shadow of a capitalist system permanently dependent for its survival on materials and markets outside itself. In the process, she shifts the fundamental onus of supplementarity from the political to the economic, and from the nation-state to empire.

Empire, to be sure, merged the political and the economic by placing public means at the disposal of private business interests. And Arendt certainly allows for a measure of affinity between capitalist superfluity and a nationalism always potentially in excess of itself. The same sense of "national mission" that had produced nationhood sometimes metastasized, she notes, into an imperial "national mission" that transformed the national myth of bounded solidarity and chosenness into a racist, messianic rationale for unbounded expansion (*OT*, 182).[27] Still, this acknowledgment of a latent supplementarity in nationalism only locates a problem in the "national" half of the nation-state equation—which is to say, in the half that Arendt always considered dangerous to begin with. The other half, the interstitial balance of relation and separation on which hinged the state and the comity of nations, goes unscrutinized.

Yet it is to this interstitial balance, tellingly, that Arendt first turns for the momentum that will sustain the narrative and analytic machinery of *Origins*. It is common to express perplexity at Arendt's decision to open her study of totalitarianism with an extended reflection on antisemitism. Seyla Benhabib proposes that to "appreciate the unity of the work as Arendt herself intended it to be read" one must begin not with part 1 ("Antisemitism") but rather with the chapter in part 3 about the extermination and concentration camps ("Total Domination").[28] Margaret Canovan observes, for her part, that Arendt's arrangement "is not a very helpful one," among other reasons because Arendt's discussion of antisemitism deploys key concepts like "imperialism" whose idiosyncratic meaning to Arendt she only later defines. Canovan chalks up Arendt's organizational decision to "her own initial preoccupation" with antisemitism, as well as to "reasons of chronology."[29]

I want to suggest, however, that the historical examination of antisemitism with which *Origins* begins serves a substantive opening purpose for Arendt. This is because the quandary of the Jews in Arendt's narrative coincides with what I have been calling the other secret conflict of the nation-state. Recall that the state requires, in order to effect the political intercourse for which Arendt valorizes it, the extension everywhere of a binding medium that relates and separates. Within the nation-state, the medium furnishes the interstitial condition for a delicate political balance gathering singular citizens together without collapsing them into the undifferentiated masses of nation and society against which Arendt warns. Above the nation-state, the medium furnishes the interstitial basis for the comity of nations and its similarly fragile balance of mutually assured sovereignty. Arendt understands these balances to possess an ontology apart from the medium that supports them, insofar as they take shape in the shifting, back-and-forth interactions among their participating elements. The medium itself, though, possesses an ontology as well. It is no mere vacuum. Historically speaking, it has needed constitution by something or someone—something or someone, moreover, irreducible to the state. After all, any individual state lacked the neutrality to facilitate the nineteenth-century comity of nations. And the "claim to be above all classes," by virtue of the local social isolation it entailed, made the state reliant on a partner that—by virtue of its own social isolation—cultivated a global solidarity beyond state control.

This partner, of course, was the Jews. But the unenviable historical role accorded the Jews by Arendt works to obscure an inherent instability in the state dynamic she relates. One easily enough appreciates Arendt's point about the precariousness of that role. Functioning as an included exclusion in a system dependent on them only to the extent that they existed apart, the Jews were vulnerable to outright exclusion once the state abandoned its class neutrality, made common cause with the bourgeoisie, and yielded to an imperial system anathema to the old equilibrium of relation and separation. Hence were they among the first consigned to superfluity by a capitalist imperial order defined by its production and management of superfluity. What Arendt's displacement thesis elides, however, is that the Jews had *already* been primed for such a superfluity by the state. As capitalist Europe both produced and required, in empire, something in excess of itself, so the state produced and required the Jews as that which necessarily exceeded it. In other words, the problem of superfluity was not limited to capitalist enterprise. It was also endemic to the state.

Origins is structured to defuse this fact. Arendt begins with the Jews in part because, put simply, they vehicle superfluity from state to empire. Earlier I examined how the displacement thesis doubles as a displacement away from the Jews of the imperial guilt assigned them in the colonial conspiracy theory that Arendt reconfigures. Now another such second-order displacement becomes evident: that of superfluity away from the state. By blaming antisemitism on the superfluity to which empire relegated the Jews, the displacement thesis diverts attention from the state's own, prior implication in Jewish superfluity. Note, moreover, how the two second-order displacements achieved by the displacement thesis complement each other. While Arendt's displacement of superfluity from the state intertwines the history of European Jews with the history of empire, a premise she shares with the antisemitic colonial conspiracy theory, her displacement of imperial responsibility from the Jews simultaneously neutralizes the antisemitism of her Hobsonian model.

What remains is an association between Jewish and imperial histories that helps Arendt locate the source of superfluity elsewhere than in the state. This inaugurates, in turn, a binary narrative structuring so much of her analysis in *Origins*: the losing battle between the modern state and the various modes of superfluity—national, social, imperial, racist, totalitarian—that overwhelmed it. One of these foils, society, offers an especially instructive point of intersection with Arendt's larger political philosophy and the tensions revealed therein. As Arendt later defines it in *The Human Condition*, modern mass society is the private made dangerously public. It organizes collective life along the principles of individual biological need, perverting citizenry into membership in a single, uniform aggregate of material production and consumption managed by a biopolitics indifferent to plurality. This "unnatural growth of the natural" overlaps with a commodity capitalism that, in transforming even the most permanent objects into evanescent consumer goods, condemns man to the cyclical transience of biological life (*HC*, 47). Reading these categories back into *Origins*, we can discern that society, by co-opting the state for bourgeois imperial gain, removed for Arendt the only viable barrier against the unnatural growth of the natural. The genie of *zoē*, of bare animal life, had been unleashed upon civilization; and in the imperial crush of superfluous commodities and superfluous men reducing individuals to their shared organic appetites, humans were retreating from the man-made "world" of true politics and permanence to the biological anonymity of what in *The Human Condition* Arendt calls the "earth" (*HC*, 134).

Yet Arendt's relative idealization of a postfeudal, class-neutral, pre-imperial state represses a crucial detail. For that state, too, unleashes a similarly uncontrollable (and, I will be arguing, similarly biological) element into the world of properly political man. The superfluity of the Jews, before Arendt identifies in it an early consequence of empire, is the unavowed superfluity always already essential to the precarious interstitial balance struck by even the benign, non-imperialized state—a balance so precarious, in fact, that it represents no balance at all, given its innate and perpetual reliance on that which escapes it. But what, exactly, makes this unavowed superfluity troublesome enough for Arendt to repress and defer?

Here again the categories elaborated in *The Human Condition* prove illuminating. Let me call particular attention to two, "labor" and "work," and to Arendt's unusual distinction between them. Labor, the province of the human being as *animal laborans*, is the toil necessary for the satisfaction of man's biological needs. Because it produces nothing more than life itself and "leaves nothing behind" (*HC*, 87), it imprisons *animal laborans* in nature's infinitely recurring cyclicality. Work, in contrast, opposes a permanent domain of man-made artifice to the ephemerality of natural existence. Through work, *homo faber* builds a world of objects and institutions that gather and yet differentiate men in the way that "a table is located between those who sit around it" (*HC*, 52). This world structures the public realm by facilitating an "in-between" where, in speech and action, men reveal themselves to each other as unique. In so doing, they enact the intangible, multiperspectival "web of human relationships" in which Arendt locates the only means for preserving individual life stories, and indeed human plurality itself, from the undifferentiated oblivion of bare animal life (*HC*, 182–83). Arendt critiques Marx for ignoring the difference between labor and work, and for consequently not having understood that the society of laborers he foresaw dangerously replaced plural individuals with "worldless specimens of the species mankind" (*HC*, 118). As it happens, commodity capitalism threatens to achieve the same result: Arendt laments that mechanization and automation make consumption so ubiquitously effortless that all human endeavor is increasingly "sucked into an intensified life process" (*HC*, 132), with biology overtaking plurality as the human world recedes against an ever-expanding onslaught of disindividuating material existence.

Critics have often contested Arendt's distinction of labor from work and some of the conclusions to which it leads her. More than one commentator argues that Arendt misreads Marx by failing to account for, among others things, the similar distinction that Marx himself draws between alienated and unalienated labor.[30] Feminist political theorists have also expressed consternation that Arendt's definition of labor extends to private household tasks typically performed by women, like cooking, cleaning, and child-rearing, which Arendt excludes ipso facto from the public realm of the world and political engagement. This has led to a number of thoughtful reflections on Arendt's implicit gendering of the divisions she advances—between private and public, labor and work, social and political—as well as on the permeability of these divisions themselves. So, for instance, does Seyla Benhabib compellingly maintain that raising children is a world-shaping activity without which no individuals could reasonably grow to occupy the public realm.[31] Arendt, though, seems preoccupied with minimizing any overlap between biology and world. One such potential overlap exists in the fact that labor, and not just work, attends the endeavor of world-building. Arendt allows for the importance of labor in staving off the encroachment by nature on the world of permanent objects and institutions:

> Equally bound up with the recurring cycles of natural movements, but not quite so urgently imposed upon man by "the condition of human life" itself, is the second task of laboring—its constant, unending fight against the processes of growth and decay through which nature forever invades the human artifice, threatening the durability of the world and its fitness for human use. (*HC*, 100)

Despite conceding the close alignment of this "second task of laboring" with world-building, Arendt is careful to reiterate the basic nonproductivity of a task that, like all labor, leaves nothing behind:

> The protection and preservation of the world against natural processes are among the toils which need the monotonous performance of daily repeated chores. This laboring fight, as

> distinguished from the essentially peaceful fulfillment in which labor obeys the orders of immediate bodily needs, although it may be even less "productive" than man's direct metabolism with nature, has a much closer connection with the world, which it defends against nature. (*HC*, 100–101)

The feminist poet and thinker Adrienne Rich likens this repeated maintenance to the "million tiny stitches" of women's household toil and stresses its importance as "world-protection, world-preservation, world-repair."[32] Arendt, in contrast, hastens to emphasize the gulf separating the labor of maintenance and preservation from actual participation in the world. However Herculean that labor may seem, "the daily fight in which the human body is engaged to keep the world clean and prevent its decay bears little resemblance to heroic deeds"; Arendt manifestly reserves such heroism only for the public action and speech that produce the "shining brightness we once called glory" (*HC*, 101, 180).

One detects a twinge of anxiety in the vigorousness with which Arendt polices the line between the world and the monotonous upkeep it demands. What accounts for this raising of the stakes, evident already in her tonal shift between a labor of self-sustenance that produces "peaceful fulfillment" and a labor of preservation that promises only an "unending fight"? Is the basic struggle for sustenance really any less violent than the labor of maintenance? One answer rests in the more obviously thankless, Sisyphean quality of the maintenance labor she describes: labor in the fields bears fruit that no scrubbing of floors ever can. Another answer rests in the importance of the effort. Without it the world would crumble, an outcome in many ways worse for Arendt than death from lack of sustenance because man would regress back among the animals. But herein lies a complication. The further man rises, in the public world, above the cyclical transience of biological life, the more labor he creates for *animal laborans* within the same natural cyclicality governing the maintenance now required. Silhouetted against the "shining brightness" of political action and speech it enables, the man-made world casts a nettlesome shadow indeed.

Arendt indirectly addresses this dilemma by clarifying that while public, political life and private, biological life should remain distinct, they are not mutually exclusive. In the Greek *polis*, she observes, a minority of citizens were freed by the labor of slaves to pursue the *bios politikos*. Unencumbered by the private, day-to-day burden of physical sustenance, citizens could circulate in the public world of fellow citizens where they claimed their political equality in deeds and words. So radical a division of roles came at a tremendous price, however. Slaves found themselves condemned to the "shadowy kind of existence" reserved for those who, consumed wholly by the recurring toils of *animal laborans*, could not participate in the common sphere (*HC*, 50). Citizens, for their part, suffered alienation from the "vitality" achieved in labor and essential in its own way to the human experience; total freedom from necessity yielded a "lifeless life" too far removed from "real life" and its biological enjoyments (*HC*, 120). Arendt never offers what a more balanced combination of public and private lives might resemble, but it seems reasonable to infer that she envisions a civilization comprised entirely of public equals in which labor is more evenly distributed. Everyone, ideally, would partake at least to some extent in both the biological satisfactions of *animal laborans* and the fully realized humanity of public man. The unending maintenance labor generated by world-building thus poses no insuperable contradiction, as long as it falls to emancipated men electing to maintain and preserve the common world whose liberating potential they simultaneously enjoy.

What Arendt does not account for is what I will be calling the problem of beginnings, which relates to the conditions necessary for the emergence of a public realm. Modernity, with its emphasis on individual freedom and equality, emancipated the laboring classes from slavery. In this fashion, mankind had moved closer to Arendt's ideal that no man exclusively inhabit either the private necessity of *zoē* or the public realm of *bios*. But civilization was also moving dangerously further, Arendt contends, from the classical distinction between the two. Consumer society had replaced the public realm with the mass organization of biological needs, ignoring the ancients' strict separation of household and civic enterprises by reducing public life to a sort of collective housekeeping (*HC*, 33). Still, modernity at least retained the potential for such a differentiation. The benign, pre-imperial modern state described in *Origins* evokes the classical separation by standing over and against disparate private economic interests to produce a common ground. In Arendt's telling, of course, the moment proved inherently fleeting. The rise of empire and capital aside, the modern conflation of state with nation quickly rendered the mode of this commonality, namely citizenship, an accident of birth and belonging—an accident at odds with Arendt's more active conception of an equality seized rather than given, and that ominously excluded from the community of rights anyone unfortunate enough to lack citizenship.

Yet the state, as I have maintained, required no help in producing a difficulty of its own, and here it starts to become clearer why. Arendt offers that the state's elevation "above all classes" necessitated financial autonomy, an autonomy achieved in its partnership with the Jews. Political equality for citizens of the *polis* had presupposed a freedom from necessity achieved by private mastery over slaves in the household. Thus, too, did the modern equality guaranteed by the state presuppose such a freedom—though not on the part of citizens. Now it was the institution of public-ness itself, rather than individual participants, obtaining the necessary autonomy. But a similarity persisted. That which had made citizenry in the *polis* possible—the all-consuming private labor of slaves—relegated these same laborers, by definition, to a "shadowy kind of existence" outside the public realm. Likewise did the Jews' pivotal contribution to the state constitute a special ostracism. To be sure, Jews were rewarded with citizenship. We have seen, though, that the condition of this inclusion in the public realm was their continued social exclusion, since the state courted the Jews precisely for their detachment from class society. Arendt reasons that "mere formal equality before the law" was no compensation for a continued social isolation that, once the state itself capitulated to society, made Jewish pariahdom total (*OT*, 12). Again, however, Arendt defers onto the social something that already begins with the state. Aligned as they were with the state, the Jews more resembled a structural feature of the common world than full-fledged participants inside it. If the state gathered and separated citizens "as a table is located between those who sit around it," so did, by extension, the Jews who made the state possible. Others might sit around the table; but the Jews *were* the table. The phenomenon is replayed in the European comity of nations dependent, for Arendt, on a neutral Jewish interstitiality grounding and facilitating exchanges among participating nation-states.

This, then, is Arendt's problem of beginnings, in which the disruption hinted by maintenance labor intensifies. Arendt obviously condemns slavery, and she bemoans the ironies of Jewish emancipation. Yet never does she offer conditions of emergence for a public realm that had not or would not create a caste of shadow men. Unjust as it was, slaves had made possible, made thinkable even, the *bios politikos* that Arendt celebrates; without them, one gets the impression from Arendt, man might never have made the Promethean leap from his enthrallment to *zoē*. And these shadow men never seem entirely to go away. The more they are integrated into the world, in fact, the further they advance the shadow zone between world and nature already evidenced in maintenance labor's constant fight to preserve the world from reclamation by the earth. It is tolerable to Arendt that the world generate maintenance labor in continuous proportion to its existence, as long as the labor does not fall exclusively to a permanent underclass of *animal laborans* denied participation in the world. Even in the unjust conditions of the *polis*, a separation persists between the world as proud locus of the public, permanent realm and as the site—along its permanently fraying edges—of daily maintenance efforts where slaves toil in the murky zone between nature and man-made artifice. But what to make of Jewish service to modern states, wherein a key facet of the common world actually consisted *of* shadow men who, at once radically indissociable from that world and alienated from it, combined the categories of world and earth outright? The binding medium that for Arendt relates and separates men furnishes the backdrop against which the "in-between" of the public realm can flourish. The medium does not, however, constitute that in-between, any more than the table constitutes the interaction of those seated around it. This is workable enough if one equates the binding medium with the inanimate objects, artworks, and institutions that Arendt envisions when she discusses the man-made world. The problem arises when men become the medium.

Consider the comity of nations mourned by Arendt. The frailty of that balance lay not just in its vulnerability to the belligerence of an individual member, as Arendt suggests, but also in the comity's dependence on Jewish intermediaries existentially removed from the in-between they facilitated. Arendt writes unforgettably about the "worldlessness" of a persecuted people who, in their age-old quest for survival, had turned inward and become "unburdened by care for the world."[33] Instead of claiming their right in the public realm, Jews manifested a "lack of political ability" (*OT*, 8)—a political naïveté that proved fatal when, having entrusted themselves to the state, they were eventually failed by their protectors and targeted for eradication. But that worldlessness had also made the world possible. This is as troubling, given the exclusion it perpetuated of the Jews from true political life, as it is paradoxical. Nations could not reasonably stake their collective equilibrium on an international Jewish solidarity that fundamentally escaped their control.[34] More to the point, the entire equilibrium turned on a contradiction. If in its supposed plurality the comity of nations guarded against the monolithic, biological existence that Arendt detested, it no less required a class of men engaged in just such a worldless existence. Arendt never takes up the paradox, though, because it indexes an aporia in her thought. She attributes to Marx a Hebraic fixation with labor's reproductive fertility, its potential for generating a surplus, that distracted him from the biological transience of this surplus and the capacity of work to combat such ephemerality by building a lasting world (*HC*, 88, 106). And yet, Arendt's countertheory reintroduces something of that Hebraic surfeit in the Jews whose biological, inward-oriented concern with survival and reproduction simultaneously enabled, coincided with, and exceeded the political world of the state. How to distinguish, in such a strange confluence, between *zoē* and *bios* at all?

This worldlessness in the world, this excess haunting the system, is the superfluity reassigned by Arendt from the state to empire. Though Arendt would prefer to think of the "channeling of natural forces into the human world" as a perversion introduced by capital (*HC*, 150), it turns out to be a feature of world-building itself. The lengths Arendt goes to contain that fact reflect the extent of the problem it poses for her political philosophy. So far I have discussed one such tactic on her part: the deferral achieved in transforming, via the displacement thesis, the Jews from a constitutive superfluity of the state into one of the many superfluities produced by capitalist imperialism. Beyond just conveniently funneling that superfluity away from the state, empire funnels it away from Europe altogether. The shadow Jews of the state become the shadow men of empire—for the most part no longer Jews, thanks to Arendt's reconfiguration of the antisemitic colonial conspiracy theory—who pour into Africa. But this does more than redirect the problem of superfluity abroad. It also presents Arendt an occasion, I will be arguing, to recoup distinctions problematically muddled for her by that superfluity when it was still attached to the state. It remains now to examine how, in part 2 of *Origins* ("Imperialism"), Arendt works to resolve contradictions emerging from her prefatory inquiry into antisemitism.

SHADOW MEN OF EMPIRE

In 1951, the year she published *Origins*, Arendt was not the only major German thinker to be contemplating Europe's past and present against the backdrop of imperial conquest. The jurist and political theorist Carl Schmitt had emerged the year before from postwar disgrace to publish *The* Nomos *of the Earth in the International Law of the* Jus Publicum Europaeum, his sweeping reflection on the evolving fortunes of the Old World in a global context. Despite obvious divergences between the two works, and the vast political and biographical difference separating their authors, there remains an interesting correspondence between Arendt's nostalgic account of the European comity of nations and Schmitt's comparably wistful theorization of a bygone European spatial order. One does not readily imagine that Arendt, a German Jewish refugee from Hitler's Germany, could have shared much of an outlook on Europe with a compatriot who became a Nazi Party member, antisemitic polemicist, and unrepentant apologist for the Reich. Still, like her contemporaries in the Frankfurt School, Arendt continued to take Schmitt seriously—if with a grain of salt.[35] In *Origins* she notes that Schmitt's "very ingenious theories about the end of democracy and legal government still make arresting reading," despite including him in the ignoble ranks of "those comparatively few German scholars who went beyond mere co-operation and volunteered their services because they were convinced Nazis" (*OT*, 339n65). And while Arendt never engages in *Origins* with *The* Nomos *of the Earth*, the ease with which certain aspects of the two works may be placed in retrospective dialogue illustrates a commonality useful for appreciating uncertainties stirring beneath the surface of Arendt's text.

Schmitt's *nomos* resembles, in its broad outlines, a more resolutely martial and geographically ambitious version of what Arendt identifies in the comity of nations. As Schmitt defines it, the *nomos* of the earth was the international spatial order introduced when, in the fifteenth and sixteenth centuries, the "Age of Discovery" prompted Europeans to think in newly global terms. The significance of the *nomos* is that "for 400 years it supported a Eurocentric international law: the *jus publicum Europaeum*."[36] Schmitt is not just interested in the Eurocentricity of this international order, though that is clearly part of its appeal to him. He is also keen to emphasize how aspects of the *nomos* worked to regulate and contain—to "bracket," as he puts it (*Nomos*, 100)—inter-European wars that might otherwise have gotten out of hand. By recognizing the new overseas lands as "free spaces," or outlets of sorts, where European powers and their proxies might skirmish "beyond the line" of normal jurisprudence, European international law headed off wars of annihilation by limiting real war to an orderly, continental affair between European sovereign states (94–95). So conceived, war became a conflict between *justi hostes* ("just enemies") of more or less equal standing between whom peace was always a possibility and who respected each other's contribution as sovereign states to the "balance of the European Powers" (141, 189). Indeed, the very existence of a European "family" (141), of Europe itself, was for Schmitt premised on this genteel matrix of hostilities among states, a system in turn premised on the colonial *nomos* that bracketed it.

Arendt has in mind the same European "family" when she writes of the comity of nations. Both thinkers, too, date the decline of this European order to the late nineteenth-century rise of high empire. Schmitt posits that once European powers began treating colonies as extensions of sovereign state territory, rather than as overseas possessions, the resulting disappearance of "free spaces" meant that the old *nomos* was defunct: war could now spread everywhere unchecked, eventually yielding a first world war that "dethroned the old world from the center of the earth" (*Nomos*, 220, 239). Arendt, on her end, details how the enthusiasm for unfettered imperial expansion militated against the precept of a European "balance of power" founded on restraint (*OT*, 15). Arendt plays down the military quality of this balance, tending to focus instead on a less agonal "inter-European solidarity" (*OT*, 15). She also values the comity of nations more for having preserved and respected plurality among peoples, sharing none of Schmitt's single-minded insistence on territorial boundaries and integrity.[37] And she never grounds the European comity of nations in any global, imperial *nomos*.

Nevertheless, Arendt's account offers a bracketing element of its own. Arendt sometimes appears to present the old inter-European solidarity as having constituted its own transcendent foundation. Nineteenth-century statesmen like Clemenceau and Bismarck, she affirms at one point, "never dreamed of seizing a monopoly over the continent or of annihilating their neighbors completely" (*OT*, 22). She seems to subordinate Jewish internationalism to this elemental European cordiality: "The Jews could not only be used in the interest of this precarious balance, they even became a kind of symbol of the common interest of the European nations" (*OT*, 22). But already here Arendt effects a meaningful slippage. The very precariousness of the balance and its need for instantiation in a Jewish "symbol of the common interest" suggest something less than an originary self-sufficiency on its part. Arendt's subsequent observation that the final dissolution of Europe in fact began with the Nazi attack on the Jews further underscores her sense of a deep reciprocality between European Jewry and the comity of nations (*OT*, 22). Ultimately unwilling simply to grant the European order a *creatio ex nihilo*, Arendt reifies European-ness itself in the Jews, who "were European, something that could be said of no other group."[38] This is in keeping with her general metaphysics, which required, as we have seen, that any "in-between" among plural actors be framed by an interstitial medium facilitating it all.

The European balance, therefore, that Schmitt overtly anchors in the external, bracketing guarantor of the *nomos*, Arendt tacitly anchors in the internal, bracketing guarantor of the Jews. Again, differences remain. Where Arendt emphasizes inter-European solidarity, Schmitt stresses the generative importance of inter-European enmity. Arendt also never countenances the right of colonial conquest that Schmitt so lustily invokes. The difference perhaps most consequential to Arendt's project, however, is this: the bracketing that, for Schmitt, places Europe on more solid existential footing actually redoubles the conundrum of Europe for Arendt.

The reason lies in the nature of the brackets. The new American, African, and Asian spaces "beyond the line" so integral to the *nomos* functioned, in Schmitt's famous formulation, according to the "state of exception" (*Nomos*, 98).[39] By providing a region of exception where anything was possible, or at least where European powers might squabble without escalating reprisals back home, these spaces guaranteed order in the more circumscribed sphere of European life and jurisprudence. Neither inside that sphere nor strictly extraneous to it, colonial spaces rendered operative the divide between legality and extralegality, "civilization" and "nature," by continuously straddling it. Giorgio Agamben, in his influential gloss of the phenomenon, has termed this a "zone of indistinction" in which the erasure of difference between inside and outside paradoxically and continuously reactivates that difference.[40] Agamben's key point is that with modernity the zone of indistinction and exception has increasingly tended to become localizable in, and even coincide with, the normal sphere—a process that culminates monstrously in the Nazi concentration camps, where the exception becomes the norm and where every crime thus becomes "truly possible."[41] Retrofitting, here, Arendt's own observation that in the concentration camps "everything is possible" (*OT*, 459), Agamben draws a line from the *nomos* to the worst contemporary horrors.

Long before Arendt gets to the Holocaust, though, the bracketing of the European comity of nations by the Jews has already introduced, from the perspective of Arendt's historico-political assumptions, a dynamic reminiscent of the *nomos*. Neither quite inside nor quite outside the common world of Europe, and manning a bulwark between European plurality and monolithic biological existence precisely insofar as they sit astride the two, Arendt's interstitial Jews collapse together the same categories (civilization and nature, inside and outside, world and biology) commingled in Schmitt's "free spaces." And they do it more disruptively, because they do so from within Europe; in Agambenian terms, they make intolerably localizable the unlocalizable. The *nomos*, as Schmitt conceived it, bracketed the European "family" by funneling away from the Old World a potentially annihilatory violence. Arendt's Jews, in contrast, bring Europe face-to-face with its otherness to itself.

Now, it may appear perverse to associate with the Jews a malady that would erupt full bore in the Final Solution. Arendt's own inclination is to do just that: likening historical Jewish "worldlessness" to a species of "barbarism,"[42] she sees prefigured in Jewish life the radical expulsion from the human world that European Jewry would experience in the camps. Along with her controversial remarks in *Eichmann in Jerusalem* about cooperation by the Judenräte ("Jewish councils") with the Nazis, this kind of analysis has evoked perennial accusations that Arendt meant to "blame the victim."[43] But my point is that her assignation of blame, such as it is, proves a red herring caused by the deferral for which the Jews simply provide Arendt a vessel. By tracing a progression from traditional Jewish "worldlessness" to the superfluity into which the Jews were cast by empire, and finally to the generalized superfluity of a totalitarianism that renders all men disposable, Arendt equates the devastations of modernity with the steady advance of a ravaging superfluity wrought by capital. As I have been arguing all along, however, the real problem for Arendt of Jewish worldlessness is not that Jews had turned away from, or been turned away by, the world. Rather, it is that they figured the paradoxical indispensability of worldlessness to the world, with all the category-collapsing consequences implied.

That the Jews should bear this burden for Arendt is not in itself especially remarkable. Zygmunt Bauman has proposed that the Jew, ever since becoming the necessary yet unassimilable supplement of Christianity, has constituted less a quintessential other for the West than a paradigmatic embodiment of the "ambivalence" intensified when modernity began unsettling age-old distinctions like class difference.

Before returning to what this ambivalence means for Arendt, let me continue with Bauman, who argues that this increased ambivalence provokes correspondingly more violent reactions against it. Ultimately, "the temptation is to 'de-ambivalentize' the ambivalence, by condensing it or focusing it onto one obvious and tangible object—and then burn ambivalence down in this effigy." Thus explained, antisemitism becomes the acutely modern limit case of "proteophobia," an "apprehension and vexation related . . . to something or someone that does not fit the structure of the orderly world."[44] A strength of Bauman's modernization argument is that it puts a finer point on the Durkheimian notion, advanced most notably by George Mosse, that antisemitism is a reaction to the anomic dislocations of modernity.[45] Adding Derrida to the mix, Bauman suggests that the Jew was made to incarnate the class of discomfiting "undecidables" ushered in by a modernity that upended traditional binaries.[46] By positing the phantasmic Jew as the psychic template for such undecidability ever since Judaism's supersession by the Church, Bauman also answers the question of why the Jews, and not some other out group, so singularly attracted this anomic backlash.

What Bauman's schema does less well is allow for the possibility that one might identify in the Jew a locus of ambiguity, and even seek to "de-ambivalentize" that ambiguity, without resorting to antisemitism (or, for that matter, to a philo-Semitism that no less marginalizes the Jew). Arendt demonstrates just such a possibility—and in a way that, fittingly enough, both resembles and departs from aspects of Bauman's modernization thesis. Attributing a vicious new antisemitism to the modern phenomena of capital and empire, Arendt's displacement thesis anticipates Bauman and others in linking the rise of antisemitism to the advent of modernity. But to the question of "Why the Jews?" Arendt rejects out of hand any answer that attempts to explain, as Bauman's does, how "a specific scapegoat was so well suited to his role" (*OT*, 5). Her reason is provocative: any such explanation, she maintains, "upholds the perfect innocence of the victim" in a way that necessarily overlooks what the Jews themselves did to elicit so much hatred (*OT*, 5). Little wonder that Arendt's posture has drawn accusations that she blames the Jews for their misfortune in much the way antisemites might.

The explosiveness of these charges, however, has prevented a more nuanced examination of how Arendt rehearses a discourse about Jews at once subjacent to and distinct from antisemitism. Bauman's criteria prove useful here. Arendt certainly does not focus every ambivalence in the Jew, the better to "burn ambivalence down in this effigy," as Bauman defines the passage from proteophobia to antisemitism. Yet the fault Arendt ascribes to the Jews—a fateful inability to overcome their political benightedness—nevertheless represents a subtle de-ambivalentizing effort on her part. To the extent that the Jews become, as I have advanced, the aporetic kernel where world and worldlessness merge in the Arendtian system, that system exhibits at least some of the modern tendency to concentrate ambivalence in the Jew. In contradistinction, though, with the antisemitic impulse to neutralize this ambivalence by neutralizing the Jew, Arendt works only to remove the Jew from the site of ambivalence. This removal also mitigates for Arendt the initial specter of ambivalence itself, since her definitive alignment of the Jews with worldless superfluity rehabilitates the world/worldlessness binary threatened while the Jews still maintained their paradoxical importance to the state.

In fact, the entire metaphor of superfluity in *Origins* might productively be understood as a device for discharging ambivalence. Its suitability to the task stems from two key properties. First, it figuratively reinscribes divisions between inside and outside, world and nature, *bios* and *zoē*. As that which by definition exceeds prescribed boundaries, superfluity draws away from Arendt's normative standard-bearers of worldliness—the state, for instance—whatever external supplements might haunt them from inside. Second, and just as important, superfluity *flows*. Though superfluity might reorder binaries for Arendt in an unacknowledged way, the flotsam and jetsam generated reproduce, nonetheless, some measure of continued ambivalence. Think of Arendt's fixation with the "mob," that destructive figure of human superfluity "in which the residue of all classes are represented." Fueled by the *déclassés* cast off from the common world in the nineteenth and twentieth centuries, the mob holds an uncanny mirror to the structure it plagues: "This makes it so easy to mistake the mob for the people, which also comprises all strata of society" but clamors "for true representation" (*OT*, 107). Arendt seems unsettled by the resemblance; after all, an always latent potential for this mob would appear etched into the obverse of the more redeemable "people" it monstrously apes. But because superfluity flows, a palliative to this lingering ambiguity emerges: imperial Africa, where the European mob may more singularly assume its destiny as untrammeled *animal laborans*.

To a point, then, Arendt locates in empire an expedient for more tolerably reorienting the *nomos*, with the zone of indistinction shifting from Europe to Africa as the mob—and alongside it Europe's uncanniness to itself—flows across the sea in the imperial settlers ejected by the Old World. Arendt does not stop there, however. She remains intent on divesting even this imperial mob of any remnants of uncanny liminality. These "ghostlike" men, we read, are mere "shadows of events" leading a "phantom-like existence" in colonies like South Africa (*OT*, 189–90). Ghosts, shadows, phantoms: every image metaphorizes the imperial mob as the distorted double of a world left behind. Arendt means to erect a dichotomy whereby the *bios politikos* still possible in Europe contrasts with the *zoē* embraced by settlers in Africa. But the metaphor subverts her intent. Harboring inside them, in their ghostly doubleness, the Europe they have left behind, these superfluous men effect Europe's continued presence as much as its absence. And if they appear ghostlike from the perspective of Europe, they also prove phantom-like next to the Africans they encounter. Arendt cites a passage from Conrad's *Heart of Darkness* in which the Englishman Marlow observes Africans in the Belgian Congo:

> The prehistoric man was cursing us, praying to us, welcoming us—who could tell? We were cut off from the comprehension of our surroundings, we glided past like phantoms, wondering and secretly appalled, as sane men would be, before an enthusiastic outbreak in a madhouse. (quoted in *OT*, 190)

Here the dichotomy opposes European civilization to African prehistoricity, with Marlow's impression of his own ghostliness intended to underscore the supposed chasm between them. Thus has Arendt suspended her imperial revenants between two poles: too superfluous to be properly European but still spectrally European enough not to be natives, they ultimately inhabit a netherworld somewhere in between. Phantoms, indeed; theirs is a condition of spectral ontology, of the "hauntology" manifested by that which, following Derrida, is "neither living nor dead, present nor absent"[47]—or that which, in the specifically Arendtian case, uncannily interweaves *bios* and *zoē*.

For Arendt, this will not do. From superfluous Jews to the superfluous men of empire, superfluity has in *Origins* successively removed *zoē* further away from murky imbrication with *bios*. And so, in another metonymic transfer along the chain of superfluity, Arendt makes phantoms of the Africans themselves:

> What made them different from other human beings was not at all the color of their skin but the fact that they behaved like a

> part of nature, that they treated nature as their undisputed master, that they had not created a human world, a human reality, and that therefore nature had remained, in all its majesty, the only overwhelming reality—compared to which they appeared to be phantoms, unreal and ghostlike. (*OT*, 192)

This ghostliness is of a different cast, so wholly absorbed in *zoē* that "when European men massacred [Africans] they somehow were not aware that they had committed murder." Arendt's Africans figure *animal laborans* in his pure state, contact with which hastens the European mob's slide toward savagery (*OT*, 192, 207). "The phantom world of the dark continent," as Arendt titles one of her chapters on the Scramble for Africa (*OT*, 186), henceforth becomes the generalized domain of a ghostlike *zoē*—threatening, no doubt, but in other ways easier for Arendt to countenance than the worrisomely uncanny admixture of *zoē* and *bios* that has haunted *Origins* until then.

Numerous critics have charged that Arendt's representation of black Africans here and elsewhere in *Origins* does not always rise above the racialist imperialism she assails. Others have demurred, offering that Arendt means only to relate the shocked perspective of Europeans arriving in Africa.[48] Whether or not Arendt exhibits ethnocentrism, however, does not change the fact that, as some of the more interesting contributions to this debate have noted, the radical naturalness ascribed to Africans in *Origins* fundamentally shapes the economy of the whole. Michael Rothberg, for instance, advances that the "human animals" encountered by European colonists in part 2 of *Origins* set the stage—and even furnish the condition of possibility—for Arendt's description in part 3 ("Totalitarianism") of the "animalized humans" produced in the concentration camps. Africa, he concludes, "serves as an unquestioned point of origin in [Arendt's] genealogy of totalitarianism."[49] The argument seems justified enough: when Arendt details the "phantom world" of the Nazi camps (*OT*, 445), her language pointedly recalls the "phantom world" of imperial Africa.[50] That said, I would caution against overlooking Africa's status as a conceptual way station, rather than simple point of origin, for the boomeranging *zoē* that in *Origins* wreaks such havoc on both continents. True, *zoē* rebounds onto Europe with a destructive force proportional to Africa's function as a limit-case reservoir of "'natural' human beings" previously absent from *Origins*' cast of characters (*OT*, 192). But Africa also serves, for Arendt, to untangle *bios* from *zoē* definitively. However unruly, the mob that descended on Africa arrived mainly from the European nation-states Arendt most admired: England and France. The emergence of *zoē* there, at least in the guise of overseas imperial expansionism, raises the difficulty that *zoē* might secretly prove immanent to the laudable *bios* these nation-states had ostensibly come closer to achieving than their contemporaries. Arendt largely diverts this troublesome *zoē* to the account of capital, nationalist excess, and various other antitheses to "the restraints of Western tradition" still embodied, she feels, in the imperial powers' state and political institutions (*OT*, 156). And yet, phenomena like the mob—molded in the uncanny image of the nation-states it plagued—linger in *Origins* to suggest the nagging anxiety that the "Western tradition" could unintentionally produce, even require, its own inverse.

Arendt arguably projects this anxiety in her anti-imperialist indictment of capitalism for likewise requiring its opposite. Rosa Luxemburg's "brilliant insight," she writes, was to have discerned that imperialism arose from the "essential dependence of capitalism on a noncapitalistic world" (*OT*, 148n45).[51] But I want to focus here on how Africa itself, despite Arendt's explicit opposition to empire, also works strategically in *Origins* to uncouple *zoē* from the "Western tradition." The local bureaucracies that administered the imperial powers' far-flung African possessions according to the tenets of raw power did so, Arendt submits, at a significant political and geographic remove from their parent institutions. The principle of consent, the basis of modern nation-states, simply did not obtain in African colonies (*OT*, 126–27), and the realities of distance meant that imperial bureaucrats enjoyed a certain freedom to impose whatever alternative they might devise (*OT*, 134). The expanding European menace of *zoē*—that is, of superfluous capital and superfluous men—here sheds the imprint of the nation-state as it becomes more uniquely "African," a process of separation and distillation accelerated by the encounter with the limit-case *zoē* of indigenous tribes.

Admittedly, Arendt's boomerang thesis ensures that Africa does not contain this newly concentrated *zoē* for long. Even resurgent in Europe, though, *zoē* remains uncoupled from the imperial nation-states that previously engendered it. Now it becomes the province of "tribal nationalisms" belonging to "those peoples who had not participated in national emancipation and had not achieved the sovereignty of a nation-state" (*OT*, 227). These are the marauding barbarians who, under the banners of Pan-Germanism and Pan-Slavism, embrace the "continental imperialism" that Arendt contends most foreshadowed totalitarianism. Thus is Arendt's cleavage of *zoē* from the nation-state doubly complete, assimilated as *zoē* has become, in her narrative, with "tribes" on two continents unlucky (or primitive) enough never to have achieved national sovereignty.

Readers of *Origins* have long remarked that Arendt proves exceedingly vague about how, exactly, overseas imperialism is supposed to have rebounded in Europe as National Socialism, given that she mostly discusses British or French—rather than German—examples of African conquest.[52] Still, the boomerang thesis continues to fascinate, especially as scholars across a wide range of disciplines turn their attention to understanding imperialism's transformative impact on European life.[53] The postcolonial turn in German historiography and the emergence of genocide studies, in particular, are prompting new conversations about whether Arendt's controversial argument holds promise as a model for inquiry. Proponents of the hotly debated "continuity thesis" in German historiography, like Jürgen Zimmerer, have taken inspiration from the boomerang thesis in their efforts to demonstrate the shaping influence of German colonial practices on the Holocaust.[54] By contrast, the historian Dirk Moses questions whether Arendt even advanced a boomerang thesis at all, arguing that it was only in what she called "continental imperialism," and not African imperialism, that Arendt really located a precursor to Nazism. Moses also doubts whether Arendt considered Britain and France to have suffered direct and lasting boomerang effects from their African empires, observing—rightly I think—that she considered the two empires to have left the more respectable institutions of their home polities largely intact.[55] Arendt's intention in doing this, he adds, was to represent "the survival of the Western political tradition that she wished to redeem," a point with which I would also tend to agree.[56]

Again, though, it is essential not to forget what I have been outlining so far: namely, Africa's key role for Arendt in redirecting *zoē* from the "Western" imperial nation-states that exported it. Why otherwise spend so much of *Origins* chronicling Europe's African misdeeds? Had Arendt wanted simply to redeem the French and British political traditions, she might logically have attended to the decolonization already on the horizon as she wrote *Origins* in the aftermath of World War II. Instead, she makes Africa into a transformative relay in the global circuit of imperial violence she sketches, exteriorizing *zoē* from the Western powers before routing it back through their totalitarian others. That African misconduct by Britain and France should echo back home in the continental imperialism attempted by Slavs and Germans has struck many as a methodologically eccentric proposition for which Arendt gives scant empirical evidence.[57] But I propose that this apparent discontinuity was in fact the point, allowing Arendt—via Europe's African interlude—to more neatly bifurcate the European political landscape into competing principles of *bios* and *zoē* than was possible from a strictly national perspective. France and England might ultimately have suffered from a boomeranging *zoē* that fortified their totalitarian foes, but at least *zoē* now threatened them from without rather than from within—still a disastrous state of affairs, obviously, but one certainly more philosophically reconcilable for Arendt with what we have seen is her valorization of the benign, pre-imperial state.

Arendt's displacement thesis parallels the boomerang thesis in this regard. Just as boomerang effects from Africa position the Western nation-state on the right side of an existential divide between *zoē* and *bios*, so does the Jews' imperial superfluity divert the troublesome ghost of *zoē* from the state. Each procedure complements the other. It becomes even clearer now why Arendt intertwined Jewish and imperial histories, occupying as they do homologous positions in the logic she develops.

So structural a concatenation by Arendt of Jews and empire also reflects a significant—and unexpectedly productive—methodological tension. Though *Origins* contains no real statement of method, Arendt later clarified that she had meant to eschew any linear, narrativizing account of totalitarianism as the inevitable last link in a chain of historical causalities. Responding in 1953 to the political philosopher Eric Voegelin, who interpreted *Origins* as "a gradual revelation of the essence of totalitarianism from its inchoate forms in the eighteenth century to the fully developed," she countered that no such inchoate, originary essence had ever existed.[58] Her intent, she continued, had been to "talk only of 'elements,' which eventually crystallize into totalitarianism, some of which are traceable to the eighteenth century, some perhaps even farther back."[59] Arendt's point is that the "crystallization" of these elements into totalitarianism remained contingent, even if the individual elements themselves might possess genealogical precursors. As some have noted, however, the contrast she draws here between crystallization and genealogy, or between contingency and causality, is not always so distinct in her work. Rothberg argues that Arendt's Benjaminian attempt to describe the "shock" crystallized in the encounter between Europeans and Africans is undercut by the terms of her description, whose hierarchical presumption of African inferiority inscribes the contingency of that shock in traditionally linear, genealogical narratives of civilizational progress and regression.[60] More sweepingly, Seyla Benhabib has suggested a fundamentally uneasy coexistence in Arendt's thought between a Benjamin-inspired "fragmentary historiography" attuned to historical moments of discontinuity and rupture, and a more phenomenological *Ursprungphilosophie*, inspired by Husserl and Heidegger, that postulates continuities between originary states and the present.[61]

This concurrence of discontinuity and continuity extends, I would add, to the story Arendt tells about empire and the Jews. The displacement thesis locates a crucial but fairly contingent relationship between imperialism and antisemitism. As noted earlier, another development than empire might equally have drawn the bourgeoisie into partnership with the state and thus equally displaced the Jews. For all the interrelation it posits, therefore, between antisemitism and empire, the displacement thesis counterposes a significant measure of contingency and discontinuity; empire here represents the sufficient, but not necessary, condition of modern antisemitism. The boomerang thesis, on the other hand, traces a more direct continuity between the two ideologies. Once imperialists had discovered in Africa that race might profitably be made a principle of social organization, the same thinking could take hold in Europe. Even this apparent continuity, however, conceals a decided discontinuity, given that Arendt never explains how racist practice aimed at Blacks "jumped" from Africa to Europe in the intensified antisemitism espoused by the pan-movements—a disjuncture compounded by the fact that Pan-Slavism and Pan-Germanism involved peoples largely not implicated in the Scramble for Africa.

I have argued that the latter play of continuity and discontinuity is in fact useful to Arendt, facilitating as it does her cleavage of *zoē* from *bios*. What I want to submit now, by way of conclusion, is that it is also useful to us. Pascal Grosse, a historian of German colonialism, has declared *Origins* "one of the constitutive books of postcolonial studies."[62] Grosse means that Arendt anticipated by many decades the scholarly acknowledgment, roughly beginning with the publication of Edward Said's *Orientalism*, of Europe's inextricability from its imperial history. Those disturbed by Arendt's representation of Africans in *Origins* might object that her Eurocentric perspective borrows too much from the imperialist worldview to offer legitimate purchase on the co-constitution of metropole and colony. But let us play devil's advocate. What if Arendt's precocious account of transoceanic continuities, rather than just tainted by its rehearsal of allegedly insuperable divides—like her Hegelian unwillingness to grant Africans a human history of their own—actually emerges *from* those presumptions of discontinuity? Must her insight still be discounted? Or can it be productive to contemplate, as I think we should, the historical importance of such reflexively presumed discontinuities for conceiving real or imagined modes of continuity? Consider, once more, Arendt's reterritorialization in and through Africa of a violent European excess come home to roost. On one hand, Arendt impressively maps the contours of a global circulation less tractable to European mastery than had been supposed. On the other hand, she conceives Europe's continuity with its imperial spaces only *because* Africa, as the constructed site of an incommensurable alterity she repeatedly restages, offers a mechanism for safely externalizing *zoē* from the nation-state.

I am not suggesting that Europe was not otherwise provincializable along these lines. In his incandescent *Discourse on Colonialism* (1950), published the year before *Origins*, Aimé Césaire had linked Nazi and imperial crimes without recourse to Africanist constructions. Europeans, he wrote, "tolerated . . . Nazism before it was inflicted on them . . . they absolved it, shut their eyes to it, legitimized it, because, until then, it had been applied only to non-European peoples."[63] W. E. B. Du Bois had remarked as much in 1947, as would Albert Memmi in 1957.[64] Nevertheless, Arendt's comparatively tortuous arrival at a parallel verdict remains valuable precisely for its embedment in, and retroactive illumination of, a fraught tradition stretching back to the nineteenth century. Late nineteenth-century antisemites, after all, had been the first to warn of boomerang effects from Europe's imperial adventure, something I document in the following chapters. But one would be hard-pressed to understand these Cassandras of global interpenetration from the usual perspective of a boomeranging continuity. The first to fear a demographic influx of imperial subjects radically heterogeneous to Europe, and yet predicating that fear on an imagined homogeneity between European and non-European Jews, antisemites racialized empire—and imperialized race—in ways that unpredictably synthesized discontinuity and continuity. Such a synthesis disrupts the usual genealogical story, shaped in part by the boomerang thesis, of a logical transfer from the colonized to the Jews (or vice versa) of a common racial animus evolving over time. Alongside this metonymic narrative must be considered what Arendt described in the displacement thesis, and what I will be describing throughout this book: namely, a relation between antisemitism and empire as dispersed across arrays of shifting, sometimes scalar contingencies and discontinuities as it is sedimented in a shared doctrine of race. And so, armed with Arendt's intuitions and mindful of their limitations, we wade into the morass.

CHAPTER 2

Colonial Conspiracies

Racializing Jews in the Era of Empire

Early in *Bel-Ami*, Guy de Maupassant's best-selling 1885 novel about bourgeois turpitude in the Paris of the Third Republic, the narrator relates a telling biographical detail. Among the damning labels affixed to the inauspiciously short and corpulent Monsieur Walter—politician, financier, newspaper owner—are that he is "Jewish and from the South of France."[1] Here is a southern variation on Baron Nucingen, the fictional banker of German Jewish origin and embodiment of speculative financial modernity who had cut a rapacious swath through Honoré de Balzac's *La Comédie humaine* (*The Human Comedy*) half a century earlier. As Balzac's Rastignac before him, *Bel-Ami*'s young arriviste protagonist Duroy will bed the wife then marry the daughter of the Jew to whom, remora-like, he attaches himself. "The tightwad says things right out of Balzac," a character helpfully observes about Walter, lest the reader miss the filiation (91).

But like one of Nucingen's fake bankruptcies, there is something counterfeit about Walter. Nucingen's thick accent, transcribed with famously mocking precision by Balzac, at least testified logically to a provenance alternately identified in the *Comédie humaine* as Alsatian or German. Walter's German-sounding name, on the other hand, belies his supposed "méridional" status as a Jew from the Midi, or southern third of France. From the Spanish Portuguese Sephardim who eventually settled in cities like Bordeaux and Bayonne after the Jews' 1492 expulsion from Spain, to the Jewish communities of Avignon and the papal states annexed during the Revolution, to those Jews exiled to Narbonne, Marseilles, and other parts of ancient Gaul during the Roman Empire, southern French Jews had arrived from many places in many different ways. They generally were not, however, Ashkenazim from Germany and eastern Europe, as Walter's name suggests him to be.[2]

What to make of this incongruence? Strictly speaking, of course, it was possible for a Jew named Walter to possess southern French origins. And Maupassant's grasp of Jewish social geography might certainly have been incomplete. Yet there is also something less than accidental at work, I think, in Walter's hybridity. By giving him the onomastic trappings of German identity, Maupassant inscribes Walter in a grand French literary tradition of German Jewish villainy. That tradition reached an apex after 1870 when the Franco-Prussian War hardened the French against both their German occupiers and the foreign-sounding French Ashkenazi refugees resettling in France from the provinces of Alsace and Lorraine lost during the conflict. The national "axis of otherness," to borrow a phrase from Fredric Jameson, here appears firmly oriented along eastern and European lines, at least with regard to German Jews.[3] But as I want to argue in this chapter, the fact of these Germanic bugbears' Jewishness also aligned them with an axis of otherness rapidly extending in the southern, African direction followed by French imperial expansion. This is particularly the case for Walter, whose Moroccan speculations in the novel recall the scandal surrounding France's invasion of Tunisia in 1881, and whose southernness therefore rejoins the creeping new threat he incarnates.

Walter's easternness, though, continues to function as well; otherwise, why not have made him a more plausibly southern Jew, or even a North African one altogether? Playing a few years later on the same suspicions about North African Jewish conspiracy, the pulp writer Louis Noir would simply make Monsieur Isaac, director of the titular bank in the novel *La Banque juive* (*The Jewish Bank*) (1888), a "Jew from Tunis" colluding from Paris with his Algiers-based Tunisian nephew.[4] But just as often were metropolitan Jews with Maghrebin connections represented as having German roots. Take the scheming Monach family in Robert de Bonnières eponymous novel *Les Monach* (*The Monachs*) (1885), published the same year as *Bel-Ami*, whose members are explained to have branched out from Frankfurt to Paris and Oran.[5] Such stock diasporic portraits doubtless owed something to the association of the 1870 Crémieux decree enfranchising Algerian

Jews with the Franco-Prussian War during which it was promulgated. I propose, however, that they also index the psychosocial role of antisemitic representations in negotiating the competing yet intertwined imperatives of late-century nationalism and imperialism. To put it in the terms developed previously in this book, Jewishness became a conceptual currency not only for constructing the national and global scales important to imperial capitalism but also for elaborating the necessary dialectic between them.

The topos of the Jewish colonial conspirator—a figure standing in for economic, political, and demographic circulations over and above what individual nations seemed able to control—offered a foil against which xenophobic nationalism could posit a national scale insulated from capitalism's leveling global force. This was not necessarily to contravene or impede the properly global functioning of capital: as I noted in my Introduction, globalized capitalism still required local fixities around which production could congeal, fixities nations historically provided.[6] Indeed, to the extent that nationalist antisemitism reinforced the cultural cohesions necessary for organizing production at the local scale, it served the world economic system decried by antisemites themselves.

But what the Jewish colonial conspirator additionally facilitated, and what I think warrants discussing all this in the parlance of scale, is the transposition of scales when ideologically convenient or required. The insular national scale could be and was constructed at the expense of various species of "cosmopolitans" beyond the Jew; consider the rootless Armenian seductress Astiné Aravian in Maurice Barrès's nationalist novel *Les Déracinés* (*The Uprooted*) (1897) or the "Levantine" grafter and speculator Sabatini in Émile Zola's finance novel *L'Argent* (*Money*) (1891), to take two of the authors I consider in later chapters. Only the Jew, however, and especially the Jewish colonial conspirator, made it possible to translate events occurring at one scale into events meaningful at another. Thus, for example, might antisemitic ire manifest an anxiety about the nation's increasing inhabitation of a world system marked by impenetrable complexity and racial alterity—something feasible because of the Jews' understood racial or conspiratorial association with colonized subalterns—while recoding that anxiety into a more tolerable encounter playing out at a national scale as a matter of national rivalry—something feasible, in turn, because of the same overdetermined Jew's continued association with German or British or any other national enemies.

The result invites us to reconsider the displacement that occurred when, according to Jameson, nineteenth-century colonial powers substituted European national rivalries for a more fundamentally unsettling axis of otherness produced in the encounter by Europeans with their imperial subjects.[7] The displacement was never absolute, and traces of uncontained colonial otherness explain how frequently European imperial nation-states figured differences among them by means of the Jewish national other. But neither, I would add, did antisemitism only provide a transitional or median category of Jewish difference against which to define national self-sameness without succumbing to the less manageable difference overseas. For if antisemitism transposed the global into the national, it conversely and crucially worked to transpose the national into the global. In the fin-de-siècle novel *La Revanche de l'honneur* (*The Revenge of Honor*) (1896), which I will be considering at the end of the chapter, an aristocratic French colonist exiled to Tunisia rediscovers his rightful patriotic verve thanks in part to his defeat of a continental Jewish nemesis who has followed him to North Africa. It is there also that, transformed into a gentleman farmer—though under only the auspices of capitalist imperial expansion—he is able to reintegrate the national body politic as both a usefully bourgeoisified aristocrat and the paragon of a sanitized industrial modernity unencumbered by "Jewish" finance capital. In other words, the novel uses the Jew to imagine the global-imperial scale as a scale at which economic and demographic circulations actually serve and enhance, rather than undermine, the hermetic stability of the national scale. Capitalism, likewise interested to balance the fixity of production with the global mobility of capital and labor, was hardly doing anything different.

It was as engines of scale, then, that Jews found themselves racialized in the era of nineteenth-century imperial conquest, and not just as another variety of colonial subaltern. To be sure, the vagaries of racial relationality meant that metropolitan Jews had been racialized in ways borrowed from those being developed to rationalize European colonial domination in places like Africa. Alphonse Toussenel, utopian socialist and anticapitalist author of perhaps the first dedicated secular antisemitic tract in French, *Les Juifs, rois de l'époque* (*The Jews, Kings of the Era*) (1845), argued by analogy that the Jew was to the "gentleman" what the black race was to the white.[8] The remark, however, was contained in an 1847 tome on zoology. In his 1845 diatribe against the Jews, Toussenel preferred analogizing colonized and enslaved Blacks to the white working class he considered enslaved by the Jewish "kings of the era."[9] It was difficult, after all, to brand the Jew with the inferiorizing and primitivizing stigma of blackness while simultaneously accusing him of financially enslaving his Gentile victims. Indeed, as I began this book by discussing, even more enlightened critiques have encountered difficulties relating the antisemitic association of Jews with money to anti-Black racism, since the two seem to function so differently. Materialist approaches to antisemitism, especially, struggle to explain the Africanization of Jews, since their convenience as economic scapegoats would seem to have been predicated on certain assumptions about Jewish superiority—in financial affairs, in international organization—apparently incompatible with received notions about African or Arab primitivity.

Yet there is a materialist perspective from which to appreciate why, with the rise of empire, the racializing primitivization of Jews in fact coincided increasingly with the myth of Jewish financial power. The reasons, I submit, stem from what I have been calling racial scalarity. Essentializing Jews affirmed the global scale at which a fancifully homogenized world Jewry was understood to operate with unwavering ethnic uniformity. And the discourse of Jewish primitivity achieved such an end by positing a kernel of age-old avarice lurking inside even the most assimilated European Jews. "One must see the *native* Jew to understand the civilized Jew," would write Édouard Drumont in *La France juive* (*Jewish France*) (1886), the century's definitive antisemitic statement.[10] Drumont delighted in looking for specimens of the "native Jew" among North Africa's beleaguered colonized Jews, something I will be returning to at length. Just as important, however, was that the Jew remain representable according to multiple and often simultaneous sets of racial codes, the better to figure in him the Möbius strip linking national and global scales seamlessly and dialectically together. Hence, for instance, could the German Jewish antagonist in *La Revanche de l'honneur* be made by the author to masquerade effortlessly (and implausibly) in colonial Tunisia as an Arabized Tunisian Jew. And hence, more mutedly, does Maupassant situate Walter at the vague but critical intersection between east and south.

So, too, in the same dialectical mode, did Jewish primitivity function both to affirm a global scale and to manage the worrisome imperial alterity introduced by the imperial nation's imbrication in that scale. For it was not just as supposed financial predators that European Jews were blamed for the dislocations caused by capital. Rather, it is also as racialized others that they attracted an even vaguer anxiety about the fundamental dislocation produced when Europeans sensed their increasing implication in and reliance on an imperial world system beyond their comprehension. Antisemitism became modern in part when a conspiracy theory about global Jewish dominance promised to explain capitalist modernity's increasingly convoluted mysteries. Here Jews were understood to possess uncommon acumen. Insofar, however, as what made the new world system so incomprehensible was the sheer otherness encompassed, Jews additionally facilitated the representation and containment of this otherness itself. Primitivized by antisemitic discourse into an attenuated version of radical imperial alterity, yet still understood to control the world, Jews made imperial otherness incorporable into exactly the kind of explanatory system it otherwise so threatened to defy. Only as Europeans *and* Africans, masterminds *and* savages, nationals *and* imperials, did Jews serve such a purpose. Hardly incompatible, the two representational extremes in fact proved interdependent.

I will return further on to my novelistic examples, which I have chosen to emphasize in part because of how uniquely effective the novel could be in exploiting conspiracy's narrative possibilities for rendering, containing, and otherwise managing alterity. But it is important to underscore as well the extent to which the trope in question circulated among different discursive registers and geographies. Drumont, we will see, was influenced by Maupassant's unkind descriptions of North African Jews in his travel writing, and probably too by Maupassant's portrait of Jewish colonial conspiracy in *Bel-Ami*. Colonially conspiring Jews would feature prominently in *La France juive*, and thereafter in Drumont's antisemitic newspaper *La Libre parole*, convincing credulous readers that Jews were pulling the levers of imperial expansion. Among the most avid such readers was the prolific Anglo-French author and social critic Hilaire Belloc, a dominant voice in twentieth-century British letters.[11] Stridently anticapitalist, anti-imperialist, and anti-Dreyfusard, Belloc published a first novel in 1904, *Emmanuel Burden*, that would have fit comfortably among the tales of Jewish imperial skullduggery dotting the French literary landscape two decades earlier. In it, the respectable British merchant Emmanuel Burden is led to his demise by I. Z. Barnett, a Jewish peddler of pyramid schemes and sham companies who sells Burden on a fraudulent plan to extract gold from the M'Korio Delta in West Africa. Barnett's activities and origin place him squarely at the familiar intersection between axes of otherness:

originally from Frankfurt, he rises through subsequent novels to lofty plutocratic heights thanks to various imperial machinations in Africa and India.[12]

Like Maupassant—whose attribution of the Tunisian invasion to Jewish finance so impressed French mentalities that Jean-Louis Bory's 1973 introduction to *Bel-Ami* still essentially reproduces the charge as historical fact[13]—Belloc helped shape the lasting fiction of Jewish imperial connivance.[14] Among the British imperial enterprises incensing Belloc was the contentious Second Boer War (1899–1902), which he considered to have been "openly and undeniably provoked and promoted by Jewish interests in South Africa."[15] In this respect he joined the British economist and anti-imperialist J. A. Hobson, who in 1900 leveled a similar claim in his book on the Boer War. As noted in the previous chapter, Hobson's iteration of the theory proved generative for Hannah Arendt. Arendt sought to recuperate his claim from its antisemitism, invoking Hobson's unwillingness later to recycle the charge as evidence that Jews had not in fact been as involved in South African affairs as was commonly assumed. Arendt's insistence on the point derives from her elaboration elsewhere in *The Origins of Totalitarianism* of what I have called her displacement thesis, in which she links the rise of empire to the rise of modern antisemitism. Arendt argues, recall, that the governmental clout of imperialist capitalists displaced Jews from their historical role as bankers to the state. Stripped of much of their public standing and influence, but still wealthy, Jews thus became easy targets for unprecedented accusations of parasitism.

Hobson's importance to Arendt lies in what he allows her to argue was the rapid displacement of Jewish economic power in South Africa by bourgeois, government-backed British investment.[16] But Hobson himself represents no easy illustration of the displacement thesis. Possessing insufficient evidence of Jewish influence over British imperial policy to pursue his accusations later, yet confronted with the very real diamond and gold wealth of a handful of South African Jewish Randlords, Hobson—under Arendt's logic—might have been sufficiently aghast at an apparent Jewish parasitism that he felt compelled to denounce it. The problem, of course, is that the denunciation took the form of suspicions about Jewish colonial conspiracy. The Arendtian reading of this would be that these anti-imperialist, antisemitic suspicions were epiphenomenal to the real cause of Hobson's antisemitism: namely, the Jews' political and economic displacement by empire and their subsequent irrelevance to imperialism or any other state project.

Yet Hobson could just as easily be cited as an example of how, as I want to argue here, the topos itself of Jewish colonial conspiracy significantly drove the antisemitic narrative in the years of state-backed imperial expansion. However involved or uninvolved Jews might actually have been in European imperialism, the *perception* of their involvement was widespread. And the very fact of increased government involvement in the imperial capitalist enterprise would only appear to have reinforced this perception, given the reflexive belief by antisemites that Jews most invidiously wielded their supposed influence in the corridors of political power.

Part of my reason, then, for turning in the present chapter to the late-century European refrain of Jewish colonial conspiracy is that it complicates the displacement thesis. This goes as well for Arendt's specific formulation of the thesis with regard to France. Keeping to her general theory about the potential of unexplained wealth to elicit charges of parasitism, Arendt argues that the loss of official state influence by French Jews after the Second Empire maps perfectly onto the increase in antisemitism presided over by a Third Republic less receptive to Jews in its ranks. If in the last chapter I questioned the latter premise, here I would question Arendt's subsequent choice not to link the Third Republic's rampant imperialism, the decline of Jewish state influence she cites, and the surge in French antisemitism. Emphasizing instead France's difficulty keeping up with England in the Scramble for Africa, Arendt credits the ultimate political failure of French antisemitism at the turn of the century to the fact that France "never developed a full-fledged imperialist party." The claim remains true to the displacement thesis by assuming the same basic connection between, on the one hand, an imperial marriage of government power with bourgeois finance and, on the other, an antisemitism directed at the Jews left out; the public-private partnership having failed in France to produce an imperial party, it follows for Arendt that French antisemitism remained correspondingly unofficial. And because French antisemitism "had been nourished principally by the purely national French-German conflict," she elaborates, "the Jewish issue was almost automatically kept from playing much of a role in imperialist policies, despite the conditions in Algeria, whose mixed population of native Jews and Arabs would have offered an excellent opportunity."[17]

Of course, French imperialist policies in the last few decades of the nineteenth century were generally set by the Opportunists at the helm of the Third Republic and not by radical antisemites lucky even to be elected.[18] For official French imperialism not to have transformed antisemitism into a dominant, state-sanctioned political force does not preclude, therefore, that the Third Republic's foray into empire exerted a profound influence on the government's antisemitic adversaries and on antisemitic sentiment more generally.[19] The available evidence certainly suggests a persistent attribution of imperial expansion to increased Jewish involvement in the state's financial, political, and electoral life. Indeed, Arendt's unwillingness when discussing France to reiterate a basic tenet of her displacement thesis—the imperial sidelining of Jews—may owe less to the absence there of "a full-fledged imperialist party" than to her unvoiced appreciation of how, in an imperial power with so many colonized North African Jewish subjects, opportunities dramatically multiplied for perceiving ostensible Jewish governmental manipulation at home and abroad.

Arendt's ascription of French antisemitism almost exclusively to the "purely national French-German conflict" merits reassessment as well. To be sure, militant antisemites often made a show in the 1880s of keeping their sights on the "blue line of the Vosges," partaking in the nationalist, *revanchiste* (revengist) objection by the right—sometimes echoed by the left—to colonial expeditions deemed a frivolous strain on limited financial and military resources. Those resources, many felt, should be dedicated to the essential task of reclaiming the provinces of Alsace and Lorraine lost in 1871, or at least to ensuring that Germany did not inflict further such painful wounds on the nation.[20] "I have lost two daughters, and you offer me twenty servants," protested the *revanchiste* nationalist Paul Déroulède about the Third Republic's colonial acquisitions.[21] The perennial radical Henri Rochefort, for his part, raised the specter of enemies like Germany who "would see us conquer not only Tunis but also Indochina and Tonkin, so that our borders be constantly emptied of the soldiers we will send there to contain the annexed and protect our nationals."[22] Yet as I have been maintaining so far, it would be a mistake to divorce what antisemites argued about Jews to rally sentiment against Germany from what they argued about Jews to rally sentiment against colonial expeditions to Tunisia and elsewhere. Motivated by a blanket disdain for the policies of the Third Republic, the two postures also represented, more subtly, complementary facets of an ongoing negotiation between nationalism and colonial imperialism belying any simple ideological opposition of the two (or, conversely, their simple equation, as propounded by zealous republican colonialists convinced of the importance to the nation of imperial expansion).

If I am obviously marking my distance from Arendt in various ways, I remain nonetheless under the general aegis of her insight that European antisemitism emerged transformed by imperial circumstances irreducible to the interrelation between antisemitism and colonial racism. Her indebtedness, as mentioned in the last chapter, to theorizations of European imperialism by Hobson and Rosa Luxemburg—who, like Marx before them, considered empire what David Harvey calls a "spatial fix" required for addressing overaccumulation and other crises endemic to capitalism[23]—also inscribes Arendt within the *longue durée* of a critical geographic tradition later responsible for the scalar perspectives I have been using here to situate antisemitism at a certain nineteenth-century ideological intersection between nationalism and imperialism. And there is an Arendtian echo as well in the attempt I will be making now to document something of a pendant to Arendt's suggestion that European imperialism conjoined racial and economic thinking with unprecedented force. Colonial South Africa, contends Arendt, proved the effectiveness of the "race principle," or institutionalized racist exploitation, at making conceivable and sustainable an economy in which "profit motives were sacrificed time and again to the demands of a racist society." That continental totalitarians like the Nazis would take to heart the African lesson about how "profit motives are not holy and can be overruled" represents the chief "boomerang effect" offered by Arendt to explain an aspect of the relationship between empire and European antisemitism different from the one proposed by the displacement thesis.[24] But it is worth asking, I think, whether independently of a boomeranging colonial "race principle"—though not independently of imperial circumstances—continental antisemitism was likewise making it possible to think race and political economy intimately together. After all, what was the accusation of innate Jewish financial villainy if not a racialized grounds for questioning the profit motive, albeit one ingenuously or disingenuously confusing Jews with capital's real nature?

Setting aside then, for the moment, the dialectic linking national and global scales, I want to trace the distinctly modern confluence of racial and economic thought as French antisemitism honed its conspiracy theories against the backdrop of empire. In so doing, I shift from modern antisemitism's ideological function to its rhetorical functioning. Among the motley cast of antisemitic characters coming to the fore at this stage—Rochefort, Camille Pelletan, Georges Meynié—Drumont stands out for having harnessed the discursive possibilities of empire in particularly transformative ways. Revisiting his massively influential 1886 antisemitic polemic, *La France juive*, I will examine how Drumont sophisticatedly exploited France's discovery of North African Jewry, along with metropolitan financial scandals that negatively implicated Jews in the rapid colonial expansion of the 1880s, to help invent a synthetic new antisemitism. By sensationalizing the imagined crimes of North African Jews, and seamlessly linking this construction to French misgivings about the role of metropolitan Jews in the colonial project, Drumont exploited the fact of empire to fuse permanently the racial and economic antisemitisms that, until then, were proceeding along somewhat distinct trajectories. But there is a longer history as well to the association in France of Jews with imperial affairs, and it begins with a favorite target of organized late-century antisemitism: the Alliance Israélite Universelle (Universal Jewish Alliance).

A CONVENIENT ENEMY

If militant antisemitism in some sense always entailed the pursuit of an absolute—of racial or religious purity, for instance, or of anticapitalist economic utopianism—France's disastrous 1870 defeat by Germany convinced many of an outer limit on just how universal an absolute might be acceptable. That limit, for antisemites quick to join the rising tide of nationalism, was the nation. This shift in metaphysical horizons pitted the national against everything beyond it, including the international, "universalist" network of Jewish power. An attendant antirepublicanism, stoked by frustration with the corrupt and unstable Third Republic, provided fodder for an even broader indictment of the universal. Drumont's *La France juive* would argue in 1886 that transnational Jewish universalism was the legacy of a Revolution whose own universalist aspirations had been hijacked by the Jews to disastrously lasting effect. And in the explicitly universalist pretentions of a Third Republic that justified its rapid imperial expansion on the grounds of an evangelical mission to export the new government's republican values, antisemites were likewise presented with a particularly concrete manifestation of the universalism they abhorred.

Of course, the Third Republic was also reviled for what it was doing domestically. The republicans' 1879 consolidation of government power, inaugurating a decade of legislative interventions in domains like divorce and education, inflamed reactionary sentiment on the traditional counterrevolutionary monarchist and Catholic right.[25] French Jews, whose emancipation had coincided with the Revolution, were perceived to be once again imposing their agenda on the nation.[26] Drumont was among those swept up in the outrage. The son of a petty bureaucrat whose institutionalization at age fifty impoverished the family, Drumont became a practicing Catholic in the same year, 1880, that he decided to write *La France juive*.[27] But if the frustrated young journalist's newfound devoutness clearly animated his antisemitism, and if *La France juive* certainly abounded with the hoariest of Catholic accusations against Jews—deicide, infanticide, usury—Drumont was also on some level wary of appearing out of step with the times. His protestation in the second volume of *La France juive* that "I am among those who respect all beliefs and who consider faith, wherever you find it, as the most priceless of treasures" has rightfully been read as rank hypocrisy, given the alacrity with which Drumont everywhere else attacks the Jewish faith.[28] Yet Drumont's pronouncement, I would argue, is just as strategic as it is shameless. Situated in a long section about the activities of the Alliance Israélite Universelle in France's imperial sphere of influence, the remark appears less intended to suggest real tolerance than to shore up what otherwise might be perceived as an outdated rhetorical arsenal. Why rely on Catholic antisemitism's old theological shibboleths, Drumont seems to be suggesting, when contemporary evidence of Jewish political and financial "crimes" is so plainly apparent in French possessions all over the globe?

No institution more epitomized the Jews' hated universalism, or its easy conflation with republican imperialism, than the Alliance Israélite Universelle. As always with any successful demagoguery, the conspiracy fantasies of Drumont and his colleagues refracted elements of the truth. French Jews themselves, emancipated by the Revolution, had enthusiastically embraced its universalist principles of liberty, equality, and fraternity. This ideological outlook found its most inspired organizational expression in 1860 with the establishment in Paris of an Alliance designed to reach across national boundaries in an attempt to "regenerate" less fortunate Jewish communities abroad. Predictably, the Alliance would become a bête noire of late nineteenth-century political antisemitism. With its global reach, explicitly universalist pretensions, and founding cadre of international Jewish luminaries, the Alliance lent very public credence to antisemitic alarmism about an international Jewish conspiracy. Drumont dedicated one of the six sections in his 1,200-page screed to the Alliance and its longtime president,

Adolphe Crémieux, and rarely missed an opportunity to implicate the Alliance in the political and financial scandals of the day. For Drumont and those he inspired, the Alliance was simply too good to be true. Drumont often even found it unnecessary to impute treachery to the Alliance, happily making his case in the Alliance's own words. Pronouncements of Crémieux's like "the Alliance is not a French, German, or English Alliance, but a Jewish one; it is universal" needed so little rhetorical adornment that Drumont smugly passed them on to his readers with minimal comment.[29] The enemy had conveniently manifested itself; now Drumont and his ilk could do battle with it in the light of day.

The Alliance's institutional nature, imaginary though the threats it posed might be, invited the organization of an organized counterweight. Drumont obliged, brashly declaring in *La France juive* that "the Universal Anti-Semitic Alliance is formed and the Universal Jewish Alliance will not prevail against it."[30] Boosted by the publishing phenomenon that was *La France juive*, Drumont assembled around him in Paris a crew of malcontents and agitators bent on making antisemitism a social and political force. Perhaps recognizing the inherent contradiction in launching a "universal" movement to combat the universalism he loathed, Drumont would shortly pare his aspirations to the national level, founding the politically minded Ligue Antisémitique Nationale de France in 1889 with fellow antisemite Jacques de Biez.[31] While the antisemitic newspaper Drumont founded in 1892, *La Libre parole*, met with periodic success and contributed heavily to the paranoid climate of antisemitism and nationalism surrounding the Dreyfus Affair a few years later, Drumont's political dreams for organized antisemitism never really materialized. But the fact remains that, given what might be hysterically perceived as an institutionalized Jewish assault, Drumont could compellingly make the case for an institutionalized resistance.

Drumont considered imperialism a different side of the same universalist coin. A fervent opponent of the Third Republic's increasingly numerous colonialist enterprises in the 1880s and 1890s, including messy and unpopular expeditions to Tunisia, Tonkin, and Madagascar, Drumont deemed the republican *mission civilisatrice* ("civilizing mission") so much universalist window-dressing on what he charged were a series of Jewish financial speculations.[32] After 1870, and especially beginning in the 1880s, the still rather timid theoretical association of Jews with empire would erupt into an explicit, full-blown association backed by the weight of historical circumstance and public perception. French antisemitism would become so bound up in this association, and so trade on it, that it is legitimate to wonder whether France's late-century antisemitic frenzy might have proven as excessive were it not for the colonialist preoccupations of the Third Republic.

In the antisemitic reaction against empire, the history of the Alliance Israélite Universelle plays a key role. Prompted, through a sort of capillary action, by the growing causeways of imperial influence and expansion, French Jewry's newly global outlook would associate Jewish internationalism with empire in the minds of antisemitic generations to come. Earlier I suggested that the Alliance's overtly institutional status invited an institutionalized antisemitic response. But it is equally important to recognize that the Alliance did so in its perceived capacity as emblem of an imperialist order that, on a more structural level, contributed to the rise of modern French antisemitism. Any Jewish alliance of sufficient scope was bound to provide antisemites a useful rhetorical foil. Beneath its rhetorical convenience, however, the special antisemitic fixation with the Alliance Israélite Universelle—conditioned, as I will discuss, by the Alliance's historical involvement in the French imperial project—reveals how Jews bore the brunt of increasing anxiety over the upheavals of the French imperial project.

Aron Rodrigue has assembled a genealogy of pivotal moments leading to the foundation of the Alliance. The first of these moments happens also to be a pivotal moment in the history of French imperialism: the 1830 invasion of Algeria. With this colonial conquest of a region containing a sizable indigenous Jewish population, French Jewry became, as Rodrigue puts it, "the first modern Jewish community which came into direct contact with a non-European one."[33] Urbane French Jews were taken aback to discover the indigence of their far poorer coreligionists to the south. Following their emancipation in 1791, French Jews had internalized the "regeneration" paternalistically prescribed them by the Abbé Grégoire in 1789, making it the slogan for Jewish progress. They had also emerged from the universalist moment of the Revolution with a heightened sense of solidarity. These notions of regeneration and universal brotherhood, when confronted by the plight of Algerian Jewry, combined to produce a kind of Jewish *mission civilisatrice*.[34] Inquiries by French Jews in 1837 about what could be done to "regenerate" the seemingly backward Jews of Algeria were followed up in 1842 with the dispatching of an official Jewish delegation to Algeria and with the formation soon afterward of central consistories in the Algerian administrative *départements* of Algiers, Oran, and Constantine charged with regularizing and modernizing Algerian Jewish life.

Subsequent episodes in the prehistory of the Alliance similarly followed a path charted by France's imperialist aspirations. The Damascus blood libel affair of 1840, according to Rodrigue a major catalyst in the foundation of the Alliance twenty years later, owed much to French dreams of imperial influence in the Levant.[35] Upon the disappearance in Damascus of a Capuchin friar, the city's Christian Arabs charged that Jews had killed him for the ritual use of his blood (an accusation that had been periodically leveled at Jews for centuries). The local French consul, whose country's patronage of the Christians of the Holy Land dated back to the Crusades, took the accusation seriously. Given France's alliance with Mehemet Ali, ruler of Egypt and occupier of Syria since 1832—an alliance born of Napoleon's own occupation of Egypt in 1798, which marked the modern turn of French colonial efforts away from the New World and toward North Africa and the Near East—the governor of Damascus elected to remain mindful of French concerns. He arrested the Jews accused, some of them prominent community leaders, and extracted confessions through torture. A horrified French Jewry responded vociferously. Having made no headway with foreign minister Adolphe Thiers or King Louis-Philippe, neither much disposed to undermine the French consul in Damascus, the Central Consistory of French Jews decided with the Board of Deputies of British Jews to send a joint mission directly to the Middle East. The mission, whose members included Adolphe Crémieux, future president of the Alliance Israélite Universelle, shortly obtained the prisoners' exoneration. A successful precedent had been set for cooperative, transnational intervention in questions of vital Jewish interest.

Alongside French Jewry's developing commitment to the "regeneration" of Algerian Jews, the Damascus affair cemented the importance to French and European Jews of an "Eastern Jewish question" that would train Western Jewish attention on Jewish communities in North Africa and the Middle East.[36] The Crimean War of 1854–56, which pitted France against Russia in an essentially imperialist disagreement over control of the Christian Holy Lands in the Middle East, gave fresh momentum to the "Eastern Jewish question" by sparking concerns about the future of Jews living in the Ottoman Empire. Once again, French imperial aspirations had created a venue for French Jewry's engagement on the part of their less fortunate coreligionists outside of

Europe. By the time the Alliance Israélite Universelle came into existence in 1860, its particular focus on the Jews of the "Orient" represented the codification of a project three decades in the making. That project would flourish into the next century as further French imperial pushes into Tunisia, Morocco, and the Levant provided ongoing opportunities for the Alliance to influence Jewish life around the globe, in particular through the establishment of schools. By World War I, 183 Alliance schools had been founded from Morocco to Iran.[37]

Overlap between imperialist expansion and Jewish philanthropy abroad contributed to the emergence of modern French antisemitism by tangibly demonstrating how transnational Jewish allegiances might concern national interests. And in France's humiliating defeat by Germany in 1870, those allegiances were seen by some to have impacted national interests indeed. Drumont charged time and again in *La France juive* that what was a disaster for France was a boon to the Jews, whom he blamed for conspiring across the Rhine to bring about the war. In league only with other Jews, irrespective of nationality, Drumont's Jews were loyal solely to their global ambition of founding the seat of a new Jewish empire in France. This imputation of imperial designs to the Jews suggests how French Jewry's activities overseas had called attention to an increasingly interconnected and global Jewry, a global Jewry onto which Drumont projected—in a sort of associative inversion—the very imperialist tendencies that produced it. Drumont's hero Toussenel, author of *Les Juifs, rois de l'époque* (1845), could not yet conceive of the Jewish threat to France in terms of an imperial Jewish destiny. If for Toussenel the Jews certainly profited from national upheaval, like that produced upon Napoleon's defeat in 1815, they did so only in their nebulous and timeless capacity as stateless "cosmopolitans."[38]

By the 1880s, however, French Jewry had drawn toward it the Jews of Algeria and Tunisia, among others, and the antisemitic imaginary could claim proof of a global, cooperative threat. The distinctly colonial flavor of that perceived threat was enhanced by the financial scandals set off by the 1881 invasion of Tunisia, which for many would render imperialist expansion synonymous with Jewish malfeasance. It also did not help that a new class of what Pierre Birnbaum calls "state Jews," welcomed into service by a meritocratic Third Republic blind to creed, officially and publicly endorsed a colonial *mission civilisatrice* they considered the extension of the republican principles that had benefited them.[39] These state Jews of the colonialist "Republic of the

Juleses" (Grévy and Ferry) encouraged antisemites to consider Jewish colonial intervention a governmental phenomenon. Drumont's sensational ascription of the 1870 defeat to an international Jewish conspiracy, then, owed at least part of its success to imperialist circumstances that made such conspiracies more believable than ever.

THE CRÉMIEUX DECREE

The extent to which antisemites would associate the disaster of 1870 with the colonies is illustrated by their reaction to another, very governmental development that fateful year: the Crémieux decree naturalizing the Jews of Algeria. Early in 1870, before the outbreak of war, the government of the Second Empire had considered administrative reforms in Algeria. Among the proposed reforms was the collective naturalization of Algerian Jews, a project dear to Adolphe Crémieux, a member of the Corps Législatif (France's lower legislative chamber at the time) since 1869 and long a proponent of naturalizing his "beloved Jews of Algeria."[40] Although the debacle at Sedan abruptly tabled the Algerian question, Crémieux's post as minister of Justice in the provisional republican government empowered him to take up the issue anew. In Algeria, the fall of the Second Empire was energizing republican attacks against the colonial military administration, or *bureaux arabes*, resented by proponents of a civil administration. Seizing this republican momentum, Crémieux enacted a six-decree Algerian constitution on October 24, 1870. One of those decrees made the 35,000 Jews of Algeria citizens of France.

Already no friends to the Jews, radicals in the colony were outraged. Suddenly, nearly 10 percent of the French Algerian electorate was Jewish.[41] The extreme left feared for its political fortunes, and the stage was set for the virulent political antisemitism that would dominate the Algerian political landscape for the next several decades. Antisemitic commentators in the metropole took notice. "Never, perhaps," writes Drumont in *La France juive*, "did the Jew prove himself more odiously indifferent to everything concerning the Nation, more implacably obsessed with himself and his race, than in the decrees emancipating Algerian Jews pronounced then by Crémieux."[42] To Drumont, the Crémieux decree represented exactly the sort of Jewish power grab the Franco-Prussian War had been organized to facilitate. Catapulted to the highest ranks of power by the war, a Jew had symbolically opened the doors of the nation to the hordes of his coreligionists in the south.

As usual, Crémieux's unapologetic advocacy on behalf of Jews served Drumont's propagandist purposes to a tee. Documenting the imagined conspiracy by French and German Jews to bring France to its knees was a tenuous, circumstantial business. In the Crémieux decree, however, Drumont could identify manifest, apparently incontrovertible evidence of Jewish national disloyalty. If the president of the Alliance Israélite Universelle had so apparently abused the nation's wartime disarray to further the Alliance's Algerian agenda—which Drumont not so subtly suggested by including his attacks on the Crémieux decree and the Alliance in the same chapter of *La France juive*—it became less of a stretch to pin the 1870 defeat on Jews who had similarly placed their transnational interests above those of the state. Concern that the Alliance, as Drumont alarmedly reported, had "over seven thousand students" in schools "in Syria, Morocco, Tunisia, Mesopotamia," or that the Crémieux decree had unjustly empowered Algerian Jews, or that French Jews had conspired with German Jews to bring about the Franco-Prussian War, became so many interchangeable accusations in an antisemitic discursive web that linked France's post-defeat trials to French Jewry's historic involvement in the imperial periphery.[43]

Drumont's suspicions about Algeria were given reverent, book-length treatment a year later by Georges Meynié, whose 1887 *L'Algérie juive* (*Jewish Algeria*) explicitly answered Drumont's exhortation to "study Algeria."[44] More vividly than even Drumont, Meynié drew a connection between the 1870 war and its colonial aftermath:

> The Jews had thus taken a decisive first step and were determined not to lose any ground. To increase their power, they gathered together all their coreligionists vegetating in Europe and obtained, moreover, naturalization for the indigenous Jews of Algeria.[45]

For Meynié, the antisemitic task was properly only understood at the global, imperial level, because that was the scale on which Jews themselves understood their mission:

> Though powerful in other states, they expect that it will be long before they can govern there. They hope thus to conquer France, which they know is divided into two parts: France and Algeria. Therefore do they require strong support from their indigenous

> coreligionists, and to facilitate the task, they must obtain naturalization.[46]

Drumont had argued in *La France juive* that the Crémieux decree betrayed the nation in several ways. For one, he was convinced that the decree had set off the 1871 Arab insurrection in Algeria, a thesis Meynié reprised at length and that became a commonplace of antisemitic discourse. Drumont also felt the decree had effectively turned the colony over to Jewish hands. But it was Meynié who most forcefully argued for the importance to metropolitan French Jewry of its Algerian counterpart. Each, according to Meynié, truly needed the other. What one lacked, the other possessed: "In Algeria, the Jews rule by numerical superiority; in France, they owe their power to their wealth. On both sides their strength lies in union, as they can do nothing without one another."[47] Meynié intimated, moreover, that the naturalization of Algerian Jews might lead to the same for many European Jews whose status as foreigners left them vulnerable.[48] Just as the Jews of Algeria had shored up their position, so might the expatriated Jews of Europe gain an even more permanent foothold in the countries they had already come to dominate. In this fashion did Meynié imagine a circuit whereby the consequences of Jewish advances in the colony would visit the whole of the imperial nation-state.

Drumont envisioned a circuit of a more optimistic sort. After arguing that the Crémieux decree instigated Muslim revolt and left Algeria at the mercy of the Jews, *La France juive* concludes that "a consolation emerges nonetheless from the spectacle of so much sadness. It is via Algeria, perhaps, that the French anti-Semitic campaign will begin."[49] Drumont goes on to cite recent antisemitic developments in Algeria, including street demonstrations, pronouncements in the press, and antisemitic organizing.[50] The electoral implications of the Crémieux decree were indeed giving rise to an unprecedented level of organized antisemitism in the colony, where already in 1871 a first anti-Jewish league had formed in Miliana to prevent Jews from exercising their newfound power at the ballot box.[51] Drumont was particularly impressed by the antisemitic demonstrations in Algiers in June and July 1884, during which a crowd of two thousand protesters had at one point attacked and looted Jewish shops.[52] Drumont obviously hoped this "genuine start of an anti-Semitic uprising" would spread to the metropole.[53] Drumont's later popularity in Algerian antisemitic circles and 1898 election as a deputy from Algiers has contributed to the perception of Algerian antisemitism as an extension of the fin-de-siècle metropolitan frenzy surrounding the Dreyfus Affair. But Drumont's Algerian hopes of the previous decade hint that antisemitic inspiration might have traveled in the opposite direction first. As the historian of Algeria Charles-Robert Ageron concludes, "One might almost suggest, like Drumont oddly prophesized in 1886, that it is via Algeria that began the French antisemitic campaign."[54]

To Ageron's assessment, I would add that if Algerian antisemitism provided Drumont an encouraging example, it provided a discursively potent one as well. Anti-Opportunist sentiment in the 1880s, shared though it was by antisemites like Drumont, was not inherently antisemitic. The tendency of the new Algerian Jewish electorate to vote Opportunist, however, increased the possibilities for associating Jews with the work of an unpopular government. This was exacerbated by the newly enfranchised Jews' heavy electoral weight—in some Algerian towns, Jews represented as much as 50 percent of the voting population[55]—and their penchant for voting as a bloc according to the directives of the Algerian Jewish consistories. Thus, in the wake of the Crémieux decree, was the existing reactionary wave against the Third Republic poised to feed a concomitant rise in metropolitan antisemitism.

THE TUNISIAN AFFAIR

The Crémieux decree and Algerian antisemitism were only two aspects of a broader confluence of imperial factors that favored the rise of French antisemitism in the 1880s. On its own, the Crémieux decree had not sparked a metropolitan antisemitic backlash in the 1870s. It was not until the 1880s, when the Third Republic entered the international expansionist fray with expeditions to Tunisia, Tonkin, and Madagascar, that accumulated developments abroad helped prompt the emergence of a "Jewish question" back home. Shot through with Jewish involvement—whether fairly or unfairly assumed—these imperial developments mutually reinforced each other to produce, through a kind of metonymic amplification, a powerful antisemitic mythology combining elements of economic and racial antisemitism in disturbing new ways. By providing a transnational context in which traditional allegations of Jewish financial connivance could be linked with new evidence of congenital Jewish behavior that crossed national lines, the rise of empire announced a dangerous new era of French antisemitism.

A tipping point in this acceleration toward the antisemitic excesses of the 1890s occurred in the spring of 1881, when the government of Prime Minister Jules Ferry sent the military expedition that led to the establishment of the French protectorate over Tunisia. Citing an incursion into Algeria by tribal Tunisian Kroumirs as the formal pretext for invasion, Ferry and the republican leader Léon Gambetta seized what they considered a golden opportunity for France to reassert a preeminence shaken since the country's 1870 defeat by Germany. Many disagreed with their wisdom. The muckraking journalist and erstwhile politician Henri Rochefort soon began accusing Gambetta, Ferry, and Edmond Roustan, the French consul in Tunisia, of having conspired in backroom financial schemes of epic proportion. In invading Tunisia, Rochefort maintained, the Opportunist government had acted at the behest of a cabal of French financiers in possession of Tunisian debt certificates that stood to increase significantly in value with the establishment of French control over Tunisia. What is more, he added, Gambetta's newspaper *La République française* had led a public campaign to depreciate the debt's stock market value in a conspiracy by a privileged few to buy Tunisian bonds on the cheap before an invasion they knew was coming. Rochefort also accused the Opportunist government of having occupied Tunisia partially out of frustration over the Tunisian Bey's refusal to countenance the creation of a private Crédit Agricole Tunisien entrusted with printing paper money in Tunisia.

Though historians have disputed their veracity, these claims resonated with Rochefort's contemporaries.[56] The Tunisian affair quickly became the political scandal of the day, with the deputy Georges Clemenceau and his radical left joining Rochefort in decrying the pursuit of economic concessions over which innocent French soldiers were dying "of sunstroke and misery."[57] Clemenceau's attacks in the Chamber of Deputies against the Tunisian expedition helped provoke the fall of Ferry's cabinet in November 1881, while Rochefort's acquittal a month later in the libel case brought against him by Roustan cast further doubts on the government and its continued work of military pacification in Tunisia under new prime minister Gambetta. Four years later, Ferry's second premiership would collapse in disgrace over an unpopular colonial war in Tonkin whose detractors could easily raise the specter of colonial profiteering that had caused him so much trouble during the Tunisian affair.

The open antisemitism Rochefort adopted later in the decade, on display in his 1889 article "Le triomphe de la juiverie" ("The Triumph of

Jewry") for Maurice Barrès's newspaper *Le Courrier de l'Est*, was not yet in evidence at the time of the Tunisian affair.[58] Still, his accusations carried antisemitic overtones. Comparing the Tunisian banker who had issued government debt to another banker, the Swiss Jecker, who purchased the Mexican bonds Rochefort similarly considered responsible for Napoleon III's disastrous Mexican expedition two decades earlier, Rochefort insinuated that "the banker in question is of the same origin and religion."[59] Rochefort's later fond reminiscences about his friendship with sixty Algerian chiefs imprisoned with him on the Île d'Oléron, where Rochefort was sent in 1872 for sympathizing with the Communards, also suggest a predisposition to view French intervention in Arab lands through an antisemitic lens. Rochefort relates in his 1896 memoirs how he learned from his new friends, recently imprisoned for their participation in the Algerian Arab insurrection of 1871, that "the Crémieux decree naturalizing Algerian Jews as French had been the cause of the insurrection in southern Oran," and writes of the "commiseration I felt for the leaders of the insurrection in southern Oran, who had fallen into traps set for them by Jews and old commanders of the *bureaux arabes*."[60] Elsewhere Rochefort disgustedly references "the monstrous Crémieux decree" and "the fateful decree, to which we owe the destruction of our colony." Attributing the decree to Gambetta, who, "Jewish in origin, always showed his affection for the old coreligionists in his family" (even though Gambetta was not Jewish), he makes it seem likely that Gambetta's Tunisian expedition rekindled Rochefort's existing suspicions that Jewish motives explained Opportunist interest in North Africa.[61] Rochefort indicated as much during the 1881 Tunisian expedition itself when, in an apologia for the Muslim insurrection taking place simultaneously in Algeria, he cited the supposed effects ten years earlier of the Crémieux decree: "We had roused them [Muslims] against the Jews who, protected by one of their own, were going to steal their flocks and money."[62]

However subdued the antisemitism of Rochefort's own public pronouncements about Tunisia, his theories clearly struck an antisemitic chord. Camille Pelletan, the radical leftist opposition journalist and deputy who seized on the allegations swirling around the Tunisian expedition, was far less circumspect in the antisemitic tenor of his conclusions. Editor of Clemenceau's radical leftist daily *La Justice*, which picked up the Tunisian story after Rochefort's September 27, 1881, bombshell "Le Secret de l'affaire tunisienne" in the Rochefort-led *L'Intransigeant*, Pelletan traveled to Tunisia in October to see for himself what conspiracies might have prompted the Tunisian invasion. His dispatches to *La Justice* about what he found provide stark evidence that, although Clemenceau would go down in history as an implacable opponent of antisemites during the Dreyfus Affair, in the 1880s Clemenceau and his socialist partisans remained under the sway of a leftist antisemitism dating to Pierre-Joseph Proudhon and Charles Fourier.

Describing his first impressions of Tunis, Pelletan gives a nasty account of the city's Jewish quarter:

> Wandering in the detours of the Arab quarter, eventually we landed in a different environment altogether. The alleys are the same, only littered with debris and unbearably dirty. The open doors reveal interiors just as appetizing. The inhabitants look oddly different. The women, especially, are noticeable. Their entire outfit consists of leggings and a short white, pink, light yellow, or light green blouse. All of them, whatever their age, wear this low-cut costume of extras in a ball, and as they tend toward the most incredible obesity, you cannot imagine what bellies, what rumps, what bloated backs hang beneath this flimsy costume! The old women in this paraphernalia cut extraordinary silhouettes. Here we are in the quarter where teems all the Jewry of Tunis.[63]

In a brief recap a few days later of the Tunisian government's recent financial misfortunes, Pelletan meaningfully recounts how "a Maltese Jew," Abbéazis, had made off with the entire Tunisian navy fleet.[64] These portraits of Jewish filth and gluttony set the tone for the subsequent revelation of Pelletan's chief discovery during his stay: that the French consul Roustan had fallen in with an unsavory, "cosmopolitan" crowd of thieving courtiers in which "the descendants of Israel" mixed with "Copts, Greeks, de-Italianized Italians." Pelletan insists especially on the general Elias Mussali, a disgraced court interpreter of Egyptian origin, and his wife, the beautiful, Tunisian-born daughter of an Italian merchant, in front of whose conjugal residence "the consul's carriage" could be seen "twice a day." Along with a certain Volterra, a "Jew originally from Livorno" and "under-Elias" whom Pelletan lengthily accuses of counterfeiting, the Mussali household allegedly exerted undue influence over Roustan in a variety of financial schemes.[65]

A month later, as a star defense witness in Roustan's libel suit against Rochefort, Pelletan would reiterate his allegations about the Mussali clique of Jews and hangers-on. He suggested that Roustan had become Madame Mussali's lover and that the Mussali/Roustan camp had personally lobbied the Bey on behalf of the proposed Crédit Foncier bank (to whose failure Pelletan, following Rochefort, partially attributed the Tunisian invasion).[66] Pelletan had previously made clear the nature of his feelings about the Crédit Foncier in an antisemitic tirade against North African Jews worthy of Drumont's or Meynié's attacks later in the decade:

> The Arab owner, improvident like all Orientals, is the Jew's prey. Imagine a country where, one or two years out of three, lack of water causes the harvest to fail! The lender arrives. He becomes master of the land.
>
> To create a lending organization with the tremendous power of European capital, such was the Crédit Foncier's first goal. The Jew already seems like a calamity to the Arab. Well, the Société Callas was to the Jew what a rifled barrel is to the harmless local barrels.[67]

Pelletan's witty and sensational testimony turned the tide of the Roustan libel suit in Rochefort's favor and helped place the Tunisian coterie of Jews and para-Jews he fingered at the center of the affair.[68] Pelletan stopped short, however, of recognizing any collusion between the Tunisian "juiverie" he despised and French Jewish financiers in the metropole. Pelletan reserved his bile for foreign Jews, citing for instance the involvement of Baron Frédéric Émile d'Erlanger, a Paris-based German banker whom he sardonically called "an honest Prussian financier." Likewise is he careful in the excerpt above to draw only a parallel, and not a connection, between the French Société Callas firm and Jewish usury in Tunisia.[69] It was one thing to attack "Oriental" Jews in the colony; it was another to take that fight to French Jews. Pelletan had a party to represent, as did his friend Clemenceau, who limited his condemnation of Tunisian Jews to a public mention of a "population made up of Levantines, Jews, Copts, Greeks, Egyptians, Turks, Italians, French, and half-breeds of all sort who live off the Muslims and side with the Bey or the consuls, depending on their interests at the moment."[70]

Of course, as I have been arguing, it was significant for a German Jew to have played so considerable a role in a North African scandal. I will have occasion further to elaborate the point below; for now, let me only highlight the vituperations d'Erlanger attracted. A more self-professedly antisemitic socialist like Auguste Chirac, a disciple of Toussenel and author of numerous antisemitic tomes, was only too happy to echo Pelletan's claims. In his 1883 *Les Rois de la République: Histoire des juiveries* (*The Kings of the Republic: History of the Jews*), an exhaustive compendium of purported Jewish financial crimes, Chirac implicates d'Erlanger in the scandal: "already in 1872, [d'Erlanger] was planning, with his intrigues in Tunisian finances, the necessity of the protectorate that cost and still costs France so much money."[71] Chirac would repeat the accusation in his 1886 *L'Agiotage de 1870 à 1884* (*Speculation from 1870 to 1884*).[72] But Chirac—an admirer of Gambetta, to whom he dedicated *Les Rois de la République*[73]—chose to remain silent on the explosive Rochefort charge that Gambetta's government had orchestrated the slide then rise of Tunisian bonds.

The most extensive suggestion that Jews were behind the Tunisian bond scheme would not in fact come from a professional antisemite like Chirac but from a writer of a different sort of fiction: Maupassant. *Bel-Ami* takes place against the backdrop of a fictional Moroccan affair meant clearly to evoke the real-life Tunisian affair that had rocked the nation a few years earlier. Walter, the Jewish editor of the fictional daily *La Vie française*, conspires with Laroche-Mathieu, a deputy who becomes minister of foreign affairs, to "bear" the Moroccan debt in the pages of his newspaper. They plan to drive down the debt's market value so they can buy low, then sell high when the French government, as they know it will, invades Morocco and guarantees its debt.

This operation obviously recalls the very same manipulation of which Rochefort had accused *La République française*, the Gambettist newspaper whose name bears a more than coincidental resemblance to Walter's *La Vie française*.[74] Given the number of Jews within Gambetta's inner circle and their contributions to *La République française*, one might charitably see a simple gesture of verisimilitude in the decision to make Walter a Jew.[75] But Maupassant's relentlessly unflattering portrayal of Walter hints at a far more organic association by Maupassant of Jews with the colonial misbehavior he despised—an association I will discuss in greater detail at the end of the chapter. Taking a cue from Pelletan's subtly implied correlation between suspect Tunisian Jews and suspect affairs back home, Maupassant goes one step further and boldly places a Jew at the center of the metropolitan scandal. More than the mere reflection of a generic antisemitic zeitgeist, then, *Bel-Ami* contributed to the substantial elaboration of that zeitgeist according to a very specific colonial context.[76]

Drumont prominently featured Tunisia a year later in *La France juive*. As usual, Drumont excels at connecting the dots, combining elements from his predecessors' Tunisian accusations into a continuous narrative of trans-Mediterranean Jewish conspiracy. In Drumont's account of the Tunisian affair, Roustan serves as the corrupt go-between in a partnership of metropolitan and Tunisian Jewish interests. Roustan's attendance at a banquet in Tunis organized by the Alliance Israélite Universelle obviously confirms, for Drumont, Roustan's vassalage to powerful metropolitan Jewish interests of the sort Maupassant had so unforgettably depicted.[77] And predictably, Drumont is enchanted by Pelletan's colorful descriptions of Roustan's Tunisian entourage, gleefully making Madame Mussali the mastermind with whom Roustan plotted the Tunisian invasion.[78]

Perhaps because of his rivalry with Rochefort, Drumont's version of the Tunisian affair remains fairly perfunctory. He focuses instead on another Tunisian scandal of the day, though to similar effect. In an exposé he would continue at length in his 1889 book *La Fin d'un monde, étude psychologique et sociale* (*The End of a World, A Psychological and Social Study*), Drumont tells the story of Mustapha ben Ismaïl, the Tunisian Bey's former grand vizier and favorite. After the establishment of the French protectorate, Mustapha traveled to Paris in 1884 and secured a personal loan for one million francs. Drumont recounts how, unable to repay the loan, Mustapha was approached by the Jewish founders of a new "Société foncière de Tunisie" (Tunisian Land Company). These financiers promised to assume Mustapha's debt in exchange for valuable land given him by the Bey. Though Mustapha agreed, the land in question turned out to be *habous*, a legal designation making the property inalienable under Islamic law. Drumont charges that, eager to take possession of the land, the Société enlisted the French resident general Paul Cambon and the usual host of shady local Jewish characters—including Volterra, the Jewish courtier familiar from Pelletan's denouncements—in a successful campaign of official pressure to enable the transaction. Drumont estimates that this graft produced a return of eighty million francs on a total investment of less than two million, including Mustapha's original debt.[79]

Similar attacks in the mid-1880s on the government's Tonkin adventures, as well as the uproar among antisemites over the Panama Canal scandal early the next decade, illustrate the lasting effect of Rochefort's seminal accusations. In its Panama crusade, Drumont's antisemitic daily *La Libre parole* would particularly hound Alfred

Naquet, the Jewish politician Drumont had previously implicated in the Mustapha ben Ismaïl affair, itself derivative of Rochefort's original Tunisian denunciations. In this manner did the invasion of Tunisia launch to new heights the economic, anticapitalist brand of antisemitism honed in previous decades by Toussenel, Paul Devaux, and a midcentury generation of radical leftists influenced by the antisemitic doctrines of Proudhon, Fourier, and Louis Auguste Blanqui.[80] Drumont's ecumenical innovation was to marry this anticapitalist, leftist strain of antisemitism (the prevalent one in Algeria) with the antimodern, traditionalist antisemitism of the reactionary right. He was encouraged to do so, I would argue, by the stimulus given to leftist antisemitism by the colonial fallout of the 1880s. In fact, it is reasonable to ask whether the antisemitic furor over the spectacular January 1882 crash of the Union Générale bank, credited today by historians with having helped spark the wave of French antisemitism in the 1880s and 1890s, was not itself prepared by the Tunisian scandal on whose heels it occurred.[81] Thousands of small investors ruined by the crash directed their ire not at the Union Générale and its criminally unscrupulous founder, Eugène Bontoux, but at the Jewish Rothschild family accused of having plotted the bank's demise. This happened, I would advance, at least in part because the antisemitic subtext to accusations leveled at the Tunisian expedition by Pelletan and others had already primed the pump. It is telling, along these lines, that while Drumont pays considerable attention in *La France juive* to Jewish misdeeds in Tunisia and Algeria, he makes almost no direct mention of the Union Générale.[82]

ECONOMY AND RACE

Drumont's emphasis on North Africa suggests that colonial questions marked a turning point in the development of modern French antisemitism. By providing sensational opportunities for the invention of Jewish political and financial conspiracies, the Tunisian affair joined the Crémieux decree in adding important new fuel to the economic antisemitism that, in an increasingly secular, capitalist world, was reconfiguring the religious antisemitism of old. But the Algerian and Tunisian contexts of these new obsessions sped up the development of another phenomenon as well: the convergence of economic antisemitism with racial essentialism.

In some socialist and Marxist quarters antisemitism had been tacitly condoned or even encouraged as a useful proxy for class consciousness, with hatred of Jews considered an early step in the war on capital. Within this logic, the Jew played a merely structural role, ideologically important less for what he was than what he represented. Chirac, for instance, was more concerned about systemic "Jewish" behavior than about Jews themselves and considered anyone capable of what he called *juiverie* ("Jewry"):

> To consume without producing, that is to say living at the expense of others, constitutes *parasitism*.
>
> The same phenomenon, elevated into a system and dependent on monopolizing the means of exchange, constitutes *juiverie*.
>
> . . . It is therefore evident that independent of all religious superstition, *juiverie* exists quite distinctly.[83]

The Jewish people constituted only a "prototype" for *juiverie*, and Chirac abhorred "Christian *juiverie*" as much as he did "Jewish *juiverie*."[84] Of course, this is not to say that such purveyors of economic antisemitism did not also often consider the Jew's supposed financial dominance an expression of inherent qualities. Ernest Renan's mid-century affirmation of the Semites' inferiority to Aryans, taken up by countless others in subsequent decades, ensured that race-thinking would color even the most clinically social interpretations of the "Jewish problem."[85]

Yet it was not until the Third Republic's embrace of empire that the true discursive potential of this combination of economic and racial anxieties was tapped. In the North African Jews who increasingly attracted metropolitan attention after 1870, a new means became available for weaving together economic and racial antisemitism in the fashion that would propel antisemitism into the twentieth century. The antisemitic discovery of North African Jewry facilitated this convergence in three ways: by offering comparative "proof" that Jewish financial and political maneuvers were common to, and coordinated across, different Jewish communities sharing a same racial bond; by providing an opportunity for the credible and hyperbolic construction of a "real," unassimilated Jew committing his financial and political crimes on a more primitive, and therefore more tangible, level; and by celebrating the supposedly deep-seated racial antipathy of Arabs for their Jewish neighbors, in hopes of transforming metropolitan compassion for these heroic Arab surrogates into a parallel racial antipathy for metropolitan Jews.

Drumont perfected these strategies, and *La France juive* wields them all. Drumont was especially adept at mining France's North African colonial experience for comparative evidence of an essential "Jewish" nature. The Tunisian affair, for instance, had provoked outrage among Drumont's contemporaries over tales of political and financial misbehavior by both Tunisian Jews (Pelletan) and French metropolitan Jews (Maupassant). Drumont's contribution was to insist on the coordination of these two Jewries in the affair. Madame Mussali, Drumont alleged, had conspired with Roustan from across the Mediterranean to harness the financial and political wherewithal of her metropolitan brethren.[86] In this fashion Drumont could suggest that Jews were everywhere the same, regardless of geography or culture. What made them the same was their innate predilection for financial crimes. Thus did Drumont draft the tenets of economic antisemitism into the service of racialism. By extending the suspicion of metropolitan Jewish behavior to the behavior of Jews in North Africa, and vice versa, Drumont took advantage of the Tunisian affair to transfer animosity against Jewish speculation to Jews themselves, wherever they might be. It has been said that Drumont wrote little that had not already been written by antisemites before him.[87] But his real genius lay in combination, not compilation. Borrowing elements of an economic antisemitism elaborated by the left and combining them with a hierarchizing cultural racialism appealing to the right, Drumont contributed mightily to the modern brand of antisemitism that would later wreak havoc in Europe. That combination, I submit, was given crucial momentum by the experience of empire.

Drumont used other tricks to blend the economic and the racial in this same comparative vein. Perhaps most memorably, he employed existing Orientalist motifs in new ways, assigning them meaning they did not completely yet possess. Of Madame Mussali, Drumont writes:

> You often see, in travel books, those African Jewesses half-lolling on cushions at the back of a secluded room in their home, resting their ring-laden fingers on a vast, flabby belly. Overcome by stoutness at thirty years of age, glistening with fat, they have but one remaining passion, to watch grow the heavy sequin necklace around their bloated neck.
>
> It was with one of these Jewesses, Madame Elias Mussali, that Roustan decided it was necessary for a certain number of our poor soldiers to be killed.[88]

The hackneyed unoriginality of Drumont's Orientalist description is matched only by the subtle originality of its purpose. Portraits of this sort had long been employed to exert discursive power over the exotic, Jewish subject.[89] More recently, Pelletan had mobilized nearly identical imagery within the context of the metropolitan Tunisian scandal. This was no accidental association on Pelletan's part. But Pelletan drew up short of explicitly positing a racial cooperation between French Jews and the Jews of Tunisia. Drumont, however, overtly hitches the corporeal quality of his phantasmagoric North African imagery to the real-life metropolitan scandal, dramatically racializing not only North African Jews but, by implication, French ones as well. Certainly, there was no shortage of precedent for the metonymic association of actual French Jews with imagined Oriental decadence. Drumont's innovation is to historicize the association, fusing the economic antisemitism unleashed by imperial brouhahas like the Tunisian affair with an Orientalist inheritance heretofore confined to more abstract, aesthetic realms. Deploying classical Orientalist imagery to newly pointed ends, Drumont transformed the racial fantasies of early imperial interaction into the racial nightmares of late imperial anxiety. The Oriental Jewess had stepped out of the tableau and into the financial and political life of the metropole.

In a second strategy enabled by the imperial context of the 1880s, Drumont made North Africa the hyperbolic staging ground for Jewish treacheries not easily demonstrable back home. Invented as they were, Drumont's accusations of Jewish crimes in France faced a potential credibility gap. Readers, confronted with the absence in their daily lives of tangible evidence of the conspiracy theories proffered by Drumont, might wonder if he had gone too far. Given that Jews represented only about 0.18 percent of the French population, many in France had never even seen a Jew.[90] North Africa did not present the same problems of verifiability. For one, the Crémieux decree had instantaneously created the most visible Jewish constituency in French history. As a proportion of the population, Jews in Algeria far outstripped Jews in the metropole.[91] Drumont's bugaboo, so demographically insignificant in France, had conveniently assumed much more impressive form in the colony.

What is more, the geographic space of empire opened a rhetorical space in which Drumont and others could depict the Jew in his "true" racial essence, supposedly practicing his trade as he had since time immemorial. Predictably, Drumont's North African Jew proved more shameless in his transgressions than did his metropolitan cousin:

> Nothing of what we see here can give us an idea about what the Jew is like in Algeria, for Jewish usury, which has reached incredible proportions in places like Alsace, is nothing next to Arab usury.[92]

The colonial spaces of Algeria and Tunisia offered Drumont and others a convenient middle ground, far enough away from the metropole not to contravene readers' everyday experiences but close enough within the orbit of French life to benefit from an assumed eyewitness plausibility. This device permitted the distillation of fairly invisible metropolitan financial crimes into more rhetorically compelling vignettes. In his discussion of the Tunisian affair, for instance, Drumont is careful to finger the Tunisian Jew Chemla, whom he identifies as the official supplier of the Tunisian expedition and accuses of "extraordinary graft committed at the expense of our unfortunate soldiers' health and lives."[93] Chemla's assault on the bodies of French soldiers, an implied manifestation of the rather more abstract metropolitan schemes held responsible for the expedition, typifies a rhetorical alchemy that used North African Jews to corporealize social anxiety into a bodily one—and, by extension, a racial one. Like nowhere else, Tunisia and Algeria provided an opportunity to strip away the social titles and complicated financial schemes with which the French Jew was felt to have disguised his authentic nature. "We have experienced the *real* Jewish war in that land," declares Drumont of Tunisia, capturing the extent to which, for a generation of French ideological antisemites, the North African colonies came to fulfill a key revelatory function.[94]

A third racializing strategy added Arabs to the mix. In what would remain a lasting theme for committed antisemites like Meynié and the Marquis de Morès (see Chapter 3), Drumont spun a passionate story of racial antipathy between the proud North African Arab and his craven Jewish neighbor. A long passage of *La France juive* tells of Arab outrage over the Crémieux decree's granting to Jews of privileges not granted to Arabs. After establishing Arab distaste for Jews—"an Arab would consider himself dishonored if he killed a Jew," Drumont dramatically relates[95]—the passage goes on to explain how, upon receiving the decree, the Arab leader Mohammed Ben Ahmed el Mokrani (who was in fact Kabyle, a distinction lost on Drumont) "spit on it" and swore that "'I will never obey a Jew!'" Mokrani went on to lead the 1871 Algerian Muslim insurrection, dying, as Drumont puts it, "a hero."[96] Drumont's hagiography of the "noble and loyal" Mokrani would shortly be recycled by Meynié in his follow-up to *L'Algérie juive*, titled *Les Juifs en Algérie* (1888), which dedicates a chapter to the Crémieux decree and a chapter to Arab loyalty and military prowess.[97] As Pierre Birnbaum has remarked, philo-Arabism was in vogue among nationalist reactionaries—most notably, Gustave Le Bon's 1884 *La Civilisation des arabes* had praised Arab civilization as a paragon of nationalist identity—and drew on existing notions of the proud, fierce Arab promoted by years of guerilla resistance in colonial Algeria.[98] Drumont's attention was further attracted by texts like François Leblanc de Prébois's 1875 *Situation de l'Algérie depuis le 4 septembre 1870* (*The Algerian Situation Since September 4, 1870*) and Louis Serre's 1873 *Les Arabes martyrs, études sur l'insurrection de 1871 en Algérie* (*The Martyred Arabs, Studies on the 1871 Insurrection in Algeria*), both cited in *La France juive*, which combined such philo-Arabism with condemnations of a Crémieux decree speciously argued to have provoked Algerian Muslims into rebellion.[99]

Drumont put this philo-Arabism to single-mindedly antisemitic use. By prompting identification with and sympathy for a noble Arab civilization "wronged" by the Crémieux decree, and by doing this against the backdrop of the Arab's supposedly violent racial hatred of the Jews, Drumont sought to naturalize a similarly violent racial loathing on the part of his own countrymen. If Arabs naturally harbored a deep-seated hatred of Jews, should not the French? In this surrogate capacity, Drumont's Arab played the role of both victim and example. As the supposed victim of a "Jewish Republic" ("République juive") that had happily enlisted Algerian *tirailleurs* (indigenous infantry) in 1870 before promptly turning its back on them, the Arab furnished Drumont a metaphor for the disappointed ambitions of a French Revolution he felt had been similarly crushed by Jews a century before. Not for nothing does he remark that the exclusion of Arab prisoners from the 1886 amnesty that freed the Communards "clearly demonstrates the end of the French revolutionary legend."[100] And as the sworn enemy of the Jew, Drumont's Arab surrogate furnished an exemplary model for the kind of chivalric, prerevolutionary qualities thought necessary for confronting the Jewish masters of the postrevolutionary age. A latter-day knight-errant reinvented for the era of empire, Mokrani was worthy of emulation because, unlike the majority of French, he "had not obeyed any Jews."[101]

What makes these strategies so notable, taken in their entirety, is that the colonial experiment offered Drumont a universally palatable "glue" with which to help cement the modern, political French antisemitism he shaped. Crafting a racialized message, as we have seen, from real and imagined current colonial events, Drumont avoided raising the hackles a more scientistic argument might have raised among antisemites on the Catholic right allergic to biological racism's materialism and underlying atheism. Anticapitalists on the socialist left and traditionalist right could relate to Drumont's narrative of trans-Mediterranean economic conspiracy. Racialists steeped in archaist philology could find contemporary, real-world confirmation of their theories. And religious antisemites could recognize in the sands of North Africa their age-old Hebrew nemesis, risen again as an unchanged race from a familiarly biblical desert landscape. The god Moloch-Baal—the pre-Mosaic golden calf-god of the Jews and the Carthaginian devourer of children and virgins so indelibly impressed on the French psyche by Flaubert's *Salammbô*—had been awakened by the French colonial empire, courtesy of France's occupation of the Carthaginian territory now contained in Tunisia. With its culturally loaded topography, aura of economic scandal, and sizable contingent of indigenous Jews, colonial North Africa was fast on its way to becoming one of the most gloriously overdetermined discursive weapons French antisemitism would ever wield.

AXES OF OTHERNESS

That Drumont was inspired by *Bel-Ami*'s fictional commentary on the Tunisian affair seems likely given his undeniable debt to Maupassant's nonfictional impressions of North African Jews. In the lengthy section of *La France juive* devoted to the Crémieux decree, Drumont, who had not yet traveled to Algeria, extensively cites a passage from Maupassant's Algerian chronicle *Au soleil* (*In the Sun*). Published two years earlier in 1884, *Au soleil* gathered together a series of articles Maupassant had written in 1881 while on assignment in Algeria for the newspaper *Le Gaulois*. France's most important colony was making headlines because of an insurrection in the south led by the tribal leader Bou-Amama, and *Le Gaulois* needed a correspondent on the ground. Fresh off the resounding success of his short story "Boule de Suif" ("Ball of Fat"), Maupassant enthusiastically accepted the challenge, eager, like so many French artists before him, to embark for the storied lands of exotic North Africa. The vignettes he produced combined the expected excesses of Orientalist description with a bitter critique of the failures of French colonial policies in Algeria.[102]

Most interesting to Drumont, however, was Maupassant's description of the indigenous Jews he encountered. In one of the longest individual citations in *La France juive*, Drumont reproduces an antisemitic tirade in *Au soleil* against the Jews of southern Algeria. "As soon as one advances into the South," writes Maupassant in an unsettling first line not cited by Drumont, "the Jewish race reveals itself in a hideous way that explains the ferocious hatred of some for this people, and even the recent massacres."[103] Drumont excerpts most of the rest of the passage, including the following:

> In Bou-Saada, one sees [the Jews] hunched in filthy dens, swollen with fat, base, and lying in wait for the Arab like the spider lies in wait for the fly. They call to him and try to lend him one hundred *sous* in exchange for a bill he will sign. The man senses the danger, hesitates, does not want to; but the desire to drink tugs at him, as do others: one hundred *sous* represents so many pleasures for him! Finally he gives in, takes the silver coin, and signs the greasy paper. After six months he will owe ten francs, twenty francs after a year, one hundred francs after three years. Then the Jew sells his land, if he has any, or else his camel, his horse, his donkey, in a word, everything he owns. . . . The Jew is master of all of southern Algeria. . . . It would take a special law to modify this deplorable situation.[104]

Maupassant's description mobilizes all of the commonplaces—obesity, insalubrity, rapacity—strewn throughout Pelletan's and Meynié's nearly identical accounts of North African Jews. Familiarly, Maupassant stresses the Jew's exploitation of the Arab to set the tone for a subsequent indictment of the Jew's exploitation of colonial circumstances. Like Pelletan, however, he remains careful to distinguish the object of his disgust from the Jews of the metropole or even Algiers: "The Jews of Europe, the Jews of Algiers, the Jews we know, with whom we mingle every day, our neighbors and friends, are men of the world, learned, intelligent, frequently charming . . . our Jews hardly resemble the Jews over there."[105] Unsurprisingly, Drumont omits Maupassant's qualification in order to close the racial loop between metropolitan and peripheral Jewries. The Maupassant Drumont admired, the Maupassant whose influence Drumont explicitly cited in the introduction to *La France juive*, was the Maupassant who in time would come to feel that the Jews of France, "frequently charming" though they might be, shared something in common with the Jews he had so loathed in Algeria.[106]

That is the Maupassant of *Bel-Ami*. Fresh from twenty-eight months in the French Algerian army, *Bel-Ami*'s antihero Georges Duroy arrives in Paris to make his way in life. An old army friend finds him a job at *La Vie française*, a daily newspaper run by Walter. In this Jewish foil, Duroy finds the most pernicious and successful of the rivals he will emulate during his meteoric ascent in society. Hiring Duroy to write seemingly innocuous journalistic reminiscences of his time in Algeria, Walter in fact makes Duroy an unwitting participant in a campaign to lower the value of Moroccan debt bonds by convincing the public that a Moroccan invasion will never occur. Such an invasion will occur, as the politically connected Walter well knows, and when it does, it makes wealthy men of Walter and others who have been stealthily buying bonds all along. Made aware of his dupery, Duroy, who has already seduced Walter's wife, gets the last laugh by seducing Walter's daughter and coercing the family into a wedding that makes him heir to the Walter fortune.

Walter's Moroccan speculation—a thinly veiled fictionalization, as noted earlier, of the real-life Tunisian manipulations suspected by many—represents a metropolitan coda to the predatory behavior by Algerian Jews Maupassant had already decried while in North Africa. Maupassant's Algerian travels lasted from July to September 1881, and it was only after his return that the Tunisian affair would explode and that Pelletan's investigations and testimony in the libel suit against Rochefort would implicate Jews in the sordid allegations swirling around the Tunisian expedition. Maupassant, who had deemed the Jews of southern Algeria "the bleeding wound of our colony," was no doubt struck to learn of ostensible Jewish machinations in yet another colonial context.[107] Three years later, with antisemitic sentiment still high in the wake of the Union Générale crash, Maupassant likely found it natural to place a scheming Jew at the center of the Parisian, colonially themed novel he was writing. Jews appeared implicated in colonial fiascos on both sides of the Mediterranean, and the kid gloves with which he had previously treated metropolitan Jews were off.

But Maupassant had not forgotten Maghrebin Jewry. Subtle cues in *Bel-Ami* suggest that Maupassant considered Walter's metropolitan crimes part of a Jewish colonial continuum defined as much by Maupassant's negative feelings about the Jews of southern Algeria as by his distaste for the unscrupulous metropolitan media and the Jews it employed. Showing off his art collection to Duroy, Walter explains his acquisition strategy: "It's the right moment to buy paintings. Painters are dying of hunger. They're without a cent, without a cent" (163). The Jewish parvenu's exploitation of artists in their moment of destitution recalls the tactic cited by Drumont from *Au soleil*, in which Algerian Jews prey on the desperation of Muslim tribes by selling back to them their own sheep looted only days before during French *razzias* (raids). Here is Drumont, still quoting Maupassant:

> When a French detachment raids [*va razzier*] some rebellious tribe, a swarm of Jews follows it, purchasing booty for a song and reselling it to the Arabs no sooner the detachment gone. . . . Then the Jews are there asking to buy, for two francs apiece, sheep that are worth twenty. The Treasury still stands to gain twelve thousand francs: the sheep are sold. Eight days later, the original owners have repurchased their sheep for three francs a head. French vengeance comes cheap.[108]

Among the first paintings indicated to Duroy by Walter is, fittingly enough, "an Algerian plain" (161). Walter might have replaced sheep with art, but his actions no less evoke those of his colonial brethren.

The camel standing on the horizon in the Algerian painting—"a big camel on long legs, resembling a strange monument" (161)—hints at another intended lesson of Maupassant's indignant *razzia* story, and indeed of *Bel-Ami*: that one colonial opportunist deserves another. Duroy's mistress Madame de Marelle will later recount to her amused lover a dream she had in which they picnicked atop a camel (330). Retroactively inserting Duroy into the painting, the moment situates him at the juncture between Walter's North African depredations and Duroy's own Algerian adventures. For Duroy is himself an aficionado of *razzias*, and real ones, having enjoyed the days when as a soldier in Algeria he "ransomed Arabs in the small southern outposts." Remembering one such episode, among whose fondly recalled spoils count the requisite sheep ("twenty hens, two sheep, and some gold"), a penniless Duroy bemoans the impossibility of engaging in the same behavior in Paris (32). But of course he will do just that, kidnapping Walter's daughter Suzanne then successfully ransoming her when Walter consents to their marriage. And like the Algerian Jews in *Au Soleil*, Walter turns Duroy's Parisian *razzia* into an opportunity to buy low and sell high, rationalizing the loss of his daughter as an investment in his ruthless future son-in-law's obvious potential for becoming "deputy and minister" (398).

Thus does Duroy's marriage to Suzanne seal, for Maupassant, an unholy alliance between Jewish finance and French military power, one begun with punitive Algerian raids against defenseless tribes and ramped up to spectacular geopolitical proportions by the Moroccan affair. Walter has borne out his worrisomely southern alterity, extending that alterity along the colonial axis toward a new North African outpost teeming with Jewish and Muslim others. Why, then, make him vaguely German too? Why locate him, as I began this chapter by observing, at the intersection between axes of otherness? The answer becomes easier now to understand. On one hand, Walter's double otherness quietly reinforces the perception of a French nation subject to coordinated forces exerted from without. The hint of Germanness muddying his nationality makes it easier for his southernness to register as something extending beyond the Mediterranean. In turn, the two geographical alterities resonate together according to existing cultural scripts. If Maupassant never claimed, like Drumont, that Algerian Jews danced in the streets upon hearing of France's capitulation at Sedan, Walter was nevertheless likely to remind certain readers of a baron other than Nucingen: Baron d'Erlanger, the Parisian Jewish banker from Frankfurt accused by Chirac of having fomented the Tunisian invasion.[109] At least in allusive form, here was another German Jew concatenating his transcontinental interests across an unsuspecting France.

On the other hand, the condensation in the Jew of national German and colonial North African alterities hints at ideological functions rather more complex than the rote construction of national identity at foreigners' expense. Drumont would later furnish a telling example in *Le Secret de Fourmies* (*The Secret of Fourmies*), his 1892 pamphlet seeking to explain why on May Day the previous year the army had massacred ten striking textile workers and injured dozens more in the northern French town of Fourmies. Among the chief culprits predictably fingered by Drumont was Ferdinand Isaac, a local subprefect and "little Algerian-German yid" whose Bavarian father Drumont claimed had moved to Algeria and been naturalized by the Crémieux decree.[110] Organicist nationalist that he was, Drumont was inveterate at attributing to Jewish non-nationals any class conflict turning Frenchman against Frenchman, and the Fourmies debacle—neither side of which, workers or soldiers, Drumont cared to condemn—proved no different. More interesting is the circuitous route taken by Isaac and his family in their infiltration of France. The transition from Germany to Algeria, then back into Europe, confirms the usual Jewish rootlessness against which to construct a national rootedness. But so, we will see, does it strategically impart to the Jew a certain unexpected rootedness of his own. The Crémieux decree had been received by antisemites as a breach through which, attracted to Algeria by the prospect of citizenship, the flotsam and jetsam of world Jewry would come streaming into the French body politic. The new demographic menace was often depicted as a diffuse North African horde converging on Algeria from neighboring territories like Tunisia.[111] One would expect this imagery to have in turn triggered representations of primitivized African Jews invading metropolitan France from the south, and to an extent it did: witness the aforementioned novel *La Banque juive* (1888), in which Monsieur Isaac, a Parisian banker and "Jew from Tunis," has arrived from Algeria.[112]

Yet it matters just as much to Drumont that Ferdinand Isaac, made an emblem of Crémieux-facilitated invasion by *Le Secret de Fourmies*, pose a danger as Isaac Seligman, the Bavarian Jew whose family's old German surname Drumont insists on reviving. The effect is not just to render the threat he incarnates implicitly military, something an indigenous North African Jew would not have done. It is also, I would offer, to complicate the apparently straightforward opposition between an international coterie of conspiratorial Jews and the French nation upon which they descend. Superficially Drumont has posited two agonistic scales: the national scale where he understands economic and social harmony naturally to reside, and the global scale at which Jews circulate and conspire to disrupt that national harmony. But of course the possibility for national harmony only exists, under this logic, insofar as the national scale participates and remains embedded in the global scale. Truly to uncouple one from the other would be to remove the antisemitic pretext for class discord like that observed in Fourmies, and with it the nationalist illusion of organic class cooperation, since that cooperation was only ever negatively defined by modern antisemitism in terms of a disruptive external Jewish element. *Le Secret de Fourmies* betrays the extent of Drumont's dialectical dependence by reinforcing it at every turn. The more Drumont makes Algeria the privileged gateway where naturalized Jews bridge global and national scales—something mirrored and enabled by France's Algerian participation as a nation in the global imperial project—the more inseparable the participation becomes from his thought. Even the supposed scale of Jewish conspiracy, global by definition, often seems to find Jews straddling the comparatively national German scale to which their origins apparently require tracing and the more global, transcontinental, imperial, and diffusely African scale across which they circulate.

As previously argued, such a dialectic reproduces in the colonially conspiring Jew something resembling the workings of a maturing imperial capitalism itself similarly dependent on balancing the dictates of national fixity and global liquidity. And it does so usefully, at least from the perspective of capital, by opening the antisemite in a controlled way to the utility of an imperial alterity against which a truly isolationist nationalism might otherwise have remained shut off completely. Here modern antisemitism's rhetorically potent combination of the racial and the economic joins an equally potent ideological function. For if racializing the Jew as a proxy for capital appealed broadly to constituencies on both the left and right skeptical about economic modernity, racializing the Jew as an attenuated avatar of imperial difference helped smooth these same constituencies' acceptance of the imperial fact and of their nation's imbrication with it.

In this acceptance, the racial scalarity instantiated by means of the Jew played a uniquely facilitative role, creating the conditions of possibility for perceived relationalities among all manner of racial, national, and imperial formations. Consider the following colonial rumination by Maupassant in a newspaper article published in *Gil Blas* the same year he published *Bel-Ami*:

> It is thus written that our colonies will always ruin us.
>
> Capable people cry out: "Where is the surprise? The French will never know how to colonize."
>
> Thinking hard about it, I have come to believe that we simply do not know how to choose our colonies. We take the worthless ones, and we are surprised that they yield nothing.
>
> If I were the government, like those with ideas about how to save France always say, I know well what I would do. I would put into a suitcase all of our colonies, Senegal, Gabon, Tunisia, Guiana, Guadeloupe, Cochinchina, the Congo, Tonkin, and the rest, and I would go find M. von Bismarck. I would say to him: "Monsieur, you are looking for colonies, and here is a supply, a heap, a complete selection. There are all kinds, in all shades. They are inhabited by Arabs, Negroes, Indians, Chinese,

> Annamites, etc. I ask you, for each one, a kilometer of Alsace and a kilometer of Lorraine.[113]

Maupassant's broadside against the Third Republic's colonial strategy echoes his dyspeptic take on the Tunisian affair in *Bel-Ami*, and his invocation of Alsace and Lorraine reproduces nationalist accusations about the government's misplaced priorities. What strikes me, however, is the extent to which Maupassant frames the discourse of *revanchisme* in terms as imperially capitalistic as they are hesitantly scalar. Stock *revanchiste* narratives usually contrasted the speculative foreignness of the government's perceived colonial boondoggles with the reassuring solidity and Frenchness of the lost provinces. Yet while Maupassant here attempts just that, he makes his point in ways subtly inconsistent with the national concreteness he otherwise means to endorse. The suitcase imagery, for example, figures both France's colonial project and national rivalry with Germany according to exactly the logics—portability, liquidity, fungibility—associated with the finance capital reviled by Maupassant and others for having embroiled France in places like Tunisia. Maupassant seems especially to seek a principle of equivalence rendering the imperial exchangeable back into the national. But if the proposed kilometric exchange rate is played for wry effect, the same thing generating the effect also partially waylays the intended structure of equivalence. The proliferating imperial difference (Arab, Black, Indian, etc.) cited with obvious dismissiveness by Maupassant helps devalue the colonies to the required satirical point. Simultaneously, though, that difference interposes itself between otherwise like objects—two varieties, colonial and metropolitan, of land or territory—in a manner unsettling the proposed exchange. The principle of equivalence making the colonies themselves interchangeable for Maupassant is the shared alterity of their populations. With what yardstick, then, really to accomplish the imagined swap, given the difficulty of finding a common unit of measure somehow translating between the lost provinces' territorial sameness and the colonies' human difference? Maupassant wants back lands belonging to France, not the Germans now living there, but of course there is no question of offering Bismarck a Congo devoid of its Congolese. How to move, in short, between a national scale defined by its self-same fixity and solidity, and a global-imperial scale understood as the domain of circulating alterity?

The answer, it should be clear by now, lies in the one alterity conspicuously absent from Maupassant's list: the Jewishness that supplies the scalar principle of equivalence necessary for translating between nation and empire. Jews get left off the list as its unthought, the thing making it possible, the condition of relationality within which Alsace and Arabs and Annamites all somehow inhabit what would otherwise quickly devolve into a Borgesian taxonomy. Only because the Jew could be both German and Algerian, national and imperial, European and African, could so many varied modes of otherness (and sameness) legibly coalesce for metropolitans struggling to make sense of an evolving imperial world and their place within it.

This is not to say that representations of Jews visibly ordered cascading representations of otherness around them. The colonially conspiring Jew's usefulness rested, on the contrary, in the figure's capacity for managing radical imperial otherness by dissimulating it without eliding it completely. Here I return to Jameson and his essay "Modernism and Imperialism," whose otherwise useful framework for thinking nineteenth-century European imperial anxiety overlooks antisemitism's unique role in mediating between empire and nation. First, a summary. Jameson argues that the nineteenth-century European novel tended to elide the incommensurable difference of the colonized other by displacing it onto the whiter, more palatable difference of the European other most threatening to a given nation's hopes of imperialist mastery—a role, he notes, often played in French novels by the German. With the advent of modernism, the elision of colonial realities continued. But instead of merely signaling an unwillingness to engage with a colonial other, Jameson adds, it signaled a grave new realization on the part of the modernist author. The metropole now seemed to depend for its economic existence on a colonial periphery that, if no more incommensurable than previously, had dangerously introduced that incommensurability into a colonizing power no longer able to grasp itself as anything but a fragmentary part of an unknowable whole. The metropole suddenly perceived itself in terms of a lack, and Jameson characterizes this lack as the material basis for nothing less than modernism's defining formal and stylistic project: its coming to grips with the inability of language to communicate an immanent, autonomous, and self-fulfilling truth.[114]

Like Jameson, I believe that imperial encroachment on the metropole's perceived autonomy elicited strategies of containment. I am less convinced, however, by his periodization. Though not entirely clear on the matter, he seems to understand the nineteenth-century substitution of national rivalries for exploited subaltern alterities—the "masking of one axis of otherness by a very different one"[115]—to have mystified the inherent violence of imperial appropriation, and thus perhaps to have forestalled anti-imperial opposition. More certain is that only after World War I, on Jameson's view, did "a significant structural segment of the economic system as a whole" come to be located far enough beyond the metropole for Europeans to feel anxiously decentered by empire.[116] But did feeling this way necessarily require sufficient development of the world imperial system for the sensation to have an extensive material basis? Or might it have been possible for the violent encounter with subaltern otherness, considerable already in the nineteenth century, to make Europeans feel problematically bound up even then with the world economic system taking shape? We have seen how in France colonial expeditions and other imperial developments were often suspected of occurring at the behest of Jewish financial interests. Insofar, then, as imperial concerns saturated the modern antisemitic imaginary, and as antisemitism manifested the anxiety produced when metropolitans felt caught up in what Moishe Postone calls "a web of dynamic forces they could not understand," it seems reasonable to attribute at least some of this anxiety to a perception that the nation was subject to worrisome global economic influences.[117]

For Jews to have been understood to constitute the chief such influence is no accident. Had capitalism remained confined to Europe, never expanding outward into African and Asian imperial markets, the French might very well have remained content to blame the "web of dynamic forces" on national others—British, German, and so forth—traditionally associated with economic modernity and external danger. But if the topos of Jewish colonial conspiracy so took hold, it was because Jews doubly made sense for negotiating the relationship between nation and empire. I argued earlier in this book that Jewishness had long been a privileged figure of Western scalarity, for reasons having as much to do with anxiety over Christian supersessionism's own scalar pretensions as with Judaism's theological commitment to bridging particular and universal. In this regard, Jews helped make representable the dialectical relation between two very different varieties, national and global, of economic scale. To the extent, moreover, that representing the relation necessarily entailed contending with imperial difference, Jews made tolerable what imperial capital therefore required: for metropolitans on some level to accept their entwinement with radical alterity. Racialized into an enemy of the nation, yet made racially contiguous with colonized subalterns, Jews ushered imperial difference into the realm of metropolitan representation by acceptably recoding it in national terms. Jameson is right that one axis of otherness required masking by the other. Only the masking was necessarily partial. Behind the German was the Jew; and behind the Jew, the colonized.

CONSPIRACY THEORIES

So imperial alterity needed defusing, not eliding. *Bel-Ami* accordingly and carefully calibrates its Jewish conspirator's otherness to standards both national and imperial, eastern and southern. But what also suited *Bel-Ami* to the task so well, and the novel form more generally, was that conspiracy itself offered a device for at once representing and managing metropolitans' dimly experienced participation in the bewildering network of global forces they themselves had set into motion. Predicated on the conceit of a secret Jewish plot to destroy France and conquer the world, the modern antisemitism perfected by Drumont and his acolytes invited its devotees to fill in the narrative blanks of a supposed secrecy—to give, if you will, a plot to the plot. Antisemitism in this way made fictional creation the guarantor of historical truth, positing as the motor of history a conspiracy imperfectly knowable by any other means than the storyteller's divinatory prowess. But conspiracy was also arguably the guarantor of modern fiction. Not for nothing, observes Peter Brooks, does plot derive one of its English meanings from the French word for conspiracy, *complot*, given the nineteenth-century novel's historical reliance on narrative plots whose "organizing line . . . is more often than not some scheme or machination."[118] And in this specifically bourgeois literary guise, I would offer, conspiracy made possible something that Drumontian pamphleteering could not. Borrowing the armature of the bildungsroman, with its Rastignac-style heroes' education into the mores, structures, and conspiracies of capitalist urbanity, Maupassant updates the genre for the imperial age by making Duroy the unsuspecting instrument of *La Vie française*'s venal campaign to convince the public that France will not invade Morocco. In contrast with a polemic like *La France juive*, which immediately lays bare supposed Jewish conspiracy from the perspective of a relatively omniscient outsider, *Bel-Ami* only belatedly reveals Walter's intrigue. Until then, save for a few hints dropped here and there by the narrator, the reader has experienced the conspiracy from the subjective perspective of its unwitting young dupe.

This is, of course, the perspective from which readers usually experienced the slow revelation to bildungsroman protagonists of society's secrets. But here also is the perspective from which Maupassant's novel understands contemporaneous metropolitan readers to experience the imperial world system. By representing to them a version of that system—as well as, crucially, their own implicitly unwitting participation in it—*Bel-Ami* at once calls into figuration the system and its mystery. By draping the system in conspiracy, however, the novel works equally hard to make containable what, having been conjured, now threatens the metropole from without.[119] That which is governed by conspiracy remains knowable, and thus manageable; one need only learn the secret.

Maupassant, too, once stood where Duroy does. Consider Duroy's struggle to write a first article for *La Vie française*, in which Walter has requested that he recount his "Souvenirs d'un chasseur d'Afrique" ("Recollections of an African Cavalryman"): "In his mind he could see the lovely bright city tumbling from the mountain to the sea in a cascade of flat-roofed houses, but he could no longer find a single word to express what he had seen, what he had felt" (65). Duroy may not be able to transcribe the scene he remembers, but Maupassant certainly had, having penned nearly identical words while on assignment for *Le Gaulois* in Algeria.[120] Lighthearted nod toward writer's block that the self-plagiarism perhaps represents, the mise-en-abîme potentially also serves notice about the status of narrative. It is as if Maupassant repurposes journalistic description as novelistic narration, the totalizing comprehensiveness of which—however nominally fictional the register—he intends to do better justice to the truth of the colonial situation than any individual eyewitness account like that Maupassant himself had provided. There is a sense as well, of course, in which Maupassant is deriding the eventual substitution for Duroy's actual experiences of narrative cliché. After all, this and subsequent articles will be ghostwritten by Duroy's colleague's wife, Madame Forestier, who judges that the reading public prefers trite Orientalism of the "fanciful excursion" variety (75). Yet Maupassant had already tried his hand at educating readers of *Le Gaulois* about hard Algerian facts on the ground, turning a jaundiced eye on mismanagement of the colony by a governor, Albert Grévy, so apparently incompetent that he seemed "chosen specially by the military party to sink the civilian government."[121] Producing here instead a novel about the failure of narrative, in particular journalistic narrative, to communicate imperial realities, Maupassant is not just bemoaning the state of newspaper writing. He is also performing a narrative substitution of his own, preferring to what he had attempted previously in Algeria a novelistic testimonial ostensibly pulling the curtain further back on the "real" secret of imperial expansion.[122]

Meanwhile, though, the expansion represented requires tempering for what it suggests about the metropole's entanglement in a world system. Maupassant thus recasts the insight in familiar, knowable metropolitan terms, deflecting imperial alterity across a variety of protective familiarities and affinities. Two vases of flowers on Madame Forestier's mantel, one from her now-husband Duroy and one from the man cuckolding him—vases that mirror, notes Nicholas White, a later description of the Tunisian and Moroccan colonies as "two vases on a mantelpiece" (312)[123]—translate geopolitical intrigue into the customary bourgeois tropes of domesticity and adultery. But something is shifting nonetheless. Chiding Duroy for dismissing her suspicion that France will invade Morocco, Madame Forestier revises the dictum made famous by Alexandre Dumas in his 1854 novel *Les Mohicans de Paris*. "In political schemes," she instructs Duroy, "one must not say: 'Look for the woman,' but rather: 'Look for the deal'" (289). She is, of course, right: lucre, not women, motivates Walter and his co-conspirators. Maupassant has ostensibly repudiated the Balzacian erotics of power, uncoupling sexual desire (for women and of women) from economic desire. The door is now opened to the possibility that something less metropolitan, less recognizably *French*, makes the system go. Yet Maupassant is only willing to countenance the possibility in safely glancing terms. Walter's Jewish greed, "other" in its venality shorn of sexuality, renders incorporable into the metropole—like the "strange" hothouse plants creating a "fantastic and stunning background" inside his fashionable *hôtel particulier* (358)—what lurks worrisomely on the imperial periphery. So, too, will Maupassant eventually recombine adulterous affair and politico-financial *affaire*, women again asserting their usual Balzacian status as conduits of knowledge when Duroy's mistress Madame Walter clues him into the Moroccan conspiracy.

For the conspiracy to prove discoverable and understandable (not to mention joinable!) by the protagonist likewise fulfills expectations raised by a bildungsroman format to whose conventions Maupassant ultimately adheres. Indeed, the very structure of Maupassant's novel perhaps furnishes the most potent code of all in which to normalize and domesticate the decentering alterity otherwise introduced. Whatever *Bel-Ami* does at the level of content to orient the nineteenth-century bourgeois metropolitan novel toward imperial circumstances, it simultaneously turns away from, qua bourgeois novel of education, at the level of form. Jameson identifies in a decentered twentieth-century metropole the anxious material driving modernist style and formal innovation, with a newly experienced lack incised on the surface of language itself. But dating, as I think we can, the early stirrings of this lack to the nineteenth century, it becomes apparent that the same sensation might also have produced formal inertia as bourgeois authors—willing, in a realist or naturalist mode, to register the economic realities of empire—clung to old models as a way of containing and managing the results.

The colonially conspiring Jew similarly functioned to reveal and conceal, at once signifying and suppressing a creeping imperial difference. In this respect, it remained important to distinguish between the axes of otherness at whose intersection the figure was located. For the Jew to mediate between national and global scales required that the corresponding alterities never bleed completely together, since the figure's utility depended precisely on translating between varieties of otherness. By the time of *Bel-Ami*, Maupassant seemed less convinced of what he had proclaimed earlier about the Jews of southern Algeria: that "our Jews hardly resemble the Jews over there."[124] But if there now appeared greater continuity between northern and southern Jewries, they also could not be conflated entirely, lest an overriding imperial otherness make it difficult to locate in the Jew a national, German enemy as well. Thus, I submit, could Maupassant not make Walter *too* southern. And thus, in less restrained hands than Maupassant's, did these complex representational requirements make for some truly bizarre novelistic Jewish villains in late-century French literature. I finish now with a brief look at one particularly identity-bending example, who stalks the heroes of Paul de Garros's potboiler *La Revanche de l'honneur* all the way from Europe to Africa.

GLOBALIZING THE NATION

First serialized in 1896, *La Revanche de l'honneur* is the second of two colonially themed novels published that year in the pages of Drumont's *La Libre parole*. The first was Baude de Maurceley's *Amour et gloire, roman franco-saharien* (*Love and Glory, a Franco-Saharan Novel*). Set during the 1871 Muslim insurrection in the Algeria, *Amour et gloire* explicitly attributes the insurrection to Muslim outrage over the Crémieux decree.[125] In this endorsement of a theory already long cherished by antisemites at this point, *Amour et gloire* inscribes itself in a relation of solid continuity with existing French antisemitic doxa.

La Revanche de l'honneur does so too, albeit with a few wrinkles worth examining more closely. The novel opens in April 1870. Pierre de Vilbraye, a young aristocrat, idles away his days in Lorraine between his aunt's château de Valfleury and his dead parents' house. Thérèse, his aunt's daughter, is in love with him. Unfortunately for her, Pierre loves Sabine, the daughter of Thérèse's German tutor. The tutor receives an inheritance and returns to Frankfurt, taking Sabine with her. Pierre visits the pair in Frankfurt, starts gambling, and badly indebts himself to the banker Nicolas Kemmerling, who lends him money at predictably outrageous interest rates. After marrying Sabine, Pierre betrays his country when he waits out the 1870 Franco-Prussian War with her in Switzerland.

The novel then shifts to Tunisia, circa 1891. Antoine de Marrancourt, a French count and upright Tunisian colonist, is a struggling widower. Ruined and forced out of Lorraine by the war, he has settled in Tunisia in hopes of rebuilding his fortune through viticulture. In Lorraine he married Thérèse—the same Thérèse left in the lurch by her cousin Pierre—and had a daughter, Irène. Thérèse died in childbirth. Adding to his misfortunes is the Jew Abou-Samara. Abou-Samara's usurious loans may soon cause Marrancourt to lose his Tunisian estate, named Valfleury in honor of his dead wife's home in Lorraine. With his "huge nose like a vulture's beak" and "hooked fingers," Abou-Samara is also terrorizing Pierre, himself relocated to Tunisia and living in humiliation under an assumed Alsatian identity.[126] Clearly her mother's daughter, Irène has fallen in love with Pierre's son Guillaume, an enthusiastic patriot (unlike his father) who wants to adhere formally to the French side.

Pierre is not the only one who has fled to Tunisia. Abou-Samara, it turns out, is none other than the banker Kemmerling, on the run from shady dealings in Frankfurt. Meanwhile Pierre, forced to face up to his past by his son's impending marriage to Irène, admits everything to his son. The way is clear for redemption. Marrancourt's trusty manservant reveals Abou-Samara for the criminal he is, saving both Marrancourt and Pierre from bankruptcy. Pierre then travels to the original Valfleury, now in German-annexed territory, to make spiritual amends. While there, he stands firm against a German *douanier*—to that border guard's "Who's there!" Pierre proudly retorts "France!"—and receives an expiatory bullet in the leg for his troubles (268–69).

When the smoke clears from the cheap melodramatic twists and neat symbolic turns, several things become clear. For one, Garros has traded on received notions among antisemites about Tunisia, and more generally about the relationship between Jews and French colonial North Africa. Pierre's exile to Tunisia in the wake of a financial gain by a rapacious banker recalls, in miniature, the familiar antisemitic accusation that speculation by Jewish bankers had motivated the Tunisian expedition. Kemmerling's easy transition between German banker and North African Jew also invokes the familiar conspiratorial fluidity between European and North African Jewries. By linking Tunisia and the Franco-Prussian War, Garros produces a set of resonances that cater not only to antisemitic suspicions over transnational Jewish collusion during the 1881 Tunisian affair but also to the triangulation, perfected by Drumont, which considered the 1870 Crémieux decree in Algeria of a piece with the betrayal of France by German Jews.

With respect, though, to antisemitism, Garros breaks new ground when he offers Tunisia as a consolation for the lost province of Lorraine. Standing before the original Valfleury, now dilapidated and in German-controlled territory, Pierre waxes triumphant:

> Luckily, Valfleury is like the phoenix. Burned here by the Vandals, it rose from the ashes in a more hospitable land. . . . On the slopes of Zaghouan, a few miles from Tunis, there is a Valfleury belonging to M. de Marrancourt. (266)

Music though Pierre's defiant Germanophobia may have been to nationalist antisemitic ears, it nevertheless remains at odds with a classic tenet of antisemitic *revanchisme*: that the colonial enterprise, especially in a pet project of Opportunism like Tunisia, only dissipated limited resources needed for reclaiming France's legitimate borders on the continent. Garros's compensatory logic is certainly not without precedent. Raoul Girardet has cited a widely read children's book from 1887, Augustine Fouillé's *Les Enfants de Marcel, instruction et morale en action*, in which Marcel, having been forced from his native Alsace after the 1870 war, moves to Algeria where he discovers a "new Alsace."[127] Even so, Garros's symmetrical proposition of a new Lorraine in Tunisia was unusual for antisemites long accustomed to considering the protectorate a symbol of the same Jewish power they held responsible for France's traumatic territorial loss.

And yet, Garros is building on ideas ambient in French reactionary thought since the previous decade. Unfettered, in his pulp sensibilities, by the relative verisimilitude and decorum observed in metropolitan realist novels like *Bel-Ami*, Garros takes a familiar notion and offers its preposterous limit case: a German Jew equally convincing as both a cosmopolitan banker and an apparently indigenous Tunisian moneylender. There was, of course, an expatriated European community of Jewish elites in Tunisia, who like the aforementioned Volterra had become go-betweens in the imperial powers' dealings with the Tunisian government. Pelletan and company had made significant hay out of this fact. Jewish North Africans, we know, were also readily believed to have insinuated themselves into French metropolitan life. Leave it to Garros, however, to imagine that a banker from Frankfurt would take the Arabic name Abou-Samara and raise his Tunisian son as Ahmed! Garros's indigenization of a European Jew hyperbolizes the racial continuity between Jewries presumed and constructed by the likes of Drumont and Meynié. Nesting otherness within otherness, Kemmerling's overdetermined Tunisian alias—derived from the root Arabic word for "black"—further underscores the Jew's intended remove from whiteness.

But in a reminder of how, as I explained earlier, it remained ideologically necessary that the African and European poles of Jewish alterity nevertheless remain distinct, Garros has Abou-Samara insist on his Europeanness. Though he has everything to lose by rejecting his own indigenous cover, Abou-Samara wants his son to remember that they are not like other Tunisian Jews. To Ahmed's claim that the establishment of France's protectorate liberated Tunisian Jews from "veritable slavery," his father replies with an impassioned Germano-Jewish racial call to arms against the French:

> Ha! I couldn't care less, sniggered Abou-Samara. Too bad for the Jews if they have suffered every snub without complaining!
>
> Good for them if France's victory marked the hour of their liberation!
>
> As for us, you know, Ahmed, we cannot be assimilated to our coreligionists long settled in the Regency. If they owe something to the French, we owe them nothing . . . nothing but hatred, that racial hatred not extinguished by the rivers of blood already spilled. (104–5)

Having posited an easy continuity between Jewries, Garros cleaves them apart again, the better to reinforce the intended racial incommensurability between German Jews and their supposed French enemies. Once more, the Jew furnishes the pivot around which to translate imperial affairs into the national terms of European rivalry.

There is another phenomenon here binding scales even more intricately together: the reconstitution of the national at the scale of the imperial. The essential principle of fungibility on which rests Tunisia's compensatory substitution for the part of Lorraine lost to the Germans weds the nation, in its very ontology, to the logic of circulation characteristic of the global scale. Changed by his colonial experience, Pierre returns to the scene of his desertion and bravely acquits himself of his debt to his country. Garros wishes to show a landed aristocracy reassembling itself after having failed the nation in 1870. Himself an aristocrat, Garros was obviously sensitive to the late-century, decadentist argument that the aristocracy had degenerated into an indolent shadow of its glorious former self (an anxiety possibly stoked by Garros's failure to gain admission to the prestigious military school of Saint-Cyr).[128] Yet for all its symbolic weight, Pierre's sacrifice accomplishes little. More important to his reintegration of the national body, at least in concrete terms, is his assimilation into the prevailing economic order. And that order is now irreversibly both imperial and bourgeois. Pierre's plan in Tunisia, he explains to his son, is "to become French again . . . through work" (177). The young Pierre indebts himself by gambling, a Balzacian topos from an era when the nobility still clung to dissipation over industry. The older Pierre indebts himself because he needs capital to play the only remaining game in town.

To be sure, Garros would have the Tunisian Valfleury resemble the old one, giving France's imperial capitalist expansion a veneer of noble, precapitalist respectability. But for the phoenix-like Valfleury estate to have risen again across the Mediterranean also necessarily implicates Garros's aristocratic heroes in the unmistakable premises—iterability, standardization, exchange—of the commodity form. The resulting anxiety generated in the text demands an antidote. Whatever precapitalist solidity and authenticity Valfleury gives up as the imperial copy of a national original, it ostensibly regains by contrast with the even more fluid finance capital embodied by Kemmerling/Abou-Samara. Such an implicit division of capitalist production into the supposedly separable components of a "destructive" international finance capital and "productive" local agro-industrial capital adopts the cynical maneuver of a bourgeois antisemitism interested to divert anticapitalist sentiment against the Jew.[129] Kemmerling likewise guarantees the new

Valfleury's perceived organic authenticity by reproducing, in his conflict with French colonists, the profoundly national stakes of the continental conflict pitting France against Germany. And if this perhaps still represents an attenuation of imperial alterity along more tolerable national lines, it also finds Garros largely unable to define the national, even as a matter of continental territorial unity, at anything other than a global, extracontinental economic scale. So extensive a transposition of the national scale into the global requires the catalyst of a Jew who, indigenized or primitivized as an imperial yet still nationalized as a German, makes it possible to toggle between scales by inhabiting them both himself.

Garros's scalar move and its attendant antisemitism camouflage bourgeois economic change in the appearance of an aristocratic continuity with a prewar past. They also reflect and contribute to the spirit of the change itself. Redefining fixity according to the dictates of mobility, Garros channels the requirements of an imperial capital concerned to balance local production and global circulation. At the planetary scale, the world system was generating new productive agglomerations as labor and capital migrated across nations and continents. For these fixities usefully to grow and endure, however, they needed to be reconstituted at the more local, domestic scales required for stability. Thus, for instance, could Tunisia be construed as a new Lorraine, naturalizing North African capitalist production in national terms designed at once to promote fixity and to render it portable whenever disruptions in one part of the world system (like territory changing national hands in northeastern France) made either necessary or seemingly justifiable the relocation of production to another. Garros's associated temporal proposition—that this distinctly modern phenomenon might be instantiated by an aristocracy making a return to past honorability and military form—suggests a related attempt at combining continuity and disruption, fixity and mobility, stasis and change. But as we will see in the next chapter, such a fusing of modernity and tradition was no simple metaphysical task, impelling reactionaries like Garros ever further toward conceiving the nation in dialectical relation with its imperial periphery.

CHAPTER 3

Men on Horseback (1)

The Marquis de Morès, Nationalism, and Imperial Space-Time

As the nineteenth century drew to a close, many in France fixated on a swampy, mosquito-invested African province known as the Bahr al-Ghazal, an Oklahoma-sized territory bordering the French Congo in the upper Nile region of South Sudan. Pierre Savorgnan de Brazza, the Italian-born explorer and naturalized Frenchman famous for securing the Congolese colony, had in 1890 conceived an occupation of the upper Nile as a bulwark against Britain's imperial Egyptian possession to the north. French attention eventually focused on the Bahr al-Ghazal—Arabic for "the river of gazelles"—and its abandoned Egyptian garrison of Fashoda. For years, Fashoda had rotted in oblivion. Then, in 1893, the engineer Victor Prompt presented an old classmate from the École Polytechnique engineering school with an audacious variation on Brazza's idea: with Fashoda under French control, French engineers might dam the Nile headwaters, seizing control of the river and forcing Britain to negotiate with France over Egypt.[1]

Prompt's former classmate was none other than Sadi Carnot, president of the Republic, and in Prompt's plan, Carnot saw a way to settle the "Egyptian question" once and for all. That very year, Théophile Delcassé, Carnot's colonial undersecretary, charged Captain Parfait-Louis Monteil with leading a mission to the upper Nile. British threats and other political complications caused Monteil to be called off his goal in 1894. Nevertheless, a tantalizingly simple way had been announced for challenging British supremacy in Egypt.

There is some doubt about just how convinced, exactly, French officials were that Fashoda held the hydrological key to the Scramble for Africa.[2] What is not in doubt is that in 1896 the French government renewed its bid for Fashoda, sending Captain Jean-Baptiste Marchand to accomplish the mission with which Monteil had previously been entrusted.[3] Marchand's arrival at Fashoda two years later, in September 1898, sent shock waves through France. Marchand and his 150 men found themselves face-to-face with the 25,000 men of Herbert Kitchener, the commander of an Anglo-Egyptian army unwilling to let France strategically bisect the axis of British colonial power that extended from Alexandria to the Cape of South Africa. Delcassé, now foreign minister, eventually opted for surrender, but not before "L'Affaire de Fachoda" had nearly escalated into war.

The crisis sent French nationalists and antisemites—already in a militaristic mood over the Dreyfus Affair—into a collective fit of jingoistic choler. Édouard Drumont's antisemitic daily *La Libre parole* considered the withdrawal an ignominious humiliation on a par with that inflicted on France by Britain's 1882 occupation of Egypt, receiving the news with the headline "La Capitulation de la France—L'Abandon de Fachoda" and long continuing to denounce the French government's betrayal of Marchand and of France's rightful claim to Egypt.[4]

The Fashoda Affair has since been identified as a turning point after which the anticolonial extreme right definitively rallied to the cause of empire. Historian Edward Berenson writes that, galvanized by Fashoda, the "new militantly pro-colonial stance of the nationalist right" helped build a "large constituency for empire in France."[5] Yet though this may be true with regard to the larger republican imperial project against which the right had often railed, it is also worth remembering that—at least among French antisemites and other reactionary nationalists—the dismay after Fashoda hardly constituted a departure from longstanding complaints about British preeminence in Egypt. Skeptical as Drumont was, for instance, about the motivations behind the Third Republic's colonial adventures, the 1875 purchase by Britain's Jewish prime minister Benjamin Disraeli of a majority of shares in the French-built Suez Canal simply furnished too tempting an apparent example of Jewish conspiracy.[6] By "abandoning" Marchand, went the continued narrative, the Third Republic had spinelessly declined to strike a blow in Egypt against the imperial jewel of world Anglo-Jewish power.

Drumont and others also spun the Fashoda story as evidence that a single intrepid soul might accomplish what the government could not. But even this part of the narrative was not new. Two years before Fashoda, another folk hero had been sainted when the Marquis de Morès, a disgraced former agitator in the antisemitic movement grouped around Drumont, was killed in Africa attempting a similar Egyptian feat. Morès intended to cross the entire Sahara desert in a drive toward the Bahr al-Ghazal, where with help from Muslim Mahdist forces already resisting the British in Sudan he hoped to threaten the economic lifeblood of Egypt. He made it no further than southern Tunisia, though, before perishing in a shootout with Tuareg highwaymen attracted to easy prey.

Metropolitan antisemites greeted Morès's death with the paroxysms of a crusade starved for a martyr. Persona non grata in Paris only a few years earlier, Morès was suddenly peering out from the masthead of *La Libre parole* and receiving solemn eulogies from the likes of Drumont and Maurice Barrès.[7] Reactionary arguments about the Third Republic's inability to harness the chivalric energies of the Marquis's one-man campaign provided a blueprint for subsequent lionizations of Marchand, whose own fateful mission began just weeks after Morès died in 1896. Drumont was later proud to point out the filiation: "Is not Marchand, the heroic Commander Marchand, Morès' dream realized?"[8] Barrès, too, saw in the Marchand mission a continuation of "Morès' unfinished deeds." "Morès," he wrote in his 1902 *Scènes et doctrines du nationalisme*, "had dreamed of conquering for France the Bahr al-Ghazl, with the help of the Mahdi of Omdurman. Marchand, with limited means and despite the Mahdi, achieved this conquest."[9]

But if I will be focusing here on Morès, it is not just because he arguably set in motion the future right-wing narrative about Marchand's abandonment. It is also because the Marquis's memorialization represents a crucial moment in the broader emergence of a new nationalist paradigm. The specificity of that new paradigm, particularly regarding what I will argue is its unique temporality, characterizes the resolutely literary mode in which Morès's contemporaries remembered him. It was de rigueur, for instance, to represent Morès's death as the dramatic last act in the "roman," or medieval epic romance, that the impetuous Marquis seemed to have lived.[10] Metaphorical at first, this time-bending literary mourning soon found practical inspiration in the *Chanson de Roland* and its titular paladin, the Charlemagnian warrior immortalized by the poem for his exploits at the Battle of Ronceveaux Pass in 778. Not content simply to consecrate a new Roland, Drumont's *La Libre parole illustrée* decided that, like Roland, Morès merited celebration in verse. Readers obliged, honoring the "valiant" Marquis with overwrought poems that would grace the pages of *La Libre parole*'s weekly illustrated supplement the rest of the year.[11]

The following few couplets capture the stylistic and ideological tenor of this poetic outpouring:

Roland, at Ronceveaux, at least had the pleasure,
Of a death dreamed by his generous desire.
You, alone in the African desert with no more army,
Than an escort—empty word!—afraid of the wind,
You rode [*tu chevauchais*], dreaming of happy projects
That, linking the two Worlds together in one fell swoop,
Of a France wounded, dying, dead,
Would make the new France, eternally strong.[12]

Touting the regenerative potential for the metropole of expansion abroad, the poem locates the source of that renewal at the intersection between two powerful imaginaries: the chivalric and the imperial. The spatial displacement produced by Morès's imperial foray into the "African desert" precipitates an accompanying temporal displacement, reviving in the present a bygone era of courtly adventure. In and of itself, this temporal effect feels expected enough. The West construed its imperial periphery as a place where time had stood still; and so, what made the aristocratic Marquis potentially anachronistic in the metropole became timely in the Sahara. Collusion between Morès's escort and the Muslim tribesmen who killed him, recalling as it did Roland's ambush by Saracens after a betrayal in his own camp, likewise consolidated the Marquis's knightly stature.

Equally important to the poem's logic, however, is Morès's simultaneous occupation of the opposite temporal pole. As a Frenchman and European, Morès also incarnated the penetration of modernity into a land untouched, as Hegel would have it, by History. Imperial space thus possessed the curious property of conferring on the Marquis a dual temporality. Even as he resurrected the past, he brought it into line with the present. This, the poem tells us, is the prerogative of the Marquis's aristocratic imperialism. The intransitive "chevauchais," a literary expression for riding horseback that here evokes knightly exploits, also dovetails connotatively—as a transitive verb meaning to sit astride—with Morès's design to link "the two Worlds together." The two worlds refer to Morès's goal of a Franco-Islamic alliance. On another level, though, the announced union represents that of the old France and the new.

At least, this is how Morès and many of his admirers would have read the tribute. A self-consciously chivalric aristocrat who catered to the proletariat, most notably by proposing a system of workers' credit, Morès fancied himself as attuned to matters of the hour as to the mores of yesteryear.[13] In Africa, he intended to place chivalry at the service of a distinctly modern enterprise that he understood was playing out as capital radiated toward new resources and markets.[14] Others had been perceived to do something temporally similar. Charles Gordon, the legendary British imperial hero killed by Mahdist rebels at Khartoum in 1885, combined a reputation for chastity—a knightly topos if there ever was one—with plaudits for advancing the cause of modern civilization by fighting against the Sudanese slave trade.[15] Why were such figures so consistently understood to bridge past and present? Morès, in whom Drumont saw a new Gordon, proves especially instructive a case because of what the hagiographic response to his death reveals about a shifting temporal landscape in fin-de-siècle France.[16] This chapter is about that complicated landscape, its influence on a strident new brand of French nationalism, and the way in which it came into especially sharp focus against the backdrop of a rapidly expanding empire.

There exists no shortage of precedents for thinking about French and European imperial expansion in light of contemporaneous temporal preoccupations, particularly those surrounding modernity. Literary critics and historians have documented various attempts by aesthetes like Flaubert and Baudelaire to seek refuge abroad from the bourgeois modernity under which they chafed at home.[17] Another influential tendency, initiated in part by work on French colonial urbanism, has found many treating the colonies as what Ann Laura Stoler calls "laboratories of modernity"—that is, experimental sites designated by metropolitan colonizers for elaborating new methods of governance, discipline, and control.[18] Of course, none of this implies an airtight distinction between exoticist, antimodern escapism and the imperial cultivation of modernity. If anything, in fact, the relationship has historically proven rather dialectical. Madeleine Dobie notes, for example, how in fantasizing picturesque lands unsullied by industrial modernity, Orientalist art simultaneously and paradoxically offered up the Orient as a "colorful plaything" ripe for modernizing imperial conquest.[19]

Late-century French antisemites, too, blurred the line between escaping and affirming modernity when, in empire, they sometimes recognized an opportunity to reconcile capitalist expansion with a traditional, agrarian past. Recall Paul de Garros's *La Revanche de l'honneur*, the 1896 antisemitic novel in which, as I discussed previously, German and Tunisian otherness coincide in the single Jewish foe dogging French aristocrats exiled to Tunisia by the Franco-Prussian War (1870–71). But it is those expatriated colonists as well who are made to incarnate another imagined continuity, one between a precapitalist model of landed aristocracy consigned to permanent irrelevance by the bourgeois Third Republic and the model's ostensible reconstitution outside the metropole. Never mind that these characters' colonial estates were necessarily inspired by the large-scale, technologically advanced, and highly capitalized exploitation characteristic of most French agriculture in the Tunisian protectorate at the time. What mattered for Garros, ideologically speaking, is that the new colonial domains evoke the old, feudal mode of noble privilege, though without exactly reproducing it. Thus might an anxious, bourgeoisified aristocracy dress its capitalist participation in the more respectable garb of landed gentility. And insofar as the sleight of hand required diverting capitalist malfeasance to Jewish account, the same antisemitic and imperial fable of economic continuity might align other constituencies against the figure of the colonially conspiring Jew. These included a bourgeoisie eager to smooth out capitalism's more disruptive qualities without endangering the capitalist order itself and recently proletarianized, urbanized masses at once nostalgic for a time before economic dislocation and wary of any return to the feudal.

So the imperial periphery had become more than just a suspicious place usefully assimilable, as I argued in Chapter 2, to metropolitan antisemites' theories of global Jewish conspiracy. It was also handy ideological terrain for managing and even producing all manner of mystifications. One such mystification concerned the status of modernity, a constructed overseas version of which antisemites could quietly endorse while continuing to denounce a degraded metropole. Yet as the defenders of Dreyfus began accusing their enemies of an ossified clericalism anathema to the modern Republic, antisemites found themselves compelled to insist more overtly on the modernity of their project. Morès, in spite of his aristocratic quirks, was taken as exemplary on this front. "No more for Morès than for us, the war against Jewry . . . was not a religious war," wrote Drumont upon learning of Morès's death, enlisting the dead Marquis to distinguish modern antisemitic ideology from knee-jerk prejudices of old.[20]

That so knightly a figure would be celebrated for his modernity is no accident, and not just because Morès's admirers worried that he might be remembered as a reckless throwback. Indeed, he proved so attractive a symbol precisely because of the compatibility his chivalric imperialism made it possible to suggest between the new French antisemitism's ostensibly modern outlook and the traditional values also epitomized by the Marquis. It was one thing to rail against economic modernity while tacitly embracing the status quo. However contradictory that state of affairs, no explanation needed offering, almost by definition, since such simultaneous avowal and disavowal required only some fetish mechanism—the Jew—for silently displacing and containing the underlying irresolvability. It was another, more difficult thing to articulate openly how past and present might be understood to coincide. For what becomes apparent in these labored fin-de-siècle ruminations about time by antisemites and xenophobic nationalists was that to posit, as they attempted, a continuity between the modern and the traditional was not simply to imagine modernity as the culmination of a gradual historical process. Neither was it merely to excavate some kind of unchanging essence binding the current nation to its previous incarnations. Rather, Morès's death occasioned a reflection about the possibilities for *both* stasis and change somehow to comprise a same historical force. And this, I will be arguing, meant reconciling varieties of time itself.

The different temporalities in question map roughly onto any number of established binaries—secular and sacred, homogeneous and messianic, linear and disjunctive—customarily employed in discussions of time influenced by the various thinkers, from Walter Benjamin to Johannes Fabian, with whom I want to engage here. Because no two of these pairings ever quite correspond exactly, part of my task will be to chart the overlaps, slippages, and distinctions in usage among them. But typology aside, such existing temporal frameworks also require some reassessment to appreciate properly the crisscrossing attitudes toward nation, race, and empire traced by the Morès story. The challenge begins with contemplating nationalism, or the radical fin-de-siècle French variant thereof, in its dimension as a convergence of temporalities. The relationship between temporalities is typically represented along contrastive lines: either an older temporal mode is understood to have given way, more or less gradually, to a newer one, or temporalities are taken to coexist uneasily and even incommensurably alongside one another. Seldom are they considered in their interaction, likely owing to the sheer conceptual gulf that tends to separate them. And yet, many in France made it their tacit goal to bridge just such a gulf.

The reasons for and difficulties entailed by this attempted temporal synthesis shed light on a host of phenomena in the hypernationalist and hyperimperialist decades before World War I. In what follows, I begin by delineating the new ideological stakes for a late-century breed of reactionaries as keen to celebrate French national modernity as to render that modernity consonant with various phenomena, like chivalry and historical constancy, whose connotations (feudalism, stasis, religion, etc.) usually furnished modernity its opposites. A subsequent part of the chapter considers how literature and narrative were deployed in hopes of the desired synthesis, promising the transmission across generations of a French essence without any recourse to fantastical, religious, or ahistorical devices that would undercut the modernity of the endeavor.

But Morès and his African adventures were useful for more than what they might do, once literarized, to help merge temporalities in the way sought. As I will argue, the Marquis's talismanic influence also suggests something about how the imperial project itself, in a larger sense, encouraged the temporal reconciliation undertaken in the metropole. This had much to do with the well-documented belief by Europeans that to travel outward into the imperial periphery was to travel backward in time to a more primitive stage of human development. The resulting conflation of space and time is justifiably cited now as a chief ideological pillar of European discourses legitimizing conquest on the grounds of civilizational and racial superiority. Yet to see in imperial space-time exclusively a strategy for dominance over primitivized subalterns is to miss how empire also made possible a new, hybrid time of the nation. At the intersection between temporalities I will describe, imperial access to the past became as much about recuperating and conjoining erstwhile aspects of the French nation as about burnishing the invading nation's modern credentials. And if it is in a space apart that empire facilitated a perceived temporal remove, it is also by virtue of this space apart, I want to conclude, that empire enabled a nationalist marriage of temporalities difficult within national boundaries alone.

Turn-of-the-century European imperialism, then, did not simply inflame existing nationalist passions within and among rival powers. In the French case, imperial expansion also gave a crucial fillip to a new *kind* of nationalism—one whose self-proclaimed reconciliation of tradition and modernity has been considered to anticipate twentieth-century French fascism but whose interconnected temporal, spatial, and imperial valences remain poorly understood. The ire directed by this nationalism at racialized metropolitan others scarcely surprises, given the infernal circuit formed between an increasingly elaborate imperial racialism, on the one hand, and xenophobic nationalism's correspondingly exclusionary tendencies, on the other. As I have elsewhere been trying to demonstrate, however, the convoluted workings of the circuit cannot simply be reduced to mutual influence on each other by hierarchizing racial systems operating in the metropole and periphery. Indeed, the present example will make clear how the new French nationalism's fin-de-siècle conceptual basis—a vision of transhistorical national solidarity realized in the present through a fusion of temporalities—required a spatial fix making it possible to address, at the scale of empire, contradictions problematic at the scale of the nation. Understanding this kind of scalar recourse to the geographic and conceptual space of empire sheds light, in turn, on the resulting construction of racial relationalities not always strictly explainable as technologies of repression and control. Such was the case, for example, when the new nationalists bolstered their notion of Frenchness with admiring references to putatively chivalric, feudal qualities among African Muslims, even as those same subalterns were simultaneously and predictably contrasted with French modernity.

The chief architect of the new nationalism, Maurice Barrès, about whom I will have much to say, has been influentially glossed by Tzvetan Todorov for what Barrès's nationalist relativism did to facilitate the "rejection of others."[21] National cultures were intrinsically different, and so peoples must be separately governed according to their own determinate sensibilities; universalism was by contrast dangerously unable, in Barrès's estimation, to take "individual differences into account."[22] But even for so parochial a thinker, such differences in kind were modulated by similarities across time. These time-spanning similarities *between* peoples mattered because of a resulting consistency suggested *within* them: once a foreign people's assumed primitivity reminded imperial observers of their own past, it became easier, we will see, to imagine a continuity of the metropolitan past with the metropolitan present. In other words, to be like others made it easier to be like oneself. The new nationalism thus sought unexpected regimes of similitude, all while hardening underlying assumptions about racial difference. It is around this key play of similarity and difference, as well as stasis and change, that an important new set of interrelated literary, nationalist, and imperial discourses crystallized in the wake of the Morès debacle.

THE MARQUIS

Antoine Amédée-Marie-Vincent-Amat Manca de Vallombrosa, Marquis de Morès, was a handsome, swashbuckling nobleman and former army officer with a history of failed business ventures in the Dakota Badlands and Tonkin. Born in 1858 to an old aristocratic Spanish clan exiled from Sardinia to France earlier that century, Morès pursued the family taste for military distinction at the prestigious French academy of Saint-Cyr. There he was classmates with Henri Pétain, future Vichy chief of state, and became fast friends with Charles de Foucauld, later famous for his spiritual peregrinations in North Africa. Upon resigning his commission in 1881, Morès lost 500,000 francs of his father's money in the Parisian stock market crash of 1882, then moved to New York to work with his new American bride's prominent banker father. Soon his attentions turned to the great cattle boom, prompting a move to the Dakota Badlands and an unsuccessful venture to cut meat shipment costs by slaughtering cattle on the range. A reputation for strong-arm business dealings and friendships with suspected cattle rustlers quickly sent him packing from the frontier. By 1888 the wax-mustachioed Marquis was at it again, this time in French Indochina, where he hoped to find riches building a railroad into China from France's new colonial possession of Tonkin. Forced out by more savvy competitors, Morès mounted a venomous and highly visible public campaign against the minster of the interior, Ernest Constans, the former governor of Indochina whom Morès held responsible for his latest investment fiasco.

Morès's political radicalization continued apace in France. Converted to doctrinal antisemitism in 1889 by Drumont's *La France juive*, which convinced him that Jews were behind both his financial undoing and the Third Republic, Morès quickly became one of the stars of the antisemitic movement assembling around Drumont. A failed 1890 run for a Paris city council seat from a heavily socialist district found Morès incorporating socialist elements into his platform, though only to the extent that he felt measures like workers' credit would promote national cohesion. Socialist leaders like Jules Guesde and Paul Lafargue were unimpressed, and Morès returned the favor by making organized socialism one of his many targets.[23]

Morès's flamboyant, combative ways would henceforth consistently land him in the headlines. When not dressed in his signature cowboy garb, intimidating Jews with his loyal gang of butchers from the slaughterhouses of La Villette, Morès provoked endless duels with Jewish journalists and army officers.[24] One of these duels, with the Jewish officer Captain Joseph Alexandre Mayer in June 1892, ended badly: Mayer died, his lung punctured by Morès's sword. The tragedy earned Morès widespread rebuke in the Parisian press and became the first in a series of events—including Morès's disloyal public revelation of Drumont's role in arranging for him a loan of 20,000 francs from Cornelius Herz, a Jew vilified by *La Libre parole* for his role in the Panama Canal scandal—that eventually cost the Marquis his welcome nearly everywhere.

Dispirited, Morès turned his energies toward Africa, where he worried France was losing its battle with England for imperial preeminence. In the metropole, Morès had styled himself a socialist, pandering to a working class he thought held the key to French national unity (a politics that, drawing on Maurice Barrès's declaration that Morès realized "the union of the socialist idea and nationalist idea," Robert Byrnes has suggested makes Morès "the first National Socialist").[25] In Africa, Morès found a new and related calling: the creation of a grand Franco-Islamic alliance, without which Morès felt France could not forestall British and Jewish dominance of the continent. Morès's assumption of African Muslims' natural antipathy for Anglo-Jewish encroachment followed in a cynical antisemitic tradition of Islamophilia that, as I have discussed previously, was given substantial currency by Drumont in the 1880s. Beginning with the invented notion that the 1871 Algerian tribal rebellion had been sparked by Muslim resentment over the Crémieux decree's granting of French citizenship to Algerian Jews, French antisemites had found it convenient to rail about mass exploitation of Muslims by their African Jewish countrymen.

Consequently could Morès and other antisemites cite the benefits of French imperial influence to those purportedly dispossessed by Jews. "Do justice, in Algeria, to the Arabs," Morès enjoined French president Jean Casimir-Perier in an 1894 open letter, invoking the familiar antisemitic trope of native Algerians "shamefully robbed of their land by Jewish usurers."[26] "He is missed by all the oppressed," *La Libre parole* would later opine about the recently deceased Marquis, explicitly grouping the interests of the economically beleaguered in both colony and metropole: "It is a noteworthy fact that the Arabs whom he tried, in Algeria, to free from the Jewish yoke mourned his death and celebrated his courage at the same time as the French workers, employees, and shopkeepers who today will walk behind his coffin."[27] Morès had indeed met with some limited success stoking antisemitic passions in Algeria, though less among Muslim Algerians than among the French and European colonists caught up in the wave of antisemitic agitation beginning to sweep the colony.[28] "Give the Arabs land, justice, and the Koran," he thundered to an assembled crowd of 10,000 at Bab el Oued in February 1894, "and walk with them in the peaceful conquest of Africa."[29]

Despite this initially enthusiastic reception, as well as the encouraging agreements he reached with Arab chieftains during a brief exploratory venture into the Algerian center in early 1896, Morès failed to muster significant support for his various commercial and military schemes to erode Anglo-Jewish influence in Africa. These included a plan to link Lake Chad to the port city of Bizerte in France's Tunisian protectorate, as well as an alliance with Muslim rebels in Libya to threaten British Egyptian forces from the lower Nile. Undeterred, Morès launched a longer, foolhardy expedition from Tunisia in May 1896, hoping eventually to wrest control of the upper Nile in South Sudan and so achieve a stranglehold on British Egypt.[30] By June 9 he was dead, ambushed by his own Tuareg escort in the sands of El Ouatia south of the last French military outpost in Tunisia.

For all his sheer eccentricity, though, Morès was hardly sui generis. As noted above, Morès's bid to dam the Nile in the Sudanese Bahr al-Ghazal province resembled official French efforts before and after him. More generally, Michel Winock is right to include Morès under the rubric of a French proto-fascism heralding twentieth-century disasters. Winock's ascription to Morès of what Ernst Nolte calls the "radical conservatism" of proto-fascists like Drumont and Maurice Barrès underscores the temporal peculiarity of what the Marquis and his antisemitic peers hoped to accomplish.[31] As self-styled guardians of tradition, they had inherited the conservative, counterrevolutionary legacy of Joseph de Maistre and Louis de Bonald. As proponents of an ersatz socialist radicalism, however, these foes of "Jewish" capital professed less interest in repealing modernity than in contesting its supposed diversion by Jews. Combined, the two attitudes produced a corporatist ideology intent on erasing class conflict without altering the underlying relations of production. An imagined prerevolutionary harmony, according to this organicist worldview, would return to redeem an economic modernity corrupted by the Revolution and its Jewish beneficiaries.

Few other figures prompted more ruminations on such temporal circularity than the Marquis de Morès. In part, this arose from the necessity of defending Morès against the perception, even by some admirers, that the uncompromising Marquis had fallen prey to his own anachronism. An unsigned article published in the conservative *Le Figaro* days after the Marquis's death proposed that Morès's "taste for action, unbalanced and excessive as it was" would have paid greater dividends had Morès been born in different times:

> Suppose a man of this caliber had been born one hundred and fifty years earlier. Circumstances allowing, he would have walked in the footsteps of Montcalm, Dupleix, or Lally; he would have died to conquer or preserve an empire for France. Placed instead in our modern society where dilettantism is the only faith, where the energetic are suspect, and where strong convictions are considered tiresome, he acted alone, and he was lost in advance.[32]

Morès launched his fatal last mission into the Sahara against the explicit wishes of the French colonial administration in Tunisia, an outcome avoidable, the article maintains, were the Third Republic as capable as the ancien régime of harnessing individual energies for the good of the nation.[33] The examples do not exactly call to mind unqualified appreciation by the old monarchy of its colonial envoys—Joseph-François Dupleix, once the celebrated governor of France's Indian colony in Pondicherry, died a ruined man after having been recalled from his post in 1754 by French authorities leery of Dupleix's expansionist ways; General Thomas Arthur de Lally, commander of French forces in India during the Seven Years' War, was scapegoated and unjustly executed for treason by Louis XV after losing Pondicherry to the British in 1761[34]—but it is these martyrs' travails, too, that the author means to evoke in his portrait of a man betrayed by his government's enervated modernity. Not that *Le Figaro* thought Morès's actual plans outmoded. Jean Hess, the colonial writer who favorably chronicled Morès's African project for the newspaper, emphasized the practicality of commercial and strategic aims that Morès had developed with the backing of "well-placed Parisians" knowledgeable about the contemporary colonial enterprise. Still, he bemoaned, most could not see beyond the labels of hotheaded "zealot" and "adventurer" to appreciate the useful but untapped reserves of action channeled by the Marquis from a more vigorous French past.[35]

Where Hess underscored the era's inadequacy to the man, *La Libre parole*'s Jean Drault wondered about Morès's adequacy to the era. The Algerian correspondent for Drumont's antisemitic newspaper, Drault concluded that Morès's colonial project had been undermined by his chivalric ethos. "But is not Morès a romance hero?" he asked on the day of Morès's widely covered funeral, acknowledging the prevailing topos surrounding the Marquis. Yes, answered Drault—but to a fault. Drault gently queries Morès's romantic conviction that the Saharan Tuareg were descended from the "knight-monks of the Middle Ages who had settled in the desert" and suggests a measure of aristocratic hubris on Morès's part: "And perhaps he thought that they would recognize him from across the ages, he who was a descendant of the Crusaders, of those who had defended the Holy Sepulcher." For this reason, Drault continues, Morès resembled a character from the "romances of the Knights of the Round Table," too archaic in his outlook to realize a goal otherwise "very modern, very realizable."[36]

Joining the tropological chorus, *La Libre parole illustrée* had likewise marveled at the "knightly romance" (*roman*) of the Marquis's career.[37] Morès's picaresque ways certainly lent themselves to the metaphor. How else to describe a man who had played cowboy in the American West, hunted tigers in Burma and Nepal, dreamed of railroads in Tonkin, cracked heads in Paris, and tried single-handedly to unify all of France's African possessions? Such a literary comparison struck a memorializing tone befitting the fallen hero that antisemites and nationalists were eager to construct, while tactfully acknowledging how Morès's intemperate idealism had perhaps consigned him to a deluded realm on the quasi-fictional margins of real-world activity. And if Morès, such as his contemporaries represented him, was so easily metaphorized as a fictional hero come to life, it was partly because of the grim literalism with which Morès himself had appeared consciously to pattern his actions after the tragic heroes of French knightly romances. The Marquis's favorite book was literary historian Léon Gautier's reverential 1884 tome about the culture of medieval French chivalry, *La Chevalerie* (*Chivalry*), among whose insights was that French knights in training had been formed by the "useful, bold fictions" of feudal *chansons de geste* (epic poems) essential to inspiring "manly feelings" in their noble young audiences.[38] Morès clearly took this didacticism to heart. The question pondered by his contemporaries was whether Morès had been reasonable to reach so far back in time for his examples.

The quandary, then, of Morès's posthumous recuperation by the Parisian antisemitic agitators he once alienated was that what in death made him so poignant a martyr—his doomed adherence to a literary, chivalric ideal—had also, in life, evidently curtailed his success. Here we might begin complicating any easy notion about how, like the fascists they have often been taken to anticipate, Morès's antisemitic comrades in arms sought to organize the world according to the principles of the artwork. Borrowing from Jean-Luc Nancy and Philippe Lacoue-Labarthe their hypothesis of a fascist "fictioning" of the political, which they trace to Plato's seminal likening of the political to a plastic art, David Carroll has suggested that, to men like Drumont, antisemitism meant subsuming material contingencies under the ordering, totalizing influence of the aesthetic.[39] The cult of Morès, however, lays bare fin-de-siècle misgivings and anxieties among seeming proponents of this aestheticizing ethos. On one hand, Morès's literary self-fashioning flattered the sensibilities of onlookers inclined to see, in their perceived struggle against a fundamentally treacherous Jewish or Masonic or Republican evil, a world governed by the reductive laws of chivalric fiction (any good example of which, as Gautier intoned, must necessarily begin with "a story of treachery," the better to give budding knights a taste for righting wrongs).[40] On the other hand, Morès's reckless and ultimately suicidal ways gave even stalwart friends pause. Was it indeed possible, let alone advisable, for literary topoi to come alive in this way? And what did it mean, anyway, for access to the storehouse of French chivalric energy and action to appear so literarily mediated?

Of course, the relentlessness with which antisemites located the Jew behind every disaster had a circular way of distracting from these questions as soon as it raised them. There was certainly no shortage of conspiracy theories suggesting that Morès had succumbed less to his own chivalric poses than to dastardly retaliation by the occult forces he was supposedly defying in Africa. Hess, Morès's Algerian mentor the Prince de Polignac, and others immediately pinned the Marquis's murder on the Arbibs, a family of Tripolitanian Jews influential in North African trade and finance whose dealings with England seemed to confirm the Anglo-Jewish power Morès imagined he was combatting. Helpfully enough, Morès himself had written a preemptive letter to the Arbibs incriminating them in anything that might happen to him in the desert.[41] Yet such conventional narratives only overlaid lingering complexities raised by Morès's unconventional life. In their more reflective moments, Morès's apologists grappled with their complicated hero's liminal place not only between past and present, or between the written page and the lived world, but also—as I want to show now—at the even hazier boundary between different ways of thinking time.

NATIONALISM AND DOUBLE TEMPORALITY

The most symptomatic reaction to the Marquis's death along temporal lines came from Barrès, the doyen of radical French nationalism and a frontline combatant in the unfolding Dreyfus Affair that would, with the publication of Émile Zola's incendiary "J'Accuse" eighteen months later, bring France to the brink of civil war. One of several high-profile eulogists joining the July 19, 1896, funeral procession of 10,000 Parisians that accompanied Morès's body from the Gare de Lyon train station to the Notre-Dame cathedral and Montmartre cemetery, Barrès rebutted suggestions that the Marquis had highlighted modern France's inability to employ the Marquis's undiminished aristocratic energies.[42] On the contrary, argued Barrès, Morès's vision of classes working together toward a common nationalist end constituted the crystallization, in a synchronous present, of exactly the historical process that linked old France and new. This process, moreover, had gained momentum over time as various forces and upheavals increasingly fixed France's geographic, political, and cultural identity:

> [Morès] thought that the elements which had contributed to shaping and distinguishing our nation, and had sustained her by developing with her throughout the centuries, are still the only ones capable of maintaining France all while adapting her to the characteristics of the period into which European societies have just entered.[43]

Barrès's superficial point is that the very principle of organicist nationalism, a solidarity among classes forged in the crucible of the nation, carries behind it the accumulated and irreversible momentum of history. The various "elements" coalescing around this common principle have contributed in different and sometimes surprising ways: later in the speech, for instance, Barrès pointedly appropriates a Revolution clearly at odds with cross-class solidarity but whose adherence to the nation form for its "general organization" he admires for having nevertheless consecrated nationality as the fundamental unit of human belonging.[44] Here Barrès confirms his basic accommodation to republican government, something that he shared with fellow radical conservatives like Morès less intent on rolling back the Revolution than on denouncing the individualism they associated with the liberal Enlightenment ideals that the Revolution had helped to triumph.

The more unsteady dimension of Barrès's historicizing argument concerns what to do with the collective national thread weaving through so many disparate elements arrayed by Barrès across the French past. A love for country common to the knights Morès idolized and to, say, revolutionary Jacobins certainly might be fashioned into a shared denominator uniting different social strata with otherwise vastly divergent class interests. But such a unifying force operated largely along a diachronic axis—that is, it connected groups and moments temporally removed from one another. How to pass from so latent or virtual a diachronic solidarity dispersed in time to a synchronic solidarity actualized in a given present?

The promise of the Marquis, for Barrès, lay in answering this critical question, though not because Morès somehow harked back to a prelapsarian Eden before the revolutions of 1789 or 1830 had riven the social body asunder. For Barrès, notes Zeev Sternhell, a wholesale turn toward the past was tantamount to denying the unity of French history and thus to renouncing the principle of national unity.[45] What Morès offered instead was a uniquely double temporality. First, he embodied the possibility of historical continuity. Barrès stressed the idea in *Le Figaro* a month before the funeral:

> . . . by a rare coincidence, [Morès] combined the brilliance and frivolity of the old ways with contemporary interests.
>
> That the France of yore and modern France should meet without rejecting each other, that they should be united in a same soul, is rare in a time when men who preserve the Past spurn the Present and even the greatest artisans of the day reject the qualities of yesteryear. Morès displays so rare and yet natural a mixture. Can you not see mixed in him, for example, a figure of the Fronde and a member of the Geographic Society?[46]

Drumont, in a similar vein, described at the Monmartre cemetery how the Marquis "seemed to have come to link the Past and the Present."[47]

Such a feat of continuity itself comprised a certain temporal doubleness by locating the Marquis astride tradition and modernity. No artifact, no atavistic relic, Morès had combined the best of both epochs. "This gentleman of old descent, who had the adventurous courage of the first Crusaders, was nevertheless no knight-errant stranded in our century," insisted Drumont in the pages of *La Libre parole*. Rather, "he had a taste for and appreciation of modern life."[48] Yet this doubleness ultimately only played out within a same diachronic temporality. Indeed, for the Marquis seemingly to have arrived from an aristocratic past happy to embrace a proletarian present confirmed that, however disjunctive the rupture produced by the Revolution, the arrow of history could contain it. The real temporal doubling emerged not from these protestations of national historical continuity but from telescoping so diachronic a unity into the synchronic present. When Barrès praised Morès for combining "the socialist idea" with "the nationalist idea," he was acknowledging more than Morès's efforts to build a social organism from class parts integrated by a contemporary sense of collective national belonging.[49] He was also conceiving this nationalist idea as something that, grown ever stronger as it produced virtual commonalities among very different kinds of Frenchmen separated in time, might consummate its potential by producing real, active solidarity among all classes in the present. If Morès usefully emblematized the process, it was because the Marquis incarnated the vision of a history minable for its unifying national energies, condensable into a synchronic distillate of those energies, and convertible into the basis for a fusional new society. Synchrony, in the radical conservative understanding of the nation, represented as much a collapsed, verticalized culmination of horizontal diachrony as a simple component within it.

This proposition differs from Benedict Anderson's familiar schema of the national community imagined by its participants as a shared, anonymous simultaneity progressing sequentially through history. The nation thus envisioned required the invention of what, citing from Walter Benjamin's "Theses on the Philosophy of History," Anderson calls "homogeneous, empty time."[50] The container, as it were, within which moments succeed one another, the past continuously yields to the present, and causality reigns, homogeneous time organizes an infinite series of cross-sectional simultaneities into a unidirectional flow. So conceived, synchrony relates to diachrony like a part to the whole. For Barrès, however, a synchronic present of hoped-for national unity would recapitulate the whole itself, collecting and reorienting along a vertical axis the combined national riches (chivalric self-sacrifice, Napoleonic grandeur, etc.) distributed horizontally throughout the past. For Morès to have tried to "link the Past and the Present," as Drumont put it, therefore meant more than reconciling old France and new by usefully reviving a noble chivalric spirit drowned by the revolutionary mob and its supposed Jewish profiteers. At another level, it meant folding *all* of the past, revolutionary and reactionary alike, into a solidary present.

Yet if radical conservative nationalists did not embrace homogeneous, empty time as their definitive temporal logic, neither did they subscribe exclusively to the "Messianic time" that Anderson contrasts with the empty time of the nation. Adapting, again, a term from Benjamin's "Theses," Anderson describes how messianic time allows for simultaneity to transpire along (or perhaps more accurately, outside) the horizontal axis of duration. Events in messianic time prefigure and fulfill, rather than precede and follow, conforming to a providentially ordained script where causality does not obtain and past, present, and future all inhabit an instantaneous now. Such a "mediaeval" logic of horizontal instantaneity, in Anderson's account, left little or no room for thinking the vertical simultaneity that came to "take [its] place" and furnish modern individuals a mental tool for envisioning their participation in a national collectivity marching concurrently through time.[51]

I will return in a moment to how radical conservatism significantly belied the conceptual dichotomy, bordering on mutual exclusivity, implied here by Anderson between the two temporalities. Let me begin first by noting, though, some existing challenges to Anderson's fairly schematic association of messianic time with a prenational, premodern mode of consciousness. Ian Baucom, for example, locates in Ernest Renan's canonical disquisition on nationalism, the 1882 lecture "Qu'est-ce qu'une nation?" ("What Is a Nation?"), an implied national redemption of the past by the present that strikes him as characteristically messianic.[52] We might also include Homi Bhabha's deconstruction of the "meanwhile" produced for Anderson when the modern novel fixed the psychological horizon of the nation by positing a shared, synchronous connection between social actors largely or wholly unaware of each other's activities.[53] Countering with the solitary novelist who, in Benjamin's "The Storyteller," produces isolation rather than community by representing the incommensurable, Bhabha bypasses the notion of messianic time only to reinscribe its linguistic equivalent. Against the "meanwhile" of a national narration presuming the smooth, continuous passage of a synchronous national community through homogeneous time, Bhabha opposes the radical discontinuity inherent in the signifying system of which narrative is made—a system that, drawing on the semiotics of Claude Lévi-Strauss, Bhabha understands to have come into being in "the sudden timelessness of 'all at once.'"[54] Bhabha's poststructuralist reminder of this destabilizing intrusion into synchrony of the "instantaneous rather than simultaneous" accords with Benjamin's portrait of a messianic "time of the now," a time "blasted out of the continuum of history" because it creates instantaneous, horizontal linkages circumventing the rigid and orderly course of homogeneous time.[55]

But while such correctives to Anderson's periodization point in a more faithfully Benjaminian way toward the ongoing coexistence of messianic and homogeneous temporalities, they also end up reproducing Benjamin's own rather absolute distinction between the two. The virile "tiger's leap into the past" attempted by the proper historical materialist bears no resemblance, for Benjamin, to the historicist's insouciant confidence in the gradual, causal, and irreversible flow of homogeneous time.[56] So too, for Bhabha, does the discontinuous temporality of signification—which he equates to cultural difference—subvert the comfortably homogeneous time of the nation with a disjunctive, Benjaminian "sudden shock."[57] The oppositional mode in which homogeneous and discontinuous time here confront one another echoes both critics' use of the latter for puncturing the bourgeois ideological fantasies of progress or totalizing homogeneity they associate with the former. Even Baucom's more detached historical identification of a mnemonic, messianic disposition in nineteenth-century European nationalism proceeds, in its explicit rejoinder to Anderson's model of a more "amnesiac" synchronic national community, from the premise of a basic variance between messianic and homogeneous time.[58]

What interests me about the double temporality of organicist nationalism, however, is that it attempts to chart a middle path between the two Benjaminian poles. Recall how Barrès predicted a fusional moment of class reconciliation catalyzed by a collective nationalist project. A horizontal sequence of nationalist energies previously dispersed in French history among various classes and eras would come flashing together in a single, unificatory present. The axis of diachrony would collapse into the axis of synchrony; latent commonalities would become manifest solidarity; time would crystallize into space. It is a dynamic reminiscent of the messianic simultaneity, or what Anderson calls "simultaneity-along-time," gathering key historical events into an instantaneous (if evidently not emancipatory) constellation of the sort Benjamin describes.[59] Yet here this simultaneity also partakes of a vertical, transverse simultaneity cutting sectionally across homogeneous time. For one, Barrès clearly imagined a national community traveling synchronously together through history. The permanence for him of the "nationalist idea" through centuries of French history meant that, regardless of social turbulences, the nation remained operative at any given point. Thus could the Revolution reinforce the political contours of the nation even as it temporarily drove Frenchmen apart. Just as importantly, Barrès pictured the national project as an incremental affair, a transformational process unfolding gradually in time:

> A transformation only yields the expected benefits, only leads to a state in turn likely to evolve further, inasmuch as every progress is linked to the most recent past. In a word, a creature is viable only to the extent that it changes in accordance with its character and hereditary habits.
>
> This historical sense, this strong naturalist feeling, this acceptance of a determinism, that is what we understand by nationalism.[60]

Such a perspective, replete as it is with the terms of a nascent Darwinian thinking—evolution, viability, heredity—presumes a homogeneous, empty time within which the "creature" of the nation grows and adapts along the unidirectional arrow of causality, every stage leading logically to the next. We are drifting away from the messianic model of noncausal, instantaneous linkages between events clustered together by a providential force operating outside and independently of diachrony.

Or at least, so it appears. For Barrès's evolutionary paradigm itself exhibits a decidedly compound temporality, one that cuts to the core of the compound mode he attempts to navigate. The determinism in which he so insistently grounds his nationalism means that, as the national evolutionary process seemingly unfolds in empty time, it remains governed by an ordering, quasi-providential power tethering the organism to a fixed hereditary script. This logic entails a variety of time internal to the process itself, much as messianic prophecy and fulfillment infuse into the very events they connect an instantaneous temporality distinct from external, empty time. Indeed, instantaneity conditions every step in the evolutionary sequence Barrès describes: observe above how "every progress" only occurs insofar as it remains simultaneously "linked to the most recent past." Progress, in other words, requires the immediate future to have been foretold in, and so essentially coincide with, the immediate past. The result is at once a paradox and its partial solution. How to conceive of progress if what is, or will be, in fact always already was? Barrès answers by displacing the mechanism of prefiguration and fulfillment from the traditional millennial scale—with its risk of mooting the apparent change observed during the intervening centuries—to the granular, almost imperceptible level between closely successive events. In so doing, he represents the nation's trajectory as a continuous series of tiny messianic flashes that, when viewed from a distance, emulates the steady, horizontal rhythm of incremental progress. Discontinuity, disruption, and instantaneity thus "hidden" interstitially away, Barrès imagines a messianic time (or his deterministic version of it) embedded in and conformable to, rather than incommensurate with, the parameters of homogeneous time.

For help considering the stability of this outcome, we may productively enlist Johannes Fabian's meta-anthropological reflections in *Time and the Other*, which tackles something resembling the curious hybridity at hand. Fabian's historical account maps at first glance onto Anderson's. As for Anderson did messianic time give way to the homogeneous, empty time of modernity, so for Fabian did "sacred time" precede in Europe a more universal "secular time" codified by the Enlightenment *philosophes*. Fabian likens the shift to the difference between linearity and tabularity: where Christian history never considered time independent from the linear chain of sacred events whose predetermined unfolding constituted time itself, later thinkers began picturing time more tabularly and capaciously, as a multidimensional vessel containing a wider variety of potentially unrelated events. This recalls, again, the familiar contrast between messianic and homogeneous time. But then Fabian introduces a crucial nuance. If the *philosophes* loosened time from its rigid Christian moorings, the better to accommodate a secular universal history suitable for describing all mankind, they nevertheless inherited from Christianity a teleological bent. The secularized result became the Enlightenment faith in human progress. In the way, then, that sacred time was bound up with the destinies of Christendom, the new, secular time remained bound up with the salvation of universal man.[61]

Secular time was thus not yet totally empty, not yet totally neutral. For it to become so required uncoupling it completely—or "naturalizing" it, in Fabian's expression—from human affairs. Though the scientific and epistemological basis for this radically dehistoricized conception of time had been laid as far back as Cartesian mathematics, Newtonian physics, and other systems that treated time as a universal independent variable, Fabian insists in particular on its formulation by Darwin, who noted unequivocally that his theory of evolution implied no inner temporal necessity. Evolution, he thought, was not compelled by chronology to produce gradual modifications or improvements, time somehow imparting to events an internal organizing telos. But Fabian does not cite Darwin to mark a definitive modern epistemic break with premodern sacrality. On the contrary, he aims to underscore how Darwin's epigones and vulgarizers so frequently continued to view evolution through the prism of sacred time, or at least its secularized equivalent. Social Darwinists, especially, but many others as well in the biological and fledgling social sciences clung to the notion that if organisms evolved, they must be evolving to some purposive end. When applied to man, such thinking spawned a now-infamous panoply of flawed chauvinistic frameworks. Not only might humankind be imagined to have passed through an ascending succession of biologically evolutionary stages, but assorted civilizations and cultures could also be assimilated to these various stages in profoundly hierarchizing ways, and all under the aegis of scientific authority.

The resulting "evolutionary time," as Fabian dubs this kind of pseudo-evolutionary outlook, clearly diverged from Darwin's vision of a properly neutral time. Fabian's understandable distaste for the epistemological and material violence wrought by evolutionary time (he singles out, in particular, its role in rationalizing the colonial enterprise) leads him essentially to identify in it a warmed-over sacred history with hypocritical pretensions to scientific objectivity. Still, in evolutionary time's replacement of "faith in salvation by faith in progress and industry"—to use Fabian's own description—I am more inclined to see a variety of secular time occupying a hybrid position somewhere along the conceptual continuum between sacred time and Darwin's truly naturalized time. If evolutionists were unwittingly repurposing an old Christian mentality, their universalizing designs, however misguided or specious, meant that they certainly considered thinkable a more empty, tabular time.

The possibility of so hybrid a temporal consciousness offers useful purchase, I think, on the radical conservative nationalism for which Barrès made Morès a posthumous model. Remember how Barrès describes tiny flashes of messianic temporality coextensive with the inner necessity impelling the nation's evolution, even while he sees in the process a gradual series contained and ordered by an outer, empty, homogeneous temporality. Put simply, Barrès conceives time as at once internal and external, catalytic and inert, determinant and detached. This is the synthesis attempted by evolutionary time. Barrès read Darwin and Darwin's best-known followers, Herbert Spencer and Ernst Haeckel—to whose collective work Barrès was exposed by his intellectual mentor Jules Soury, the high priest of French biological racism[62]—and he enthusiastically harnessed evolutionism to political and ideological ends. But what makes Barrès's evolutionist musings so important is not just the revision his temporal backbends suggest to Benjaminian accounts of nationalism insensitive to historical gradations between messianic and homogeneous temporalities. The terms and circumstances of Barrès's attempted synthesis also make it different, in its messianic approach to the nation, from anything envisioned by Fabian. This invites us, we will see, to rethink Fabian's account of how Europeans located in colonized peoples a window onto bygone, more primitive eras in human evolutionary time. I pause now, though, to consider briefly again why the "roman" of Morès's life, in its specifically literary quality, offered so tempting a vehicle for tackling the contradictions of Barrèsian nationalism.

FROM LITERARY HERO TO NATIONAL MESSIAH

Morès represents a key figure because he places into such sharp relief the hybrid temporality presumed by Barrès, as well as the tensions associated with it. Some of the tensions, I have noted, revolved around the status of the written word. Playing the role of chivalric hero in life and death, Morès proceeded under a resolutely textual sign. Honoré de Balzac famously vowed to finish with the pen what Napoleon had begun with the sword. Morès seemed bent on finishing with the sword what began with the pen, and not just because insults traded in the press so often finished, for Morès, on the dueling grounds. The Marquis's apparent acceptance of literature as his blueprint was taken by some to mark the distance separating the fanciful, headstrong Morès from the present and its practical realities. Whether he had in fact set out to make life imitate art, or was merely understood to have done so, the message remained the same: the world did not conform easily to the dictates of literary representation. Others, however, in interpreting the Marquis to offer unifying temporal possibilities, found themselves broaching—with complicated results—a more reciprocal relationship between literature and the real.

Such were the efforts of radical conservatives interested to code Morès's sheer literariness as a temporal example for the nation. Barrès had not yet hit, at the time of Morès's death, on the idea of "the Land and the Dead" ("la Terre et les Morts") that he would make famous in a lecture written three years later for anti-Dreyfusard colleagues at the Ligue de la Patrie Française. To render it in the terms I have been developing, Barrès's nationalist slogan superposed messianic and homogeneous modes. Rootedness in "the Land," that classic requirement for nationalist belonging, facilitated a messianic, instantaneous communion with and among the successive generations of "Dead" whose continuous occupation of that land over homogeneous time made rootedness possible to begin with.[63] The messianic and homogeneous, in other words, each furnished the other's condition of possibility, a point to which I will return. For now, let me only observe that Morès offered Barrès a similar device. When Barrès admired how "everywhere [Morès] took his romance [*roman*], he brought charm and chivalry," he was remarking more than just poetically or metaphorically on the Marquis's knightly graces.[64] He was also contemplating literature's potential, via a living text like Morès, to engender something unique. An avatar sprung from the pages of chivalric romances, Morès seemed to have brought those around him into immediate, tangible contiguity with a former time. Think of this as a kind of nineteenth-century, culturalist *Jurassic Park*: from a literary artifact surviving through the ages, fragments of viable cultural DNA still locked within it, a latter-day knight might spectacularly be reconstituted. And yet, for all the messianic potency of such a figure come flashing into the present from a distant past, no religious or magical explanation was necessary. One need only accept the existence of a literary inheritance passed from generation to generation, linking them together through chronological, homogeneous time, and capable of making fantastically palpable the linkage itself in any given, achronological, instantaneous moment.

To reason in this way, of course, was to make deterministic assumptions about literature's necessary fidelity to some sort of cultural essence. Let us not forget that the godfather of French biological determinism—Hippolyte Taine, whom Barrès long admired[65]—formulated his influential doctrine of *race* (heredity), *milieu* (environment), and *moment* (historical moment) in a work of literary history, *Histoire de la littérature anglaise* (1863), which stressed the primacy of literature for discerning the unique character of a people or nation. Within the "complete series of great expressive monuments" comprising, for Taine, a truly notable national literary output, each literary "monument" expresses a cultural unity operative at a synchronic point in time; the "series" constructed expresses, in turn, a national cultural unity operative along the diachronic axis of history.[66] Barrès does Taine one better, however, by proceeding as if literature might not simply reflect but in fact help produce cultural unity. Such a porosity between literature and the real facilitates Barrès's ultimate goal: a better translatability between synchronic and diachronic unities. On Taine's view, literature best revealed a deep, determinant set of "racial" qualities common to a people, qualities that guaranteed cultural coherence both at any given moment and over time. Barrès sought to make these two axes of coherence more directly interdependent. Rather than remain passively correlated together by a same underlying racial factor, they might act on one another causally and directly. Starting from the premise of a historical continuity expressed in a literary inheritance, Barrès posited that someone willing, like Morès, to be "the last reader of chivalric romances"[67]—to be more willing, in other words, than anyone else to *live* these texts—could actualize the cultural unity accumulated diachronically therein and use it to foster contemporary national cohesion. This is the familiar, hybrid collapse of homogeneous time into the messianic now, the sudden pivot of the horizontal into the vertical.

Evidently, though, Barrès was still grasping for the best way to conceptualize the combination. It certainly presented no a priori contradiction for Morès to have revived a knightly French sensibility while maintaining, as a "practical 'Americanist,'" the bona fides of a modern reconciled to the doxas of world capitalism and scientific positivism.[68] Indeed, what better place than the horse-dotted plains of the American West to imagine the Marquis updating Old World chivalry with a contemporary taste for novelty, expansion, and innovation? Morès's trademarked Stetson hat seemed to signal as much. The same man might channel an age-old *courtoisie* while remaining shaped by the forces of the era in which he lived. Taine had reasoned no differently when he theorized that the characteristics of a *race* underwent various inflections depending on the historical *moment*.[69] The problem lay in Morès's literary reconstitution of tradition. For Morès and his radical conservative admirers to conceive cultural continuity as at once encodable in and extractable from literature was to externalize that continuity, at least in some measure, from man himself. Literature perhaps offered a plausible mechanism for transmitting a heritage steadily through time. Morès hence need not seem excessively atavistic, since he was only expressing something that had lingered all along. Yet the mechanism offered no account, as it was being deployed here, for how chivalry might have evolved in the real world and in accordance with each era (though it certainly could reflect the changes incurred). Morès's hagiographers likened him indiscriminately to a seventeenth-century nobleman in the Fronde revolt against the king (Barrès) or to a member of the medieval Crusades (Drumont).[70] Chivalry thus construed simply became a static, transhistorical constant at odds with the kind of evolutionist paradigm Barrès otherwise attempted to cultivate.

Sensing this, Barrès wondered what contemporary factors besides literature had combined with Morès's noble blood to produce so blended a character. Implied was that chivalry must have survived among men and their affairs, and not just on the page:

> I would like to research how certain milieus, certain educations maintain in some contemporary men a feudal way of thinking, as exemplified in the increasingly rare notion—of which the *Discourse on Universal History* offers the most famous literary expression—according to which there is between the leader of men [*l'homme-chef*] and God the direct and continuous relationship of a loyal vassal to his lord.[71]

Note the reference to Bossuet's celebrated 1681 affirmation of monarchical divine right in his *Discours sur l'histoire universelle*, which Barrès takes, in thoroughgoing Tainian fashion, as a privileged literary expression of the "feudal" mentality in question. Note, too, Barrès's subtle recontextualization. Where Bossuet had defended the divine right of kings, Barrès substitutes the faith in Providence of *l'homme-chef*. This is the Carlylean hero, the man on horseback, the autocratic savior and populist leader anticipated by late-century radical conservatives prepared neither to reinstate the monarchy nor to embrace parliamentary democracy.[72] Barrès's sleight of hand situates Bossuet within a genealogy of chivalric man stretching from the vassal knights to the likes of General Boulanger, whose brief flirtation with a coup d'état in 1889 had set so many hearts aflutter among young political idealists and nationalists of Barrès's generation.[73] And it is with the adaptability common to this whole genealogy, he means, rather than some calcified feudal spirit, that "certains milieus, certains educations" have imbued men like Morès. In other words, it was not acceptable for a Morès simply to read and emulate the monarchist program prescribed by Bossuet, lest his politics turn out anachronistic. Some environment must have helped Morès adapt the underlying principle to the sensibilities of the era. That environment, moreover, must itself have evolved and adapted throughout the centuries and with it an evolving conception of chivalry. After all, had such an environment or formation emerged spontaneously, in a sort of instantaneous messianic linkage with Bossuet's epoch—and had it not, therefore, traversed the intervening period of profound historical change—how would it "know" to adjust the message for a post-monarchic age?

Once more, change poses a metaphysical challenge to the messianic. Barrès's solution, as in his version of evolutionary time, is to embed the messianic in the steadying, incremental context of the homogeneous. While for Barrès it remains key that Morès has brought flashing into the present a knightly fervor worthy of Bossuet and the Sun King he served, it remains equally important that this sudden messianic contiguity occur against the tempering backdrop of a logical progression. Previously I have discussed how literature offered such a graduated backdrop, insofar as it provided a smooth mechanism, enduring through homogeneous time, for plausibly making accessible to one another eras separated by vast temporal expanses. Obvious already is a sense in which Barrès deems homogeneous and messianic modes more compatible than conflictual. That time unfolds in orderly, homogeneous fashion furnishes the condition of possibility for it to fold messianically back onto itself; conversely, the commensurability between discontinuous eras become contiguous reinforces the unified progression in which they remain inscribed.

But though for Barrès literature facilitates such temporal complementarity, it does so asymmetrically, in a way that subordinates the homogeneous to the messianic. Literature becomes a potent method for producing something approximating a messianic instantaneity (even if this version of the messianic remains, to invert Benjamin's familiar phraseology, shot through with homogeneous time). For one, it makes it possible to bring the distant past into messianic contiguity with the present. It also messianically condenses and translates an accumulated diachronic tradition into a blueprint for synchronic social unity. Literature does not, however, similarly produce the nation's unified diachronic progression, as much as it indexes and expresses it. And so, because the nature of this progression remains refractory to literary explanations—recall Barrès's uncertainty over how, exactly, the spirit of chivalry had adapted and evolved—Morès's messianic evocation of the Fronde or the Crusades leaves huge gaps unaccounted for in the evolutionary record. A tension persists, in short, between a messianic time content to jump among centuries and a homogeneous time concerned with the countless events intercalated throughout.

One way Barrès proposes to relieve the tension is by narrativizing it. We have seen already how Barrès's evolutionary time merges temporalities by relocating messianic instantaneity from its usual millennial scale to the level of successive events. Steps in the nation's evolution proceed both as increments added in homogeneous time and as tiny messianic flashes in which each event prefigures the next to produce an instantaneous now where past, present, and future coincide. This is but the limit case, I would add, of a more general principle: the shorter the temporal gap between messianic moments of prefiguration and fulfillment, the less those moments appear to short-circuit the steady march of homogeneous time. The gap need not shrink to the distance between successive events. What matters, really, is that a sufficient number of messianic moments add up to provide a narratable sequence tracing a change—or more precisely, that they tell a story. "It will be up to a few good writers," insists Barrès, "to show all of French chivalric history reflected in Morès' willingly spilled blood."[74] Barrès's martyrological exhortation performs the familiar messianic gesture of collapsing diachrony into synchrony, summoning up an entire chivalric tradition from a single Christlike act of self-sacrifice. But he is calling as well for a more densely emplotted diachronic narrative, one affixing Morès iteratively to an ordered sequence of messianic men who tell the gradual story—stretching homogeneously across the national saga—of a chivalric spirit both surviving into and evolving with each subsequent age.

Such a narrative would mediate temporalities, rendering Morès's messianic discontinuity in the mode of homogeneous continuity. Literature, for Barrès, had done something similar by facilitating messianic linkages (between eras, between diachrony and synchrony) within the parameters of the secular. Yet if literature in this way marked a temporal convergence, it did so largely as a channel or vehicle translating among more putatively concrete social phenomena. Here Barrès hints instead at a temporal hybridity achievable rather more hermetically inside the confines of narrative itself. To erect a historical series of messianic men was to assume their interrelation within messianic time, each figure conceptually superimposed on his successor and predecessor by a general rhythm of prefiguration and fulfillment. But alone, this temporal logic assumed too narrow a subjectivity. For all their importance to France, chivalric men by definition embodied an aristocratic nobility to which, from Barrès's fundamentally republican perspective, the nation was irreducible. The subjective, messianic, specific time they inhabited therefore needed splicing to the comparatively objective, homogeneous, general time of the national collectivity.

Barrès submitted the potential of narrative to satisfy such requirements. Grouped together as elements in a series, messianic men would emerge reinforced in their shared constancy, cementing a simultaneity-along-time claimable as part of the nation's determinate trajectory. To do so, however, they must exist more than in and for themselves; they must also be placed into sequence against the larger, shifting national context to which each hero had adapted his iteration of the chivalric spirit. That is to say, an essentially achronological constellation of messianic events required chronologization as episodes in an evolving national story. Hence might Morès's "willingly spilled blood" extend Christlike redemption to an entire national community rather than simply reflect the accumulated sacrifices of his forebears.

Barrès's imagined result calls to mind Paul Ricoeur's account in *Time and Narrative* of narrative's unique capacity for reconciling two age-old ways of thinking about time. The Aristotelian way, relates Ricoeur, was to conceive time as a cosmic, chronological succession of instants relative to which human life threatened to seem fleeting and meaningless. Augustine, in contrast, reflected on time from the more psychological perspective of the individual for whom it is possible to think of the past, present, and future all at once. Ricoeur argues for the privileged importance of narrative, especially history and fiction, in offering a poetic resolution to what otherwise represents the speculative aporia between cosmic and psychological temporalities. By setting individual, subjectively experienced episodes into an impartial chronological sequence governed by the ordering principle of plot, storytelling creates a median category of "narrative" or "human" time where psychological and cosmic time combine to redeem human existence and give it meaning.[75] A parallel can be drawn to Barrès's attempts at reconciling the messianic and homogeneous into a hybrid national time, insofar as the two poles of this dialectic correspond roughly to a subjective Augustinian mode in which past, present, and future are experienced together at the level of events themselves, and an objective Aristotelian mode in which all events are contained by chronological, impersonal time. Significant differences obviously remain, not least among them that the meaning achieved for Barrès rests on the exclusion from the national project of all but the select individuals comprising a transhistorical, Tainian *race*. We have seen, too, how Barrès misreads Darwin, thereby mistakenly claiming the power of science and reason to effect a temporal reconciliation only really approachable—at least according to Ricoeur—by poetic means.

Still, Ricoeur offers a useful reminder of the obstacles facing Barrès, as well as the temptation to resolve them in narrative. Ricoeur's framework also better approximates Barrès's vision of a nation-reinforcing, hybrid narrative time than does Anderson's description of the modern novel's contribution to national self-fashioning. In Anderson's telling, the modern novelistic "meanwhile" helped integrate individual subjectivities into an impersonal, synchronic national collective perceived to be moving as one through homogeneous time.[76] This model does not consider whether characters might from their subjective perspective experience time rather differently, contemplating past, present, and future together in the mode of Augustinian or messianic instantaneity. Neither does Anderson's model exactly preclude the possibility, since on some level, it would be consistent with what he deems the novel's contribution to a shift in temporal consciousness for the novel to have performed such a shift itself. Depicting many characters engaged at the same moment in different activities and different places—as only a novel could—a Balzac or a Henry Fielding wove multiple subjectivities into a new, objective whole. But Anderson proceeds as if any lingering subjective experience of time ceased thereafter to obtain, at least from the standpoint of the resulting imagined community.[77] Barrès, in contrast, postulates a nation dependent not only on the abiding coexistence of messianic and homogeneous temporalities but also on their permanent entanglement. I would add that Barrèsian nationalism, however idiosyncratic, hardly represents a trivial iteration of the nationalistic idea. Quite to the contrary, Barrès's influence reverberated deep into the twentieth century, his name venerated by proto-fascistic and fascistic revolutionaries whose efforts would be rewarded in Vichy France's 1940 suspension of the Republic.[78] We are therefore wise to explore the strategies with which Barrès and other radical conservatives tackled the difficulties facing the temporal alchemy they undertook.

RETHINKING IMPERIAL SPACE-TIME

It is a measure of the aforementioned difficulties that Barrès's effort to understand the nation's evolution in more than just its literary expressions ends up circling back, ironically enough, toward storytelling. The Marquis's eminently retellable adventures certainly invited such treatment. The extravagance of his ambitions aside, though, their specifically imperial nature highlights another key outcome of the paradoxical relation between stasis and change produced when radical conservatives so resolutely juxtaposed messianic and homogeneous temporalities. For if the kind of temporal duality instantiated by Morès demanded to be narrativized, it also demanded to be spatialized. What this reveals, further, is that conventional approaches to the space-time of empire make assumptions more suited to explaining the imperial outlooks shaped by bourgeois liberalism, capitalism, and even Marxism than those associated with the complicated brand of reaction I have been examining here.

Critics almost always consider imperial thought, especially of the nineteenth-century variety associated with the second great wave of European colonial conquest, only ever to have woven together space and time in service to a confident claim of European civilizational superiority over non-Europeans. What results is a simplified account of Europeans' own temporal self-fashioning. Europeans certainly designated Europe as the privileged space of modernity, traveling away from which seemed equivalent to traveling back in time. Hegel codified the point in his *Lectures on the Philosophy of History* (1837), and the only big disagreement regarding the matter over subsequent decades concerned how to act on it. Might slumbering colonized peoples be nudged back into the flow of history by their white tutors, as affirmed by the liberal center and republican left in ways that yielded the civilizing mission variously articulated by French, British, and other European colonial powers? Or was such intervention even possible, let alone worthwhile, as argued by those on the right more interested in continental affairs and skeptical about universalizing claims of human perfectibility?[79] The trouble with this basic historical picture, however, is not that it presumes a former European unanimity about modernity's distinctly European nature. Indeed, one would be hard-pressed to find noteworthy exceptions to so hegemonic a belief in nineteenth-century Europe; even those seeking to flee modernity did so abroad, according to the tenets of the same spatiotemporal schema. The problem, rather, is that this account filters events through a single temporal lens. Because we are still inclined to imagine ourselves moving gradually through linear, homogeneous time, we see in the European imperial imaginary a simple extension or expression of a homogeneous temporality possessed of spatializing tendencies from the outset. By definition, after all, homogeneous time's linearity mapped time onto an abstract spatial dimension, opening the way to mapping time onto the more concrete surface of the globe. And while we may now find this imperial space-time deeply objectionable, we remain prepared to accept that it made historical and conceptual sense, since the underlying spatiotemporal architecture proves so legible to our contemporary consciousness.

What if, though, as I have been endeavoring to demonstrate, temporality constituted for some Europeans a more vexed question than is customary to assume? Considered from this standpoint, empire's fusion of space and time does not just represent the logical ideological counterpart to homogeneous time's European rise. It also bespeaks a comparatively anxious strategy for negotiating that rise itself, particularly in relation to an older but abiding messianic paradigm. In a moment I will reflect on how a certain fin-de-siècle variety of French imperial enthusiasm can be productively understood in terms of this spatializing response to temporal uncertainty. For now, let me begin with a few more observations about why such uncertainty and its consequences have escaped critical notice and about some basic frameworks useful for rethinking imperial space-time.

First, a word of clarification. I do not mean to suggest that the spatializing anxiety in question functioned in lieu of or apart from the more straightforward relegation by Europeans of distant peoples to a distant past. As will become clear, radical conservatives incorporated this topographic chauvinism into their elaboration abroad of a temporal amalgam difficult to accomplish at home. But I want nonetheless to distinguish between imperial space-time, at least in its conventional definition, and the very different spatiotemporal imaginary—let me call this hybrid space-time—of those Europeans navigating the hybrid temporality described so far. Typically speaking, imperial space-time posited a temporal distance between peoples at the rough level of nation and ethnicity. So, for instance, were Englishmen or Frenchmen reflexively understood to have progressed further along the arrow of history than their Indian or Algerian subjects. It was of course possible to impose temporal taxonomies at more local, finely segmented levels, as when the French deemed Algerian Kabyles less removed from European civilization than the Arabs populating the same colony.[80] And Europeans could receive the same treatment: consider, for example, Anne McClintock's demonstration of how Victorian capital constructed its British others (women, the working class) into atavistic remainders using the same evolutionist schema deployed to justify economic exploitation overseas.[81]

Yet to focus exclusively on such taxonomies, prevalent though they were, foreshortens our historical perspective. Imperial space-time manifestly served an imperial capital concerned to transform various subalterns into the superseded relics necessary for corroborating white European man's place in the historical vanguard. Surveying the globe, Europeans might assess humanity's diachronic history at a single glance and so explain contemporary imperial conquest in terms of the victims' putative historical obsolescence. Thus, too, were domestic others deemed fit for proletarianization or exclusion. By contrast, hybrid space-time revisited the past in ways more recuperative than hierarchizing, something on display when French radical conservatives prescribed a nationalist solidarity coalescing in the present moment various nationalist energies hitherto dispersed in time. The difference was that, so conceived, the nation depended as much on the past as empire required superseding it. But we can see now another significant difference at work. If imperial space-time opened a supposed temporal gap between peoples operative only along the linear, homogeneous arrow of history, the hybrid space-time of the Barrèsian nation spanned the gap between temporalities themselves. Such is, indeed, what made the project hybrid, given its idea of the nation as a space where instantaneous messianic linkages across history might somehow coincide with the incremental advance of homogeneous time.

What made this project doubly hybrid is how difficult, ultimately, it was for the same national space to accommodate both temporalities, producing a result as poised between national and imperial spaces as between varieties of time. However much Barrès or Drumont protested that Morès's timeless chivalric sensibilities had fueled distinctly modern exploits, the construction of Morès into a new Roland implied precisely the kind of messianic jump across centuries that so contravened the principle—change over homogeneous time—on which depended the very idea of modernity. One solution, we have seen, was to shrink these messianic jumps to a size embeddable in the homogeneous temporal fabric. But tracing France's connection to past glories back through a long chain of tiny messianic flashes dulled the rhetorical éclat of the

Roland metaphor. How could such an attenuated display compete with the real pyrotechnics of a second coming? How, in other words, to blend temporalities in a way that still felt inspiringly messianic but sustained the radical conservatives' professed commitment to modernity?

Morès's imperial trajectory suggested an answer. Beyond the continental nation, in the space of empire, Morès could more easily be imagined to have flamboyantly revived the past without breaching the confines of the present. There he and other neo-paladins might pursue an unchecked idealism impossible in the modern, rational metropole. Barrès thought this just as well, remarking diplomatically that "Morès, so accentuated in his type, was not easily usable in normal surroundings."[82] Yet if extraordinary imperial "surroundings" freed men of action from metropolitan strictures (and, hinted Barrès, metropolitans from tempestuous characters in their midst!), the point was not simply to remove their atavistic behaviors to locales correspondingly arrested in time. Empire also made it easier to inscribe those behaviors within the framework of a modern European endeavor. At home in France, the hybrid space-time of organicist nationalism struggled to reconcile chivalry's century-hopping ways with the quotidian, step-by-step progress through homogeneous time of the contemporary national collective. Abroad, though, the contradiction receded against the backdrop of an imperial space-time more sweeping in its approach to homogeneous temporality. However distant the French past Morès evoked, he remained modern relative to peoples understood never to have emerged from the past at all. As a matter of proportion, too, Morès's knightly persona scanned more easily in Africa, where imperial space-time already measured the temporal distance between peoples in millennial terms. Messianic jumps required no shrinking overseas.

In fact, imperial space-time suggested that the messianic need not entail jumps to begin with. Much as, for Barrès, literature could link distant eras from within the boundaries of homogeneous time, imperial space-time invented a way for past and present plausibly to coincide without overtly invoking a temporality other than the homogeneous. One must only accept that contemporaneous cultures had made it different distances along the same universal arrow of homogeneous, linear history for travel in space to become travel in time. Note, however, the distinctly messianic cast this thinking retained. After all, was not the basic premise—that cultures representing different stages in diachronic time simultaneously inhabited the planet—conceptually akin to a sacred temporality grouping successive events into the instantaneous now of a simultaneity-along-time? Following Fabian's argument about evolutionary time, which he considers to have secularized the messianic into the telos of progress, we might therefore consider imperial space-time to have secularized the messianic into the space of empire.

Insofar as the conquest of that space was justified on evolutionist grounds, the peoples encountered were consigned by Europeans to an outmoded human past. Yet the same circumstances also enticed those who hoped to revivify a specifically French past while maintaining from it the decorous distance necessary to their claim of modernity. Hence was Morès so willing, as Drault noted in *La Libre parole*, to recognize in the Tuareg mores reminiscent of the European feudal aristocracy.[83] French discourse largely owed the parallel to explorer Henri Duveyrier, whose famed 1864 volume about his Saharan travels, *L'Exploration du Sahara: Les Touâreg du Nord*, profoundly influenced a generation of adventurers, imperialists, and policymakers.[84] Duveyrier's admiringly fanciful account of Tuareg knights-errant roaming the desert south of Algeria and Tripoli has been read as a rejection of metropolitan bourgeois modernity, and Drault likewise took the Marquis's belief in Tuareg chivalry as evidence of an unfortunate archaism.[85] The real picture, I think, was more complex. If in the Sahara chivalry appeared quite literally not to be dead, the interest of this to a Morès or a Barrès proved twofold. Like his mentor the Prince de Polignac, who as a young French officer had in 1862 signed the commercial Treaty of Ghadamès with the Tuareg in Libya, Morès believed friendship with the Tuareg key to securing for France the Saharan trade routes they patrolled.[86] To that end—especially for those more aristocratically inclined—a natural kinship could be adduced between the French and what, in the words of historian Benjamin Brower, seemed a nomadic "ancien régime that had survived deep in the desert."[87] Jules Delahaye, a journalist and former deputy hired by the Marquis's widow to investigate the murder, reported later in his book on Morès that Polignac dreamed of "Tuareg chivalry defended, popularized, by a knight like Morès."[88] But to project such nobility onto the Tuareg, or for that matter onto the topos of the more generically Muslim "desert knight" about whom Barrès and other radical conservatives waxed so romantic, was also not to prescribe for France a return to feudal ways.[89] Rather, a grand Franco-Islamic alliance promised to rekindle France's own chivalric fires without requiring any attendant turn from modernity.[90]

Drumont implied this much when he posthumously applauded Morès for having announced that "the Islam that we were told was exhausted and worn would make a sensational return."[91] As I examined in Chapter 2, Drumont had long taken North African Muslims as surrogates for an old France supposedly beleaguered by the same "Jewish" Republic. Substitution that it was, the surrogacy functioned like a metaphor: the regeneration of an "exhausted" Islam meant, really, the regeneration of an exhausted France. And yet, practically speaking, a chivalric partnership with Islam in Africa against "England's appalling encroachments" afforded protection against too brutal a recrudescence of feudal vigor at home.[92] No more than Barrès did Drumont think it easy for chivalry to come messianically surging back into a modern national body having moved, in homogeneous time, long and irrevocably beyond the feudal order. At the scale of empire, however, the balancing act became less precarious. Not only did imperial space-time make it possible to visualize concretely how metropolitan France might overlap in time with some African version of its own chivalric past, it also ensured that the two would remain conveniently separated in space.

As radical nationalists looked to empire for solutions to their temporal quandary, what was their relation to a colonialist republican nationalism more exclusively committed to the single temporality of linear progress? The prevailing historiographic narrative recounts that the French right, having resisted colonial expansion by Opportunist republican governments brought to power by the 1870 Franco-Prussian War, embraced the project of empire on nationalist principle in the tumultuous decade and a half before World War I. As noted previously, Berenson locates the pivotal moment in France's 1898 showdown with British imperial forces at Fashoda.[93] Raoul Girardet situates the definitive turning a point a bit later, when the First Moroccan Crisis nearly caused a war between France and Germany over imperial predominance in Morocco. *Revanchiste* nationalists had previously objected to an overseas expansion they felt distracted from France's continental duty to reclaim from Germany the Alsace and Lorraine territories lost in 1870. By 1905, however, the Germans threatened as much from the other side of the Mediterranean as they did from the Rhine. The result, argues Girardet, was a convergence between what he identifies as two nationalisms: a traditionalist one preoccupied with continental security and an expansionist one bent on colonial conquest.[94] Girardet mentions Barrès among the *revanchiste* converts to the imperial cause. If in 1911 Barrès could still gripe that Opportunist colonialism had in the 1880s diverted "the elite from our Rhine army," and that previous imperial motivations had been too Anglophobic and insufficiently Germanophobic, he was now prepared to see in Morocco "France's destiny."[95]

Yet Girardet's two nationalisms had perhaps been converging for some time. Berenson's account, for one, suggests that Fashoda-driven Anglophobia swayed *revanchiste* sentiment in favor of empire a few years before Germany began its Moroccan saber-rattling. And already in 1896, Barrès himself seemed torn between nationalist imperatives. Speaking at Morès's funeral, Barrès cited French depopulation as an argument against territorial expansion: "Our nation, with its declining birth rate, needs no additional territories."[96] This was consonant with *revanchiste* natalism and the belief that if France had declined relative to Germany because of demographic weakness, it could ill afford further population loss overseas. But French national interests, he added, were still very much at stake in the Scramble for Africa. The trick was to lay economic and strategic claim to the continent in a way different from the British and French republican models of military conquest:

> So it was not wars of conquest and extermination that Morès envisaged. His project was the weakening of English influence through an alliance between Islam and France. He pursued, in Africa, his constant concern for preserving, growing, and affirming the nation in the face of other nations.[97]

Barrès's vision of an imperialism without colonialism borrows from both nationalisms. Accepting the global scope of competition between European nations, he calls to mind no less a bête noire to the radical nationalists than Jules Ferry, the former Opportunist prime minister who in an 1885 speech to the Chamber of Deputies had famously labeled overseas imperial expansion necessary for France not to "descend from the first rank to the third or fourth."[98] Hoping, however, to replace conquest with a proxy war in which Muslims would do the fighting, Barrès remains within the bounds of a nationalism concerned to husband France's military resources for the replay of 1870 to come. His triangulation between different nationalist attitudes toward empire nuances Girardet's bipartite schema. But I am more interested in this triangulation for the further illustration it provides that, in the hands of radical conservatives, empire mediated temporalities. As dismissive as Barrès, Morès, Drumont, and others were of the Third Republic's innumerable colonial wars against indigenous peoples, the imperial space-time both presumed and reinforced by these conflicts furnished a means for messianic and homogeneous time to coexist. It certainly might be that the republican rationale for empire eventually lent itself to appropriation by radical conservatives similarly preoccupied with French prestige. Yet it was also the case, I am arguing, that empire beckoned simultaneously as a device for managing the temporal quandary immanent to their particular style of nationalism.

The usual mode of conceiving imperial space-time overlooks this important last phenomenon by only ever assuming that Europeans saw in imperial subalterns some degree of primitivism beyond which the colonizing powers had advanced. The misprision owes much, I have suggested, to our own bias in favor of homogeneous time. It also owes something to Fabian, from whom I am otherwise borrowing here. Thinking, with Fabian, of evolutionary time as a secularized messianism, one better appreciates how radical conservatives might have instinctively seen in evolutionism a way to combine the messianic and the modern. Fabian's widely cited reflections on the hierarchizing tendencies of evolutionary time have, however, obscured the mechanism by which the resulting combination occurred. This is because his narrative of temporal secularization privileges the prophetic, forward-looking dimension of the messianic over its other key quality—simultaneity-along-time—to which I have been arguing radical conservatives remained attached. Secularized, in the manner Fabian describes, into the evolutionist telos of progress, what most obviously remained of the messianic was its directionality: that is, the sense that everything was still moving toward a single, future goal. The awaited messianic event was spatialized as the endpoint of a civilizational race, a transformation further spatializing because time furnished the seemingly empty container for the race itself. In its contradictory nature, then, as something teleologically determined, and yet ostensibly neutral enough to encompass all humankind, evolutionary time fostered a regnant mentality according to which "not only past cultures, but all living societies were irrevocably placed on a temporal slope, a stream of Time—some upstream, others downstream."[99] Distances in space became convertible into differences in time, the telos of progress making it possible to perceive a Europe leading the evolutionary or civilizational advance while cultures elsewhere distributed across the globe lagged behind.

Fabian calls this the "denial of coevalness," an influential coinage that has since entered the conceptual lexicon of postcolonial and globalization studies. From McClintock's Fabian-inspired reflections on the "anachronistic space" imagined by the Victorians to house colonial and other subalterns, to Walter Mignolo's observation that contemporary U.S. imperialism still denies the coevalness of "underdeveloped" peoples, critics have seized on the complicity of evolutionary time and its afterlives in various incarnations of empire.[100] But what about those imperialists who, in the anachronistic spaces of empire, saw an opportunity for the nation to come safely into messianic contiguity with its own hallowed past? As important to them as the occasion for cultural chauvinism—itself important, again, for safeguarding their modernity—was the occasion for reimagining simultaneity-along-time. Secularizing the messianic spatialized its future-orientedness into a goal from which some cultures were deemed further than others. The same process, though, no less thoroughly spatialized messianic simultaneity-along-time in the way I have already proposed: namely, by positing that multiple societies representing various stages of human development occupied the planet at the same time. And this denial of coevalness in turn provided the condition of possibility for affirming simultaneity-along-time within the nation itself. Not only could Europeans enter, by traveling in space, into contemptuous relation with supposedly anachronistic others, but a similar logic also helped stage a comparatively recuperative encounter with their own previous European natures (or some constructed version thereof). It is in the coincidence of these two different but mutually reinforcing simultaneities—one juxtaposing the contemporary nation with significantly "earlier" stages of human development, and one more narrowly juxtaposing the nation with its former selves—that radical conservatives endeavored to look toward the past without seeming to lose sight of the present.

FINAL CAUSES

Thinking with and against Fabian brings into focus a hybrid national time that might otherwise escape notice, and this requires recognizing how messianic simultaneity-along-time seemed to preserve access to the past even after it had been secularized into the forward-looking doctrine of progress. Messianic time has, in other words, left divergent modern legacies. I want to finish now by better accounting for these, as a way both of more carefully calibrating the conversation about time itself and of introducing another, related temporal tension whose importance to radical conservatives I will be taking up in the following chapter. First, the recalibration. Fabian's oversight is to treat messianism mostly as if only its goal-oriented dimension had been secularized and to forgo any attendant explanation of what happened to messianic simultaneity-along-time. Better than Anderson, Fabian understands what Benjamin calls homogeneous time to have reconfigured the messianic rather than simply displaced it. Fabian's story remains partial nonetheless. I have tried to demonstrate that if evolutionary time secularized a messianic telos, the accompanying elaboration of imperial space-time assumed a simultaneity likewise adapted from the messianic. Radical conservatives seized on this simultaneity to fashion a hybrid space-time for the nation. Considered thusly, simultaneity-along-time did not so much disappear as reemerge under its own secular guises.

Crucially, those guises were multiple, and understanding this makes it easier to combine insights inherited from Benjamin, Fabian, and others whose differing assumptions and temporal vocabularies can bog down attempts at placing them into conversation. Benjamin, like Fabian, uncouples the messianic telos from messianic simultaneity-along-time. Unlike Fabian, though, he opposes the teleological and messianic altogether, going so far as to deny that messianic time was ever teleological to begin with. Absent any messianic prehistory, the telos becomes, for Benjamin, the exclusive domain of homogeneous time and the associated ideology of progress, while the messianic retains only its capacity to effect simultaneity-along-time. I will return momentarily to this cleavage from the messianic of the teleological, which in its own way poses no less significant a set of problems than Fabian's relative silence on what happened to messianic simultaneity when the time of salvation was secularized into the time of progress. Let me only note now that even stripped of any messianic precursor, Benjamin's homogeneous time provides a framework comparable to Fabian's for explaining the dispossessions inflicted by teleological thinking. Dipesh Chakrabarty, for instance, identifies in a Benjaminian "secular, empty, and homogeneous time" the constitutive means by which various historicisms—that of classical bourgeois liberalism, but that of classical Western Marxism too—automatically conflate history with progress and write out of history those who supposedly fail to keep up.[101] Historicisms deny the coevalness of victors and the vanquished, and they do so according to the tenets of homogeneous time.

Benjamin's homogeneous time can be mobilized in this way because it in fact never exhibits the real emptiness of what Fabian calls the more strictly neutral, naturalized time divorced entirely from human affairs.

Like evolutionary time, homogeneous time, at least in Benjamin's definition of it, performs a teleological violence. Fabian denounces evolutionary time for presuming that the simple passing of history imparts to events an inner necessity, progress, in whose name even the worst European colonial excesses might always be rationalized. Benjamin, taking a different tack, warns that what looks like progress always conceals the "barbarism" at which cost "civilization" has been achieved.[102] Yet the basic argument remains the same, since for both critics progress proves no more inevitable a historical outcome than the disasters required by it.

Benjamin departs from Fabian, however, in drawing a distinction between the inner necessity held to drive progress in teleological, homogeneous time, and messianic time's own inhabitation of events. Viewed from Fabian's perspective, any messianic thinking—whether in the classic mode of sacred time or in the updated mode propounded by Benjamin—shares with homogeneous time the fundamental assumption that time acts on and through events, rather than simply furnishing a neutral, empty container in which they occur. It is in this sense that Benjamin's description of homogeneous time as "empty" constitutes a misnomer and that Fabian dismisses pseudo-Darwinian temporality as warmed-over sacred time. But where Fabian would discern an epistemic continuity between messianic and homogeneous temporalities, Benjamin locates a contrast. Benjamin's historicist looks backward simply to confirm that homogeneous time only moves forward in the direction of progress. Benjamin's unforgettable angel of history, on the other hand, looks backward and sees something quite different: the "wreckage upon wreckage" left by the storm of progress. Were the angel's wings not so violently pinned open by the storm carrying him forth, he might "stay, awaken the dead, and make whole what has been smashed."[103] Such is the messianic task assigned to the historical materialist, charged by Benjamin with redeeming the sacrifices of history's proletarian victims. These sacrifices only achieve their meaning after the fact, according to a process that it has become de rigueur to compare with the Freudian mechanism of deferred action, or *Nachträglichkeit*, whereby a second event invests a first one with a significance not initially present. The retroactivity produced reverses cause and effect: what appears from a diachronic perspective to come "after" now comes "before," engendering a simultaneity or instantaneous discordant with the linear causality of homogeneous time. On this reading, Benjamin combats the blind tyranny of progress by short-circuiting its temporal logic.

Bhabha, in a comparable vein, considers the psychoanalytic phenomenon of retroactivity to challenge the violence of foundationalism, opening the future to a play of possibilities freed from determination by an originary past.[104] Taking his cue from Benjamin, Bhabha posits a disjointed temporality both antipodal and antidotal to a homogeneous time assumed to convey peoples along a linear historical trajectory where origins determine outcomes. Yet alongside Bhabha's deconstructive preoccupation with the linguistic sign, such a psychoanalytic bent diverts attention from the possibility that, following Fabian, one might identify in Benjamin's homogeneous time a secularization of the old sacred time whose orientation toward salvation morphed into the *philosophes*' worldly faith in progress. That is to say, Benjamin arguably sets homogeneous time against a messianic time historically and metaphysically entwined, via a shared origin in sacred time, with the very temporality he understands his messianism to undercut.[105]

Benjamin himself, of course, takes special care to contest this. The Jewish anticipation of the Messiah, he writes in the crucial last sentences of the "Theses," does not mean that "for the Jews the future turned into homogeneous, empty time," since "every second of time was the strait gate through which the Messiah might enter."[106] So uncertain an eschatology—echoing, as Fredric Jameson notes, the disillusioned Jewish messianism chronicled by Benjamin's friend Gershom Sholem[107]—stirs Jacques Derrida to draw a cautious parallel with his own location of justice in the "unpredictable future-to-come."[108] Derrida ultimately remains wary that Benjamin's messianism perhaps still too much resembles, if only as a "simulacrum," those various eschatologies and teleologies (Jewish or Christian, Marxist or neoliberal) blinded by their anticipatory "calculation of a program" to the real justice enacted in the singular, unforeseen event.[109] These are the precursors and manifestations of homogeneous time, a time from which Benjamin's messianic time would therefore not be completely detached.

But let us for the moment accept Benjamin's firm distinction between messianic and homogeneous temporalities, while likewise accepting Fabian's identification of a continuity linking sacred (messianic) and evolutionary (homogeneous) time. The two schemas are only reconcilable if what lends itself in the messianic to secularization as homogeneous time proves different from what, for Benjamin, lends itself in the messianic to precisely the opposite, radically heterogeneous or disjunctive temporal effect. And indeed, Benjamin and Fabian together offer a basis on which to trace the required divergence. That basis is both theological and metaphysical, I would offer, and understanding it begins with understanding what is putatively Jewish about Benjamin's messianic time. Benjamin famously describes his idiosyncratic, Jewish-inspired messianism in terms of a "*weak* Messianic power" premised on "a secret agreement between past generations and the present one."[110] The agreement's secretive quality twice subtracts the underlying structure of prophecy and fulfillment from the teleological temporality of progress. Just as, in Benjamin's understanding, an old Jewish uncertainty over the Messiah's arrival differed from the certainty associated with predictions made in homogeneous time, so could past generations not know which future generation(s) would work to redeem an earlier class suffering. What is more, the sufferers' possible failure altogether to anticipate their pain's future redemption—a redemption thus "secret" because it is never articulated as a prophecy in the first place—means that, according to the aforementioned logic of retroactivity, the suffering only ever achieves meaning after the fact. Neither event, then, actually occurs in a way quite congruent with linear, homogeneous time. Unanticipated or imprecisely anticipated, the redemption proves refractory to insertion before the fact into a homogeneous temporal continuum. Meanwhile, the suffering's retroactive significance causes it to "happen," in a strange but very real sense, after the redemption it otherwise appears to precede. Hence are the two events linked together by an instantaneous, bidirectional simultaneity-along-time alien to homogeneous time's linear unidirectionality.

Whether or not Benjamin's messianic time truly achieves such temporal subversion is the subject of a long and familiar critical debate. For my purposes here, I prefer to consider a different if connected question: that of the relationship between the non-homogeneous, Benjaminian simultaneity-along-time just described and what, following Fabian, is the simultaneity-along-time inherited by homogeneous temporality from sacred temporality and metamorphosed into the telos of progress. From Benjamin's standpoint, the two simultaneities—one enacted by the weak messianic power, the other presumed by what we might call this power's "strong" teleological counterpart—could not be more opposed. Yet one can also be forgiven for thinking, like Anderson, that the old, sacred time of divine providence or final cause represents "something close to what Benjamin calls Messianic time, a simultaneity of past and future in an instantaneous present."[111] Divine final cause means that two events occurring at different times on earth essentially happen at once in the mind of God, where they coincide as part of an eternal, preordained script indifferent to the more or less illusory passage of mortal time. This kind of simultaneity-along-time finds an echo in Benjamin's messianism, which likewise brings into contiguity events or generations forced apart by a homogeneous time of progress illusorily marking an insuperable distance between the present and a past deemed obsolete. One difference, obviously, is that Benjamin's weak messianic power invokes no extrinsic, divine final cause. But neither does homogeneous time, secularizing as it does the extrinsic final cause of divine providence into an intrinsic final cause impelling events from within, as part of their very nature, toward progress.

What, then, separates Benjamin's messianic time from the homogeneous time with which he so passionately contrasts it? The answer lies in their relative recourse to an intrinsic final cause. Homogeneous time calls that intrinsic force progress. Benjamin understands messianic time, on the other hand, to exhibit no such inner necessity. Whether Benjamin's messianism definitively dispenses with an intrinsic final cause is, of course, open to discussion. One could argue that he simply relocates the facilitation of simultaneity-along-time from an extrinsic, organizing divine logos to a more earthbound site: the memory or consciousness of the historical materialist. But let us again read Benjamin for what seems to be his intended meaning and accept the possibility of a simultaneity-along-time not facilitated by any final, organizing cause or telos. We might then identify two different kinds of simultaneity-along-time branching in separate directions from a same initial monotheistic root. Benjamin's appeal to an uncertain Jewish eschatology would describe the path of a disjunctive simultaneity-along-time ungoverned by, and promising liberation from, any determinant telos and the violence it imposes. Diverging from this emancipatory temporality would be the path taken by a comparatively confident Christian eschatology more certain about a Messiah already come once down to earth. Indeed, it is precisely in the Christian confidence in salvation that Fabian locates the precursor of evolutionary or homogeneous time's similar confidence in the foregone conclusion of progress. And with this secularized confidence comes the attendant variety of simultaneity-along-time implied by any such genealogically Christian, self-assured teleology. Divine or secular, extrinsic or intrinsic, final causes superimpose what will be on what is and has been.

For teleology and simultaneity-along-time to prove so conceptually interrelated explains why one cannot help but look for the absent logos grounding Benjamin's messianic instantaneity. Even Derrida, whose overtly post-Benjaminian notion of "messianicity" more rigorously eschews any logos than does Benjamin's messianism, acknowledges the "irreducible ambiguity" surrounding the question of whether a teleological, biblical messianism might have been necessary to make messianicity eventually thinkable.[112] But where others have investigated the difficulties inherent in disentangling an emancipatory simultaneity-along-time (or instantaneity, or singularity) from stifling determination by a telos, I would remind us that late nineteenth-century French radical conservatives' teleological commitment to progress cannot be considered apart from the simultaneity-along-time with which it likewise remained entwined. The typology I have just outlined helps differentiate the simultaneity-along-time mobilized by such pseudo-socialists and superficial anticapitalists—politically intent on currying favor with capitalism's losers but not really interested in class struggle—from the more revolutionary mentality animating Benjamin's messianic twist on historical materialism. Benjamin's poststructuralist admirers would likewise contrast the deterministic foundationalism of the radical conservatives' temporally hybrid nationalism with the postfoundationalist turn anticipated by a messianic time beginning, in Benjamin, to detach itself from determination by a logos. Yet by calling attention to the kinship between these two divergent mobilizations of messianic instantaneity, I mean also to highlight the complexities that arise when extrinsic final causes become intrinsic. Dispensing with any divine final cause, Benjamin's schema leaves one to wonder whether that cause resurfaces or not in an organizing revolutionary consciousness privy to the secret agreement between generations and without which no retroactive meaning can emerge. Already, too, we have seen how the telos of inevitable progress, catalyze though it might an accompanying simultaneity-along-time, does so more complicatedly than a divine final cause. Unlike the mind of God, progress is not external to the passage of earthly, diachronic time; arguably, in fact, it requires that time to unfold. Such was the challenge posed to radical conservatives seeking to resolve how the same telos of progress could at once intrinsically inhabit all events—producing a relation of instantaneous simultaneity-along-time—while concurrently behaving as a gradual process of diachronic change.

This was tantamount, I have discussed, to a paradoxical belief that time might at once act on and neutrally contain events. Similarly paradoxical was the fact that the process itself of progress could be taken as an organizing goal or telos rather than some finite outcome toward which progress would ultimately lead. Concerned about the Marxist appropriation of Hegel's teleological historicism to announce the collectivist end of history, Barrès used Hegel instead to define history as an infinite, dialectical pursuit of social perfection. Historical change was therefore always legitimate and desirable, insofar as Barrès understood it to be inevitably moving toward an ideal. And because that organizing ideal, progress, was at once process and goal, the simple movement of history became the continuous realization of the ideal: "truth is continually realized for all of eternity."[113] The tautology is evident, the conflation of process and goal recalling his strained identification of a tiny, instantaneous messianic ideal driving each incremental step forward in the nation's evolutionary change. We know as well that such stratagems less easily accommodated bolder messianic leaps of the sort Barrès and others thought Morès had incarnated, and that doing so required the spaces of empire.

But if these were complexities introduced when the old metaphysics of divine providence became the ideology of permanent progress, they in fact constituted only one class of difficulty presented to radical conservatives by the shift from extrinsic to intrinsic final causes. When considered as extrinsic and godly, final cause oriented events in the single and obviously salutary direction of salvation. Once final cause had been rendered intrinsic, however, events might be understood to unfold along a different kind of path. The optimism inherent in the doctrine of Christian salvation most easily and naturally translated into the equally optimistic doctrine of necessary progress. Absent God, though, nothing now prevented some from being convinced that an intrinsic final cause might act less beneficially on and through events to impel men toward decline instead. And just as radical conservatives wrestled to reconcile varieties of time, so did they find themselves pulled between varieties of intrinsic cause. In the next chapter I consider how the resulting, distinctly modern uncertainty created fertile terrain for antisemitism, as well as for related notions about the imperial regeneration of a metropole supposedly beset by Jewish decadence.

CHAPTER 4

Men on Horseback (2)

Melchior de Vogüé, Imperial Regeneration, and the Dialectic of Determinism

In the last chapter I discussed a new kind of nationalism that emerged in the fin de siècle as French chauvinistic thinking labored to reconcile species of time. On one hand was a traditionally messianic Christian temporality assuming a providential final cause extrinsic to time because emanating from God; on the other, a modern variant reimagining that final cause as an intrinsic feature of time itself ever driving events forward in the direction of progress. If the teleological quality common to both temporalities made them tempting to combine, the task was not easy: messianic simultaneities across time quite conceivable, for instance, under the conditions of extrinsic, divine final cause became significantly less intuitive under the conditions of linear, incremental progress. I have examined how empire eased the effort, facilitating the intersection between temporalities by situating the nation between differently constructed varieties of space. That an older, "truer" France might hence have been anticipated to reemerge in imperial endeavors abroad, while leaving untouched the metropole's privileged position at the forefront of progress, is one way to understand the even more zealously imperial nationalism I will be examining now.

But another, equally significant temporal complication was also shaping imperial and racial thought. For in the wake of Lamarck, Darwin, and rapidly developing notions about evolution and heredity, there emerged not one but two ways of thinking about how biological organisms—and, by extension, social organisms—might be impelled from within toward determinate ends. The first represented a scientific, nineteenth-century iteration of the Enlightenment faith in progress, translated now as a conviction that organisms necessarily improved as they evolved in time. The second closely mirrored the first. Where the *philosophes* had announced the triumph of reason and progress, the French Revolution and subsequent European upheavals brought a jaundiced retort from conservatives like Joseph de Maistre and Louis de Bonald. To them, ostensible advances in the scientific and political arenas had only produced moral, religious, and social decline. Such warnings about the "the dark side of progress" laid the foundation for what became degeneration theory, pioneered in the 1850s by French psychiatrist B. A. Morel (*Traité des dégénérescences physiques, intellectuelles et morales de l'espèce humaine* [*Treatise on the Physical, Intellectual, and Moral Degeneracy of the Human Race*], 1857) and French race theorist Arthur de Gobineau (*Essai sur l'inégalité des races humaines* [*Essay on the Inequality of Human Races*], 1853–55) and according to which organisms, men, or races could exhibit decreasing complexity and robustness over time.[1] Readable, at a general level, as a secularized version of the Fall and its narrative of deterioration from an ideal state, degeneration theory more precisely interests me here for having taken a divine final cause rendered intrinsic—the idea of progress—and inverted it into a determinant, heritable, and degradative force.

This chapter examines what happened when a late-century generation of ambiguously scientifically minded reactionaries wrestled with the implications of subscribing to both varieties of intrinsic final cause. One could not, after all, credibly maintain that the same entity or organism was destined at once to decay and thrive. Antisemitism, I will be arguing, seemed to promise a way out of the double bind by safely delimiting the bodies and spaces on which time might act with the wrong kind of determinant force. If Jews seemed naturally to lend themselves to the tactic, it is perhaps because, by figuring them as the frozen remnants of Christianity's past, the West had long been accustomed to imagining time acting differently on the Jews. But if I mean here to propose an explanation for a more specifically modern antisemitism, it is also because Jews were now being made to bear the burden of the distinctly modern problem of conflicting determinisms.

To begin tracing this problem's modern contours, let us for a moment revisit a few key antisemitic figures—among them the Marquis de Morès, Maurice Barrès, and Édouard Drumont—whose complicated political subject position I grouped in the previous chapter under the rubric of radical conservatism. Degeneration theory offers another measuring stick against which to measure the sheer complexity, novelty, and precariousness of the ideological space they were attempting to carve out. That theory gathered momentum following France's humiliating 1870 defeat in the Franco-Prussian War, after which Frenchmen across the political spectrum broached the possibility of a deep-set national decadence. Different remedies were prescribed: while republicans advocated a revival of the democratic ideals eroded when Louis-Napoléon's 1851 coup d'état derailed the 1848 revolution, royalists called for turning the clock back to an era before the revolutions they blamed for national decline. Radical conservative nationalists like Morès, Barrès, and Drumont were no strangers to the discourse of degeneration, painting the xenophobic picture of an ailing national organism beset from within and without by enemies. Their self-professed modernity, however, militated against the classically reactionary solution of returning to a prelapsarian past. Instead, they espoused an organicist corporatism combining the fantasy of a bygone, prerevolutionary social stability with the idea of a collective, future-oriented response to present economic and political realities. The attendant dream of class harmony predictably ran afoul of real-life class divisions. Morès's political failure in France, which hastened his exile to Africa and solitary campaign against imperial Britain, certainly illustrates the point. Conservatives were appalled by Morès's socialist bluster and unsavory associations with anarchists and other agitators. Meanwhile, the socialists with whose ideas the Marquis flirted mistrusted his wealth and doubted his commitment to real class struggle.[2]

Morès's knack for ruffling feathers in all quarters mirrored the basic problem afflicting the radical conservatism elaborated in the early 1890s. Too radical for the conservatives and too conservative for the radicals, proponents of this composite ideology courted relegation to the farthest fringes of national life. In antisemitism, though, they could salvage from their alienated politics a more successful politics of alienation. Rather than seek implausibly direct cooperation among classes, they cultivated an indirect solidarity by turning various disaffected constituencies against the same Jewish enemy. Indeed, it was a hallmark of the modern, Drumontian brand of antisemitism to gather all manner of malcontents—antirepublican Catholics, anticapitalist atheists, disaffected aristocrats and workers alike—with otherwise conflicting sensibilities. Many such odd bedfellows would march together under the anti-Dreyfusard banner in the waning years of the century. But as large a tent as this antisemitic movement produced, it also suffered from mounting internal contradictions. Barrès and other anti-Dreyfusards' various invocations of degeneration theory to depict a French nation infected by Jews, and to allege an accelerating deterioration within Jews themselves, wedded them to the determinism of intrinsic causes.[3] Negative or positive, these causes were of a philosophical piece: much as degeneration theory held an inverted mirror to the ideology of permanent progress, the narrative of an increasingly diseased "Jewishness" reflected back the myth of necessary Aryan genetic health. Yet by taking the nation as an organism subject to both determinisms, antisemitic nationalists faced a dilemma. If, as Barrès thought, the nation was destined to progress over time, how to separate this intrinsic final cause from competing forces supposedly and simultaneously rotting the national body from within?

The easy answer was excision, in terms of which we are accustomed to representing the associated discourse of national purity. When in the ominous conclusion of *La France juive* Drumont called for the army to fall upon French Jews, he was suggesting that only then could France return to health.[4] After all, the appeal of antisemitism was precisely to render seemingly excisable what ailed the social body by condensing it all in one place. In what follows, though, I examine how complicated it actually proved to offload so massively and decisively the specter of degeneration onto a single racialized site. Barrès, for instance, considered it quite possible for French society to decay without any help from the Jews. Noting the degenerative danger posed by "the old hereditary prejudices of caste or parish" mining the individual geographic regions (Alsace-Lorraine, Brittany, Provence, etc.) whose traditions he otherwise glorified, the great bard of "The Land and the Dead" conceded that the dead made competing claims on the living. One claim promised continued vitality, while the other—evident in continued hereditary prejudices among the various Estates—threatened a "departmental torpor." To negotiate this double inheritance, Barrès prescribed a "circular movement" stimulated by regional universities designed to reinforce the more salutary local sensibilities while dissipating any attendant stagnancy in a restorative, modernizing bath of postrevolutionary French cultural solidarity.[5] As intensely, then, as Barrèsian regionalism fixated on the inexorable force binding man to the locality of his birth, it also quietly required each region's integration into the national collective.

Here Barrès was offering a spatial solution to the temporal and metaphysical problem posed when the past was represented as exercising conflicting determinant influences on the present. The strategy constituted a conceptual pendant of sorts to xenophobic antisemitism: echoing and inverting the process by which a negative determinism might usefully be confined to the excisable body of the Jew, Barrès proposed that the more unpleasant inherited local particularisms could first be isolated from their beneficial counterparts, then dissolved by salubrious exposure to a modern (though decentralized) national enterprise. But these twin processes of racist exclusion and regional integration were also not necessarily so easy to combine, as Barrès tried to do. What if, rather than disappearing, the various local hereditary prejudices were in fact only exacerbated when introduced to one another in the collective national project? And what if, among those undesirable parochial hatreds, a historical animosity between Jews and their enemies—of the very sort Barrès otherwise hoped to construct and exploit—came simultaneously to signal a decadent nation's vulnerability to inherited discord?

These were the questions asked by Barrès contemporary and fellow literary celebrity Eugène-Melchior de Vogüé, on whom I will be focusing in this chapter. Vogüé's influential musings drive home another key phenomenon I want to explore: how, among the complementary ideological formations crystallizing around the fin-de-siècle intellectual malaise in question, antisemitism and imperialism came particularly to interact. Conceived in the manner above, French Jews were made to figure the problem of contradictory determinisms that, at the regional level, prompted Barrès's circulatory remedy for local stagnancy. Except increasingly the prescribed movement reached further afield, to a larger world system within which the metropole might enter into a morally productive exchange with its imperial periphery. From this ideological perspective, insufficient geographic movement posed as much a problem as deracination, given the exposure risked by the sedentary to accumulated internecine enmities poisoning the metropole. Inducting Barrès into the Académie Française in 1907, Vogüé used his congratulatory speech to tweak Barrès's signature insistence on the virtues of rootedness. Deracinated conquering races, suggested Vogüé, had also made France great:

> Man or people, you think that the most "racinated" are also the strongest. Beautiful and wise verity! Why must the inconvenient exception always trouble the best rules? You spoke to us earlier of Normandy: I could not help thinking that they were

> exemplarily deracinated, these tall Normans arriving by boat from Scandinavian fjords and scattered across every coast, every ocean, every island. Grant me that if they had not been perpetual wanderers, what great pages would be missing in the history of the world, as well as several elements essential to the formation of the French type.[6]

Vogüé argues by reductio ad absurdum for the senselessness of fetishizing supposedly rooted peoples who, if one goes back far enough, inevitably turn out to have immigrant ancestors. But Vogüé was hardly making the case against foundational notions of identity. His real concern was that too complacent a rootedness carried the abovementioned costs. In empire, he imagined a tonic for a Frenchness withering in an increasingly polluted native soil. No more than Barrès, however, did he hope to roll back modernity. Rather, empire became a space where a chosen caste of apostle-soldiers could flourish outside the determinant metropolitan time of decay long enough to return fortified with a dose of regenerative vigor incorporable into the contemporary nation.

Important, too, we will see, is the extent to which Vogüé reveals how antisemitism itself was coming to figure the growing late-century contradiction within which he and others found themselves. Often he treated antisemitism as a symptomatic phenomenon, one evidencing the very kind of social decomposition about which railed programmatic antisemites like Drumont. Yet Vogüé also happily and extensively blamed Jews for France's late-century descent into chronic governmental instability, political scandal, and social crisis. Such apparent inconsistency perhaps owed something to rhetorical expedience: condemning the kind of strident antisemitism offensive to Vogüé's aristocratic gentility, he could impart an aura of comparative respectability to his own antisemitic ruminations. At a deeper level, though, this simultaneous avowal and disavowal of antisemitism also reflected the fundamental conundrum facing Vogüé and many of his peers. Seeking, in the twilight of the century, alternatives to the scientific positivism whose paradigms still prevailed, they frequently ended up reproducing the models they rejected. Thus could Vogüé locate in organized antisemitism the throes of a degenerating society, even as he excoriated the positivist abjection of the same degeneration theory he invoked.

What remained of these lapsed positivists' positivism, I will be arguing, was intended to justify a decidedly fair-weather determinism on their part. As long as, say, the Darwinian doctrine of survival of the fittest conformed to a Maistrian might makes right conception of aristocratic primacy, Vogüé had no problem espousing Comtian positivism's erosion of the boundary between the individual and collective; against the accumulated genetic or cultural backdrop of the right ancestry or clan, the individual could acceptably represent a mere drop in an ocean. The difficulty rested in mitigating the more ideologically inconvenient aspects of contemporary deterministic thinking, like for instance the possibility that even the noblest men were constrained by deterministic forces producing ignoble results.

Indeed, even a less conflicted positivist like Ernest Renan had struggled a few decades earlier with the apparent tendency of racial inheritance to render its desirable and undesirable outcomes frustratingly interdependent. I will return at length to this point, which I think cuts to the aporetic core of a pseudoscientific nineteenth-century racial thought predicated in part on an older mode of aristocratic reaction. Let me only say now that, like Renan, Vogüé sought an imperial, spatial fix to what I will be calling the dialectic of determinism. Though reminiscent (as I intend it to be) of Max Horkheimer and Theodor Adorno's dialectic of enlightenment and associated theory of antisemitism, the dialectic of determinism explains in more historically contextual terms—that is, without relying on the kind of transhistorical psychobiological explanation to which Horkheimer and Adorno appeal—how modern antisemitism partially emerged as a spatializing response to a temporal impasse become increasingly untenable. Empire represented an iteration of this spatializing response, promising even further distance between a "good" determinism and the "bad" variety displaced onto the Jew. But as I conclude, it also set these determinisms spinning back into a dangerous new dialectical relation with one another, portentously linking the Jewish question with imperial expansion in ways more typical of the twentieth century than the nineteenth.

IMPERIAL CHAMPIONS

Seduced by the military's growing enthusiasm in the 1890s for African exploration and conquest, those previously inclined to consider empire an extension of the hated Third Republic now increasingly saw a potential overseas staging ground for that government's demise.[7] Political antisemites' on-again, off-again relationship with Boulangism in the late 1880s and early 1890s, complicated though it was, had at least convinced them of the possibility that the proverbial man on horseback might, like General Boulanger, materialize to rally the nation against its enemies.[8] Boulanger gone, the search for a new such figure turned naturally enough to the imperial periphery, the sole theater of French military activity and the place where Boulanger himself had built his legend fighting in Algeria, Cochinchina, and Tunisia.

Caution reigned at first. Of General Dodds, commander of the French forces sent to conquer Dahomey, Drumont opined that "it will not be this one, but maybe it will be one who resembles him somewhat." Those military leaders who, like Dodds, "had been heroes in Africa" appeared to Drumont too excessive in their "obedience" properly to threaten the government.[9] With the death of Morès, however, antisemitism could claim a figure who had truly gone it alone in Africa. Captain Jean-Baptiste Marchand's abandonment at Fashoda two years later in 1898 provided an even better opportunity for political antisemites, in concert with other strident nationalists, to anoint a maverick savior. Forced by a recalcitrant French government to retreat from his position on the upper Nile from where, like Morès, he had hoped to threaten British supremacy in Egypt, Marchand returned to France a martyred hero. Drumont's *La Libre parole* trumpeted Marchand's return with a four-page illustrated supplement in which Lucien Pemjean announced that a "wind of valor and pure glory arises to sweep away the unhealthy air and noxious miasmas that we have breathed for so long." Reflecting the extent to which the Fashoda Affair crystallized the emotions of a Dreyfus Affair at its apogee, Pemjean indulged in a pointed, side-by-side comparison of Marchand with his Jewish antithesis Dreyfus.[10]

Marchand ultimately declined to play the role of Napoleon returning from Egypt.[11] But what Marchand himself might not accomplish, literature could now all the more convincingly predict. First serialized in 1899 in the pages of the well-respected *Revue des deux mondes*, Vogüé's successful novel *Les Morts qui parlent* (*The Dead Who Speak*) elevated to the level of doctrine the notion that empire would save a Republic overrun by Jews.[12] Other French novels had exploited the contrast between a more or less avenging imperial figure and his Jewish foe.[13] Never before, however, had a work so explicitly and categorically located in the imperial periphery a last chance for national salvation. And no other document, I would submit, better lays bare the contradictions and anxieties of an era in which so many proclaimed the reconciliation of tradition with modernity.

The Vicomte Eugène-Melchior de Vogüé made a logical and effective spokesman for this credo. An influential man of letters and scion of one of the noblest families in France, Vogüé is most remembered for having written *Le Roman russe* (*The Russian Novel*) (1886), the book that introduced Gogol, Turgenyev, Tolstoy, and Dostoyevsky to a wide French public and earned Vogüé a seat in the Académie Française in 1889. One of the architects, with Paul Bourget and Ferdinand Brunetière, of the backlash against French literary realism and naturalism, Vogüé preached a reconstructed conservatism that sought to place modern scientific and democratic principles under the guiding influence of religion. *Les Morts qui parlent*, the second of Vogüé's three novels, registers Vogüé's disgust with the parliamentary system he discovered as a member of the Chamber of Deputies from 1893 to 1898. Elected from the administrative department of Ardèche with conservative support, Vogüé embarked on an indifferent legislative career during which he refused to join a caucus, intervened in parliamentary debate on only two occasions (one of them to defend his own contested election), and eventually declined to seek reelection.[14]

The bitter antiparliamentarianism of the resulting novel organizes several of Vogüé's fixations into a shrill, if reasonably well-written, *roman à thèse*. Vogüé's longtime antisemitism—already in 1882, he had concluded about the Union Générale bank's spectacular failure that the bank had been "killed by the Jews"[15]—achieves its crowning expression in Vogüé's detailed account of the high-level manipulation of parliamentary democracy by a Jewish cabal bent on financial and political domination. As an antidote to this state of decadence, Vogüé proposes something near to his heart: the French imperial project. A high-ranking member of the Comité de l'Afrique Française and influential proponent of colonialism, Vogüé was a mentor to Hubert Lyautey, the renowned colonial officer and administrator of Tonkin and Madagascar, whom Vogüé encouraged to write and to develop his Catholic conservatism. Vogüé was in turn influenced by Lyautey's faith in the regenerative potential of the imperial periphery for the metropole. Vogüé's portrait in *Les Morts qui parlent* of a colonial "nursery of men," from which a cadre of virile supermen forged in "the school of action and responsibility" will return to shake up a stagnant France, echoes identical notions elaborated by Lyautey in the two men's correspondence.[16]

Little of this will surprise anyone familiar with the fin-de-siècle climate in which Vogüé wrote his novel. Antiparliamentarianism on both the left and the right expressed widespread frustration with the instability of a Third Republic whose governments came and went with debilitating frequency.[17] Those inclined to reaction considered this upheaval one more symptom of a French decadence seeming, with the Dreyfus Affair, to have reached crisis proportions. As is often the case, such decadentist alarm went hand in hand with a distinctly messianic tendency, one that had already almost catapulted General Boulanger to power. Against the backdrop of the imperialist rivalry in Africa that, at Fashoda, brought France and England to the brink of war, it is understandable that this secular messianism should pin its hopes on the saga unfolding overseas. Imperial space furnished the key elements of such a narrative of redemption, representing as it could a place from which, untainted by the torpors of the metropole and steeled in the imperialist fires of national rivalry, a savior (or saviors) might arrive to heal the nation of its decrepitude. Barrès's influential notion of "national energy" stoked matters further.[18] According to the thermodynamic principles that, as Michel Serres has demonstrated, so informed the late nineteenth-century French conception of the world, imperial contact appeared to offer a means for tapping this resource.[19] Dormant in the metropole, "national energy" would be released by the contiguity of two vessels—a metropolitan space with a surfeit of energy and an imperial space perceived to lack it—across whose energetic difference the potential promised to become actual. Vogüé implied as much in 1891 when, arguing passionately for an aggressive French annexation of Africa, he affirmed that "presently, Africa is the dynamometer where each race comes to test its energy."[20]

Only the smallest of mental steps separated this thinking from the conclusion, on display in *Les Morts qui parlent*, that the energy released would sweep back into the metropole to regenerative effect. Between center and periphery "a circuit is thus formed," wrote Vogüé's friend Lyautey.[21] Such a circuit granted the nation an ability to auto-correct: nurtured away from the ailing metropole, the "true" France would return, strengthened, to assert its due. I would like to suggest, however, that the proposed auto-correction, and in particular its imperialist correlate, represented less a remedy to a perceived fin-de-siècle decadence than the major manifestation of a constitutive tension at the heart of the ideological project that prescribed it. The antisemitic, anti-Dreyfusard mobilization that drew Vogüé closer to the more doctrinal antisemitism of a Drumont considered Dreyfus, as a Jew, hereditarily inimical to the national body. This unapologetic racialism was the spawn of a positivist and materialist intellectual revolution that, as the century progressed, had increasingly deemed man a product of inexorable deterministic constraints. Yet even as they embraced a deterministic account of the permanent incompatibility between the "Semite" and the nation, many anti-Dreyfusards attacked the philosophical climate that had produced such determinism in the first place. Positivism, they charged, had failed to deliver on its scientistic promise of infinite progress. Limited in its capacity to remedy the ills it diagnosed, it had yielded to an impotent, pessimistic nihilism. Against the perceived bankruptcy of reason, an important fin-de-siècle current—counting Vogüé among its standard-bearers—championed the virtues of religion, spirituality, and affect.

This reaction's contradictory appetite for the determinism whose philosophical foundations it otherwise questioned represents more than a matter of simple, hypocritical political expedience. It also reflects the movement's own filiation, at a fundamental level, with the paradigm it critiqued. Having cut their intellectual teeth under the pervasive influence of Comte, Taine, and Renan, partisans of the antirational, anti-Dreyfusard right like Vogüé and Brunetière were just as imbued with these giants' positivist, determinist, and materialist methodologies and assumptions as they were critical of their supposed effects.[22] Accordingly, antirationalists frequently attacked positivism and its avatars in terms borrowed from the targets themselves. Even the decadentist premise of their reaction had its roots in a discourse of biological degeneration elaborated over the previous decades by positivists in the medical community. Thus could Vogüé bemoan "the incurable weakness of our political and social organism, what doctors would call its physiological misery"—a textbook example of degeneration theory—before citing "the tight correlation" between "this social infirmity" and the epistemological structures whose authority he had indirectly just invoked, like "scientific positivism" and "practical materialism."[23]

If in moments like this Vogüé seemed to lack reflexivity, he could also be candid about his positivist inclinations. Approving "the wise habit of measuring everything exactly against experience and reality," he even went so far as to attribute France's "recent disappointments" to its "resistance to realist disciplines that ensured others military, political, and economic success." Vogüé's charitable assessment here of the positivism he elsewhere denounces hinges on a bold caveat: for behind his embrace of scientific advances, Vogüé reveals, rests a conviction that "the latest findings of experimental analysis . . . approached traditional truths, when they did not confirm them expressly."[24] Faced with the contradiction of elaborating a critique from a vantage point indebted to the object of that critique, Vogüé simply turns the epistemological tables, subordinating the object—empiricist positivism—to a set of timeless verities that transcend it. In this fashion does he illustrate what Pascal Ory and Jean-François Sirinelli have dubbed the "ratio-traditionalism" of peers like Barrès, who vehemently argued for the compatibility between rational modernity and the traditions of the past.[25] These were the spiritual inheritors of a conservative traditionalism elaborated early in the century by Maistre and others. But thinkers like Vogüé also deemed their intellectual forebears' faith in divine providence an extrinsic variety of final cause reconcilable with the intrinsic sort popular since Darwin, whose social Darwinist vulgarizers understood evolutionary theory to mean that life contained its own teleological script. Hence, declared Vogüé, could part of Maistre's *Soirées de Saint-Pétersbourg* easily have been written by "a disciple of Darwin and Pasteur," and hence were French reaction and materialist determinism of a logical piece: "A Darwin founds amid our democratic societies an aristocratic and traditionalist doctrine par excellence; a Renan, a Taine, arrive at the same place by different routes."[26]

Vogüé's confidence notwithstanding, his fusional metaphysics represented no easy task, and *Les Morts qui parlent* finds him at arduous pains to address the fissures in the path on which he and fellow fin-de-siècle ideological travelers like Barrès had embarked. To the complexities that dogged the reconciliation of tradition with modernity, *Les Morts qui parlent* offers a sweeping resolution. A traditional French vigor reawakened in the imperial periphery would remedy the decadence Vogüé felt had taken hold in the metropole, though in a way that, suffused with the inherent contemporaneity of the imperial project, promised less a return to the past than a new, self-consciously modern lease on the future. In this regard, Vogüé participates in the realization by late-century reactionaries discussed in the previous chapter—namely, that figures like Morès and Marchand might, in the imperial crucible, more convincingly alloy radical nationalists' and antisemites' contradictory attachments.

But *Les Morts qui parlent* contributes a substantial twist to the proceedings, breaking new ground in French antisemitism's developing ideological dependence on empire in a way that complicates, as I will go on to propose, received assumptions about the positivist underpinnings of European imperial expansion. To be sure, Vogüé subscribed to the imperial corporatism increasingly typical of antisemites. Registering admiration for imperial soldiers "indifferent" to the "sickly worry" plaguing the metropole, *Les Morts qui parlent* proffers an imperial panacea to the class divisions subtly invoked by the novel's indictment of socialism (375). Unlike more radical compatriots, however, the genteel Vogüé did not seek in empire to attenuate suspicions raised on both sides of the political divide by the Drumontian brand of populist, para-socialist imprecation against modern economic upheaval. Instead, Vogüé's recourse to empire explicitly addressed a rather more deep-seated quandary: the double-edged sword of a determinism that, while pivotal to modern antisemitism's reactionary contention that Jews were innately toxic to an otherwise glorious nation, simultaneously raised the possibility that France's still-traumatic 1870 swoon might reflect a more generalized, national disposition to fail in the global struggle for survival.

This predicament gives *Les Morts qui parlent* its title. Elzéar Bayonne, one of the novel's two main protagonists and the assimilated heir of a wealthy Jewish family of dung purveyors, becomes a Socialist leader in the Chamber of Deputies (rising, as it were, to the top of the heap). There he is joined by a school chum, Jacques Andarran, who hails from a proud line of aristocrats and soldiers. Cajoled by countrymen into a reticent but successful election campaign, the delicate Jacques wonders bemusedly at the parliamentary venality and mediocrity he finds in the Chamber. He turns for guidance to his fellow deputy and former professor Ferroz. An atheist and positivist clinician, the supercilious Ferroz admonishes Jacques to consider the spectacle around them in terms of an uncompromising determinism:

> Ah! My friend, you think you are seeing the gestures and hearing the words of five hundred and eighty contemporaries, and nothing more, contemporaries who are conscious of and responsible for what they say and do? Undeceive yourself. You are seeing and hearing so many mannequins passing for an instant on the world's stage, who move reflexively and are the echoes of other voices. Look behind them at an innumerable crowd, the myriads of dead who impel these men and control their gestures . . . *these are the dead who speak*. (176, emphasis added)

Meanwhile, Elzéar goes about proving Ferroz right. Dandyish and ambitious, he recognizes in socialism's political ascendance an opportunity for private gain—a natural consequence, the narrator helpfully offers, of a Jewish "ethnic character" typified by a "financier's shrewdness about the best choice of exchange currency, an assured discernment regarding the price that would best prime the political market" (42). Elzéar also succumbs to the more sinister cupidity of his shadowy, Machiavellian extended family, whose members exploit his position, charisma, and naïveté to seize the reins of power. Doubly determined, in this fashion, by his race, Elzéar confirms Ferroz's observation about Jews that "it is in them that speak the most ancient dead, those most active and unchangeable" (365).

Justified as the narrative proves Ferroz in Elzéar's instance, the old professor's determinism otherwise prompts malaise for Jacques when applied to the whole of the national body. Jacques politely objects to Ferroz's baleful portrait of a nation in thrall to the "centuries-old divisions" bequeathed by previous generations. Are not, Jacques asks, the "new winds" of liberty, science, and progress capable of reclaiming the present from the clutches of the past? Perhaps so, Ferroz concedes, but only for "healthy peoples"—among whose ranks he does not count the French (178–79). Jacques's more sanguine assessment nevertheless foreshadows the conquering arrival of the novel's key figure: Pierre Andarran, Jacques's officer brother fighting an imperial war in the Sudan. As steely and phlegmatic as Jacques's legislative colleagues are craven and excitable, Pierre incarnates a revivifying African project entrusted by Vogüé not only with righting the metropolitan ship but also, at a more telling level, with negotiating a determinism that threatens dangerously to spill beyond the confines of the novel's Jewish straw men.

Les Morts qui parlent lurches onto this ideological high wire with more brio than finesse. Jacques visits his wounded brother in Senegal, where he discovers a hardy and purposeful corps of "Sudanese" recomposing in Africa what has decomposed in the metropole. "When you have accumulated enough ruins," Pierre tells Jacques, "you will come looking in our ranks for reorganizers" (225). Jacques returns home transformed by the experience. Pierre, for his part, symbolically makes good on his own prediction by returning to Paris and killing his counterpart Elzéar in a duel late in the novel. Elzéar's pathetic death at the hands of this champion of the "hereditary patrimony" confirms that the deterministic cacophony produced by "the dead who speak" threatens only as a multitude of voices (231); reduce those voices to one, that of the Christian warrior France Pierre represents, and the din subsides (though only provisionally, we will see). Ancestrally disposed as Pierre is to heroism, his gesture obviously proves no less determined than

Elzéar's decadence. But the fact of such a determinism concerns Vogüé less than the possibility of picking and choosing among its effects, a principle of selectivity countenanced by Ferroz when he opines that the aforementioned "healthy peoples" know how to make a "judicious choice of past traditions" (178). Vogüé submits, in other words, that the nation combat determinism's more debilitating consequences by favoring that same determinism's constructive facets.

One marvels at this eleventh-hour entrance of choice, or free will, into a schema otherwise so thoroughly defined by its determinism—that is, by precisely the absence of choice in a novel whose characters largely proceed according to hardwired ancestral scripts. That the choice Vogüé prescribes further boils down to an embrace, *manu militari*, of a warrior heredity itself facilitating this embrace (witness Pierre's predictably superior dueling skills) propels the whole enterprise into the familiar tautology of nationalist chauvinism: the true nation abides because it is the true nation. The speciousness of the move bespeaks its precarious epistemological footing. Proponents of a timeless and religious "ideal," Vogüé and the ratio-traditionalists bridled at positivism's willingness to stoop for its truths into a fallen world of contingent particulars. Yet one of the most dramatic conclusions born of that very same positivism—the deterministic conviction, in a Darwinian age, that a man's actions were dictated by biological imperatives beyond his control—captivated men like Vogüé at least as much as its attendant atheism offended them. After all, what was determinism if not a confirmation of the inevitable persistence into the present of the past, in a mode of continuity reminiscent of the ideal? What is more, the corporeal manifestation in determinate man of this continuity suggested mankind's ability to incarnate the ideal as such, rather than simply to aspire to it. Just as Aristotle's empiricist turn had recuperated Plato's timeless, universal Ideas, but only insofar as they were instantiated by particulars in the material world, so did positivism promise new heft and immediacy, on a palpable human level, to abstractions like the nation.

The devil was in the details. It was difficult to condone determinism as a terrestrial vehicle for celestial ideals without also accepting its perpetuation of traits more unsavory. Further wedding the ratio-traditionalists to determinism's grim obverse was the necessity to their idealist project of a materialist foil. As a rhetorical construct, the struggle of the lofty nation against its foes required that those foes appear as congenitally predisposed to mischief as their counterparts to heroism. If the Manicheism of this strategy relied dialectically on determinism's less pleasant implications, however, it also policed those implications by confining their appearance to a single out-group. Modern antisemitism delivered especially well on this count by positing a racialized, essentializing binary—the intrinsically noble Aryan and the innately craven Semite—that usefully uncoupled deterministic promise from deterministic curse. Thus did antisemitism inevitably appeal to those who, at the fin de siècle, looked back with ambivalence on previous decades. Deferring onto the Jew determinism's more threatening dimension, one could reject positivism's accused excesses without undercutting its contributions to modernity. Antisemitism made it possible, amazing though it may now seem, to be reactionary without being retrograde.

Yet Vogüé sensed the tenuousness of the compromise. Was it really possible to critique positivism for its indifference to transcendental ideals while simultaneously invoking a dispassionately materialist determinism to condemn the Jews? *Les Morts qui parlent* confronts this question in a fascinatingly self-conscious exchange about antisemitism itself. Shocked by the antisemitic fulminations of several colleagues, Jacques refuses, out of "native generosity," to support a xenophobic law targeting Jews. Ferroz interjects that antisemitism represents less an ethical question than a matter of scientific certainty: past a certain "proportion of foreign elements," he explains, "the zoological law" dictates the expulsion from the national body of the foreign pathogen. "But one must prefer the moral law!" protests Jacques emphatically, arguing not that Ferroz is wrong but rather that man ought not tolerate the violence Ferroz's analysis predicts. The student here surpasses his master, Jacques standing in for a generation of ratio-traditionalists convinced and dismayed that the positivism whose diagnostic acumen they admired offered little in the way of cure. Positivism's presumed apathy on this front—Ferroz repeatedly proclaims his scientific neutrality ("I neither like nor dislike a phenomenon, I study it")—prompts a stinging rebuke from Vogüé along ethical lines (363–64).

The ostentation of the rebuke hints at a more complicated unease on Vogüé's part. Jacques's ethical objection aside, Ferroz's mechanistic justification of racial animosity flatters Vogüé's evident antisemitism. The fact that Ferroz's measured rationale for antisemitism compares so favorably to the ravings of his less reflective colleagues confirms as much. But Vogüé also recognizes the inherent difficulty of selectively ascribing determinism's more disagreeable consequences to the Jewish people. Jacques's preference for "the moral law" does not mean he contests Ferroz's deterministic certainty about an inherent Jewish difference, which Jacques indeed takes for granted. What Jacques resists is the extension of this determinism to the rest of society. Predictably for such a double standard, the boundary Jacques draws proves logically porous, and Vogüé realizes it. To declare the Jew constitutionally parasitic was implicitly to risk considering the Aryan constitutionally susceptible to parasitism. Viewed in this light, Jacques's outrage betrays anxiety over a negative determinism breaching its arbitrarily assigned Jewish limits.

Vogüé responds by reaffirming these limits with the help of empire. In the metropole *Les Morts qui parlent* depicts, the hereditary predisposition of Jews for evil suppresses the equally hereditary predisposition for good of their more allegedly French neighbors. The novel's shadowy Jewish cabal, exploiting parliamentary antagonisms to its own corrupt ends, leads a chorus of "dead who speak" whose atavistic squabbles ensnare even the past's more salutary voices. As I submitted above, however, it is only in relation to each other that these voices threaten all parties with negative determination by the past. The inherent spatiality of this relational logic implies that, absent a contiguity between determinism's negative and beneficial variants, the latter might regain its proper influence. And where better to escape such contiguity than in the open spaces of empire, far from the Jews of the teeming metropole?

The banality of the solution belies what, at the time, was the usefulness of the balance it strikes. Marveling at his brother's African accomplishments, Jacques bemoans the wasted potential of colleagues in the Chamber of Deputies who "would do wonders if you changed their environment" (227). Here Vogüé advances the fundamental proposition already incipient in his model of "the dead who speak": while the forces of inheritance exert determinant influence along a vertical, temporal axis, the manifestation of that influence remains subject to interactions occurring along a horizontal, spatial axis as well. Able to intervene with some decisiveness along this spatial axis—for instance, by sending soldiers into an African proving ground—man thus retains some measure of control over the forces that determine him. Empire, in this regard, accomplishes a double coup. First, it makes possible the "judicious choice of past traditions" Ferroz prescribes. By manipulating the environment, Vogüé proposes, one might selectively nurture a true France in the colonial theater. Critically, empire also makes it possible to do so without too overtly contravening the deterministic principles with which such a discourse of choice could otherwise seem at odds. This was important because Vogüé's project ultimately depended on the deterministic conviction that certain qualities remained indelible because inherited. The true Frenchman's true Frenchness, after all, could not emerge in the imperial crucible were it not always latent. Vogüé's spatial manipulations in fact reinforce that latency: the more he purports to choose from among different inherited traditions, the more he naturalizes their irreducible and abiding particularity.

Jacques's rumination on the importance of environment likewise burnishes its determinist credentials by indirectly invoking the authority of Hippolyte Taine, whose theory on the determinant impact of *race* (heredity), *milieu* (environment), and *moment* (historical moment) had ushered radical determinism into French thought nearly four decades earlier. Typically for a ratio-traditionalist, Vogüé engages this positivist intellectual heritage from within, exploiting the scientific cachet of its basic tenets only to turn them against the supposed positivist fatalism he disliked. Rejecting as bygone the closed metropolitan system in which *milieu* might have seemed as inescapable as *race*, Vogüé seizes on the spatial possibilities opened by empire—that is, the opportunity to manipulate radically the variable of *milieu*—in order to corroborate "traditional" values with modern scientism. It was one thing for Vogüé to maintain breezily in his nonfiction writing that "the latest findings of experimental analysis . . . approached traditional truths, when they did not confirm them expressly"; it was another, more seemingly substantiated thing for him to deploy empire, with a pseudo-empiricist verve that would have made even Zola blush, to validate reactionary theses on contemporary, colonialist grounds.

Imperialism, then, like antisemitism, offered an apparatus for stabilizing a unique fin-de-siècle admixture of reaction and self-congratulatory modernity. This explains in part why the two ideologies should prove so concurrent in *Les Morts qui parlent*. But if antisemitism and imperialism had evolved into such a tandem, it was because they represented more than just twin variations of a same tortured logic. They had also begun to demonstrate an increasing measure of interdependence. The motivated nature of the relationship plays out in the novel at two different levels of visibility, both of which I have touched on but that merit elaborating. In its broadest triumphalist strokes, *Les Morts qui parlent* combines antisemitic and imperialist preoccupations into the easily digestible schematic of a *roman à thèse*. The antisemitic canards the novel endlessly deploys—from Elzéar's unbridled ambition to the deceitful ways of his courtesan cousin Rose Esther—diagnose a stereotyped social malady the more simply to propose its neat imperial resolution. Antisemitism, in this formula, furnishes the raison d'être of a discourse of imperial regeneration, which in turn further naturalizes antisemitic assumptions about the metropole.

On a subtler level, however, *Les Morts qui parlent* outlines a relationship between antisemitism and empire even more symbiotic. Men like Vogüé and Barrès had been antisemites before they became imperialists. As recently as the preceding decade, most sharing their general reactionary bent had denounced a colonial project too associated with the Third Republic and too distracting, they felt, from the more proper nationalist goal of reclaiming Alsace and Lorraine. Now empire offered a position from which reactionary antisemites might more directly confront the fraught ideological inheritance of a modern antisemitism Drumont had assembled from sources on the left and the right. Nowhere was this more in evidence than among the ratio-traditionalists, whose embrace of modern French antisemitism's heavily deterministic precepts posed a collateral ideological risk. How was the God-fearing Vogüé to countenance an antisemitic determinism perfected by thinkers on the atheist, materialist left like Eugène Gellion-Danglar, Gustave Tridon, and Albert Regnard?[27] Furthermore, how was he legitimately to harness that determinism without unleashing a veritable Pandora's box of consequences for the rest of the nation? Insofar as it might defer onto Jews the full onus of a negative determinism, antisemitism tempered for the ratio-traditionalists the very concerns it stoked. Still, the fact remained that modern antisemitism counted among its tributaries the same positivist epistemological paradigm that had led some to hypothesize—unacceptably for the ratio-traditionalists—a biological degeneracy on the part of more than just France's Jews.

Considered from this perspective, Vogüé's imperial response to Jewish encroachment conveys perhaps less alarm about the Jews than about the specter of a negative determinism for which modern antisemitism had made the Jew a defining figure. The Jew offering an easily targeted symptom of that larger positivist threat, *Les Morts qui parlent* certainly dispenses antisemitic bromides with willful abandon; and yet, to the extent that Vogüé believes it symptomatic of the same threat, antisemitism itself comes in for substantial censure as well. Formulated too acutely, Vogüé advances, antisemitism drags the whole of society toward a degraded, deterministic fatalism: to a colleague repeating the antisemitic mantra that the French are "eaten alive" by the Jews, Ferroz sardonically retorts that "it is apparently that you are edible flesh" (364). Empire furnishes a corrective to the defeatism Ferroz mocks. It matters very much that the blow that kills Elzéar comes from the hand of Pierre, who in his imperial remove gives no indication of antisemitism. Motivated, rather, by a militaristic code of honor (the duel occurs after Elzéar publicly affronts him), Pierre simply strikes Elzéar from the picture in a way that makes no concession to an overt antisemitism that otherwise might have tainted the gesture with the deterministic fatalism it metaphorically seeks to excise.

One can obviously debate the intellectual honesty of an act intended to keep at decorous arm's length an antisemitism it simultaneously enacts. Such was the paradoxical modus operandi of a ratio-traditionalism destined to inhabit the paradigm it critiqued. But I most want to emphasize that empire here represents as much a rejoinder to epistemological difficulties posed by antisemitism as it does its unproblematic expression. In Chapter 2 I discussed how empire contributed to the ideological development of modern French antisemitism by furnishing new discursive opportunities for racializing the Jew. To this I would now add that empire also helped manage the consequences of that racialization. The more antisemites racialized the Jew, the more they lent credence to a materialist, positivist, and deterministic current of thought that had helped codify racial thinking but that remained antipodal to the religious idealism to which so many antisemites subscribed.

POSITIVISM AND EMPIRE

The preceding introduces an interesting wrinkle into the complicity so often automatically assumed between positivist reason and empire. Imperialism, we have seen, presented an opportunity to attenuate positivism's unintended consequences without disavowing it outright. Historically, though, this has been obscured by the extent to which empire and positivism otherwise proved so closely associated. The racial hierarchies legitimized and popularized by positivist thinkers like Renan furnished the republican architects of France's late nineteenth-century colonialist project a powerful, pseudoscientific rationale for imposing the white man's will on peoples of color. Renan's influential formulation of a colonialist might makes right doctrine remains particularly notorious for its starkness. Seeking, in his *Réforme intellectuelle et morale de la France* (1871), to make sense of France's crushing defeat the previous year by the Germans, Renan included a grand policy of colonization among the various strategies he prescribed for returning France to glory. It was in the natural order of things, he urged, for a "European race . . . of masters and soldiers" to govern a Chinese "race of workers" and African "race of peasants."[28] These are the flatly racist terms for which his reasoning is usually remembered.

Less frequently examined are the political benefits to France, for Renan, of colonial conquest. In an argument he helped make into a commonplace of late-century colonialist discourse, Renan labels colonial expansion a necessary remedy to class conflict in the metropole: "A nation that does not colonize is irrevocably doomed to socialism, to the war of rich and poor." But the problem for Renan is not inequality itself, which he is perfectly willing to tolerate—even promote—as the overseas prerogative of a European "conquering race." The problem, rather, emerges from the subjection to inequality of Europeans not hereditarily inclined to accept it. That is because, as Renan explains, "the common man is almost always a declassed nobleman." Recalling the nobiliary historian Henri de Boulainvilliers, who the previous century had traced the historical and legal basis for France's aristocracy to the Frankish conquest of Gaul, Renan cites various Germanic tribes—Franks, Lombards, Normans—that swept across Europe in the fifth and sixth centuries and whose blood still flows in even the humblest European worker.[29] Impose on this fallen nobleman a "task against his nature," warns Renan, and revolt necessarily ensues. The only solution is to substitute for metropolitan labor a colonial labor performed by subalterns more racially suited to the task.[30]

Renan means here to found a colonial right of conquest on the Germanic right of conquest beneficially asserted when, for instance, Norman "bandits" unexpectedly brought feudal stability and security to the lands they claimed. Little wonder that commentators from Hannah Arendt to Benedict Anderson have identified in colonial racism a reconfigured philosophy of aristocratic privilege.[31] Yet if Renan appears confident in a hierarchizing racial typology that deems the Chinese or Arabs "happy" to do the labor Europeans inherently cannot abide, his urgent colonialism otherwise betrays an unspoken anxiety about the positivist assumption on which the entire system rests.[32] Renan evidently takes seriously the injunction by Comte, the father of positivism, against what in 1852 Comte termed "the subversive tendencies that, focusing on sociability's synchronic aspect, ignore today the necessary influence of previous generations."[33] By introducing the dimension of time into the debate about society's organization, Comte meant to propose the importance of solidarity and continuity across generations for maintaining social order in any given present, and vice versa. But what if, asks Renan in the manner above, an intergenerational national inheritance also contributes to contemporary discord?

The question loomed less for those conservative enough to discount the present in favor of the past; renew past ways of being, they thought, and the present would sort itself out. So assumed the monarchist and ultranationalist Charles Maurras, leader of the far-right political movement Action Française, who would later invoke Comte's enjoinment about "the necessary influence of previous generations" to advocate for the precedence of what Maurras called "solidarity across time" over "solidarity across space."[34] A fin-de-siècle ratio-traditionalist himself, Maurras amalgamated Maistrian reaction and Comtian positivism into a "purposeful empiricism" intended to place positivist-inspired systematic laws in the service of identifying and retaining useful continuities with an idealized past.[35] Maurras's reading of Comte was opportunistic, since Comte had never sought to privilege one solidarity over the other. Renan, by contrast, started from a more faithfully Comtian premise. Treating France's shared heritage as a phenomenon ignored at the country's peril, Renan raised the prospect of social dissolution to indicate how solidarity across time—in his version, a conquering aristocratic temperament passed down from generation to generation—remained an ongoing condition of any achievable solidarity in the present. But by the same token, he underscored the extent to which the diachronic solidarity in question could also threaten the synchronic national collectivity. France's common aristocratic inheritance was precisely what made it impossible, under the socially stratified conditions of modern industrial capital that Renan acknowledged, for the French laboring classes ever peacefully to accept their lot. In other words, the determinant weight of the past caused significant problems in the present, even as it still offered powerful (if latent) conditions for social unity.

Maurras's tacit solution was to roll back the clock to the days of absolute monarchy. Absent the individualism and egalitarianism that he felt had nefariously taken hold in France with the Revolution, and whose origins he located in Judaism, inequality would cease to be perceived as a problem.[36] Such was the familiar antisemitic deferral onto Jews of the quandary posed by a double-edged determinism. Renan, more willing to accept the Republic as a fait accompli ("let France therefore remain what she is," he grudgingly declared in *La Réforme intellectuelle*),[37] regarded instead that the contradictory implications of Comte's diachronic, intergenerational "sociability" required novel strategies to manage. In espousing perhaps the most dramatic of these, systematic colonial expansion, Renan certainly looked to the ancient right of conquest for legitimacy and inspiration. Yet by considering it a structural necessity, for the sake of metropolitan social stability, that France subjugate Africans and Asians en masse, Renan was also proposing a national investment in and dependence on the imperial periphery unlike anything previous.

No such innovation seemed necessary to Maurras, who doubted that France need do anything it had not essentially done before and who long remained steadfast in his opposition to the Third Republic's acquisition of a vast new colonial empire.[38] For those ratio-traditionalists, however, struggling more genuinely to alloy modernity with tradition—that is, for those conservatives reconciled to the irrevocability of post-Revolutionary actualities—the complications arising from Comtian solidarity across time could not just be glibly rewound. Failing a temporal solution, only spatial solutions remained. And if spatial (i.e., synchronic) solidarity was threatened by the temporal (i.e., diachronic) forces of determinism, space itself required reconceptualization. Now it was the shared conquest of space abroad, rather than its shared occupation at home, that would produce social cohesion. By 1891, Vogüé was already summing up the proposition thusly: "What purpose would virgin lands serve, if not to . . . reunite men divided by sterile quarrels and tired of fighting in the night without knowing where they are going?"[39] Though Renan had said much the same twenty years earlier, Vogüé formulated things in even more aggressively spatial terms. For Renan, France's shared inheritance of aristocratic *germanité* (Germanness) meant that social friction owed more to what work was asked of certain classes than to where they performed it; he seemed unconcerned whether, once the onus of labor was transferred to the colonized, France's newly emancipated laboring classes remained in the metropole or not. Because Vogüé, on the other hand, conceived the Comtian weight of the past a bit differently, the colonial solution he proposed differed as well. For Vogüé, the key temporal issue was not that of a single, national, aristocratic solidarity across time but rather that of multiple solidarities binding different constituencies to their respective traditions. If individually these ties could be salutary, together they could also calcify into a system of what Barrès called the "old hereditary prejudices of caste" pitting generations of Frenchmen against each other in the same perennial conflicts. Relocating the best of these Frenchmen overseas, Vogüé thought, would break the deadlock.

So globalizing a solution to a continental problem expresses the metaphysical predicament in which many late-century French conservatives and reactionaries found themselves, and it explains why I have chosen to focus here on Vogüé instead of on the better-known Maurras. To be sure, Ferroz's scientific pretension to make a "judicious choice of past traditions" evinces a certain Maurrasian tendency. But Vogüé, like Renan, does not share Maurras's confidence that untangling the Comtian legacy might remain an exclusively metropolitan affair. Historians like Zeev Sternhell and Ernst Nolte have argued for the importance of Maurras and the populist ultranationalism of his Action Française in shaping European fascism's later combination of socialism and nationalism.[40] It is Vogüé, though, who I think offers a more telling early insight into another fateful combination—antisemitism and imperial expansion—that would also come to define twentieth-century fascist movements.

Not that Vogüé ever embraced programmatic antisemitism of the sort his contemporary Drumont had developed: indeed, *Les Morts qui parlent* finds Vogüé as intent on distancing himself from antisemitic rabble-rousers as he is willing to condone their basic ideas. But this is also the point, since it was only from the perspective of empire that Vogüé was able at once to castigate Jews *and* their antisemitic foes. Vogüé thus sought in empire to escape the ramifications of his own antisemitism, even as his imperial vision worked to reinforce the perception that the metropole suffered no greater danger than from the Jew. The contradictory nature of the effort reflects the contradictory position of the ratio-traditionalists. And in subtle but important ways, empire suited the task. Granted, the concomitance of the Dreyfus Affair and the Fashoda Affair made it likely that a nationalist commentator like Vogüé would so thoroughly entwine two of the great issues of the day—the Jewish question and the imperial question—if only because both affairs afforded such an opportunity for military chauvinism. Yet something more caused empire to hold such a growing fascination for Vogüé. We have seen, now, the spatializing panacea offered by imperialism to ratio-traditionalist ambivalences and obsessions. As for Barrès would local "old prejudices" fade in the circular movement between region and nation, so for Vogüé would metropolitan "sterile quarrels" dissipate in the circuit linking nation and empire. A similar conversion of time into space was characteristic, according to Max Horkheimer and Theodor Adorno, of the later, fascistic antisemitism they worked so hard to understand. I turn now to their analysis, from which I think one can work backward into the nineteenth century to appreciate better how antisemitism and imperialism came to be conjoined via the interrelated spatial solutions they offered to temporal problems.

THE DIALECTIC OF DETERMINISM

In the extended meditation on modern antisemitism that closes the *Dialectic of Enlightenment* (1947), Horkheimer and Adorno liken disgust for the Jew to Western man's abhorrence of what they term the "idiosyncratic"—that is, of everything that resists civilization's subjugation of nature to the laws of purposeful utility. Like the "grating sound of a stylus moving over a slate," the Jew reminds his tormentor of an elemental nature refractory to domination by civilized man. What makes the reminder so visceral is that this ineffable nature lingers, repressed, within the antisemite himself, who projects onto the Jew the responsibility for the inchoate unease the repression produces. The depth of the unease corresponds to the primordial quality of the experience it recalls: an encounter between man and nature that did not always obey a logic of domination. Horkheimer and Adorno posit a primitive time when, rather than submit the environment to his will, man contended with a threatening nature by imitating his surroundings. Inspired by Roger Caillois's biological theories about mimicry, they describe a yielding of the animate to the inanimate that blurs Cartesian distinctions between subject and object.

Such a near fusion, continue Horkheimer and Adorno, brings man into proximity with an inanimate world whose only mode of existence—a purely external spatiality—threatens man with "absolute alienation" from his sentient interiority. Man therefore rejects mimicry, sublimating the experience via an increasingly sophisticated array of mechanisms meant to transform surrender to nature into dominance over it, and to assert the ontological difference between ego and environment. Descended as these strategies of differentiation remain, however, from a prehistoric brush with absolute sameness, they reprise that experience in order to contain it. Thus, in their common reliance on repetition, do the universal concept, mathematics, and technology all transmute alterity into attenuated and predictable instances of the same, even as they further extend man's dominion over nature. Such sublimations "rationalize" idiosyncrasy, affording man the adaptive benefits of mimicry while maintaining a safe remove from alienating space. With modern antisemitism, Horkheimer and Adorno conclude, the historical process of rationalization reaches its apotheosis in a dizzying welter of pretexts for controlled mimetic indulgence and repetition—the disciplined uniformity of fascism, for instance, or the racial stereotype's repeated reduction of difference to the same—in ways that at once reproduce and manage the more unsettling ontological consequences of the primordial mimetic experience.[41]

As an explanation for modern antisemitism, Horkheimer and Adorno's account perhaps hinges too precariously on its psycho-anthropological premise of archaic man's partial foray into inanimate existence.[42] This said, theorists of racism have productively abstracted the Freudian fetish from the ur-trauma of castration anxiety that classically defines it, adapting the more general mechanism at work—a simultaneous recognition and disavowal of difference—to explain the encounter with racial otherness.[43] We might similarly abstract Horkheimer and Adorno's explanatory framework from the ur-trauma of spatial alienation that sets their narrative in motion. But how to describe the basic mechanism remaining? At a fundamental level, I would propose, the authors describe a temporal solution undertaken by man to a spatial problem: encroachment by the inanimate spatiality of "circumambient, motionless nature" on animate man.[44] Primitive man responds to the terror experienced by setting the process into diachrony, relocating the dissolution of boundaries from space to time. Now it is repetition over time, instead of mimicry in space, that produces an adaptive sameness—albeit one henceforth produced from adapting nature to man, rather than man to nature.

This temporal substitution established, Horkheimer and Adorno aim to highlight the fragility, if not futility, of the resulting civilizational edifice. Thus does bourgeois reason's instrumentalist emphasis on rote classification and calculation confuse repetition and real thought.[45] Enlightenment, they famously conclude, merely redeploys the strategies of an older myth and magic similarly concerned to ward off spatial mimicry with ritualized imitations of mimicry repeated over time. The "true," spatial mimesis of adaptive mimicry becomes the degraded, temporalized mimesis of domination over nature, which in turn degrades into the puerile "mimesis of mimesis" undertaken when fascist rituals ape shopworn magical ones (disguises, drumbeats, etc.).[46]

Notice that however far the temporal response to traumatic space progresses along historical time, it never ceases retracing its steps. The repetition enabled and contained by the response seems to overtake time itself, which now threatens to repeat until the point of standstill where—to describe things in the terms I have been developing so far—diachrony essentially reverts back into the synchrony of pure space. Such a point, write Horkheimer and Adorno grimly in 1944, was reached when fascist antisemitism caused the civilization-long domination of nature to come full circle by buckling under the weight of its contradictions.

I will return to this momentarily; let me pause here, though, to begin suggesting what Horkheimer and Adorno's spatiotemporal framework, in its general contours and divorced from its Cailloisian starting point, might actually better describe about fascist antisemitism's late nineteenth-century precursor. For the ratio-traditionalists, too, grappled with the ramifications of setting into diachrony a foundational spatial event: namely, the conquest of French territorial space by Frankish invaders. The confidence with which a Boulainvilliers or a Renan judges that conquest to have inaugurated the temporal system of inherited aristocratic privilege (whether at the level of class or nation) tends to obscure how the temporalization works to defuse, but also subtly and continually to reinscribe, the structuring trauma beneath. The repeated transfer of land and title from one generation to another endlessly replays the initial conquest. Except instead of risking death to violently appropriate space, as their forebears did, subsequent generations need only ever receive it. The sublimating inversion recalls that temporalized false mimesis postulated by Horkheimer and Adorno, for whom a nature that once required man to relinquish something of himself now appears freely given, in a sense, to him as possession.

But a parasite gnaws both sublimating inversions from within. Back, first, to the *Dialectic of Enlightenment*. Encountering remnants of untamable nature, and confident about civilization's mastery over them, Horkheimer and Adorno's modern man occasionally gives himself over to the idiosyncratic in temporary indulgence of an unconscious desire for regression. If we recognize here the Freudian death drive, it stays relatively confined: "anyone who seeks out 'bad' smells, in order to destroy them, may imitate sniffing to their heart's content."[47] The hallmark repetition of the death drive, while certainly in evidence, remains trumped by the larger societal structures of repetition designed to repress "bad smells" rather than luxuriate primitively in the communion they facilitate with base, organic nature. Not so in fascist antisemitism, which elevates the obsession with bad smells—condensed, of course, in the body of the Jew—to the level of repeated collective ritual and that therefore renders the temporal structure of containment increasingly indistinguishable from the spatial threat it was designed to contain. Eventually, in other words, "the victory of society over nature . . . changes everything into pure nature" as diachrony sputters, skips, and finally collapses back into synchrony.[48]

That fascist antisemitism, more specifically, should precipitate the return to space constitutes a metaphor for the self-parasitizing process described, since Horkheimer and Adorno consider the system ultimately to have turned against its own progenitors: none other than the Jews themselves, whose ancestors were among the most systematic and effective at transforming "adaptation to nature . . . into a series of duties in the form of ritual."[49] The argument proves troublingly tantamount, notes Jonathan Judaken, to a suggestion that "the Jewish civilizing impulse" is ultimately "responsible for the victimization of the Jews."[50] But strip from Horkheimer and Adorno's logic its Freudian and Cailloisian trappings—the relationship of mimesis to ritual sacrifice drawn and reconfigured from *Totem and Taboo*, yes, but especially the death drive impelling man back to a primeval mimetic flirtation with inanimate matter—and what remains offers purchase on modern antisemitism without inadvertently blaming the victim. It also sheds light on what I am arguing is the related modern impulse toward empire. At base, Horkheimer and Adorno usefully describe an oscillating reversibility between space and time, or synchrony and diachrony, set into motion when the temporal solution to a spatial problem encoded the possibility of that solution's unraveling. Nineteenth-century thinkers presumed such a reversibility when, finding unforeseen consequences in Boulainvilliers's temporalization of spatial conquest, they sought remedies in antisemitism and empire.

It is important first, however, to unravel the abovementioned unraveling from the psychobiological assumptions woven throughout Horkheimer and Adorno's account of it. Otherwise we risk offering an explanation for antisemitism that reproduces the nineteenth-century dilemma considered so far and from which Freud himself adapted the idea of the death drive. This is a critical point. The two Frankfurt School philosophers do not locate in modern antisemitism, as I have been proposing, a response to the *constructed*, historically contingent quandary of conflicting intrinsic causes or determinisms. Instead, they identify in modern antisemitism's eventual fascist elaboration the inherent culmination of a system whose contradictorily generative and degenerative tendencies they in fact naturalize into an *actual*, civilization-long feature of human life itself.

Consider again how a latent entropy always already permeates, on Horkheimer and Adorno's view, a system designed to transpose the axis of sameness from the spatial dimension of mimicry into the temporal dimension of repetition. I have characterized the phenomenon thusly: Become sufficiently repetitive in time, and time itself appears to repeat. Cancel its forward momentum with enough such repetition, and time "stops." Stop time, and synchronic space takes the reins back from diachrony. The passage from latent to actual further requires, to use more faithfully Frankfurtian terms, that (1) a refractory nature keep revealing itself in every metaphorical scrape of the "stylus moving over a slate," and that (2) the sound (or smell, or other unpleasantness) produced remain compelling enough eventually to dominate, rather than be dominated by, the temporal structure of institutionalized mimetic repetition. The stylus shifts, if you will, from the slate to the phonograph, paralyzing the whole apparatus as the jarring scratch repeats and settles into the endless loop of the skipping record.

Horkheimer and Adorno make plain the Freudian-cum-Cailloisian aspect of the regressive compulsion at work, explaining in the associated fragment "A Theory of the Criminal" how criminals

> represented a tendency deeply inherent in living things, the overcoming of which is the mark of all development: the tendency to lose oneself in one's surroundings instead of actively engaging with them, the inclination to let oneself go, to lapse back into nature. Freud called this the death drive, Caillois *le mimétisme*.[51]

Here it becomes apparent just how indebted Horkheimer and Adorno remain to a nineteenth-century degeneration theory inverting expectations of steady biological improvement into the teleology of decline. What contemporaries found so "bizarre," to borrow Daniel Pick's assessment, about Freud's 1920 postulation of "a vital trajectory toward death" recalled the paradox that life might somehow simultaneously evolve *and* devolve—a double bind Freud clearly had taken to heart, though he could be critical of degeneration theory's specific tenets.[52]

The fragment's implicit engagement with nineteenth-century criminology, the province par excellence of degenerationist notions about biological atavism, conjures up the same debate. Of course, Horkheimer and Adorno evoke the criminological enterprise against the grain: if criminology, like antisemitism, helped spatialize away the problem of conflicting determinisms by confining degeneration's effects to an aberrant subpopulation, the two critics' "theory of the criminal" invokes Freud to do just the opposite. Freud associated the death drive with all life, generalizing the basic degenerationist idea into a principle harder to divorce from the related, more sanguine teleology of flourishing life. Horkheimer and Adorno echo this de-pathologization of regression in their dialectical model binding instrumental reason and mimicry, marking their distance from classical degeneration theory even as, in a certain sense, they build on its aporetic force.

The Cailloisian spin given by Horkheimer and Adorno to Freud achieves a similarly intensifying effect, outlining a specific phenomenon—the sublime frisson of spatial mimicry—that more tangibly explains regression's lasting unconscious lure. But the biological specificity of the phenomenon also undercuts the historical specificity of the modern discourses in question. To believe in regression is to miss how a conflicted belief in something similar, rather than any actual regression itself, sufficed to alter and expand antisemitism's ideological footprint. We might debate the importance, even existence, of primeval human mimicry and its phylogenetic hold over civilized man, but we need neither to understand how a newly perceived conflict between antithetical determinisms stirred a newly functioning animus toward Jews. For what makes certain manifestations of late nineteenth-century European antisemitism so truly modern is not just their mobilization of scientific racism, or their political organization, or their codification of the world conspiracy narrative. What matters, too, is their emergence with freshly destructive potential at the intersection between reason and reaction heralding the twentieth century's own distinctly modern descent, following Zygmunt Bauman, toward genocidal "social engineering" that harnessed rationalist technological means to irrationally purificatory, idealist ends.[53]

Where Horkheimer and Adorno's framework remains valuable, however, is in conceptualizing the spatiotemporal fallout from the conflict that developed as degeneration theory settled uneasily alongside its twin narrative of increasing biological perfection. The question was especially germane for anyone already wedded, like the ratio-traditionalists, to Boulainvilliers's conjugation of spatial conquest into the principle of inherited legitimacy. Insofar as the notion allowed for an initial physical superiority in space to be continually replicated as an ongoing and heritable class superiority over time, it harmonized naturally with, and had arguably even anticipated, similarly hierarchical theories of inherited racial superiority.[54] In their more scientific guises, these reinforced the narrative of biological progress by situating certain races higher up the evolutionary ladder. But notions stemming from the right of conquest also introduced the specter of decline. The double bind of degeneration, as theorized by its founding father Gobineau, was that the basic metaphysical guarantor of racial superiority—the conquest by a stronger people or race of a weaker one—immediately began eroding the same superiority by deleteriously mixing the blood of conqueror and conquered in the inevitable subsequent process of intermarriage.[55]

The temporal consequences occasioned by a spatial victory thus appeared at once capable of reproducing the victory (by yielding the system of inherited aristocratic privilege) or steadily undercutting it (by yielding an increasingly miscegenated weakness over time). The first scenario, rendered into the terms of scientific racism, assumed intrinsic biological improvement in the way indicated above; the second scenario, on the contrary, posited permanent decadence. Now imagine that in the fin de siècle you were as intellectually indebted to one Boulainvilliersian scenario as the other, because the first allowed you to look as a "modern" toward future advances, while the second allowed you to linger simultaneously and nostalgically as an "ancient" on past glories. How, then, to reconcile the two corresponding, apparently contradictory principles of intrinsic societal progress and intrinsic societal decline?

The answer lay in manipulating the reversibility between space and time so fundamentally presumed by both versions of intrinsic final cause. Here I return to Horkheimer and Adorno, who I think have best adumbrated that reversibility. What in the *Dialectic of Enlightenment* makes it possible for history to collapse back into "pure nature," or time into space, is the lingering into diachrony of the pure synchrony it both imitates and contains. The scrape of the chalk stylus (*ein Griffel*) so closely shadows the temporal structures of mimetic repetition that we imagine the sound emerging, in Horkheimer and Adorno's carefully chosen figure, from the very gesture used to record (only to erase and record again!) the mathematical or other formulae facilitating the "recognition in the concept" that "takes the place of physical adaptation to nature."[56] To trace the line between space and time is to find it as thin and brittle as the chalk itself. But if we leave aside the Cailloisian content of the figure, we are left with a nineteenth-century habit of mind—within which, again, I believe Horkheimer and Adorno themselves remain—regarding spatiotemporal reversibility. And in the nineteenth century, so easy a reversibility represented both poison and cure. The quandary of Gobineau, for instance, was that movement in space became indistinguishable from the degradative potential of time, the superior races diminishing in purity and strength as conquest led to miscegenation. Others inspired by Boulainvilliers's setting of conquest into diachrony were likewise haunted by the spatiotemporal complications of dominance. Consider only the example of Renan, for whom a first Germanic spatial conquest, once temporalized into the homogeneous European prevalence of aristocratic blood, necessarily required a second: the conquest of colonial spaces that would shift to a global scale the modern division of labor rejected in the metropole by white working classes too atavistically and Germanically "noble" for peaceful exploitation.

These are the complex stakes of what, from the outset of this book, I have been calling racial scalarity. One might alternately think of Renan's scheme in terms of the racial relationality I have also described. After all, Renan's colonial call to arms would seem the logical and sequential outgrowth of a theory of Aryan superiority worked out, most influentially by Renan himself, at the Semite's expense.[57] The Jew (or his Muslim fellow Semite) having furnished an initial and more familiar continental template for devalued otherness, Africans and Asians were next—or at least so goes the narrative of a European racial system incorporating one subaltern after another as it fanned out from center to periphery. Renan was doubtless thinking along these relational lines, if only tacitly. But by linking colonial expansion to the old European Germanic invasions, Renan was not just situating Africans and Asians alongside Gauls and Romans as the latest victims of a conquering *germanité*, though this too was part of his justificatory agenda. Nor, even, was he merely and confidently reproducing, at the new global scale of racialized imperial subjugation, an aristocratic privilege heretofore confined to the continent. What was truly scalar about Renan's imperial turn, in the specific sense I want to employ, is that it nervously offered a resolution to internal contradictions dogging the supposed Aryanness of Europeans themselves.

Renan's spatial fix to a racial problem was, evidently enough, also a spatial fix to an economic problem. After all, he conceived the entire apparatus in response to and explanation of class strife. We might thus be tempted to conclude that Renan's elaborately racial schema simply constitutes so much window dressing designed to rationalize a hard truth: capital's necessarily predatory expansion into the periphery to stave off the inevitable crises it produced in the metropolitan center. Vogüé, too, suggests an economic basis to his racial obsessions by making Elzéar a socialist firebrand, implying both a racial explanation for and solution to the problem of class. Yet it would be a mistake, I think, to consider these racial fictions purely epiphenomenal to the material processes they worked to manage and contain. As much as they sprang from material circumstances, they had a way of taking on a life of their own. Though the underlying cause of empire might have been material, the *way* in which empire was imagined, approached, and ultimately practiced still had something to do—even much to do—with perceived tensions in the metropole surrounding the question of Europeans' own racial purity.

Crucial to these tensions is what happened when in the nineteenth century spatial events were so reflexively and routinely translated into temporal terms. And if imperial scale came to address the resulting ideological complications, it should come as no surprise just how resolutely empire was figured as a way of turning time back into space. Well known, of course, is how Europeans thought themselves capable of turning time back *in* space: history having supposedly passed "primitive" Africa by, one needed only travel there to glimpse the past. But I mean to document something different. For the Renan of *La Réforme intellectuelle*, and even more for the younger generation of ratio-traditionalists formed at the altar of his 1871 post-defeat cri de coeur, empire represented an opportunity less to travel backward in time than to stabilize and concretize a problematic supposed inheritance by reorienting it along spatial lines. So, for instance, did Renan take a volatile genealogical conceit—the centuries-long dispersal across social strata of French aristocratic blood, with its conflicting metropolitan outcomes of both solidary racial homogeneity and class unrest—and propose to mitigate the latter consequence by spatializing the former into France's imperial dominance over colonized subalterns.

Similarly did Vogüé invert the basic Boulainvilliersian proposition by suggesting how a new era of conquest could bring a generation of young colonial Frenchmen into communion with their proud military ancestry. Where Boulainvilliers had demonstrated how to set the synchrony of conquest into the diachrony of inherited nobility, the diachrony now would retroactively be strengthened and renewed in space. The difficulty, recall, was that shared national space might also bring one insalubriously into contact with other, less desirable ancestries, plunging the whole into the dangerously cross-pollenating melee of various "dead who speak." Here threatened a Gobineau-style degeneration, since proximity in space spelled degradation over time. Yet such civilizational degeneration only proved intrinsic when considered from Gobineau's globalizing perspective: as initially pure races were given to move and circulate around the world, so were they destined to intermix and decline.[58] Gobineau's individual races themselves, however, were not predisposed from within to degenerate. Assume, then, as Vogüé did, that the contamination of "true" Frenchmen by lesser ancestries was reversible by separating those lineages across imperial space, and it became possible to achieve something like rewinding Gobineau's script.

The anticolonial Gobineau would of course have countenanced no such imperialist solution, since for him conquest was by definition the catalyst of degenerative racial mixing.[59] Yet there is also a sense in which Vogüé himself seems to recognize just how easily degeneration might set in again. What matters about empire, to Vogüé, is the fact of conquest itself rather than what follows. After all, any subsequent colonial civilization might fall prey to the same metropolitan complications ostensibly incurred when synchrony was first set into diachrony by the imperialists' barbarian Germanic forebears on the continent. And so Vogüé suspends the world he describes in a state of constant conquest, attempting permanently to occupy the impossible vanishing point where, for Gobineau, racial superiority simultaneously begins and ends. Subjugated by the French, Africa's inhabitants will provide vast, compliant new reserves of manpower equipped with the necessary savagery for prevailing in the savage new era of colonial and European wars to come: "If you furnished us the means," Pierre lectures his brother,

> we would make available to you, tomorrow, one or two hundred thousand incomparable Senegalese, Sudanese, and Hausa soldiers; bayonets that do not reason, back down, or forgive; docile and barbarous forces of the sort always necessary for winning the barbarous and inevitable struggle that is war. (226)

Slated for conquest, too, is France itself. From whom? The Jews, of course. The metropole will not be rid of its Jews, however, any more than Vogüé can allow conquest to end in Africa. If Elzéar's death certainly portends a change, Pierre does not stick around for the "national recovery" he has predicted, leaving again for Africa with his childhood love in tow (225). To Jacques's giddy request of his brother that he expand the metropolitan regeneration beyond Elzéar—"Pierre, sweep away! . . . Sweep away, Pierre!"—Pierre expresses confidence in the needed change happening "by itself" (382). But when the even more explicit Marchand figure Tournöel returns from Africa a few years later in Vogüé's subsequent novel *Le Maître de la mer* (*The Master of the Sea*) (1903), he will find Elzéar's cousin Rose Esther enjoying a greater "social triumph" than ever over a Parisian society still in thrall to her sexual charms and Jewish family influence.[60]

Tournöel, too, heads back to Africa, churning through one more revolution of what begins to look like a perpetual cycle. One engine of that cycle is modern antisemitism, a theory of which I have tried to offer by identifying in it a response to the joint claims of reason and reaction. Such a response facilitated the ratio-traditionalists' ambivalent embrace of determinism by artificially dichotomizing the notion into opposing variants. The negative variant safely confined to the Jew, the Germanic Frenchman was free to exemplify determinism's more tolerable possibilities. Of course, he also increasingly seemed most free to embrace his preordained destiny abroad. Dependent as the overall system was, therefore, on physically cleaving a negative determinism from a positive one—first by assigning opposing intrinsic final causes to different races, then by assigning the results to different spaces—it offered a doubly spatial solution to the temporal predicaments inherent in the very idea of Germanic superiority (and, indeed, of race more generally, to whatever extent racial thought was descended from the historical might makes right rationale for aristocratic privilege). This solution, I have shown, involved setting diachrony back into the synchrony from which it had emerged, or at least into some updated version thereof. But doing so also engendered the strange new cycle in question. Where for Horkheimer and Adorno space and time recombine at enlightenment's fascist endpoint to yield the skipping record, as I put it before, of "pure nature," here the spatial pursuit of positive determinism enters into a recursive, dialectical loop with that determinism's unwanted negative other. For the destiny of the positively determined Aryan is not only to escape the negatively determined Jew's contaminating presence but also to return and conquer him; to do otherwise, after all, would be to abandon the metropole to its "Jewish" fate. And yet neither can the Jew be conquered entirely, since the end of conquest would mean the temporalization of space so previously problematic to begin with.

So if antisemitism provides the first condition for the perpetual cycle, the second is that the regenerative Aryan conqueror arrive from—and, just as importantly, periodically return to—some place beyond the metropole. Yet in a way I am here still only describing the cycle itself. The real other condition necessary for the cycle to take hold is that the place at hand, rather than simply exist as a geographic materiality, in fact be continually produced as the *possibility* of an "elsewhere" exceeding the metropole yet amenable to its needs. That possibility was scale, and the ability to produce it was empire. Aryan imperial conquest, as the ongoing production of scale, functioned in space to resolve the temporal contradictions of Aryanness or *germanité*. The consequences of a Boulainvilliersian historical construct, these contradictions were inherent; they required no Jews to occur. But if the contradictions' eventually attempted scalar resolution entailed antisemitism, it is not just because of a later, reflexive definition of the Aryan against the Semite. That the whole process should pass through the Jews also attests to their historical construction by the West into a privileged figure over and against which to produce scale. Such was the enduring legacy, as I have previously noted, of a Christian supersessionism intent on redefining the Church's former containment by Judaism into a scalar leap beyond it.

I will return at length in the next chapter to how Marx, Nietzsche, and others considered Jews themselves paradigmatic makers of scale who subsequently and stealthily remade Christian society in their own image. Let me finish now, though, by underscoring how for the ratio-traditionalists antisemitism and empire represented more than two comparably spatial solutions to the same temporal problem. They also worked together to entangle the global-imperial scale with the national one. In 1871, Renan could still think of a spatial fix occurring in absolute space and stabilizing the nation by bringing excentric regions—and the labor of the peoples therein—under metropolitan control. By the time of *Les Morts qui parlent*, however, the globe had been more or less partitioned, and the era of internal, relative differentiation of spaces and scales had begun.[61] In such a fully globalized regime, any attempted spatial fix like Vogüé's functioned less like the straightforward solution Renan envisioned than as the first step in a permanent new dynamic of constant spatial redifferentiation. Consider Vogüé's vaunted army of colonized soldiers, whose job it will be not to provide a stabilizing labor to the nation but rather to help the nation prevail when drawing the skittering mosaic of African or continental boundaries contested by imperial powers in a permanent state of war. The continual, racialized policing of internal boundaries extends into the nation, too, where Jewish decadence must be quarantined from the rest of the putatively healthy national body.

The latter phenomenon is reminiscent of how, for Michel Foucault, racism became a technology of state power when war was relocated from the external frontier to the "interior frontier"—if I may insert an expression of Johann Gottlieb Fichte's[62]—by positing a permanent conflict between a dominant national race and its internal others, then grounding the state's legitimacy in its biopolitical authority endlessly to prosecute that war.[63] Foucault briefly mentions a "boomerang effect" produced when European colonialism reinforced this state strategy with the possibility that "the West could practice something resembling colonization, or an internal colonialism, on itself."[64] Ann Stoler, extrapolating from Foucault's observation, speculates that internal French racism on the continent might have been in part "modeled" on hatred directed by French colonists at Algerian Jews for integrating the body politic when naturalized en masse by the 1870 Crémieux decree.[65] But the ideas about racial scalarity I have been trying to develop here bring to light two additional dynamics different from (though not unrelated to) the relational "modeling" of continental racism on colonial racism. The first, we have seen, is the parallel deployment of antisemitism and imperialism as spatial fixes—one internal, the other more classically external—to various tensions and anxieties internal to the metropole. The second is the very possibility of an internal spatial fix, which ceases to be a contradiction in terms once the global and national scales are understood in their interrelation as complementary facets of the maturing imperial world system. What happened abroad was now imbricated, as a material and economic matter, with what happened at home. And as I argued in previous chapters, it was no coincidence to find representations of the Jew at the point of imbrication, given the Jew's historical importance to Europeans as a figure through which to negotiate how scales might inhere in one another.

Continental antisemitism and colonial domination therefore worked intimately together, in the regenerative imperial circuit envisioned by Vogüé, to produce an ominous new national logic. That logic took

Jewish degeneration as a pretext for the linked projects of constant internal *and* external war. National Socialism would not do something dissimilar. Of course, Vogüé's looping machinery requires the circular conquest and reconquest of the same French metropolitan Jews, and thus implicitly their preservation; but keep substituting different successive Jewries for the initial one, and none need be preserved. Vichy France behaved accordingly when, a half century later and with little prompting from the Nazi occupiers, it extended metropolitan antisemitic legislation to Jewish subjects in the French colonies.

Whether or not we read Vogüé's antisemitic imperialism as anticipating Vichy's, the brisk success of *Les Morts qui parlent* closely associates it with the French right's general late-century conversion, particularly after Fashoda, to the imperial cause.[66] In this sense did modern French antisemitism contribute to the ongoing political project of empire rather than simply profit from the scalar opportunity to negotiate its own internal ideological conflicts. But there is another conflict still through which, indirectly but importantly, a burgeoning French and European antisemitism encouraged the production of scale: the confrontation between antisemites and their detractors, who sought in the scale of empire to leave the Jewish question behind once and for all. As I examine in the following chapter, the imperial imaginary's anti-antisemitic turn paradoxically furnished the basis for a new racialization to come—one that would soon concern colonized Muslims and whose effects still ripple through a contemporary Europe struggling to overcome its colonial and antisemitic histories.

CHAPTER 5

Bigger Pictures

Anti-Antisemitism and the Politics of Scale

On January 11, 2013, French jet fighters and helicopter gunships launched air strikes against Islamic militants in northern Mali. So began Operation Serval, an offensive designed to reclaim Mali's vast northern desert from a coalition of Islamist groups in control of the area since wresting power from Tuareg separatists the previous year. French air and ground forces quickly retook most of northern Mali but continue, as I write, a grinding war (now known as Operation Barkhane) against insurgents in the Sahel region spanning southern North Africa.

France's military intervention in its former colony was motivated in part by concerns that northern Mali might become a staging ground for terrorist attacks on European soil. Speaking on the eve of his first official trip to Africa in November 2012, newly elected French president François Hollande linked instability in Mali to concerns about domestic terrorism. Hollande noted the possibility of "French nationals in Mali . . . who can decide to come back to their home country with terrorist goals," as well as the government's decision to pursue charges against seven of the twelve French Muslim converts arrested some days earlier in a nationwide raid on a suspected Islamist cell.[1] DNA from the cell's leader—killed in a shootout with police during the raid—was found on the remains of a grenade thrown the preceding month into a kosher grocery store in the Parisian suburb of Sarcelles, and the cell was reported to have been planning further antisemitic attacks. With memories still fresh of the March 2012 shooting spree in southern France by self-styled Islamic extremist Mohammed Merah, four of whose victims were murdered for being Jewish, media coverage of Hollande's remarks painted a convergence between an Islamist threat to Europe and a burgeoning peril to Jews. International news service France 24, for instance, set Hollande's interview against a backdrop of "rising concern over homegrown religious extremism and anti-Semitism," locating jihadists at the intersection between two looming menaces whose conjugation has increasingly provided the terms on which Islam is understood to perform its incommensurability with European norms of tolerance.[2]

These norms assumed their contemporary shape when the "new," postwar Europe defined itself as a bulwark against the recurrence of Nazism and the Holocaust, and tolerance of Jews became a sine qua non of European belonging. In its perceived role as a continental vehicle for programmatic antisemitism, Islam thus reengenders the existential internal threat constitutive of the new Europe. This chapter treats the corresponding instrumentalization of Muslim antisemitism both as a specific product of Europe's recent postwar and postcolonial conditions and as a symptom of what I will be arguing is a deeper pattern in the long history of European responses to antisemitism. Twenty-first-century fears of violent Muslim antisemitism are reconfiguring the new Europe's antithesis—a voracious Jew-hatred that once sundered the continent—into something less congenitally European. The highest-profile attacks and plots against European Jews now seem imposed from without by ideologies and actors foreign to Europe. At least, this is the impression given by theorists of the "new antisemitism," who cite a shift from the racist antisemitism of yore to a more abstractly political antisemitism aimed at Jews by Muslims and assorted other third-worldists angry with the Israeli state.[3] Critics of the notion reply that it too conveniently absolves Europe of its historical responsibility for antisemitism, obscuring continuities between an older, indigenously European antisemitism and a newer, more globalized variant admittedly shaped by transnational Muslim solidarity against Israel.[4] Yet what will occupy me more here than the interwoven sources of a hybridized Euro-Islamic antisemitism—on whose hybridity, incidentally, the two sides often agree, though they may differ on the nature of the phenomenon produced—is how the figure itself of contemporary Muslim antisemitism follows a much older tradition of casting European reaction in external terms. Just as postcolonial migrations today encourage worried parallels between the historically internal other of continental fascism and an Islamist threat less presumably intrinsic to Europe, so did colonial circumstances prompt mappings of European reactionary thought onto subalterns in the imperial periphery.

I will return in a moment to such colonial mappings and to how they persist. Let me begin, though, by considering a different possible parallel, this one between Muslims and Jews. For Muslim antisemitism to supplant, or appear to supplant, an older, European brand of antisemitism calls to mind a dynamic usually associated with the Jewish victims—rather than the perpetrators—of antisemitism itself. Islam exteriorizes from Europe something heretofore interior, and yet paradoxically does so in the mode of internality, since (1) it is only as a presence within Europe that Islam furnishes a suitable analog for the internal fascist threat around which the new Europe coalesced; and (2) it is, at the same time, only as an interior presence arrived from without that Islam makes the exteriorization of this threat possible. Spaces fold together, contours warp and blur: Have Muslim migrations activated anew the unclassifiable liminality that so many theorists, generally operating under the umbrella of poststructuralist thought, understand antisemitism to locate in the Jews? Take Julia Kristeva, for whom antisemitism projects onto the Jew the monstrous indeterminacy between inside and outside that defines what she calls abjection.[5] Or consider Zygmunt Bauman's similar characterization of antisemitism as a "proteophobia" directed at an abstracted Jewishness made to condense every uncategorizable, undecidable ambivalence precipitated by modernity.[6]

Think, too, of Giorgio Agamben, who locates in the Jewish concentration camp victim the degree zero of a "zone of indistinction between outside and inside" where the sovereign at once destroys and reassembles the boundary separating nature from the law. By including the radically excluded bare human life of a *homo sacer* denied all rights, the sovereign symbolically contains what exceeds it and so reveals biopolitics' essential conjuring trick: a juridical order ostensibly set off against, yet predicated on the management of, biological existence.[7] Jean-François Lyotard imagines another inclusive exclusion when he describes antisemitism as a variety of the anxiety produced by what Freud called primal repression (*Urverdrängung*). Inaugurating the unconscious under the effect of an initial external shock, primal repression both enables and exceeds the system's capacity to represent, leaving the sensation of an ungraspable "stranger in the house" who "'from the exterior' lies in reserve in the interior." The Western mind responds by personifying this unsettling inhabitation as the Jew, that quintessential stranger in the house of Christianity, thereby making reassuringly visible and excisable what otherwise escapes representation and control.[8]

All of these propositions explain antisemitism as a strategy for displacing a difficult or unbearable boundary transgression onto the Jews. Do European Muslims now function the same way? The internal mark of an Islam that once defined Europe from without, might they instantiate the queer ontological merger of inside and outside, attracting a familiar revulsion? Have they become, in short, the "new Jews of Europe," as the increasingly common formula goes?[9] At least by the foregoing definition of antisemitism, the answer is no. For it is as category-reaffirming antisemites, rather than as category-confounding "Jews," that Muslims have been constructed according to the new rules of European identity. We will see how in this regard they are taken to reinscribe, not dissolve, lines of demarcation—like a division of the world into colonizers and colonized—that Europe presumes to have eclipsed. Far from being made figures of boundary transgression, Muslim antisemites have in fact been represented as static paragons of the bounded, over against which Europe elaborates the dream of its own boundarilessness.

But I do not mean the European boundarilessness that, for Jean-Claude Milner, animates a postwar European antisemitism intent on identifying the Israeli state with a recalcitrant, anachronistic nationalism thwarting the new supranational European project of an ever-unfolding "*pax europaea*."[10] "With the move toward the post-Nation-State globalization," as Slavoj Žižek puts it in a discussion of Milner, the Jew is "cast in the role of being stuck onto a Limit . . . as the obstacle on the path toward unification (not only of Europe, but also of Europe and the Arab world)."[11] Writing in 2003, before the European debt and migrant crises cast doubt on the future of the European Union, Milner underestimates how a violent resurgence of European nationalisms would come to interact with a wounded continental collectivism. In the conflict between nationalism and continentalism, another dream of European boundarilessness is taking shape, one whose desired unifications operate more as a scalar matter—in an ideological interplay between national and continental scales—than as a matter of absolute space. Žižek chides Milner for overlooking how "today it is the Muslims, and not the Jews, who are perceived as a threat and an obstacle to globalization."[12] Yet what Žižek overlooks himself is that, as I have been maintaining throughout this book, the circulations and liquidities producing ever-tighter global economic integration are as likely to reinforce as to dissolve local fixities. Fixing labor power at the national scale, for instance, is the chief brake against a generalized global migrancy in which workers would never stay long enough in one place for their labor power to be extracted. So if Muslims are fetishizable as the fly in the ointment of capital's smooth global functioning, they are equally and perhaps more importantly fetishizable, in the European context, as the object around which scales (especially, I will be arguing, the national and continental ones) can be integrated anew.

It is in their increasing status as Europe's paradigmatic antisemites, especially, that Muslims are playing the role described. And however unsurprising it might seem for Europe to put lingering colonial-era prejudices in the service of postwar continental concerns, less obvious is that the specific notion of Muslim antisemitism possesses a colonial history as well. This history is in turn framed by a broader European search, the first sketch of which I will be attempting here, for imperial paths beyond antisemitism, radical nationalism, and other hidebound impediments to internationalist and Europeanist visions emerging in the nineteenth century. In previous chapters I discussed what I call the Crémieux myth, the supposed and still widely cited resentment by Algerian Muslims over the 1870 conferral of French citizenship on Algerian Jews—a resentment only localizable, in the historical record, as a strategic construction by European antisemites. I want to add now that the figure of the Jew-hating Muslim once propagated by antisemites enjoyed such lasting purchase because of another, contemporaneous phenomenon: a European discourse *against* antisemitism, one equally molded by the imperial context and that likewise constructed Europe's colonized others into vectors of antisemitic intolerance.

If, then, nineteenth-century European antisemites peddled projections of their hatreds onto the colonized, anti-antisemitism simultaneously worked to render those projections convincing. The most vocal present-day champions of the anti-antisemitic fight—Alain Finkielkraut, Pierre-André Taguieff, Shmuel Trigano, and Emmanuel Brenner, to mention only some of the more prominent French intellectuals aligning themselves against the "new antisemitism"[13]—need not establish the plausibility of the Muslim antisemitism on which they often focus, since it genuinely exists.[14] Still, appreciating that Europe's colonial endeavors influenced early denunciations of antisemitism helps illuminate why contemporary anti-antisemitic voices so often stage the new Europe in terms of Muslim difference.

Étienne Balibar has marveled that critiques aimed specifically by Taguieff and others at Muslim antisemitism fall prey, as he puts it, to "transposing the 'Jewish conspiracy' into the 'Arab' and/or 'anti-Semitic' conspiracy." Hypothesizing the interdependence of antisemitism and Islamophobia within a same "historical and ideological complex," Balibar considers the recent notion of a Muslim conspiracy against the West to reproduce and reinforce the familiar narrative of international collusion among Jews. Should not, he asks, a scholar of antisemitism like Taguieff know better than to ape this hoariest of topoi?[15] Perhaps so. But if indeed Taguieff senses a conspiracy afoot (and he might debate the point), the model for that concern seems also traceable to fascism. After all, what is the new Europe's negative premise—the permanent latency of National Socialism—if not an eternal, internal possible conspiracy forever held at bay? And given the relative infrequency these days with which even the European extreme right makes antisemitic claims, what better totemic figure and replacement for that latency than Islamists appearing to plot inside Europe against its Jews?

My point is that current European anxieties about an intolerant Islam require analysis not only in terms of the antisemitism they might draw from and reinforce but also in terms of the foundational European anti-antisemitism with which they significantly coincide. Understood thusly, Europe's diverging attitudes toward its two Abrahamic others become less incongruous. Glossing an essay by Matti Bunzl on antisemitism and Islamophobia, Brian Klug writes of the "hidden contradiction within the supranational idea of the 'the new Europe'" produced when this idea is doubly grounded, as Bunzl proposes, in an embrace of Jews and a wariness of Muslims.[16] To the extent, however, that Muslim antisemitism is feared to encroach on a defining European tolerance, the embrace motivates the wariness, and some of the contradiction recedes. Jewish assimilation and Muslim marginalization become reconcilable, even coterminous, dimensions of the same project: a Europe ever keeping "an eye on itself," in Finkielkraut's words, the better to navigate between the Scylla of its fascist past and the Charybdis of its putatively antisemitic Muslim present.[17]

That Muslims should face exclusion not just as Muslims but as antisemites recalls Europe's history, chronicled by Gil Anidjar and others, of triangulating its identity across perceived enmities, distinctions, and similarities between Muslims and Jews.[18] Still unexplored, though, is the precedent for this exclusion set when in the nineteenth century anti-antisemitism made European hatred toward Jews a springboard for offering supranational alternatives to antisemitism's parochial attachments. The imperial project catalyzed the resultant politics of scale, affording anti-antisemitism a global frame of reference from which to contest and relativize antisemitism's narrative of Jewish dominance. This is not to forget that antisemites were themselves thinking at a global scale. As I argued in Chapter 2, the late nineteenth-century frenzy of European imperial conquest furnished modern antisemitism an opportunity to concretize the existing but abstract notion of world Jewish power into the more geopolitically persuasive threat of international Jewish colonial conspiracies. Indeed, part of what made that emergent antisemitism modern was precisely its inflection by a high imperial modernity coalescing with Europe's partitioning of the entire globe.

But this is also not to suggest that anti-antisemitism merely challenged antisemitism for a chance to steer in one ideological direction or another the European "planetary consciousness" dating, for Mary Louise Pratt, to the Age of Discovery.[19] Rather, the terrain of contention became scale itself. The late nineteenth-century debate between antisemites and anti-antisemites coincided with the moment when, according to the critical geographer Neil Smith—whose notion of a politics of scale I adapt here[20]—the European powers were reaching the apotheosis of their capitalist and territorial expansion. After that point, contends Smith, the global boundaries of space had been set, beyond which nothing larger might be discovered. Henceforth what mattered most was how, within this global context, space would be internally redivided into a shifting hierarchy of sometimes competing, sometimes overlapping scales (urban, regional, national, etc.) at which social organization unfolded.[21] Smith's early work presented these interlocking scales as products of capitalism and its requirements, rather than as abstractly given. I will be somewhat less interested here, however, in the material production of scale than in early discursive sites of scalar representation and contestation, sites falling under the broader rubric of the "social production of scales" coined later by Smith to account for scale-shaping actors, agons, and ideologies beyond capital.[22] The imperial vantage point adopted by nineteenth-century anti-antisemites certainly drove claims that antisemites failed to see the bigger picture. Yet just as important were related claims that antisemites supposedly did not understand their own embedment in the cultural and economic structures they condemned; that this was in part because they failed to recognize how the sequence of embedment or nestedness was fundamentally subject to change; and that to ignore how elements might climb, descend, or exchange places within a scalar hierarchy was to relinquish analytical credibility by misapprehending scale's very nature. Thus, for example, was the accusation of "Jewishness" sometimes made against antisemites more than just a barb thrown for easy satirical effect. What anti-antisemites were acknowledging and waging as well—albeit in ways frequently also unfriendly toward Jews—is what sociologist Neil Brenner has much more recently described as the constant, intrinsically political battle by societal forces over the "*hierarchization* and *rehierarchization*" of scalar units.[23]

It is no accident that antisemites should especially have prompted this sort of reaction from their contemporaries, since the Jewish question had begun as a European rumination on the Jews' fitness to occupy one level of social organization (citizenship) without simultaneously operating seditiously at another (religious belonging). Smith credits Marx's dialectical materialism and theory of value with helping to recognize the man-made production of space, and by extension of scale.[24] When it comes, though, to the associated idea of scalar rehierarchization, Marx seems to have been ahead of the curve as well and to have found special inspiration in discourses about Jews. So far I have used the term "anti-antisemitism" to describe opposition to a modern ideological movement that, after Wilhelm Marr began using the German neologism *Antisemitismus* in 1879, was understood as such. But already in 1844, Marx had taken a critique of German Jewry as his foil in an essay calling for a more expansive approach to human liberation than what the state might accomplish. No one would mistake that essay, "On the Jewish Question," as an indictment by Marx of anti-Jewish sentiment per se; indeed, Marx takes a view of the Jews dim enough ("What is the secular cult of the Jew? *Haggling*")[25] for Bernard Lewis to label the essay "one of the classics of anti-Semitic propaganda."[26] Others have maintained that Marx's comments on Jewish emancipation, and attendant pronouncements about Jews, merely constitute an unfortunate device for offering an otherwise legitimate reflection on the deficiencies of liberal political philosophy.[27] Yet either to discount Marx's essay as an embarrassment or to qualify it by bracketing off his choice of signifier for economic greed is to stop at the most pedestrian formulation of Marx's prejudice—that Jews love money—without considering his more conceptually pregnant insinuation that a European Jewish minority had made everyone else love money, too. Once enveloping Christianity, then enveloped by it, Jewishness had, in this understanding, risen quietly back up again to contain its surroundings.

Such a reversal, spurious though we obviously recognize it to be, everywhere shadows the fundamental rehierarchization that Marx himself prescribes. In the essay, he chastises his former mentor and fellow Young Hegelian Bruno Bauer for proposing that German Jews were unworthy of political emancipation by the German state since they were not first willing to emancipate themselves from the yoke of religion. Bauer, counters Marx, is guilty of a category mistake, having confused political emancipation for general emancipation. While the modern state might confer certain useful freedoms, like freedom of conscience, it nonetheless largely relegates questions like religion and property to the private realm of "civil society" (220). Real general emancipation, Marx concludes, would function at the level of that larger civil society—at the level of humanity's basic and collective "species-life," as he puts it (230)—to emancipate man from man by transforming the nature of economic relations.

If Marx's objection to Bauer turns on Bauer's too-narrow fixation with Jewish religiosity as a barometer of human enslavement, Marx hardly leaves the Jewish question behind in the passage he imagines from political to general emancipation. "The *emancipation of the Jews*," he notoriously declares, "is, in the last analysis, the emancipation of mankind from *Judaism*" (237, original emphasis). Marx means that the Jews, like everyone else, will be free only once the shackles of "money" are broken (Marx had not, at this point, begun to think in terms of "capital") (236). And implicit in this declaration is a tactic that later in the century would become explicit. Bauer, Marx suggests, fails to appreciate fully how the Jews' monetary "self-interest" has woven its way into the social fabric (236). For Bauer to place his hopes in the German state is hence to trust an institution that, by virtue of its falsely universalizing abstraction from the material, civil particulars that really matter, in fact mystifies its own subsumption under the larger, "Jewish" social order. To put it simply, at least according to Marx, Bauer's anti-Jewish critique finds him unsuspectingly operating within a Jewish paradigm.

Marx's basic stratagem would receive more overt expression by a coming generation of commentators appalled at antisemitism's emergence as an organized, self-conscious force. The rise of empire increasingly shaped this reaction. Taking antisemites as dupes of the "Jewish" system they attacked, and therefore as figures of a stubborn boundedness oblivious to the real workings of scale, anti-antisemites made antisemitism a common measure of rigidity against which to perform—but also around which to negotiate—empire's complex scalar gymnastics. Once antisemitism had been fashioned into a standard of blinkered ignorance, it became possible, for example, to paint vastly different peoples and places with the same brush. Thus might antisemitic Frenchmen or Germans whose resolute particularism frustrated attempts at national or European cohesion provide a template for thinking the obstacle posed by colonized subalterns to imperial cohesion. And thus, in turn, might projects awkwardly playing out at different scales be made to appear more self-consistent, despite flagrant contradictions between, say, democratic institutions on the continent and tyrannical colonizations undertaken abroad in their name. Jean-Paul Sartre famously described how the latter tension was managed by considering the colonized less human than their European masters, and hence exempt from the protections of universal human rights.[28] It could be just as ideologically advantageous, however, to treat the colonized as precisely *like* certain elements in the European population.

The outcome ought not be confused with those transcontinental circulations of prejudice usually theorized under the dominant conceptual premise of what, after David Theo Goldberg, I have been calling racial relationality: namely, the assumption that racializing logics and technologies directed at one people have historically been transferable to another.[29] Critics often document, for example, how Jewishness at times provided a ready domestic category through which to apprehend other kinds of difference (Muslim, black, etc.) encountered by Europeans in the imperial periphery.[30] Largely overlooked, however, is that antisemitism, too, became a flexible designation for marking some of the same difference as anathema to metropolitan ideals. For nineteenth-century French antisemites so confidently to report Muslim antisemitism in North Africa obviously evinced some relationality, since they were essentializing colonial subalterns in terms consonant with French antisemites' own cavalierly reductive attitude toward Jewish difference. Anti-antisemites, on the other hand, embraced the trope of Muslim antisemitism only after white European antisemites had first been treated as excessively nationalist or otherwise provincial obstacles to sweeping imperial visions.

I will have further occasion to reflect on the resultant, centuries-long projection of European prejudice onto Muslims, as well as on the continuing inducement that projection offers to decolonize the fight against antisemitism. Let me only say now that there is more than just a historical irony in judging Muslims' capacity for postcolonial European assimilation on the basis of their tolerance toward Jews, whose own fitness for assimilation into the secular body politic once animated eighteenth- and nineteenth-century European debates about citizenship. There is also a historical linkage between the Jewish question and imperial domination that eventually positioned Islam—and the Islamophobic reactions it elicits—at the nexus between Europe's postwar and postcolonial trajectories.[31]

One can complicate, on this basis, the central distinction drawn by Bunzl between modern (or "old") European antisemitism and the comparatively recent phenomenon of Islamophobia. The former, he holds, came into being as a nineteenth-century racializing attempt at "national purification," while the latter questions Islam's more broadly civilizational compatibility with the new Europe.[32] Though certainly fair, the distinction nevertheless obscures how reactions against the first cultural logic anticipated the second. In the pages that follow, I explore how responses to modern antisemitism provided key conceptual scaffolding to those who in the nineteenth century sought to think beyond nationalism and the nation-state. Over a century before France's postcolonial military operation in Mali, the French novelist Émile Zola made colonial Mali (then known as French Sudan) the linchpin of a utopic imperialism envisioned as a rejoinder to antisemitic corruptions of nationalism back home. Likewise did Friedrich Nietzsche's Europeanism, Marx's socialism, and other supranational outlooks emerge reinforced from an encounter with Jews that, filtered through the lens of anti-antisemitism, offered the potential for a metaphysical rescaling of perspective. Precisely because modern antisemitism so fixated on national purity did anti-antisemitic thinkers seize on imperial circumstances to develop new vistas on the world. And it is partly on the basis of such vistas that Islam would be constructed into a cosmic threat to supranational Europe.

What was the supranational, however, that it should evolve in this fashion? Turning especially to Zola and Nietzsche, the following readings situate these authors' oft-discussed pronouncements about Jews and antisemitism within their lesser-noted relation to empire. The supranational visions that subsequently come into focus differ in kind.

But they also resemble each other in method. Exploring this shared modality, or politics of scale, I am especially interested to examine the structural role it created for an antisemitic other deployable across a broad range of geographic and ideological contexts. Neither Zola nor Nietzsche devoted much attention to Islam. I will be demonstrating, nonetheless, how Islam was only too easily made to play the antisemitic role they conceived and how a modified politics of scale still troublesomely underpins contemporary anti-antisemitic responses to Muslim antisemitism.

BEYOND THE BOURSE: ZOLA, EMPIRE, AND THE JEWS

Seeing some people to his left, two women and a man, he thought he would ask them. But as he approached the woman fled, and the men warned him away with threatening gestures. He saw yet more, and they all avoided him, running off into the bushes like creeping and furtive animals, sordidly dressed, unspeakably dirty, with bandits' dishonest faces. Realizing then that the dead, where this horrid lot had passed, were shoeless with pale, bare feet, he finally understood that these were the prowling thieves who followed the German armies, the looters of cadavers, a coarse and predacious Jewry following in the wake of the invasion.

In 1892 when it was published, this forbidding literary tableau depicting the corpse-strewn aftermath of France's 1870 defeat by the Germans would have felt familiar in more ways than one. The apocalyptic tenor of the description suited the hand-wringing with which had been received the loss that cost France its provinces of Alsace and Lorraine. To readers of Édouard Drumont's best-selling 1886 antisemitic treatise *La France juive*, the passage also inevitably recalled a central argument of Drumont's polemic, one he had not invented but that he probably did more than anyone to propagate: namely, that the Franco-Prussian War had unleashed on France a horde of German Jews bent on exploiting their host country. Specious though it was, this narrative could draw reinforcement from the very real emigration toward the center of France of the approximately 10,000 Jews who chose French citizenship upon Germany's 1871 annexation of Alsace and Lorraine. Settling primarily in Paris, these displaced French Jews keyed resentment among their new neighbors.[33] The resulting myth of Judeo-Germanic invasion gained sufficient currency that even Émile Zola gave it some measure of credence—a fact evinced by the passage above, drawn from his novel *La Débâcle* chronicling the final collapse of the Second Empire in the mud of Sedan.[34]

Such an occasional brush by Zola with Drumontian conspiracy theory explains why Theodor Adorno could once remark that "no matter how energetically Zola, the defender of Captain Dreyfus, fought against hatred of the Jews, elements can be found in his own works which could be classed as identical with official anti-Semitism."[35] Adorno perhaps overdramatizes the case, but not by much. How is it that so eloquent and renowned a foe of antisemitism as Zola—progenitor of the modern public intellectual, author of the 1898 cri de coeur "J'Accuse," steadfast denouncer of the "infamies" spread by antisemites[36]—continued to populate his novels with coarse Jewish stereotypes even after he had taken his impassioned public stances in support of French Jews? How, for instance, could Zola declare so reasonably in his 1902 novel about the Dreyfus Affair, *Vérité* (*Truth*), that "there was no Jewish Question, there was only the question of hoarded wealth," only immediately to proffer as archetypally vampiric a Jew as the predatory financier Baron Nathan, with his "thick nose" and his "predator's eyes sunken beneath deep brows"?[37] Why this schizophrenic rhythm of exoneration and indictment?

Zola's famous biological determinism offers a preliminary answer. In "Pour les juifs" ("For the Jews"), an 1896 article published in *Le Figaro*, Zola takes antisemites to task for denouncing Jewish avarice—but not because he considers the accusation untrue. Of the Jews' supposed "need for lucre" and "love of money," Zola declares flatly that "all this is true." The abruptness of the concession to antisemitic discourse functions rhetorically to contrast the implied banality of these observations with the depth of Zola's impending diagnosis. "If one states the fact, one must explain it," he scolds, before citing the historical relegation of the Jews to the financial trades by their Gentile oppressors as evidence that "the Jews, in their present state, are our own doing, the outcome of eighteen hundred years of idiotic persecution." Yet the content of the concession proves no less starkly literal. Jews love money, Zola postulates, because centuries of usury have produced accumulated physiological results in the usurer: "With nimble brains, trained by centuries of heredity," Jews are conditioned in their very biology to turn a profit.[38] If, then, Zola grants the Jews an exculpatory asterisk next to the antisemitic thesis of innate Jewish avarice, he simultaneously legitimizes the slur by furnishing it an elaborate socio-scientific basis.

Thus did Zola's denunciations of antisemitism not preclude representing Jews in unflattering terms. Zola could deploy essentializing fantasies about Jewish cupidity while disagreeing nonetheless that such apparent racial shortcomings justified programmatic hatred. Adorno's two Zolas, in other words, coincide plausibly (if not pleasantly) enough, to the point that the whole question emerges as something of a red herring. Sensational as the juxtaposition between Zola's antisemitic caricatures and denunciations of antisemitism remains, little is gained from contrasting the two. Or rather, little is gained from sketching the contrast in absolute terms, as if Zola's best and worst tendencies were locked in a duel for the soul of the author. This is because Zola's anti-antisemitism does more than temper the blame he elsewhere ascribes to Jews. It also triggers a perspectival shift that finds him looking beyond the Jew for world-explanatory answers. The effort, we will see, requires for Zola an imperial frame of reference. Yet despite Zola's conscious and creditable attempt, in his anti-antisemitism, to look beyond the Jew, the nature of the undertaking has a funny way of rediscovering the Jew at every turn. For what matters as much to Zola as antisemites' misreading of the larger planetary economy that contains them is their own ironic, unheeding participation in the smaller "Jewish" economy that Zola still mistakenly considers to exist. And it is only together that these two scalar blind spots—one belonging to Zola, the other to his antisemitic targets—make antisemitism so effective a foil for Zola's saccharine vision of French global hegemony.

Zola's 1891 novel *L'Argent* (*Money*) opens in 1864 on its protagonist Aristide Saccard, a veteran speculator who has lost the real estate fortune accumulated earlier in the twenty-volume *Rougon-Macquart* cycle that made Zola a literary superstar. Awed by the possibilities of the Bourse, the Parisian stock market exchange reaching new heights of popularity during this time, Saccard decides to launch a gigantic Banque Universelle. Saccard subsequently meets Paul and Caroline Hamelin, a brother and sister back from a long stay in Egypt and Syria. His imagination inflamed by Caroline's poetic accounts of her travels and her engineer brother's ambitious but underfunded industrial plans for the renewal of virgin lands in Turkey and the Levant, Saccard decides to focus the Banque Universelle's attentions eastward. This strategy proves irresistible to investors fascinated with the Orient in all its imagined biblical and Arabian Nights splendor. After a stunning ascent comes an even swifter fall, as the backroom manipulations of Saccard and his equally larcenous coterie of insiders precipitate the bank's spectacular demise. Even as things crumble in Paris, however, a few of the bank's Eastern projects continue to flourish, marking the utopic stirrings of a "humanity of tomorrow" in an Oriental world far away.[39]

France's relation to that world in *L'Argent* can only be characterized as imperialist. Despite Zola's wry commentary on the avidity of an investing public whose Ali Baba dreams make the Banque Universelle's Oriental projects so initially successful, the unquestioned suppositions of those projects—that Turks or Levantines are incapable of fructifying their own lands, and that by extension it falls to the West to accomplish what the East cannot—remain the suppositions of imperialist logic. Projecting back onto the Second Empire the colonial chauvinism of the age of empire in which Zola wrote his novel, *L'Argent*'s narrator punctuates Paul Hamelin's exposition of his plans for a vast Eastern transportation syndicate with the breathless assessment that "it was a scheme worthy of a savvy organizer and great patriot: this was the Orient conquered and given to France" (62).

Henri Mitterand suggests that the unaccomplished Turkish designs of Eugène Bontoux, president of the ill-fated Union Générale bank upon which Banque Universelle is modeled, might have steered Zola toward the Orient.[40] Whether or not this is true, there is no doubt that Zola set out in *L'Argent* to fictionalize one of the resounding French financial disasters of the second half of the nineteenth century. Founded in 1878, the Union Générale benefited from the charismatic salesmanship of Bontoux, an engineer and entrepreneur who pitched the bank to investors as a Catholic enterprise. The bank, Bontoux claimed, would restore financial security to a dispossessed papacy whose last remnant of the Papal States had been wrested away in 1870 by the recently unified Kingdom of Italy (an event received in France as both a religious and a national affront, since the seizure occurred when France, occupied by the Franco-Prussian War, could no longer hold the garrison Napoleon III had used to maintain protective sovereignty over the pope's Roman enclave). With unprecedented financial backing from the clergy, conservative nobility, and other fervent Catholics both humble and rich, the Union Générale engaged in all manner of industrial investments stretching from France to the Balkan outskirts of the Austro-Hungarian Empire. Unfortunately, Bontoux proved less scrupulous in his business practices than in his attendance to Catholic anxieties. Following an epic period of feverish speculation that allowed the bank to quadruple its capital in just a few short years, 1882 brought total collapse. Gnawed from within by its own risky penchant for speculating on its own stock shares, as well as by a host of other likely chicaneries large and small, the bank left in its wake a swath of financial destruction that would loom large in the French psyche for years to come.

In the aftermath of the Union Générale's demise, many attributed the crash to short selling by the Rothschild family and the usual shady cabal of Jewish financiers. Bontoux himself helped shape this fiction, first by overtly positioning his enterprise as a challenge to the "big Jewish banks" and later by accusing the Rothschilds of having targeted his bank in retaliation. Historians of French antisemitism generally cite the crash as a trigger for the wave of antisemitism that swept over the country during the remainder of the decade.[41] Novelists did their part to ensure that the failure of the Union Générale, and the lessons supposedly to be drawn from it about Jewish treachery, lodged deeply in the national consciousness. Mitterand catalogues nearly a dozen novels produced in the subsequent few months and years that were directly or likely inspired by the crash.[42] *L'Argent* represents the best-known entry in this literary corpus.

Readers of *L'Argent* need not look long for evidence that Zola had internalized the easy association between the Union Générale episode and the commonplace of Jewish financial domination. Zola populates the world of the Bourse with a veritable taxonomy of Jewish speculators and middlemen as united in their essentialized typicality as in their obsessive love of money. Kolb, "whose nose, like an eagle's beak . . . betrayed his Jewish origin," spends his days surrounded by shovelfuls of gold pieces that he converts into ingots for the purposes of arbitrage (109). The villainous Busch, who makes a disagreeable living enforcing debts he has purchased on the cheap, is first introduced as he peers "in ecstasy" at the way a ruby catches the sunlight. Around him teems

> a group of unclean Jews with fat, shiny faces and the desiccated profiles of voracious birds, an extraordinary assembly of typical Jewish noses, huddled together as if gathering over a prey, fighting amid guttural cries and seemingly ready to devour each other. (24)

Nathansohn, whose "Jewish flair" causes him to bet successfully against the Banque Universelle even if it means betraying his associate Saccard

(327), inspires another character to remark that "you have to be a Jew" in order to successfully play the stock market; "without that, no sense trying to understand, one doesn't have the knack" (30). And above them all reigns Gundermann, the novel's James de Rothschild figure and the undisputed "master of the Bourse and of the world" toward whose fortune flow inexorably "all the rivers of gold" (21, 90–91).

Yet having established the novel's panoramic backdrop of low-level, reflexive antisemitic caricature, Zola suddenly offers up a rebuke of overt antisemitism. Saccard's hatred of and rivalry with Gundermann, patterned after Bontoux's bitter antagonism for the Rothschilds, occasion antisemitic rants by the banker designed to mark a distance between Zola and the prejudices of his flawed hero. On his way to see Gundermann, Saccard launches into an antisemitic mental tirade whose irrationality and hypocrisy the narrator pointedly underlines:

> Ah! The Jew! He felt toward the Jew the old racial rancor that is found especially in the south of France. It was like a revolt of his very flesh, a revulsion of the skin, which, at the idea of the slightest contact, filled him with uncontrollable disgust and violence beyond all reason. But the peculiar thing was that he, Saccard, this fearsome mogul, this financial headhunter with unclean hands, lost all self-awareness as soon as a Jew was involved, speaking caustically of the Jew with the vengeful indignation of an honest man who lives from the sweat of his brow and is innocent of any usurious dealings. (91)

In a second jeremiad against the Jews, Saccard blames his bank's failure on the "dirty Jew" Gundermann, just as Bontoux had accused the Rothschilds of toppling the Union Générale (384). But the saintly Caroline, Zola's mouthpiece throughout the novel, calmly demurs:

> "What a strange thing!" Madame Caroline murmured quietly, with her vast knowledge and universal tolerance. "For me, the Jews are men like any others. If they are apart, it's because they've been put there." (385)

This is the Zola so fondly remembered for later entreating his readers to eschew what in 1897 he termed the "fierce monomania" of antisemitism.[43]

Evidence points to a change of heart by Zola during the preparation and writing of *L'Argent* that perhaps explains the novel's herky-jerky discourse about Jews. Critics have observed that *L'Argent* does not reprise Bontoux's version of events, according to which Jewish financiers had joined with other anti-Catholic forces to sink the Union Générale.[44] In the novel, Saccard's own illegal manipulations are enough to send the Banque Universelle hurtling toward disaster; Gundermann simply profits from the inevitable, delivering a coup de grâce to the bank in the process. It seems, however, that Zola began the project amenable to Bontoux's antisemitic conspiracy theory. Richard Grant has shown that according to Zola's detailed notes for the novel, the novelist initially reserved for Gundermann a rather more sinister role:

> I see that the simplest thing would be to make my Jewish banker a Prussian Jew who plainly hopes for Germany's triumph, and who gladly supports her financially, while remaining careful enough not to give himself away.[45]

Grant rightfully points out that the sentiment might as well have belonged to Drumont, who accused Protestant Germany of making common cause with the Jews against Catholic France.[46] Thus motivated, the treacherous first iteration of Gundermann would have had every reason to behave according to Bontoux's delusional script. But Zola's mania for research led him away from this temptation. The court case prompted by the crash furnished Zola with accounts of the bank's various imprudences and illegalities. Zola's interviews with the banker Georges Lévy disabused Zola of any remaining notion that Jews had orchestrated the downfall of the Union Générale. Given the sheer scale of the forces at work in the Bourse, Lévy explained to Zola, one might profitably predict—but never actually provoke—a given shift in the market.[47] "Truth, at the Bourse, is an all-powerful force," noted Zola in summary, adding that "logic reigns. It is it that ultimately prevails."[48] Lévy's assessment enters the novel in the form of Gundermann's patient, calculating investment strategy:

> His theory was that one could not provoke events at the Bourse, one could at most foresee and profit from them once they had happened. Logic alone reigned, and truth, in speculation as everywhere else, was an all-powerful force. As soon as the share prices became too inflated they would collapse: the fall would then happen with mathematical certainty, and

> he would simply be there to see his calculation through and pocket his gain. (202)

Having initially flirted with a more villainous Gundermann, Zola ultimately opted for a version of events in which his Rothschild figure merely capitalizes on the damage Saccard has already caused himself.

Zola, however, was of too eschatological a cast of mind to accept that Jewish behavior might prove subordinate to so abstractly neutral a force as "logic." Mankind, for Zola, must be moving toward some destiny or another. "Without lust, would there be many children?" asks Saccard early on, advancing the analogical formula that will become the novel's touchstone: without the excesses of speculation, modern industrial progress would be impossible, just as the excesses of lust render possible the propagation of the species (135). Money, according to Zola's dialectical reasoning, is the fertilizing dung heap from which a new humanity will spring in the East from the ruins of the West. Typically for the era of decadentist alarm in which he wrote, Zola advances that the metropole has fallen prey to a devouring capitalism for which the Jew represents a privileged signifier; and typically for the era of empire, he prescribes the magical counterproperties of a growing imperial periphery.

But unlike, say, Melchior de Vogüé, a contemporary who later in the decade would seek salvation abroad for a supposedly Jew-ridden France, Zola never considered the imperial periphery a regenerative staging ground from which to purge the metropole of its Semitic decadence.[49] Rather, he located in empire an opportunity to transcend a metropolitan level of analysis dominated by fears of the Jew—a gesture that, though certainly conditioned by unsavory assumptions about Jewish financial preeminence in France, also represents an attempt to exorcise his own dependence on the reductive explanatory power of antisemitic ideology.

Zola's notes for *L'Argent* reflect his desire to transcend antisemitic ideology's obsessive explanation of every phenomenon in terms of the Jew. Writing in his preparatory *ébauche* (plan), Zola recorded his ambition to find for the developing story "something in the end that shows the power of money above even this question of the Jews, which in my opinion shrinks everything."[50] That "something" required a scale that would allow Zola sufficient perspective from which to pan back and reveal the epic order of things. Though Zola was already a past master of the technique—a defining aspect, indeed, of the Zolian style—his new novel would approach things on a supranational scale unprecedented in the *Rougon-Macquart*. At first, Zola simply imagined a vaguely defined "deserted scrubland where a city, a new people, would grow thanks to speculation, while back in Paris gambling would make everything fall apart."[51] From there the Orient logically imposed itself. Bontoux's real-life Oriental designs aside, no such "deserted scrubland" was more readily available to the French imagination than the topos of the fertile but neglected Oriental desert, its biblical fecundity dormant beneath what *L'Argent*'s narrator calls "the ignorance and dirt of centuries" (75). The nineteenth century's "Oriental Renaissance," as Raymond Schwab has dubbed it, had consecrated the Romantic notion of a fusion of Occident and Orient in which mankind would be reborn, a notion dear to the Saint-Simonians whose mystical progressivism saturates Zola's novel.[52] If Zola was to pick a virgin site for the cradle of a new civilization, it was hard to miss the archetype of such renewal into which the Orient had long been constructed.

All of this explains why the same character, Caroline, articulates both the novel's defense of the Jews and its vision of Oriental renewal. The two in effect represent different facets of a same project. Caroline closes the novel with a rhapsodic meditation on the "new harvest of men" emerging in the East from the "still-warm ruins" of the Banque Universelle, capping her role throughout the novel as an ambassador for Zola's vitalist conviction in the circle of life (397–98). The more of the world Zola manages in this fashion to include in his philosophical frame, the easier it becomes to dismiss Jewish financial domination as something rather less primordial than the world-moving force antisemitic doctrine held it to be. Measured against the (imperial) ebb and flow of life itself, Zola proposes, Jewish influence becomes but a detail in a grander metaphysical scheme.

Zola had not always been, nor would he always be, an imperial enthusiast. His zeal in *L'Argent* for an "Orient conquered and given to France" revises the skepticism about imperial investments previously on display in the *Rougon-Macquart*. Sixteen novels earlier in *La Curée* (*The Kill*), Zola had ridiculed the "Arabian Nights" delusions peddled to investors in the "Société Générale des Ports du Maroc" (General Moroccan Port Company), a colossal boondoggle helmed by one of Saccard's many dubious associates.[53] Though Zola again mocked the Ali Baba dreams of Saccard's hapless shareholders in *L'Argent*, he now added a caveat: in the virgin promise of a conquered Orient, the basest of motives might still yield civilization-enhancing results. During the rest of his career Zola would toggle between these two dialectical poles of empire in unpredictable fashion. The political intrigue of *Paris*, the 1898 coda to Zola's three-novel *Trois villes* (*Three Cities*) cycle, revolves around systematic graft associated with an African railroad project. This did not stop Zola from doubling down the following year on the nascent imperial fervor of *L'Argent*, delivering in his 1899 novel *Fécondité* an extended panegyric on the colonial bliss awaiting France in French Sudan. Three years later, in *Vérité*, the pendulum swings back toward skepticism, with the reader learning that the Jewish Baron Nathan has emerged "fattened again by a recent theft of one hundred million, a colonial affair."[54]

There is, nonetheless, a certain consistency about Zola's representations of empire. Subtly but steadily, Zola works to uncouple the imperial from the realm of Jewish financial domination. To be sure, Baron Nathan's "colonial affair" in *Vérité* at first seems to recycle the theme of the colonially conspiring Jew, a figure that had emerged from suspicions about the financial motives for France's late-century frenzy of imperial expansion into Africa and Southeast Asia.[55] Significantly, however, Zola goes on to describe Baron Nathan's ill-gotten colonial gains as "a colossal pillaged booty *that he had been obliged to share with a Catholic bank*."[56] The oblique reference to the Catholic Banque Universelle in *L'Argent* recalls how, in that novel, it was in fact the Catholic speculator Saccard—and not the panoply of Jews surrounding him—who hatched various imperial schemes.

In *Paris*, Zola likewise makes the kingpin of the African railroad conspiracy a degenerate Gentile bourgeois, Duvillard, rather than his Jewish rival Steinberger. One of four brothers who, like the actual Rothschild brothers, are spread across various financial capitals in Europe, Steinberger is said by the narrator to participate in his brothers' "secret association" wielding "a fantastic power, an international and omnipotent sovereignty over Europe's financial markets." But there is a chink in the armor: Steinberger is "nevertheless the least wealthy of the four," and his financial dominion is contested by a Gentile peer, Duvillard, who counters the Steinberger family's continental influence with an intercontinental influence all his own.[57] My point is that what matters more to Zola than the probity or justifiability of the imperial project is that it exists, that it does so more or less independently of the Jewish sphere, and that it consequently affords him a totalizing perspective over and above the antisemitic conspiracy narrative "which shrinks everything."

"JEWISH" ANTISEMITES

Hence do the anti-antisemitic pronouncements in *L'Argent* coincide with an Archimedean recalibration in vantage point. Against the romanticized canvas of an economically colonized Orient, Zola purports to look beyond the excesses of the Bourse and its Jews for a larger, more optimistic human truth. That such a truth should come at the expense of an imperial subaltern, effaced throughout, marks the enterprise as naive. That this truth should come at the expense of antisemites, however, otherwise reveals a fairly sophisticated rhetorical mechanism at work. Zola rejects the characterization by modern antisemitism of the Jews as prime movers at the center of a world conspiracy. At the same time, though, his attempted imperial transcendence of antisemitism encodes no less questionable a construct: namely, that Jewish financial hegemony in France is sufficient to blind even antisemites to their own participation in the resulting order. "I know for one some Christians who are very distinguished Jews," he ironizes in "Pour les juifs."[58] Zola means superficially to suggest that financial acumen is accessible to non-Jews, and he does so within the context of a reasonable-sounding entreaty to French Gentiles that they simply work harder rather than complain about Jewish successes. Yet by designating as "Jewish" the very notion of financial ascendancy, whether or not that ascendancy belongs to actual Jews, Zola naturalizes the idea of the imposition by Jews of their ethos on society at large.

Sounding like Marx, Zola implies that capitalist France marches to the tune of its most potent minority. It is a weak version of the strong antisemitic thesis: rejecting, to his credit, any literal notion that "the Jews, as we are told, [are] the absolute masters of power and money," Zola nonetheless posits a systemic uptake of the "Jewish" temperament.[59] And especially key is that, for Zola, antisemites themselves prove least aware of this synecdochic annexation of the national whole by an ethnic part. Devoid of perspective on the possibility that if the Jews "are apart, it's because they've been put there," Zola's antisemites similarly lack perspective on their complicity in the Jewishness they decry.

In fact, to hear Zola describe them, antisemites might as well *be* Jews. We have seen how *L'Argent*'s narrator tweaks the antisemitic Saccard for hypocritically railing against "Jewish" behavior he himself exhibits (a reciprocality reinforced by the fact that, as Mitterand proposes, Saccard's adventures may also have been inspired by those of the disgraced Jewish bankers Jules-Isaac Mirès and Émile and Isaac Péreire).[60] Antisemites elsewhere become Jews, at least figuratively, when in *Vérité* Zola makes the Jew-baiting Catholic Church exploit the murder of a Jewish child. Turning on its head the ancient blood libel according to which Jews ritually sacrificed Christian children, Zola here slyly inscribes the Dreyfus-era antisemitic Church within what in *Paris* he calls the "old Semitic dream" of its Jewish forebears.[61]

Taking antisemites as his target, Zola is simultaneously at pains to underscore the Jewish influence they unwittingly reproduce. The result may seem contradictory, and justifiably so. For Zola, it is also productive. Had he focused in *L'Argent* solely on Jewish financial chicanery in the Bourse, Zola would merely have indulged in xenophobia, flogging the usual narrative of a host nation beset by German Jewish aliens like Kolb, Busch, Nathansohn, and Gundermann. By tackling antisemitism as well, however, he turns further afield. What Zola's myopic antisemites misapprehend is scale: just as they obliviously inhabit a greater "Jewishness" risen from below, they are also incapable of the lofty analytical remove from which, for Zola, the Jewish question recedes in importance. Considered from this standpoint, the imperial tenor of Zola's anti-antisemitism establishes an interesting symmetry. If, at the national level, the sensibilities of a Jewish part have unduly permeated the French whole, Zola proposes to rectify matters by infusing an even larger whole—*L'Argent*'s Oriental empire-in-progress—with the still-salvageable energies of French ingenuity that will replicate for mankind what has degraded at home. To a theological model of Jewish exemplarity that, in his secularized and corrupted version of it, sees Jewish particularity deleteriously translated into a social universal, Zola opposes the more Christlike leadership of a nation that patiently sets the example for all. Zola would later recapitulate this distinction in similarly imperial terms. In his notes for *Justice*, the planned final novel in his aptly named *Quatre Évangiles* (*Four Evangels*) cycle, Zola metaphorizes the struggle for global preeminence as a contrast between the violence of the Old Testament and the benevolence of the New: the British, "having taken from the Jew his Jehovah" by anointing themselves an imperial "chosen people," must cede the global crown to a new Gallic Messiah, "a messianic, savior, redemptive France" charged as a "directing nation" with exporting democracy and science to the world.[62]

The intended fate of the Jews in any such supersessionary script, even a secularized one like this, is to fade away. Zola prescribes their disappearance into the social body: "Embrace the Jews, in order to absorb them among us without a trace. Enrich ourselves with their qualities, since they possess some."[63] That is what comes to pass in *Vérité* when, in a future Republican utopia racially homogenized by generations of intermarriage, the descendants of Zola's noble Jewish stand-ins for the beleaguered Dreyfus cease to exist as Jews.[64] Yet to erase the Jew in this fashion, however peaceably, is only to reprise the commonplace of the Jew as impediment to national cohesion. At the global-imperial scale of France's messianic redemption and reshaping of the world—the scale to have been embraced by *Justice*'s never-completed portrait of peace on earth—it is actually antisemites who, unable to see beyond the Jewish question and their racial prejudices, impede the cohesion of Zola's greater Humanity.

Stepping into the fly-in-the-ointment role typically reserved for their antagonists, antisemites here again become Jews. But the two are not exactly interchangeable. The Jews' understood status as a "nation within the nation" and an "international sect, with no real homeland,"[65] qualities that rendered them suspect in the century of national unifications, poses a less obvious threat to supranational solidarity than the "antisemitism, nationalism, Boulangism" and other such manifestations of what Zola considers a reactionary archaism anathema to human progress. If France is to realize its civilizing imperial destiny by counterposing an internationalist gospel of justice and industry to the "Anglo-Saxon" model of militaristic, Kiplingesque colonial conquest, it must renounce these parochial withdrawals into God and country.[66]

The advantage for Zola of this international-cum-imperial perspective is that it facilitates his ideological venture beyond the blinders of the national without sacrificing the gains achieved when the egalitarian nation rose from the ashes of the monarchy. Marrying political gradualism with an idealized economic expansionism, he tackles the quandary articulated in *Paris*, his rebuke of the anarchist bombings that shook France in 1892–94 and culminated with the fatal 1894 stabbing of President Sadi Carnot. Zola disputes the wisdom of the tabula rasa sought by that novel's hero, Guillaume Froment, a brilliant chemist and revolutionary anarchist out to blow up the Sacré-Coeur basilica, and eventually the social order, with a terrifying new super-bomb. There is no guarantee, warns Zola, that a violently leveled civilization might not just reconstitute its previous iniquities or produce worse ones still: "But what danger, what delay even, if one went back without knowing by what road, amid the ruinous chaos, one would regain lost time!"[67]

Better to start anew while preserving the legacy of 1789. But where, and how? The imperial periphery furnished a temptingly expeditious answer to both questions. There France might selectively extract the best in itself, a century of sociopolitical progress emerging reinvigorated from the accumulated sludge of metropolitan decay.

The silver quarried at the Banque Universelle's Carmel mine (in what is today Israel) resonates doubly in this context, modeling the extraction of hidden value while providing a silver lining, literally, to the debasement of *l'argent* (the metal) into its corrupting metonym *l'argent* (money). The bank's grasping French investors count on precisely that debasement, convinced that the bank will in fact coax money from the earth itself, and the mine's riches are certainly drawn into a circuit of capitalist exchange originating with the Bourse.[68] But alongside that circuit Zola reports the birth of "a whole civilization" in the formerly desolate Carmel valley, with "roads, factories, schools" surviving the bank's Parisian demise (397). So providential a miracle in the desert smacks of what André Wurmser calls a "utopic capitalism," with Zola envisioning a redeemable industrial result branching off, in this "people regenerated by work" (63), from a less savory finance capital emanating from the metropole.[69] One is reminded of corporatist fin-de-siècle reactionaries who, as I examined in a previous chapter, saw in empire an opportunity to wrench a "good" agro-industrial mode of capital from the metropolitan clutches of "bad" Jewish finance. Zola's valorization of silver also echoes nineteenth-century European and American debates about the gold standard, which pitted the interests of a rising industrial urban class touting gold's non-inflationary merits against a traditional agrarian class favoring silver's inflationary properties.[70] In 1890, the year Zola began writing his novel, "silverites" were already doing battle with "gold-bugs" in the United States to position silver, in the words of one historian, "as the money of the people, as contrasted to gold, the money of the rich."[71] Zola draws the same basic populist distinction, contrasting gold's unnerving fungibility (think of Kolb melting gold pieces into ingots) with the more reassuringly concrete benefits derived by working men from honest labor in the silver mine.

Zola, however, resisted some of the more extreme temptations associated with reductionist panaceas to the depredations of capitalism. Unlike the preeminent American silverite William Harvey, Zola considered Jewish financiers' tentacular grip on the world less than absolute. Gundermann's enviable position at the juncture of "all the rivers of gold" notwithstanding, these international tributaries of wealth nourish upstream outposts of solidity, like the Carmel valley, whose potential for self-sufficiency hints at something beyond the ambit of world finance and its vicissitudes. Despite, or even because of, his influence, Zola's Jewish oligarch has neither the inclination nor the imagination to bother with such developments beyond his chosen domain. For his situation makes him, at bottom, risk-averse. Gundermann "was no speculator, no master adventurer handling other people's millions and dreaming, like Saccard, of heroic battles in which he would prevail and win for himself a colossal booty." Instead, he wields the implacable market-making power granted by the "inexhaustible merchandise" of his personal fortune (94–95). Like a casino owner confident that the odds tilt inexorably in his favor, Gundermann has no truck with anything beyond the closed system of guaranteed profit over which he presides.

Saccard, by comparison, is sustained by a gambler's mentality, envisaging a big score proportional to the odds he thinks are stacked against him by his Jewish nemesis. It seems reasonable, in this light, for Emily Apter to suggest that Saccard's Napoleonic visions of Eastern conquest represent the psychological obverse of his fixation with the Eastern Jew's imagined conquest of France. Apter credits Zola with diagnosing the twisted reflection produced when "bizarre as it might seem . . . the paranoid vision that imagined Jewish banking interests controlling world finance inspired French capitalists to think globally."[72] Bizarre indeed—enough so, in fact, to give pause about the innocence of Zola's implied symmetry between antisemitism and economic imperialism. Theorists have often connected the bourgeoisie's capitalist ambitions with its imputation of financial misdeeds to Jews. Marxist and neo-Marxist schemas, for example, classically explain antisemitism as a way of scapegoating Jews for bourgeois crimes.[73] Yet if these interpretations make antisemitism the effect of capital, Zola submits the opposite causality entirely, antisemitic hatred in fact prompting grand new capitalist designs when the "lash of a whip" of an early taunt from Gundermann provokes Saccard to announce the establishment of his new bank (22).

Zola attributes the bank's eventual stock crash to risk-taking driven in part by its founder's antisemitic monomania. What results is an apologia, on the grounds of Saccard's antisemitism, for the destructive volatility of the global capitalism he pioneers. Represented thusly, the boom-and-bust vagaries of capital become less the product of intrinsic instability in the system than of a constitutional imbalance in the man who abuses it. Such a mystification calls to mind Georg Lukács's reproach of Zola for attributing sudden catastrophes to various factors—most notably heredity—removed from the material processes governing bourgeois society. Like Flaubert, charges Lukács, Zola fails to recognize that these capitalist processes necessarily produce catastrophes of their own, offering instead a false distinction between an "even-tenored" bourgeois existence and the apparently external, "abnormal" events (like revolution) that disrupt its comfortable monotony.[74] Though Lukács takes as an example the unsettling rape committed by Saccard's atavistic son Victor, he might more aptly have cited how the combustible banker's antisemitic eruptions shift blame for the Banque Universelle's demise from quintessentially capitalist overextension to the "old racial rancor" subtending Saccard's obsessive personal campaign against Gundermann.

And yet, *pace* Lukács, Saccard's hereditary distaste for Jews provides more than an alibi for the convulsions of capital. Able, from his chosen imperial perspective, to go a step further, Zola normalizes the convulsions themselves by assimilating the bank's lurching trajectory to a constructive planetary cycle of death and rebirth. Antisemitism and capitalist empire here become twin manifestations of a same vitalist telos, Saccard's obsession assuming a generative role when sublimated and focused abroad. Thus is capital made wishfully by Zola to serve a logic other than the cold calculus of profit. As Marxist theory would have it, Saccard's self-justificatory attacks on Gundermann certainly resemble the bourgeois antisemite's attempt at mystifying the relations of production in the effigy of the rapacious Jew. Zola, though, supersedes that possible anticapitalist reading by exploiting antisemitism *itself* to paper over, in Saccard's mythically repurposed antisemitic energies, the real business of economic conquest. It is a mystification of a mystification, and one that requires a consciously global perspective. That Zola understands prejudice to spur Saccard's imperial designs ultimately proves more ideologically expedient than historically insightful. That Zola's own anti-antisemitism prompts his imperial turn, however, captures the real appeal of empire's big-picture possibilities to someone keen to refute not only antisemitism but also (and perhaps even more so) the anticapitalism frequently characteristic of it at the end of the century.[75]

Much as Zola notes the antisemite's hypocritical participation in the Jewish economy, he proposes the antisemite's simultaneous, unwitting participation in the planetary economy of life. Both maneuvers boost Zola's critical authority, arrogating to him an imperial command of scale unavailable to the comparatively near-sighted antisemite. But if along the way he transvalues Saccard's antisemitic passion into something more worthwhile, it is not really to suggest that antisemitism somehow might contribute to a larger good. More than anything, Zola's recuperation of Saccard's misguided fervor is an artifact of the French imperial philosophy that frames it. Before there was Saccard's Banque Universelle, there was Ferdinand de Lesseps's Compagnie Universelle du Canal Maritime de Suez (Universal Suez Canal Company), the international French investment venture that, after a decade of constant diplomatic and technical challenges, completed the Suez Canal in 1869. Derided in some quarters for sinking their savings "in the mud at the mouth of the Nile," thousands of patriotic middle-class French shareholders saw their quixotic bet pay off, and this seems to have confirmed for Zola the power of French ingenuity to redeem even the most speculative excess.[76] Caroline's rapturous account of the "miracle" of Port Said (77), the real Egyptian port spawned by the French-led construction of the canal in the 1860s, presages the analogous miracle in Carmel. The French mythology surrounding the Suez Canal mitigated the trauma inflicted when Britain effectively seized control of the canal in 1882. France's empire might not radiate as far as Britain's or generate as much wealth, but in what Edward Said drolly characterizes as a "political second best," the French could at least take satisfaction in having allegedly breathed life into the desert.[77] *L'Argent* rallies to this call. To the stock market masses' dilettantish excitement that, thanks to the Banque Universelle, "one would someday see Persia, India, China acquired for the West" (233)—a bulimia of possession for possession's sake—the novel offers an alternative, Suez-inspired model of empire that requires only the smallest implantation of life, wherever it occurs, to succeed. Never mind that Port Said began as a work camp populated by indigenous forced laborers excavating the canal.[78] Never mind, too, that in *Son Excellence Eugène Rougon* (1876), Zola had previously referenced the fictional collapse of an unnamed Egyptian canal company guilty of duping investors for two years without ever breaking ground.[79] What mattered to Zola, at least from 1890 on, was that developments in the French imperial periphery obey a grander design than either Jewish financiers or their antisemitic foes could fathom.

It is fitting, therefore, that the imperialist vision first sketched in *L'Argent* should reach a zenith of full-blown colonialist fervor in

Fécondité, the novel Zola wrote while in self-imposed British exile following his 1898 conviction for libel against Dreyfus's accusers. In it, Zola waxes ecstatic about populating a vast swath of Northwest Africa with one hundred million new Frenchmen. Dominique Froment, grandson of the novel's virile farmer-hero Mathieu Froment and a scion of the Froment family's African "second dynasty," breathlessly predicts a high-tech network of electric trains and river steamboats transforming French Sudan (present-day Mali) into a dynamic new corridor between France's Algerian hub on the Mediterranean and its Senegalese possessions on the Atlantic.[80] Critics have marveled that Zola would glorify a Sudanese colony with a lamentable reputation in France,[81] speculating that he succumbed to imperialist passions stoked when the 1898 Fashoda Affair pitted a handful of French soldiers against the entire Anglo-Egyptian army for control of the Nile.[82] Yet his paean to French colonialism likely had as much to do with the other *affaire* raging when the Fashoda Affair broke out. Dejected by his lonely existence in the London suburb of Norwood and pessimistic about the troubled Republic, Zola turned to an African expanse where "the ancient homeland" promised to reinvent itself as an "unlimited empire."[83] Zola's concerns about France's low birthrate are well-documented.[84] If, however, Zola's colonial idyll was meant to dispel neo-Malthusian worries about natural continental constraints on French population growth, it also implicitly imagined a nation unencumbered by what he felt were the more abstract impediments—antisemitism, Catholicism, xenophobic nationalism—posed to the Republic's global-historical destiny by anti-Dreyfusard obscurantists. It was, in short, a bid to liberate a properly universalizing Republic from the particularistic shackles of continental, ethnic, and religious attachment.

Zola's efforts at once borrow from and reconfigure the terms of the "civilizing mission" institutionalized the previous decade by Prime Minister Jules Ferry's expansionist Third Republic. Rather than construct republican universalism in relation to the subaltern particularities it was understood to supplant and absorb overseas, Zola conceives colonial expansion as the antidote to provincial loyalties thwarting that universalism in France. It is commonplace now in colonial and postcolonial studies to note how domestications of colonial and European difference overlapped, a process that for instance subjected Europe's internal others (women, the working class, Jews) to racializing grids of intelligibility fine-tuned in the imperial periphery.[85] Zola, by contrast, prescribes imperial conquest to contain and marginalize precisely the opposite metropolitan demographic: anti-Dreyfusards and antisemites who, in preaching the eternal sanctity of the nation against its enemies, styled themselves the apostles of sameness. By opposing an infinitely expansive idea of the nation to the antisemites' more restrictive, closed formulation, Zola's imperial France gestures toward dissolving the national altogether. The nation, he writes in *Fécondité*'s high-flying coda, is but one stage in a concentric series of allegiances radiating beyond empire toward an eventual whole: "the family incorporated in the nation, the nation incorporated in humanity, one fraternal people making the world into a single city of peace, truth, and justice."[86] Quibble though we might that the national hardly disappears from an arrangement in which France makes the world into a mirror of itself, Zola foresees an imperial solution to the nationalist reaction plunging France into disarray at the close of the nineteenth century.

Zola's utopic, internationalist imperialism highlights a neglected dynamic between Europe's inward self-fashioning and its outward imperial push. Recent decades have seen critics productively examine various dialectics linking metropole and periphery, including the aforementioned reciprocality between colonial and domestic disciplinary regimes; the imperial making of bourgeois and consumer cultures;[87] the colonial development of new European political and social rationalities;[88] and the twentieth-century "boomeranging" back from colonial Africa of genocidal techniques.[89] Still to be given its due, though—perhaps because of the frequent assimilation of nineteenth-century imperialism to a kind of metastatic nationalism[90]—is how imperial circumstances beckoned to those intent on questioning their European peers' increasing withdrawal into national and nationalist paradigms. Anti-antisemitism emerged in tandem with this imperial, supranational outlook as a potent rhetorical tool for anyone who, like Zola, sought in the nineteenth century to think beyond the nation.

I turn in a moment to another such figure, Nietzsche, who was even more dismissive of national boundaries and whose globalizing outlook similarly dovetailed with his iconoclastic take on the Jewish question. The resolutely democratic Zola and profoundly antidemocratic Nietzsche make for strange bedfellows. Yet Nietzsche's attempted "revaluation of all values"[91]—inspired by the Jews, worked out at antisemites' expense, and utterly central to Nietzsche's philosophy—is of an epistemic piece with Zola's scalar rehierarchizations. A half century earlier, Marx had likewise reached beyond the conceptual horizon of the nation-state to offer a critique that, unlike the one offered by his interlocutor Bruno Bauer, purported not to inhabit the (Jewish) system it denounced. Granted, Marx would have scoffed at Zola's version of this project. Predicated as the Zolian international program was on French republicanism's evangelical mission to liberate all peoples, Zola's world utopia still represented the kind of political approach to emancipation for which Marx chided Bauer. It bears mentioning, too, that Marx demonstrated far more sensitivity to the destructive effects of colonialism on its victims.[92] Zola, for his part, was no enthusiast of Marx's socialism, something made clear by the feeble Marxist dreams of *L'Argent*'s other Busch, Sigismond. And Nietzsche, theorist of the Overman, was allergic to anything resembling Marxism's egalitarianism. But this is all also the point. Whether from the political left (Marx), center (Zola), or right (Nietzsche), discourses against the critique of Jews could be flexibly deployed to equally ambitious rescaling effect.

BETWEEN JUDEA AND ROME: NIETZSCHE'S "ANTISEMITIC SCREAMERS"

"I am just having all anti-Semites shot," scribbled Nietzsche to his friend Franz Overbeck as he slipped toward madness in January 1889.[93] The imagery was extreme, even by the standards of Nietzschean bravado, but it was telling. Zola's only real competition for the preeminent voice of anti-antisemitism in the nineteenth century, Nietzsche considered German antisemites the epitome of everything he reviled. The stakes were both personal and philosophical. His painful break with Richard and Cosima Wagner, for instance, was sealed in part by the young philologist's public repudiation of the *völkisch* antisemitism obsessively espoused by his former protectors and by the Bayreuth circle that coalesced in the 1870s around the Wagners' Jew-baiting cultural nationalism. In the spring of 1878, Nietzsche sent the Wagners a copy of his new book, *Human, All-Too-Human*, which denounced nationalism and the "literary obscenity" of antisemitism.[94] The couple would never see or communicate with Nietzsche again.

Nietzsche spent the next decade at odds with a German antisemitism whose rapid mutation into a modern political movement coincided with its unwelcome intrusion into his private and professional life. A rightward turn in the German political climate, manifest in efforts by Kaiser Wilhelm and Chancellor Otto von Bismarck to inculcate national belongingness after Germany's 1871 unification, had produced an environment conducive to antisemitic ferment.[95] German Jews' full legal emancipation by the new Reich sharpened the attacks, as did the financial downturn of 1873. In 1879, the longtime anti-Jewish agitator Wilhelm Marr published what has been called the first antisemitic best seller, *The Victory of Jewry over the Germans*. Later popularizing the term itself (*Antisemitismus*), Marr propounded a brand of antisemitism informed by the pseudoscientific race theories of the day. The specter of Jewish infiltration raised by the anti-Christian, atheist, and secularist Marr is often cited as a turning point in the shift from traditional Christian anti-Jewish prejudice to the modern, racist antisemitism that spread throughout Europe in the final decades of the century. Marr's Christian counterparts in Germany were not to be outdone, though. Adolph Stöcker, the Imperial Court Chaplain in Berlin, preached openly against the Jews—for a time with Bismarck's and the Kaiser's tacit approval—and transformed the Christian Social-Workers' Party he founded in 1878 into an organ of antisemitic demagoguery. Violence broke out in Berlin and the provinces as organized gangs attacked Jews, their property, and their synagogues in 1880–81. Young intellectuals, emboldened by a series of antisemitic articles penned in 1879–80 by the respected historian and university professor Heinrich von Treitschke, banded together under the auspices of the so-called Berlin Movement to defend German culture. The subsequent proliferation of antisemitic parties and associations (including Marr's own Antisemitic League) even produced electoral results: after sending only one successful candidate to the Reichstag in 1887, antisemitic parties secured four seats in 1890 and sixteen in 1893 before declining in influence at the turn of the century.

Particularly galling to Nietzsche were the activities of the Wagner acolyte and antisemitic agitator Bernhard Förster. Förster spearheaded the Antisemites' Petition, which gathered about 265,000 signatures across Germany before being presented to Bismarck in 1881. The petition called for limits on Jewish immigration, a census for registering Jews, and the exclusion of Jews from certain teaching and governmental positions. Bismarck summarily rejected it. Förster did, however, find a receptive audience for his politics in Nietzsche's beloved sister Elisabeth, whom he met in Bayreuth in 1882 and married in 1885. Nietzsche could not hide his consternation. Writing to Overbeck in 1884, he lamented that "this accursed anti-Semitism . . . is the reason for the great rift between myself and my sister."[96] Three years later, as the Försters struggled to found the antisemitic colony of Nueva Germania in Paraguay, Nietzsche reproved Elisabeth for the marriage he had been unable to prevent:

> You have committed one of the greatest stupidities—for yourself and for me! Your association with an anti-Semitic chief expresses a foreignness to *my* whole way of life which fills me ever again and again with ire or melancholy. . . . It is a matter of honor to me to be absolutely clean and unequivocal in relation to anti-Semitism, namely *opposed*, as I am in my writings.[97]

Nietzsche never prevailed on his sister to relinquish her familial and ideological attachments to antisemitism. Förster committed suicide a few months after Nietzsche's syphilitic insanity had taken hold, and Elisabeth Förster-Nietzsche famously went on to preside enthusiastically over the wholesale Wilhelmine and Nazi distortions of her brother's legacy.

Nietzsche's entanglements with professional antisemites extended beyond Förster and the Wagners. Ernst Schmeitzner, publisher of *Human, All-Too-Human* and subsequent works by Nietzsche, embarrassed and frustrated his client by publishing antisemitic journals (including the Bayreuth circle's *Bayreuther Blätter*) and by neglecting the publication of *Thus Spake Zarathustra* in favor of antisemitic propagandizing. Adding insult to injury, especially considering *Zarathustra*'s underwhelming initial sales, Nietzsche was irked to find "the name of Zarathustra" mentioned "in every *Anti-Semitic Correspondence* sheet" sent to him in 1887 by the antisemitic publicist Theodor Fritsch.[98] "Perhaps it will help assuage your mind," Nietzsche testily replied in a letter to his insistent admirer, "if I say, finally, that there are no Jews among my friends, but neither are there anti-Semites."[99]

Nietzsche's gibe reminds us that his own opinions about Jews were notoriously complex.[100] The qualifier he appends to his 1878 attack on antisemitism in *Human, All-Too-Human*—counseling tolerance "in spite of" his observation that "perhaps the young stock-exchange Jew is altogether the most disgusting invention of mankind"[101]—illustrates how, as critics have noted, Nietzsche's distaste for antisemitism did not automatically make him a friend of the Jews.[102] It is true that the kinds of anti-Jewish clichés that dot his correspondence and writings from the 1860s and 1870s frequently came to reside, after the break with Wagner, next to more admiring assessments of the Jews.[103] In *Beyond Good and Evil* (1886), Nietzsche even asked forgiveness for his "brief daring sojourn in very infected territory" during which he succumbed to the "disease" of anti-Jewish, anti-French, and other nationalistic prejudices rampant in Wagner's circle.[104] At the very same time, though, Nietzsche was elaborating a moral history that held Jews to account for the "calamity" of Christian morality—in his judgment the greatest disaster to befall man. That disaster "became possible only because a related, racially related, kind of megalomania already existed in the world: the *Jewish* one."[105] In bequeathing Christianity to the world, the Jews had unleashed a reactive, vengeful rancor antithetical to the noble self-assurance of their classical Gentile masters. The master stroke of the "Jewish priesthood,"[106] Nietzsche maintained, was disguising its twisted new values in the seductive garb of Christian love. With the (Jewish) Redeemer's martyrdom on the cross, the slave's defeated embrace of deprivation became the universal doctrine of altruistic sacrifice. History henceforth boiled down to the ongoing struggle between aristocratic and slave moralities: "Rome against Judea, Judea against Rome."[107]

So unkind an account of priestly Judaism, indistinguishable for Nietzsche from early Christianity, contrasts with his generally favorable opinion of the biblical Hebrews. These he admires for their "self-affirmation," much as he admires other warrior peoples confident in their naturally ordained primacy.[108] Nietzsche also reserves extensive praise for contemporary Jewry. After "an eighteen-century schooling such as no other nation of this continent can boast of," he writes in *Daybreak* (1881), "the psychological and spiritual resources of the Jews today are extraordinary." He predicts a gradual process of intermarriage and assimilation through which the Jews will become "the inventors and signposts of the nations of Europe and no longer offend their sensibilities," and foresees a time when present-day Jews, strengthened by centuries of tribulation, reach back beyond priestly Judaism to rekindle their former Old Testament glory:

> Then, when the Jews can exhibit as their work such jewels and golden vessels as the European nations of a briefer and less profound experience could not and cannot produce, when Israel will have transformed its eternal vengeance into an eternal blessing for Europe: then there will again arrive that seventh day on which the ancient Jewish God may *rejoice* in himself, his creation and his chosen people—and let us all, all of us, rejoice with him![109]

What critics make of the consequent tension between Nietzsche's respect for modern and ancient Jews and his excoriation of priestly Judaism depends on which is taken as the dominant lens. Viewed through the prism of his attribution to the Jews of Christian decadence, his prognosis of fruitful Jewish assimilation has been treated by more suspicious commentators as "a gentle final solution" and as a disingenuous overture intended to "energize 'Rome' and neutralize 'Judea'" by incorporating Jewish qualities into a hybrid new caste of European overmen.[110] Viewed through the prism of his kind words for contemporary Jews and the Kingdom of Israel, on the other hand, his animus for the priestly Judaism of the Second Temple has often been treated as epiphenomenal to Nietzsche's hatred for Christianity, his real target.[111]

It is possible as well to read Nietzsche's feelings about Jews in relation to his abhorrence of antisemitism. The ailing, itinerant philosopher may have identified with the suffering, wandering Jew, preferring the Semitic underdog to the antisemitic bully.[112] His equation of antisemites with everything he detested—socialism, democracy, Christianity, nationalism, and other "herd mentalities"[113]—likely also strengthened Nietzsche's contrarian identification with the antisemites' chosen target. To be sure, the identification is grounded in representations of Jewishness that remain highly clichéd, when they are not borrowed from the antisemitic lexicon outright. But this is also intentional: ever the perspectivist, Nietzsche delights in turning his enemies' rhetorical arsenal against them. Take Jewish cosmopolitanism, the hobgoblin of antisemitic nationalists. Nietzsche might have questioned the myth of Jewish antipathy toward the nation. Instead, he validates the stereotype so that he may valorize it, hoping to shock antisemites with their own co-opted idiom when he celebrates the Jews' potential for catalyzing an eventual European amalgam: "A thinker who has the development of Europe on his conscience will, in all his projects for this future, take into account the Jews as well as the Russians as the provisionally surest and most probable factors in the great play and fight of forces."[114]

While one can certainly charge Nietzsche with reinforcing the antisemitic conventions he exploits, to stop there is to miss the larger optic. He is unconcerned with demonstrating that antisemites are wrong to consider Jews cosmopolitan, or unusually powerful, or hereditarily disposed to making money—all legitimate reasons why, in fact, he believes the Jews could attain "mastery over Europe" if they wanted.[115] Rather, he castigates antisemites for their particularistic attachment to national configurations grafted willy-nilly onto the deeper

Greco-Roman tradition that unites Europe to begin with. Nietzsche credits Jewish scholars with having conserved this tradition when, in the Dark Ages, "the Asiatic cloud masses had gathered heavily over Europe."[116] Now the Jews can again help preserve Europe, this time from a nationalist storm welling up from within. Of course, they would be acting to restore what their priestly ancestors overturned when Rome was "defeated beyond all doubt" by Judea.[117] But the irony is perhaps not so great: as we know, Nietzsche considers contemporary Jewry still as potentially imbued with Hebraic grandeur as with the slavish instinct of revenge.

The same cannot be said of the "anti-Semitic screamers" whom Nietzsche would gladly "expel . . . from the country."[118] These enemies of Europe are priestly Judaism's worst legacy, since as "men of *ressentiment*" they incarnate the massive inversion orchestrated by Judeo-Christian morality.[119] That inversion, Nietzsche alleges, occurred when an enslaved people perversely elevated their own worst qualities—weakness, poverty, abnegation, and every other obverse of their masters' noble vitality—into values that conquered their masters and eventually the world. Antisemites best illustrate the extent of the inversion not only because, in their *ressentiment*, they most recuperate the slavish resentment of priestly Jews but also because they so blindly malign the very people whose forebears they most resemble: "even today the Christian can feel anti-Jewish without realizing that he himself is *the ultimate Jewish consequence*."[120] For Nietzsche to attack antisemites is hence to attack the "revaluation" effected by priestly Jews and, in proposing to reverse it, to advance a revaluation of his own.

What Nietzsche undertook in the 1870s and 1880s, Zola continued in the 1890s. Zola's explicit anti-antisemitism attempts a similar rescaling of perspective partially aimed at the Jews he simultaneously defends. Just as Nietzsche pulls back from the Judeo-Christian revaluation of morals and its antisemitic dupes to reveal a longer Greco-Roman tradition within which more rightfully to inscribe Europe, so does Zola offer a sweeping, imperial context against which to relativize the Jewish metropolitan influence he concedes. And as much as both take inspiration from the Jews' ostensible knack for turning the tables of scale—namely, for remaking society in their financial or moral image—these maneuvers require more than a discourse about or against Jews. They also demand a rejoinder to the critique of Jews, a rejoinder that endeavors to demonstrate, at antisemitism's expense, how one's perspective must continually radiate outward or risk entanglement with the object of critique. Thus do Zola's myopic antisemites prompt him toward a supranational, imperial point; and thus do Nietzsche's parochial antisemites confirm, for this self-proclaimed "incorrigible European and anti-anti-Semite," the importance of looking to a more meaningful, lasting European ethos beyond what he considers the trivial vagaries of national life.[121]

That ethos dates to antiquity, and Nietzsche envisions it drawing on energies latent in contemporary European peoples, like the Jews, the French, or the Germans, somewhere still possessed of a "will to power" concordant with the ancients' self-affirming nobility.[122] The significant complication, however, at least in regard to the Jews, is that they stand to contribute in two very different ways. The first way, we have seen, is as survivors. In their centuries-long cohesion, the Jews offer Europe a deep experience absent from the comparatively fledgling European nations that for Nietzsche constitute more a superficial "*res facta*" ("something made") than a self-immanent "*res nata*" ("something born").[123] Traceable to their Hebraic forefathers' inborn aristocracy of temperament, this cumulative storehouse of vigor was once diverted by slavery into Judea's revaluation of noble ideals; now, hopes Nietzsche, it might partake in the no less ambitious revaluation of Christian decadence by the coming European Overman (*Übermensch*).

Yet Nietzsche's new revaluation does not necessarily augur Judea's disappearance, and neither is it meant to. For Judea, too, hints Nietzsche, has its ongoing role to play. In this regard, Jewish priestliness unexpectedly represents a second, more covert contribution by the people of Israel to the pan-European project. Nietzsche certainly believes that the Judeo-Christian era has wrought incalculable damage. "But it is only fair to add," he offers in a pivotal aside,

> that it was on the soil of this *essentially dangerous* form of human existence, the priestly form, that man first became *an interesting animal*, that only here did the human soul in a higher sense acquire *depth* and become *evil*—and these are the two respects in which man has hitherto been superior to other beasts![124]

The observation requires some unpacking. The soul, Nietzsche explains later in the *Genealogy of Morals*, emerged when the first peaceful civilization forced man's natural, predatory instincts inward. This "internalization" (*Verrinerlichung*), this discharge of a man's drives against himself—rather than against other men—opened an interiority to which were now removed, in the hidden enclave of the spirit, the violences formerly performed in the external world. The resulting "bad conscience" ushered in every kind of guilt and fear, an attendant thirst for meaning, and eventually the most sublime bad conscience of all: the *ressentiment* of the Judeo-Christian believer convinced of his eternal guilt before God. If it is an illness, though, bad conscience is "an illness as pregnancy is an illness." With it, something is "announcing and preparing itself."[125] This is because man's incipient interiority marks the stirrings of a newly spiritualized life, one in which the individual, without surrendering the natural vitality of life's given instincts, drives, and passions, nevertheless overcomes their givenness by actively shaping them into meaning—real meaning, that is, of the sort buoyed up by life, and not of the variety imposed from without by God or some other false, life-denying "ascetic ideal" determined to cleave the spirit from the body.[126]

The ascetic ideal comes to historical prominence, for Nietzsche, with the introduction of its priestly, Judeo-Christian form. Never before had a doctrine predicated on the unnatural suppression of natural instincts ascended so far. And never before had a program of self-overcoming proved thoroughgoing enough to generate a set of new ideals—meekness, poverty, and the like—sufficiently robust to unseat the aristocratic, self-sufficient ideals they negatively mirrored. In the latter respect, priestliness wields a uniquely generative power derived from the very life it militates against. The sick shepherd of an even sicker flock, the priest defends his charges against the healthy but also from themselves: for if nothing else, the doxa he instills tempers their worst tendencies, preempting the explosive, even anarchic possibilities were an accumulating *ressentiment* to remain unchecked. In so doing, Nietzsche concludes, the denier of life actually affirms it, inasmuch as he embodies the circuitous stratagem by which a weakened life forestalls its extinguishment.

This is why in the passage above Nietzsche considers the priestly soul to have acquired depth "in a higher sense." The priest's unprecedented ability to fashion new values from the raw material of life, albeit indirectly, signals the advent of humanity as such by confirming the human animal's sui generis potential for molding nature into meaning. To the extent that Judeo-Christian meaning is false meaning, the soul's priestly emergence from its prehistory represents, for Nietzsche, a monstrously abortive start. But Judea also becomes an ongoing metaphor for the Overman's eventual opportunity to get it right. In that capacity, the Jews have contributed to Europe qua Judea:

> What Europe owes to the Jews? Many things, good and bad, and above all one thing that is both of the best and of the worst: the grand style in morality, the terribleness and majesty of infinite demands, infinite meanings, the whole romanticism and sublimity of moral questionabilities—and hence precisely the most attractive, captious, and choicest part of those plays of color and seductions to life in whose afterglow the sky of our European culture, its evening sky, is burning now—perhaps burning itself out. We artists among the spectators and philosophers are—grateful for this to the Jews.[127]

Antisemites, nationalists, Christian moralizers: these are "ambitious artists who like to pose as ascetics and priests but who are at bottom only tragic buffoons."[128] They perpetuate the most debased, popular variety of *ressentiment* coursing through Judea's erstwhile slavish masses. Alongside them, however, subsists the promise of Judea's finest, the real priests, those cunning rivals to (and potentially even onetime members of) the knightly aristocratic caste from which Nietzsche understands the priestly mode to have "branched off."[129]

The result is considerable opacity in the outcome Nietzsche imagines for the epic conflict between Rome and Judea. He himself never adjudicates the matter, even when he seems to. Rome was right, he submits, to see nature's "antipodal monstrosity" in Judea, "provided one has a right to link the salvation and future of the human race with the unconditional dominance of aristocratic values, Roman values."[130] But does Nietzsche in fact grant himself that right, and if so, what might "unconditional dominance" look like, anyway? True, he makes clear that most modern upheavals—like the French Revolution, which for him inaugurated government by the herdlike majority—have deleteriously expanded Judea's initial victory over the Romans. At the same time, though, he notes that in places where the battle still rages, the struggle has "risen ever higher," producing "a '*higher nature*,' a more spiritual nature" than in places where the die is already cast.[131] The struggle itself, it seems, possesses inherent value, recapitulating at the societal level the same spiritualization of life that he prescribes for the individual—much as, for Freud, civilization constitutes the larger battleground for the war between Eros and Thanatos waged in every psyche. Nietzsche evidently hopes to reverse Judea's historical preeminence over Rome. Less clear is whether Judea's eventual defeat would mean its disappearance; its sublation by Rome into some new configuration preserving Judea's genius for self-overcoming while reaffirming Rome's aristocratic embrace of man's natural, conquering drives; or its continued existence alongside Rome as a tolerable, even useful appendage.

Such uncertainty preconceives Rome and Judea as binary opposites entering into an all-or-nothing confrontation, a dialectical synthesis, or a dynamic system. In choosing among these alternatives, however, it is instructive as well to situate Rome and Judea along a same continuum of degenerating life, since for Nietzsche Judea would never have gnawed Rome from within had the empire not already become decadent.[132] So arranged, the two value systems represent more or less diminished counterparts to the raw animal life from which the soul first alienated man. Nietzsche detests modernity for having strayed too far from the animal health still vibrant in the "blond beasts" of yore who, like the Vikings and the Homeric heroes, proudly and uncomplicatedly took what was theirs.[133] But neither does he advocate any simplistic chronological return to a previous, more natural state. On this point he is explicit: "There has never yet been a natural humanity . . . man reaches nature only after a long struggle—he never 'returns,'"[134] he writes in his notebooks, adding later that "I too speak of a 'return to nature,' although it is really not a going back but an *ascent*."[135] If Nietzsche's dueling narratives of ascent and decline can give the impression that, paraphrasing one critic, he never quite decided whether man represented an evolution or devolution from bare animal life,[136] his equivocation is not really so total. He proves sufficiently anthropocentric to grant mankind a unique and salutary role in life's elevation to a higher, spiritualized plane, despite remaining phlegmatic enough about humanity to deem man less a "goal" than "a way, an episode, a bridge."[137] Still, it is useful to remember that *both* Rome and Judea mark historical moments in what Nietzsche considers a generalized civilizational decadence to date, even as they circumscribe this temporary failure by together portending tremendous future possibility. Rome was individually inadequate to producing the Overman not only because it suffered, in attenuated form, from the same malaise epitomized by Judea but also because it lacked Judea's gift for harnessing that malaise. The "recurrent symbolic contest" between the two, to borrow Howard Eiland's formulation, therefore rules out Judea's total effacement before a resurgent Rome.[138] Rather, each ostensibly compensates for the other. Judea's self-disciplining example induces Rome's surfeit of life ever higher, heading off stagnation by locating within

Rome elements of slavishness for it constantly to overcome. Rome, for its part, ensures with its healthful instincts that Judea's life-denying *ressentiment* does not prevail.

This complementarity's emergence from the problem of degenerating life, insoluble by either Rome or Judea alone, rules out the possibility that Nietzsche understands Rome's hoped-for "unconditional dominance" to mean Judea's complete destruction. Choosing between the remaining two options—that Rome and Judea are to produce a dialectical synthesis or settle instead into some kind of dynamic, back-and-forth system—requires a closer look at degenerating life's own complicated status. In what follows, I argue for the dynamic hypothesis, endeavoring to show how Rome and Judea come to play complementary roles in a cyclical process of accumulation and release without which Nietzsche's idiosyncratic conception of life threatens his philosophical edifice. The process sets in motion a play of forces inimical to any tidy, Hegelian resolution, something broadly consistent with Gilles Deleuze's appraisal of Nietzsche's project as an "anti-dialectics."[139] At least as regards the Rome-Judea tandem, however, I am less sanguine than Deleuze's postcolonial admirers about the promise of such multiplicity for a pluralistic alternative to the domineering Western narrative of progress. For if Rome and Judea resist synthesis, it is not because their interplay captures something in life happily refractory to dialectical thought's teleological violence. It is, instead, because the system they help constitute subtly but repeatedly expels from itself a mounting entropy that would otherwise muddle the distinction between them. This recursive noise, this degenerative feedback in the system, never just disappears, pretend though Nietzsche might that it does. A succession of outlets internal and external to Europe merely draws it away. The internal variety, we will see, culminates in the Jew; the external variety, in colonization. And both modulating presences converge to place their respective others—the antisemite and the colonized—into a structural equivalence anticipating what Zola would propose a few years later.

EMPIRE AND THE DOUBLE BIND OF LIFE

A degenerative entropy haunts Nietzsche's genealogy from the moment mankind splits into conqueror and conquered, master and slave. As he would have it, Rome and Judea represent the most significant world-historical manifestations of master and slave moralities. These dual modes date back to the original domination achieved when "some pack of blond beasts of prey" first "lays its terrible claws upon a populace."[140] That domination, he tells us, gives birth to the first state and to its constitutive ailment: the bad conscience nascent in the tamed and enslaved, and eventually even their masters, newly compelled by the requirements of a peaceful existence to turn their animal instincts in upon themselves. Nietzsche was nothing if not consistent in his denunciation of the state as an impediment to life-enhancement. But there is something telling about the haste, even by the lax standards of Nietzschean methodology, with which he here equates the abrupt and infelicitous "leap" into bad conscience with the equally radical discontinuity that is the first state.[141] By blaming the man-made state for the degeneration of healthy animal life into the sickness of bad conscience, Nietzsche obfuscates the role of life in producing its opposite. After all, such a *pax bestialis* and the internalization it yields occur because, in subduing his enemies, the blond beast has acted in perfect accordance with his nature. Life's paradigmatic expression in one place thus requires its curtailment in another.

On the surface, this poses no problem to so unapologetically antidemocratic a thinker. Life's ascent requires just that it flourish somewhere, not everywhere. Such asymmetry even reflects a necessary condition of the whole: "life itself is *essentially* appropriation, injury, overpowering of what is alien and weaker; suppression, hardness, imposition of one's own forms."[142] Nietzsche defines life as the compulsion to dominate, or what he calls the will to power, in order to underscore the primacy of a life unbeholden to the reactive injunctions against violence dreamed up by its slavish victims and codified in Judeo-Christian morality. Yet the definition is itself quietly reactive. Life is only really life for Nietzsche if it expands, which requires that the strong overtake the weak. He means this to have the ring of a natural first principle. But he also tacitly acknowledges that predation upon the weak by the strong usefully addresses an attendant complication: the danger posed by a latent violence, within the pack of aristocratic blond beasts, of the strong against the strong. Nietzsche presents that latent violence as maintaining a healthy equilibrium among peers "held so sternly in check *inter pares* [among equals]" by, above all, "mutual suspicion and jealousy"[143]—which is to say, by aggression sublimated into a grudging respect. Turn that aggression too consistently in against the self, however, and sickness sets in. To compensate and remain healthy, the aristocracy "has to do to other bodies what the individuals within it refrain from doing to each other."[144] Conquests must be achieved, victories won, peoples and territories subjugated.

The expansion of the strong at the expense of the weak is thus only part of the equation. Life's other fundamental principle, its other truth, is that intercalated among these radiating expansions are contractions when, according to Nietzsche, life by necessity turns against itself. The blond beasts are successful predators because of an "ability to organize" absent in their "formless and nomad" victims.[145] They manage, as he elsewhere writes of the Greeks, to "organize the chaos," assimilating and imposing form on the disordered prey they encounter.[146] But first they must organize the chaos among themselves, and herein lies what will become a creeping difficulty for Nietzsche. Life turned indiscriminately and permanently outward by every man, he makes clear, would have mired the species in a Hobbesian war of all against all. For civilization to emerge, a clan of naturally dominant and equally matched men had to turn their warrior instincts sufficiently inward until some pocket of aristocratic stability emerged. Henceforth was life free to progress, through them, beyond the diffuse and primitive business of animal survival. Only, life now labored under a double bind. The very thing that propelled life onward and upward—its aristocratic avatars' critical self-control—also threatened to collapse life under the strain of its accumulated inward-facing weight. To forestall that entropic regression into sickness and chaos, the blond beast must periodically unleash his accumulated aggression; the "hidden core needs to erupt from time to time, the animal has to get out again and go back to the wilderness."[147]

Suppose for a moment that some pack of blond beasts managed, over countless waves of accumulation and release, to bring the entire world under its decisive control. What then? Where might accumulating life go, failing any new wilderness in which to discharge it? Nietzsche has such a limit case in mind when he anticipates a "master race, the future 'masters of the earth'" risen from Europe to rule the world. And his solution to the problem of accumulating life is at the ready. With no earthly conquests left to make, and equipped with souls at last capable of funneling life healthily and indefinitely inward, the coming race of Overmen will be free "to work as artists upon 'man' himself."[148] That is because, in fulfilling the interrupted promise of imperial Rome, they will have learned from Judea what the Romans did not: how to generate new values from the turn within. Every other conquering people in history has been weakened by its own triumph, as each successive expansion required a correspondingly draining feat of restraint. After the example of the Jews, the first to wrench sublimity from self-denial, the new Rome will at last mold its vigor's internal accumulation into unprecedented feats of the spirit.

To the Overman, then, as to any aristocracy, Nietzsche makes available a crucial outlet for the discharge of accumulating life. Previous aristocracies have possessed an external such outlet, healthy life venturing periodically afield to impose its form on others. The Overman's version of that outlet is internal, life now able to impose form on itself without incurring the price of degeneration. But what of the vast majority of "future Europeans" who, Nietzsche concedes, "will be poor in will" and "prepared for *slavery* in the subtlest sense"?[149] What will their outlet be? For the problem of accumulating life is not just the rarefied burden of the best among men; it is also the burden forced by the conqueror upon the conquered, the master upon the slave. Worse, the aristocracy's outward releases of accumulated life produce a more insidious accumulation in their conquests, consigned as these victims are to internalize their every natural drive—including, especially, the "instinct for freedom"[150]—with no comparable means of relief. This is the origin of bad conscience, later to sour further into *ressentiment*. The double bind of expanding life, offloaded from a temporarily alleviated aristocracy, returns with a vengeance in the pacified slave for whom the master's cure translates into an intensifying poison. "The most dangerous of all explosives, *ressentiment*, is constantly accumulating," warns Nietzsche, and with it the threat of chaotic eruptions like the French Revolution. Hence does he see, in the priest he otherwise maligns, a partial solution that usefully "*alters the direction* of *ressentiment*" by channeling it into the less immediately dangerous form of Judeo-Christian morality.[151] Though this morality certainly poses a long-term threat of its own, it at least furnishes a bulwark against sudden anarchy.

Nietzsche makes no similarly explicit provision for defusing the European masses' pent-up life in the post-Judeo-Christian era of the Overman. We learn only that the "evolving European" manages at once, as a type, to improve on and further enervate the old *ressentiment*-ridden herd.[152] In his supranationality, the new European provides the raw material from which a handful of truly superlative men, unfettered at last by the state and other parochialisms, can finally emerge. That said, whosoever thus emerges will do so alongside a vast, compliant population more etiolated than ever. Indeed, the two outcomes are interrelated:

> The very same new conditions that will on the average lead to the leveling and mediocritization of man—to a useful, industrious, handy, multi-purpose herd animal—are likely in the highest degree to give birth to exceptional human beings of the most dangerous and attractive quality.[153]

These new causal "conditions" boil down to growing deracination, a specter Nietzsche borrows from the discourse of reactionary nationalism but to which, in typically contrarian fashion, he assigns as much promise as portent. Less clear is what quantity of generalized decadence he believes that promise to justify. Is Nietzsche content, as one critic concludes, to reduce most Europeans to a "standing reserve" useful only for generating and supporting a caste of Overmen?[154] Nietzsche's fervent anti-egalitarianism certainly does not preclude it. Yet my sense is that he remains as suspicious as ever of slavish docility—one now threatening, according to his own predictions, to resonate in baleful unison across the entire continent.

Granted, the sweeping European acculturation that Nietzsche prescribes transcends the state and its supposed impediments to life's healthy outward expression. No state, no bad conscience, goes the theory. But on closer inspection, this really just applies to exceptional men. Recall that Nietzsche's account of the first state transfers the onus of accumulating life from the act of conquest, with its life-constraining effects on the conquered, to the internalization required by peaceful governance. Thereafter are beast and prey alike subjected to the tyranny of the state. Then comes the pan-European moment when, poststate, the beast escapes his national cage. No such efflorescence, however, awaits the evolving European herd from which the new masters will arise. Where there are masters, there are slaves. And where there are slaves, the conquering drives of the few thwart the natural instincts of the many. Just because life might supersede the state, in other words, does not mean it escapes its own chaotic cycle of accumulation and release. What prevents the stateless Overman from suffering the fate of the Romans, or of the French aristocracy, at the hands of a European multitude roiling with frustrated life?

The answer is empire. Nietzsche's observations about the European masses' growing pliancy suggest a certain hopefulness that the danger posed by their *ressentiment* might dwindle in proportion to their eroding will to power. But Nietzsche's insistence on the strictly European nature of the enterprise ultimately betrays his skepticism that any such rosy equilibrium between future masters and slaves could emerge unaided. If he foresees a time when slaves permanently know and accept their place, it is not because the basic law of accumulating life will somehow have ended. Rather, it is because the local master-slave dynamic will have settled into a global imperial context tasked, like a giant regulatory system, with maintaining order at its European core. Thus, for instance, might energies that otherwise threaten continental disarray be safely diverted abroad. Nietzsche offers "swarming trains of colonists" bound for "distant lands" as an antidote to the proletarian unrest fomented by an emergent labor movement, exhorting working men to "inaugurate within the European beehive an age of a great swarming-out such has never been seen before":

> If, on the other hand, you have always in your ears the flutings of the Socialist pied-pipers whose design is to enflame you with wild hopes? which bid you *to be prepared* and nothing further. . . . In contrast to all this, everyone ought to say to himself: "better to go abroad, to seek to become *master* in new and savage regions of the world and above all master over myself."[155]

Nietzsche has not yet, at this point, prophesied a comparatively tractable, pan-European working class more safely in thrall to the Overman, so his invitation to imperial conquest targets a restless proletariat still in danger of becoming "either the slave of the state or the slave of a party of disruption" and hence redoubling in *ressentiment*. Already, though, he imagines a healthier Europe sustained by a less obstreperous breed of worker. An influx of Chinese might furnish the "industrious ants" Europe requires, bringing with them an Asiatic contentment with their lot.[156] Nietzsche eventually concluded that the emerging European masses made pretty good ants after all, obviating the rationale for mass emigration. Yet his approach remained imperial. The imported Chinese worker's presumed docility, born of an innate subservience that holds across geographies, is the conceptual precursor to the docility of a Europeanized proletariat that, shorn of local attachments, likewise reduces to pure obedience. Nietzsche just reverses the causality: whereas Chinese deference transcends borders because it is so supposedly innate, the European multitude becomes more innately pliable as its interior boundaries dissolve. Some empires divide and conquer; Nietzsche's amalgamates and waits, its hierarchy ever cemented as spatial divisions fall away to reveal the continent's palimpsestic Roman unity.

So, too, does that hierarchy benefit from its imperial extension into non-European spaces. Nietzsche gives an ominous colonial example:

> What means one has to employ with rude peoples, and that "barbarous" means are not arbitrary and capricious, becomes palpable in practice as soon as one is placed, with all one's European pampering, in the necessity of keeping control over barbarians, in the Congo or elsewhere.[157]

King Leopold's brutal Congolese demonstration, "in practice," that might makes right puts "rude peoples" everywhere on notice—including the European rabble, should they be tempted again by revolution.[158] Observations like this prompt Horkheimer and Adorno to comment drily on Nietzsche's willingness to "elevate imperialistic raids to the level of world-historical missions."[159] Recorded in his notebooks in 1887, Nietzsche's remark coincided with the wave of German expansion into the Pacific and Africa that followed Bismarck's reticent 1884 decision to join the European powers in carving up the earth. Though Nietzsche never took up the colonial question in any detail, one can reasonably assume—as commentators have—that he disdained nationalist justifications for entering the colonial fray.[160] His documented ambiguity toward Förster's colonial efforts in Paraguay was doubtless not helped by his antisemitic brother-in-law's stated intention to refound abroad a purer German nation.[161] As a matter of philosophical principle, however, Nietzsche saw in the colonies a collective European "right to growth" necessary to any healthy society.[162] He expresses this right in the same biologistic terms underpinning his belief that, since the dawn of history, aristocratic clans have asserted the prerogative of the strong over the weak. Like those warrior forebears, Europe must project power afield in order to avoid collapse at home. But at the planetary level, Nietzsche tweaks his aforementioned premise that conquering the weak prevents disastrous internecine war among the strong. More refined than the beasts of old, the coming imperial Overmen do not risk cannibalizing one another. It is the European masses who instead become the abiding problem, since whatever remains of their restlessness will, absent the domesticating blandishments of a discarded Judeo-Christian morality, threaten the new continental order.

What results is Nietzsche's recourse to a structuring absence: the colonial subaltern through whom Europe's two future castes mediate a lasting détente. Understanding this begins with appreciating how for Nietzsche "dominion over the earth" holds promise "as a means of producing a higher type."[163] Not only does the grandeur of the task necessarily require a superior being, an "heir and continuator of Napoleon,"[164] but its eventual accomplishment also frees the victor to pursue even more elevated goals befitting an Overman. Nietzsche equates the global consolidation of empire with the end of earthly conquests and a resultant focus on internal, spiritual frontiers. Yet this works, I would offer, solely insofar as the permanent practice of European imperial domination ever interpellates and implicates the European masses. As we have seen, Nietzsche intends colonial violence to deter continental unrest, the example of, say, a Congo sparing eventual European Overmen the quotidian task of domestic repression that might dangerously exacerbate *ressentiment* at home. In turn, the relative privilege of the European masses qua Europeans further dissipates *ressentiment* by granting their thwarted life some limited outlet. What the industrious ant's slavish continental lot costs him in freedom, it at least partially returns to him in mastery over a colonial other. And the multitude need not, as Nietzsche initially proposed, actually leave Europe to enjoy this birthright. In the emerging global hierarchy among peoples, *ressentiment* is displaced onto faraway regions of degraded life over which all Europeans—Overmen and herd men alike—manifest their collective will to power.

In conceiving the imperial periphery as a release valve for social pressures building in the metropole, Nietzsche was traveling well-worn territory. It was a commonplace of European imperial thinking that colonial expansion might alleviate everything from overpopulation to class conflict. The key manifesto of the German colonialist movement, Friedrich Fabri's 1879 book *Does Germany Need Colonies?* framed the question in precisely these terms. More idiosyncratic—though certainly also in keeping with a politics of scale—was Nietzsche's implicit assumption that what empire most usefully expanded was less the boundaries of space than the relativity of lived power. Rather than funnel away from Europe a politically threatening demographic excess, the colonial periphery could placate the European masses by offering them someone, somewhere over whom to experience mastery, if only at a distance. Even when calling for a working-class colonial exodus, Nietzsche had shown himself most interested in the overseas possibility of the slave becoming master—the principle itself of aristocratic domination presumably emerging reinforced because, as Benedict Anderson puts it, colonialism afforded restless classes a chance to "play aristocrat off centre court."[165] The fortification of continental class hierarchies by racist colonial regimes offered Nietzsche a solution to the threatening *ressentiment* indistinguishable for him from the socialist, egalitarian rabble-rousers, including antisemitic German demagogues like Eugen Dühring, against whom he openly railed.[166] By contrast, colonialist antisemites like Förster saw in colonization a radical expression of their antisemitism, German cultural renewal and purification overseas seemingly promising an escape from the Jews.[167]

Along different axes, then, colonialism lent itself to antisemitic and anti-antisemitic designs alike. Nietzsche acidly noted one manner in which colonialism might simultaneously contribute to both agendas, declaring himself "so happy" that colonialist antisemites would "voluntarily exile themselves from Europe."[168] Yet by insisting here on the comparatively oblique way in which Nietzsche's distaste for antisemitism inflected his own imperial perspective, I want to underscore the unique results of this more glancing, contingent encounter between worldviews than that achieved when antisemites simply turned their racist sights abroad. For one, Nietzsche's anti-antisemitic imperialism allowed him to neutralize Judea's most dangerous supposed attribute, the powder keg of its herdlike *ressentiment*, while recuperating its more useful qualities for the coming order. Europeanization and overseas empire having defused the threat posed by antisemites, nationalists, and other "ambitious artists who like to pose as ascetics and priests," the path would be clear for the original priestly class—the Jews—to assert their pacifying influence once again.[169] These future "inventors and signposts" of the Europeans would not rule absolutely over Europe, any more than their forebears had ruled absolutely over imperial Rome.[170] Nietzsche seemed to hope instead that they would mediate between the Overman and the masses, containing and redirecting to less destructive account whatever thwarted life might otherwise explode in revolutionary energy. As Judea's priests had once used religion to fight "anarchy and ever-threatening disintegration within the herd," so would their cosmopolitan descendants minister preventively to the European multitude.[171] Only this time they would not do so in the name of a specious morality but rather in the name of their transhistorical depth as a supranational people, the best of Judea prodding the new Rome ever higher with its complementary brand of spiritual profundity.

Echoing the way in which global empire yielded Nietzsche a distant subaltern across which to stabilize relations between European master and slave, his dream of continental empire located a domestic intermediary caste in the imagined new Jewish spiritocrats.[172] Such homologization of continental and colonial racial others certainly appears familiar. Balibar has argued that the "very idea of Europe" was cemented by modernity's double racial exclusion: internally, as nation-states forged a common European belonging in their shared, nationalist reaction against the Jew; and externally, as European nation-states cohered together in a collective, "White" project of racist colonial subjugation.[173] Yet Nietzsche inverts as much of this schema as he reproduces. The Europeanization he prescribes indeed implies an external racial foil, to the extent that the "grand politics" required envisions a world dominion made thinkable by Europe's existing colonial conquests.[174] At the internal level, however, Nietzsche takes the provincial likes of nationalists and antisemites, rather than the Jews, as constitutive European foils. An immediate correlate to this is Nietzsche's valorization of contemporary European Jewry, made to embody as a people everything that nationalist antisemites are not. But there is a subtler consequence to his system as well. By aligning antisemites and the colonized on the same, non-European side of the ledger, Nietzsche points the way toward conflating the two. I have discussed already how in the 1880s French political antisemites were busy propagating the trope of the Jew-hating Muslim, the better to naturalize antisemitism as a universal religious and racial imperative. After Nietzsche, this simultaneous attribution to the colonized of intolerance and difference could be redeployed as the inscription of twin stigmata on a single guarantor of European self-consistency: the antisemitic colonial subaltern, whose similarly constructed postcolonial Muslim descendants today furnish Europe an overdetermined other.

I return in subsequent sections to early examples, in the years of high empire, of diverting European antisemitism to colonial subalterns' account. First let me pause, though, to take stock of this phenomenon in the *longue durée*. As medieval military foe, Islam framed what Anidjar, borrowing categories from Jacques Derrida, calls the "being-political" and "being-Christian" constitutive of Europe.[175] That process evolved when the extension of colonial power over racialized Muslim others (Arab, Kabyle, Black) helped confirm Europe's being-White in the biologistic mode of modernity. The horrors of World War II eventually reconstituted "Europe" as a shared vigilance against Nazism. And while decolonization simultaneously attenuated Europe's collective imperial sense of self, postcolonial migrations toward the metropole renewed European claims to being-Christian and being-White. Europe, in other words, had adopted something resembling Nietzsche's bipartite vision, defining itself against the antisemite even as it continued to presume a (post)colonial other.

Given this, what more potent a bugaboo than what Taguieff calls an Islamist "new 'fascism'" that, in combining the specters of antisemitism and Islam, so thoroughly condenses two of Europe's great historical foils?[176] The construction of Muslims into Europe's preeminent antisemitic force usefully cleaves antisemitism from its modern European origins, staving off the potential for self-estrangement when, in its repudiation of antisemitism, postwar Europe paradoxically takes as its negative image something profoundly *European*. But the figure of the antisemitic Muslim also resolves a tension between the new, chastened Europe united by the cautionary memory of the Final Solution and the old Europe forged in the common projects of empire and Christendom. Formerly external others rendered demographically internal, Europe's millions of Muslim citizens and immigrants provide a site in which to translate an earlier paradigm of Europeanness—still operative in anxieties about the Islamic threat to European cultural, religious, or racial identity—into more contemporarily palatable terms. Muslims need no longer be marked as different according to discredited logics of racial or religious intolerance. Instead, they are marginalized as bearers of intolerance itself, un-European because antisemitic and thus foreign to the new postwar ontology of democratic Europe. Their presence inside Europe further facilitates the transition, since as a now-internal danger Islam can be aligned with a fascism likewise organizing European identity from within.

The translation of an older, lingering model of European identity-production into the codes of the present accomplishes two related kinds of work. It becomes possible to pursue an official anti-antisemitic project of inclusion in the unofficial mode of Islamophobic exclusion, ensuring a European coherence otherwise jeopardized by competing definitions of Europe as a locus of ethnic embrace and rejection. And it becomes easier to posit a European self-sameness over historical time, in particular by creating postwar rationalizations for colonial-era racializations. The old figure of the Jew-hating Muslim represented an imperialist gesture—the attribution to one racialized subaltern of existential hatred for another—in terms legible to a present-day European sensibility accustomed, since the war, to considering antisemitism the antithetical guarantor of the thesis that is now Europe. It seems to make historical "sense" that a longtime ideological shorthand for the non-European, Islam, should always have coincided with what, in antisemitism, would become such a shorthand later. Here we begin to understand why contemporary anti-antisemitism can take for granted the topos of a historical Muslim antisemitism elaborated in the imperial nineteenth century by antisemites themselves. It is not just because the topos has come unmoored from its discursive origins to acquire the aura of objective truth, or because the current, very real problem of Muslim antisemitism lends the notion retroactive credibility. It is also because this older location of anti-Jewish prejudice beyond the continent flatters a newer self-fashioning premised on an existential war against antisemitism by the European collective.

The new Europe's organization along anti-antisemitic lines is thus at once a response to the concrete traumas of the mid-twentieth century and the iteration of a nineteenth-century discourse locating in anti-antisemitism a site of European cohesion. I use the pluralized "traumas" to emphasize how the public memory of the Holocaust developed in relation with the contemporaneous upheavals of decolonization. Recent work by Michael Rothberg has demonstrated the conjunction of these two histories in a "minoritarian tradition of 'decolonized' Holocaust memory" elaborated by thinkers like W. E. B. Du Bois and Aimé Césaire, whose work productively combined reflections on colonialism, racism, slavery, and the Holocaust.[177] Rothberg's conceptual decolonization proceeds by correctively (re)situating Holocaust memory within the longer context of the colonial and postcolonial memories that prepared, inflected, and incorporated it. Still to be decolonized, however, is the similarly longer arc of European anti-antisemitism within which Holocaust memory remains simultaneously embedded. The sheer weight of the Holocaust ensures that early European expressions of anti-antisemitism are often globally contextualized in terms of the future catastrophe they did not prevent, rather than in terms of the imperialism that shaped them. Zola, writes his biographer Mitterand, "understands and condemns in advance the monstrosities of chauvinism and institutionalized racism," but "others will rapidly cease to listen." Little wonder that Mitterand struggles to explain why, "strangely," Zola did not accompany his late notes against militarism and war with a renouncement of *Fécondité*'s lust for imperial conquest.[178] From the Holocaust-enabled vantage point that identifies in Zola a Cassandra for institutionalized antisemitism's modern destructive potential, it certainly appears strange for him to have remained so unfazed by the institutionalized racism of empire. But what if, as I have already begun to suggest, Zola was able to think beyond and against antisemitism—along with other anti-Dreyfusard staples like militarism, jingoism, and reactionary Catholicism—precisely only *because* of an imperialist outlook whose utility to him as an abstraction blinded him to the material, racist realities of colonial violence?

Zola's imperialist naïveté might alternately be understood as an illustration of how antisemitism's temporary defeat in the Dreyfus Affair made possible a "colonial 'good conscience'" on the Republic's part that rendered plausible the dissociation of racism from colonization.[179] Yet Zola's own significant contribution to this defeat was itself made possible by what we might instead term a colonial consciousness—that is, a politics of scale animating his anti-antisemitic project by staking out a global, imperial perspective designed to reveal the shortcomings of antisemitic thought. Such a consciousness, insofar as it enabled a critique of metropolitan racism, perhaps inevitably occulted its own racist premise. It also subtly expanded the machinery of colonial discursive violence. By making antisemites into recalcitrant obstacles to a global order promised by a benevolent French empire, Zola's anti-antisemitism contributed to a new, roving category of imperial perception. That category accommodated a wide range of possible others—including colonized subalterns—whose antisemitism, real or not, could now be taken to obstruct imperial harmony and to justify their inclusion alongside metropolitan reactionaries in a rehierarchized disciplinary regime. Lamenting, in *Fécondité*, the obstacle to an African "new France" posed by the "fanaticism" associated with "this terrible problem of Islam," Zola certainly echoed longstanding Western notions about an intransigent Muslim religiosity.[180] Henceforth, though, such a description resonated just as contemporarily with the metropolitan antisemitic "fanaticism" that Zola had been lambasting for years.[181]

We have seen how Nietzsche's Europeanism, too, traced a conceptual contiguity between antisemites and the colonized, opening the way for a prejudice against (post)colonial others justified as an antiprejudice directed at their antisemitism. Once such second-order discourses about Jews (that is, discourses about discourses about Jews) permeated Europe's approach to its colonial project, strange alchemies ensued. In the remainder of the chapter, I consider various imperial figures made to incarnate an antisemitic threat and ask what this might mean for rethinking contemporary anti-antisemitism.

RELOCATING ANTISEMITISM

The year after Nietzsche's death and one year before Zola's, the plasticity of antisemitism as a label for imperial difference found a showcase in Louis Bertrand's 1901 novel *La Cina*. Arriving in Algiers in 1891 to teach high school, Bertrand embarked on a literary career that eventually earned him a place in the Académie Française. His master idea, to which he repeatedly returned in Algerian novels like *Le Sang des races* (*The Blood of Races*) (1899) and *Pépète le bien-aimé* (*Pépète the Beloved*) (1904), was the notion of a "Latin Africa." The contemporary North African melting pot of colonists hailing from places like France, Spain, and Italy represented, for Bertrand, a revival of the pre-Islamic era of Roman occupation. After twelve centuries of stagnant Muslim rule, a new settler race of Mediterranean, pan-Latin Overmen was emerging to reclaim the Latin world's rightful preeminence in Africa.

Bertrand later congratulated Nietzsche, whom he claimed to have discovered during World War I, for having appreciated the restorative gifts of the sun-kissed Mediterranean to the enervated Northern soul.[182] He doubtless also recognized something of his vision in Nietzsche's Europeanism, whose premise of a resurgent continental Rome anticipated Bertrand's own fantasy of a pan-European amalgam seizing its due from a millenary rival. For Nietzsche, of course, that rival had been slavish Judea. For Bertrand, it was the "old enslaved race" of Islam.[183]

Bertrand's schema relegated indigenous North African Jewry to the same archaic somnolence as Muslim Arabs and Berbers. The Jews did, though, retain for him some specificity. Bertrand seems initially to have considered that in their capacity as a lightning rod for the ire of European colonists, Jews could at least produce a consolidating effect. In *Le Sang des races*, Algerian colonists from all over the European Mediterranean mingle guardedly at an inn until the passage of two unfortunate Jews unites the disparate factions in a single, hearty chant of "Death to the Jews!"[184] Much as a decade earlier Maurice Barrès had cynically identified, in metropolitan antisemitism, a potent "formula" for rallying the crowd[185]—or Drumont, now a deputy representing Algiers, had in 1898 declared before the French National Assembly that in Algeria "all, sons of Frenchmen and sons of foreigners . . . are brothers united by a common feeling: hatred of the Jew"[186]—Bertrand here suggests the potential of antisemitism as a unificatory social and racial force. Nietzsche, needless to say, would have been appalled.

In *La Cina*, however, Bertrand offered a more wary assessment of Algerian antisemitism. The preceding few years had seen that antisemitism come crashing down from its 1898 zenith, when Algeria sent four radically antisemitic representatives (among them Drumont) to the National Assembly, and agitators like the charismatic young mayor of Algiers Max Régis fomented violent antisemitic riots in the colony. By 1901, the year in which *La Cina* appeared, political antisemites on both sides of the Mediterranean had fallen into discredit as the case against their bête noire Dreyfus unraveled in France and colonial authorities cracked down on antisemitic activity in Algeria.[187] Bertrand, likely annoyed that antisemitism had temporarily captured more imaginations than his vision of a Latin Africa, and clearly feeling empowered by the waning fortunes of Régis and his ilk, sensed an ideological opportunity. Amid Bertrand's usual themes of a "new people" and "Latin continuity," *La Cina* launches a cleverly co-optive attack on organized antisemitism.[188] Two young French friends, Michel Botteri and Claude Gelée, arrive in Algeria to launch Michel's political career. Their lives play out according to the familiar script of imperial regeneration: having wasted their youths so far in the torpors of the Third Republic, that bugbear of conservatives like Bertrand, they remake themselves in the vigorous colonial air. Along the way, Claude counsels Michel to ally himself with the local antisemitic movement. Michel's conscience resists:

> First of all, from a Christian standpoint, I cannot! And the party chiefs repulse me. . . . Besides, you agreed with me: antisemitism only ever seemed to us a disguise for the old conservative party at its most retrograde and basely greedy. (128)

The novel's antisemites do little to prove Michel wrong. Among them, the Prince de Lamballe cuts an especially grotesque figure. Patterned after the very real Prince de Polignac, whose vicious antisemitism and crackpot schemes had made him a natural Algerian advisor to the Marquis de Morès's doomed antisemitic African crusade (see Chapters 3 and 4), the Prince de Lamballe is overwhelmed by his hatred for Jews. Shaking with a "crazed laughter, his mouth convulsing, his fingers febrile" as he dispenses slogans like "Yes, yes! The guillotine for the Jews," he inspires horror in those around him (196). The real-life rabble-rouser Max Régis fares somewhat better. Transposed here as Carmelo Xuereb, a preening rube whose affectations nearly prompt

Claude to laugh out loud, he at least possesses the merit of the animal virility so prized by Bertrand.

Carmelo possesses another, more surprising trait as well. He himself, it turns out, descends from Semitic stock—an inheritance on display in the "strongly accentuated Semitic nose" of his Maltese father, Ange Xuereb (301). With this twist, Bertrand uses the word "Semite" in its original nineteenth-century sense as a label for speakers of Arabic, Hebrew, or one of the other Semitic languages of North Africa and the Near East. Ange has disowned his son for turning against a Jewish people with whom, according to Ange's theory of a Phoenician origin for his Maltese dialect, Carmelo in fact shares a common Semitic origin. Carmelo will go on to provoke the ironic spectacle of a climactic and bloody antisemitic riot propelled by none other than Semitic passions: "the devouring breath of the old Semitic Moloch inflamed the blood of the races and blended them in a same dizzying whirlwind of bloody madness" (295).

Bertrand's chutzpah recalls Nietzsche's. Attributing antisemitic violence to the Semitic tendencies of those who perpetrate it, *La Cina* subordinates antisemitism to the racial metanarrative of a North Africa divided into new Latins and everyone else. Just as Nietzsche sardonically branded antisemites the unsuspecting instruments of Judea, Bertrand wields the politics of scale to reduce antisemitism to a variety of Semitism from within which Carmelo cannot see the new Latin plebs taking form. Paul Hartmann, a respected archaeologist whom Michel and Claude befriend, gives a patina of scientific authority to Bertrand's theory that the new colonial Latins have been "Semitized" by the indigenous Jews and Muslims around them:

> we have here, as in every period of African history, a jumbled multitude comprised of every Mediterranean race, which seeks in this moment to define and affirm itself as a homogeneous people. In the meantime, what strikes me is that the future people is already thoroughly Semitized . . . is it not the Jew and the Arab, among whom they lived, who have fashioned the character of our colonists? (194–95)

As the paradoxical manifestation of this Semitization, antisemitism is not completely at odds with the temporarily salutary excesses that—in the words of Bertrand's fellow literary evangelist for Algerian "energy," Robert Randau—were enabling Algerian colonists to escape a "European senility through the very exuberance of their vices."[189] But neither does Bertrand consider it a permanent organizing force.

Antisemitism, under this logic, is expected to recede from the Latin crowd, returning back to the "Semitism" from whence it came. Nietzsche's version of the tactic had remained more definitional than anything. What mattered for him was that European antisemites be properly inscribed in the genealogy of a Judea whose worst expression they represented. Without literally making them Jews, this removed their antisemitism to the proper camp in the historical and metaphorical Rome/Judea divide. By turning the imprecision of political antisemites' pseudoscientific terminology against them, however, Bertrand locates the real impetus for violent, fanatical antisemitism in a tangible and contemporaneous racial site: the "Semites" whose own supposed violence and fanaticism explained, for midcentury philologists like Ernest Renan, their inferiority to Christian Aryans in the hierarchy of cultures.[190] Though superannuated, these Semites were certainly not understood to have disappeared. Thus can Algerian antisemitism manifest, according to Bertrand, the temporary infection of European colonists by a Semitic fever transmitted through colonial contact.

Bertrand's anti-antisemitism only targets a very specific Algerian political antisemitism aimed at Jews. Characterizing this antisemitism as a narrow, primitive violence traceable to Semites themselves—those colonized in Algeria by Europeans—Bertrand eschews it for a more capacious antisemitism that, literalizing the notion in a way self-styled antisemites never had, extends to Muslims as well. Here again we are reminded never automatically to equate anti-antisemitism with friendliness toward Jews.[191] As Jonathan Judaken points out, even formulations of anti-antisemitism in good faith by Sartre and others have not always proven immune to duplicating the terms of what they combat.[192] But my more immediate point is this: by introducing Muslims into the equation, Bertrand uncouples anti-Jewish antisemitism from the "Mediterranean" Latins whose harmonious future it threatens. Zola hoped the antisemitic obstruction to French national and imperial unity would simply disappear. Nietzsche mediated and attenuated the obstruction via the colonized periphery, without exactly forecasting its disappearance from Europe. Bertrand, by contrast, relocates it squarely in the realm of a subaltern other. Externalizing antisemitism from what remained an essentially European (if resolutely southern European) enterprise understood by Bertrand and fellow "Algerianists" like Randau to be fusing French, Spanish, Italian, and other

Mediterranean bloodlines into a vigorous new race, Bertrand's project crudely portends the future convergence of anti-antisemitism and Islamophobia into a joint basis for European cohesion.[193]

An early such cohesion was in fact already underway, since the apparent hatred of Jews by Muslims was the one thing on which so otherwise heterogeneous a group of European actors—antisemitic and anti-antisemitic, nationalist and Europeanist, continental and Algerian, liberal and reactionary—seemed able to agree. This indexed a larger discourse, in the Foucauldian sense, circumscribing seemingly contradictory ideological projects within a same condition of possibility: the flexible projection of European prejudice onto a non-European other. Something of that elemental European discursive unity remains today in Europe's shared anxiety, fueled by the spectacular actions of an extremist minority, about an intolerant Islam.

TOWARD A NEW ANTI-ANTISEMITISM

One might draw a cautious parallel between the current moment and the early years of the twentieth century when, in post–Dreyfus Affair France, a spirit of evangelical vigilance likewise coalesced around a flare-up in the Jewish question. Consider the reaction by the *Archives Israélites*, the French Jewish newspaper of record, to various attacks on Europeans and Jews throughout Morocco in 1906 and 1907. The March 1907 murder by a mob in Marrakech of French doctor Émile Mauchamp especially outraged European opinion, prompting France's occupation of the eastern Moroccan town of Oujda near the Algerian border.[194] In July Europeans were again horrified to learn that eight French, Italian, and Spanish workers had been murdered in Casablanca. France invaded the city on August 3; Muslim Casablancans responded by sacking the *mellah*, or Jewish quarter, the same day.[195] The *Archives Israélites* promptly called for the kind of definitive colonial conquest that, with the establishment of the French Protectorate over Morocco five years later, would indeed come to pass. The Moroccan Arab's "atavistic hatred of the Jew," wrote editor in chief Hippolyte Prague, was presently compounded by Muslim frustrations at Moroccan Jews' cooperation with European economic penetration. France must act to protect its natural Jewish allies.[196]

French metropolitan Jews, of course, had been energetically (albeit paternalistically) advocating on behalf of North African Jewry since

France's 1830 conquest of Algeria (see Chapter 3). But by using, in an impassioned conclusion, the pillage of Casablanca's *mellah* to caution against the continuing peril of "antisemitism," Prague views North African Muslim-Jewish relations through the post-Dreyfus lens of a France held to have affirmed its commitment to the Jews. In the process, he reaches beyond and redefines the otherwise stock arsenal of Orientalist tropes—"fanaticism," "despotism"—with which he consigns Moroccan Muslims to the wrong side of progress. Now Muslims most flagrantly disqualify themselves *as antisemites* from "this European civilization" that they "reject with horror" and whose recent containment of an antisemitic, anti-Dreyfusard threat fortifies its collective difference from a rebarbative Islam.[197]

To designate anti-Jewish Moroccan hostilities as "antisemitism" was, in 1907, still a misnomer. A European invention, antisemitism in its modern, ideological form had only just started reaching the Muslim world and even then mostly via Levantine Arab Christians.[198] True, Jews' traditional second-class legal status as *dhimmi* under Islamic law meant a certain level of institutionalized cultural disdain for Jews in the Muslim world (though something similar could certainly be said of European states, several of which only emancipated their Jewish populations decades after the Ottoman Empire's 1856 declaration of legal equality for its subjects improved the lot of Jews in Muslim lands from North Africa to the Middle East).[199] And the Algerian Crémieux myth notwithstanding, it would be inaccurate to deny that imperial domination in some cases sparked tensions between North African Muslims and Jews. Events in Morocco certainly corroborated the *Archives Israélites*' concern about Muslim anger at Jewish economic elites protected by their European patrons and on whose behalf the Great Powers even appeared willing to intervene militarily. Michel Abitbol has observed that, across North Africa and the Middle East, Muslims were starting to perceive once-isolated Jewish communities as part of a coordinated international Jewry[200]—fertile circumstances indeed for the implantation of nineteenth-century European antisemitic notions about a global Jewish conspiracy. "Muslim antisemitism" henceforth became a self-fulfilling prophecy of sorts, projected onto Muslims by antisemites and anti-antisemites alike, then produced for real when anti-antisemitic incitements to conquest like Prague's made plausible to Muslims what French antisemites had spuriously alleged since the 1880s: that France might be colonizing Muslims at the behest of its Jews.

Europe risks something like this circularity today. The sociologist Michel Wieviorka has explained French Muslim antisemitism as the frustrated reaction by some members of a disenfranchised minority to their impression that being Jewish and French is allowed, while being Muslim and French is not.[201] How much more frustrated must Muslims be, then, to discover not only that Jews have easier access to a hyphenated Europeanness than Muslims but also that the new Europe's very self-understanding requires this disparity, since the postwar inclusion of Jews and postcolonial rejection of (antisemitic) Muslim difference have become so thoroughly enmeshed? What to do about the vicious cycle produced when the expectation of Muslim antisemitism potentially breeds the thing itself?

One solution is to think, in the way I have tried to here, of anti-antisemitism in historical context. The paradox of the insistence by some on the "new antisemitism" as the real enemy in the anti-antisemitic fight is that, while associating the "old antisemitism" with a largely bygone era of biological racism and nationalism, the new term generally targets a population—Muslims—whose construction as antisemites dates precisely to the erstwhile era in question. In other words, the rubric may not offer so "new" a way of conceiving antisemites after all. Yes, the antisemitism currently exhibited by some Muslims and non-Muslims takes an anti-Zionist form distinguishable in certain tenets (blaming Jews more for the policies of Israel than for being Jews) and methods (a discourse of anticolonial resistance) from the xenophobic antisemitism invented in the nineteenth century. But we have seen how, over a hundred years ago, antisemites and anti-antisemites alike already considered Muslim anger at Jews an expression of anticolonial outrage. What is really new about anticolonial antisemitic Muslim anger, or at least about its representation, is that it now threatens Europe from within.

Even on this point the novelty dissipates. However new Europe's internal Muslim antisemitism might be deemed, it certainly has elicited a familiar response. Nietzsche and others once ridiculed European antisemites for embodying the very thing they denounced. A similar charge is being leveled now at "new" antisemites, though it is of course no longer Jewishness that they are accused of reaffirming. Rather, it is their justification of anti-Zionism on the grounds of antiracism that makes them unsuspecting agents of the racism they condemn. "In the last three decades of the [twentieth] century," offers Taguieff, "Judeophobia based on racism . . . gave way to Judeophobia based on anti-racism." What he means is that by designating Israel's treatment of Palestinians as "racist," critics of Israel cynically imbue antisemitism with moral authority. The result is "a tragic reversal of the 'struggle against racism,' which since the end of the nineteenth century had included the struggle against anti-Semitism."[202]

Condemning terroristic, antisemitic "jihadists," Taguieff cites Nietzsche's distaste for martyrs. A more subtle measure of Taguieff's debt to Nietzsche, however, is the Nietzschean language in which he reproves Muslim antisemites for their "herdlike submission."[203] They are as unconscious of their racism as, for Nietzsche, German antisemites were bovinely oblivious to their *ressentiment.* Nietzsche despised these antisemites' nationalism, while Taguieff proves more suspicious of the new antisemitism's "anti-nationalist" rejection of Israeli self-determination and attachment to a transnational Islam.[204] But both justify their condemnations from the self-accorded vantage point of a world-historical perspective unavailable to their foes. Nietzsche claimed such perspective by setting Europe's Judeo-Christian heritage against the longer arc of its Roman imperial past and global imperial future. Taguieff simply inverts the premise: what the new antisemites do not properly appreciate now, he intimates, is the *end* of European empire, a historical horizon against which their indictment of Zionism as "colonialism" or "imperialism" proves anachronistic. Frozen in time, they perpetually represent Muslims in France and in Palestine as "resistance fighters" struggling against an eternal imperial injustice.[205]

Finkielkraut adopts a similarly updated politics of scale when he argues that the anticolonial championing of the aggrieved colonial subject has, since decolonization, calcified into a dangerously Manichean habit of mind. Unable to recognize that the world has changed, postcolonial European Muslims and their ideological sympathizers still view various conflicts—especially the one between Israel and Palestine—as pitting racists against a victimized, intrinsically blameless "Other."[206] Thus, for Finkielkraut, do Israel and the Jews become targets of antisemites whose self-described antiracism blinds them to the anti-Jewish racism they perpetuate. And thus do these new antisemites disqualify themselves from the new Europe, not only as antisemites but also as anachronistic anticolonials inhibiting Europe's collective "disavowal" of its colonial, racist, and antisemitic past.[207]

Finkielkraut proposes a familiar dialectic as well between the nation and its supranational guarantor. Recall how Zola conceived, in his utopic imperialism, a space where the nation might resume a noble trajectory foreshortened at home by the particularistic nationalism of antisemitic jingoists. Empire would rescue the nation from those whose narrowly ethnic definition of it corrupted its more properly political, universalizing form. Likewise does Finkielkraut's Europe fortify the nation against antisemites, though from antisemites now endangering it in the opposite way. As antinational adherents to a stateless "transborderism" and "wandering," the new antisemites reject, for him, the capacity of nations to represent their transnational political interests.[208] To this supranational vision that dispenses with the national altogether, Finkielkraut offers a supranational European alternative that, standing collectively against fascism, reaffirms the national by asserting democratic principles with which the nation remains "consubstantial."[209]

Neither national nor European, the new antisemites join the ranks of the "mixed *society*" dismissed by Finkielkraut.[210] Here he channels Hannah Arendt's distinction between "society" and the state, or between the "social" and the "political." Society, in Arendt's definition, is the monolithic realm of mass consumption and cultural conformism, where the collective economic satisfaction of mankind's biological needs substitutes itself for authentic public life. The state, by contrast, offers the opportunity for a real, shared political experience compatible with, and indeed premised on, the manifestation of human plurality.[211] In Chapter 1 I examined the double correspondence Arendt draws between this European society, which she argues provided the raw human material for fascism, and the imperial project. Society lent itself to the emergence of an authoritarian "continental imperialism" at once "tribal" in its resemblance to a supposed African primitivity, and profoundly reflective of the racist logic governing the European colonial empire. Finkielkraut's antisemitic "mixed society" offers a comparably strange, overdetermined repository for both racial otherness and its racist counterpart. Only now the two collapse into a single, hybridized, postcolonial amalgam comprised by the Muslim antisemite and his various European sympathizers.

Finkielkraut's indebtedness to an Arendtian framework situates Arendt's own anti-antisemitism within a longer genealogy of European anti-antisemitic thought conducive to the externalization of antisemitism's real onus from white Europeans onto colonial or postcolonial others. Arendt notoriously seemed to intimate that the imperial encounter, in causing colonizers to lower themselves to the purely biological, prepolitical existence of Africans, had infused continental antisemitism with a ruthless new disregard for the plurality fostered and safeguarded—however imperfectly—by the European system of nation-states. Gnawed from within and without, the "comity of nations" succumbed for good, she argued, when a racist, expansionist fascism violently erased whatever remained of a delicate historical balance among mutually respectful European powers.[212]

Writing in the immediate aftermath of World War II, Arendt contemplated the European comity of nations as a thing still defunct. A half century later, Finkielkraut considers it renewed, and with it the counterforces merging once again under the primary ideological umbrella of antisemitism. This resemblance of Finkielkraut's "mixed society" to Arendt's swarming continental masses offers a useful reminder that, for Finkielkraut, Taguieff, and similar thinkers, the new antisemitic threat to Europe does not simply pit a supranational, antidemocratic Islam against national democratic bastions in the West. Thus conceived, the threat would amount to little more than an updated version of old xenophobic fears about a supranational Jewish threat to the nation, and Muslims would indeed have become the "new Jews." At stake instead, I propose, is something more like what Arendt held dear: the profoundly scalar claim, following Finkielkraut's formulation, of a European "consubstantiality" between nation and comity, each surviving only insofar as it inheres and trusts in the other.

So the new Islamophobia differs from the old antisemitism—but not just because, as Bunzl would have it, Islamophobia questions Muslims' suitability as Europeans in a way distinct from how antisemitism once questioned Jews' suitability as national citizens.[213] Muslims and their allies are also, and maybe even especially, taken to endanger the scalar oscillation between national and European belonging. Islam, in this regard, represents less the fittingly supranational other of a postnational Europe than a magnet for displaced European anxieties about reconciling potentially incompatible national and supranational sovereignties, cultures, and interests. Indeed, Muslim antisemitism comes to figure every possible boundedness inhibiting or contrasting with the new Europe's scalar flexibility in time and space. Hence do Muslim accusations of a lingering European colonialism in Israel disturb because they understand Europe to be contained by—and not to contain—its imperial past. Hence, as well, do Muslims become a conveniently European-wide proxy for an antisemitic intolerance whose rejection furnishes individual European nations and the new Europe a shared, scalable sense of purpose around which to cohere.

Of course, Jews themselves have also long been associated with the comity of nations. Arendt considers a transnational caste of elite Jews to have facilitated crucial diplomatic relations among modern European nation-states.[214] Balibar, in a different vein, cites the nationalist rejection of Jews as a common exclusionary principle from which the collection of like-minded nations called "Europe" emerged in the nineteenth century.[215] The latter phenomenon perhaps makes it most plausible to label European Muslims the "new Jews," insofar as European nations might be understood today to collectively perform a Europeanness by each excluding (or at least marginalizing) some part of their respective Muslim populations deemed unable to respect norms shared by the nation and European community alike. But these shared norms also illustrate how different a dynamic the principle of shared exclusion has come to produce, and not just because that updated dynamic now works officially to protect the Jews whose exclusion it once required. Antisemitic nations in the nineteenth century did not necessarily need to perform and honor their individual Europeanness, since Europe was not yet endowed with the supranational political institutions that now exercise some measure of coercive control over member states; Europe was still more of an idea than a fully realized political program. Since World War II, however, and especially since the advent of the European Community, the balancing act between nation and collectivity has grown immeasurably more complex. Shared norms become essential when states must somehow harmonize national and supranational interests and projects so frequently otherwise at odds.

Accordingly, the most apt prewar comparison for how Muslims figure ideologically into the new Europe is not antisemitism but anti-antisemitism instead. For colonial empire, too, caused European states to engage in frequently divergent projects at the national and supranational level, particularly when a democracy like France reverted to feudal measures in its conquests abroad. As contemporary denunciations of Muslim antisemitism work to bridge nation and European collectivity, so Muslim antisemitism once proved a usefully scalable device for negotiating the precarious ideological relationship between nation and empire. Witness Prague, for whom Moroccan Muslims' antisemitism justifies an immediate French colonization on the grounds that "it is the destiny of inferior civilizations to be absorbed by superior ones."[216] Conjuring away tension between this chauvinistic rationale and his Dreyfusard objections to similar such racializing outlooks in France, Prague invokes a single domestic and overseas enemy—the antisemite—around which to reconcile the otherwise discordant endeavors of national Jewish assimilation and imperial Muslim marginalization.

Derived in part from this historical metropolitan conflation of the antisemite at home and the Muslim abroad, today's figure of the Muslim antisemite haunts Europe from within. Only now the tension resolved by the figure lies increasingly between a resurgent European nationalism and the European collective that, in the era of the United Kingdom's "Brexit" from the European Union, is viewed with increasing suspicion by populist national movements in France, Austria, and elsewhere. Islamophobic xenophobia serves those nationalist movements' purposes well, demarcating the nation as it does against both a Muslim other and a supranational European Union deemed by some incapable, since the beginning of the European migrant crisis, of protecting individual member states from the flow of Muslim refugees into and across the continent. Yet precisely because Europe's shared external and internal borders require a coordinated response to the migrant crisis, nationalist movements remain committed to some sort of "European identity" useful for rationalizing a continent-wide rejection of populations displaced overseas by war and economic immiseration. Particularist European nationalisms thus remain at least partially continentalist, retaining aspects of the new Europe even as they reject certain supranational strictures (a common currency, an unelected European Union bureaucracy) associated with it. As Muslims, Muslim antisemites furnish xenophobic nationalisms a non-national other coded in terms of a "cultural incompatibility" more discursively acceptable to many Europeans than a balder racism might be. As antisemites, they furnish a non-continental other coded in terms of a "post-criminal" Europe (the term is Finkielkraut's)[217] that therefore need not rely on whiteness, Christianity, or other unifying logics discredited by history. And as both Muslims *and* antisemites, crucially, they make those nationalist and continentalist postures psychosocially compatible, despite the evident contradiction between the return of aggressive nationalisms and a new Europe predicated on banishing the continental violence those nationalisms once unleashed.

Such questions are hardly academic. To decolonize certain influential tendencies in European anti-antisemitism is to acknowledge the risk that anti-antisemitism can produce its own object, including some portion of Muslim antisemitism generated by a self-fulfilling prophecy structured into the very concept of a new Europe (or, for that matter, into what we might call a "new new Europe" perhaps emerging as reactionary nationalisms at once scuttle and co-opt the postwar European order). How to proceed from there? Advancing a corrective understanding of Europe from which less complicitly to examine and tackle contemporary antisemitism is a subject for another book. I see no reason, however, not to call now for a new anti-antisemitism unburdened by accumulated biases inherited from the colonial encounter. Unsurprisingly enough at this point, such a reconsidered anti-antisemitism would doubtfully prove so truly new. For inspiration we have no further to look, already, than one of Prague's more temperate colleagues at the *Archives Israélites*, who just a few months before Prague's anti-Muslim outburst cautioned that Muslim antisemitism was at least partially a construction by French antisemites eager to depict aggrieved Muslims bedeviled by local Jews conspiring with European powers.[218] And there is admittedly something about trying to locate anti-antisemitism's problematically unavowed influences that potentially mirrors old anti-antisemitic attempts at turning the tables of scale on "Jewish" antisemites. But either way, to appreciate European anti-antisemitism's original and ongoing flaws requires assessing discourses about Jews and empire in all their knotty historical relation. That is what I have endeavored to do here and throughout this book. Only thus may we loosen the double grip encircling, like two weathered talons, a European present still prey to its antisemitic and imperial pasts.

Acknowledgments

A project like this is no individual endeavor. Fellowships from the National Endowment for the Humanities, the University of California Humanities Research Institute, and the Hellman Family Foundation made much writing and research possible. Many generous colleagues also contributed along the way. Maurie Samuels was a beacon of support and guidance. Susan Gillman and Dick Terdiman championed my work when I needed it most. Nick White's encouragement has been unwavering, and Mayanthi Fernando's contributions key. Gerry Prince, Lydie Moudileno, and Mary Donaldson-Evans were kind early mentors. In Debarati Sanyal, Cathy Nesci, Alex Wettlaufer, Vilashini Cooppan, and Steven Englund, I have been graced with incomparable readers. Patrick Bray, Bettina Lerner, David Carroll, Ellen Burt, Dan Edelstein, Heidi Brevik-Zender, Andrea Goulet, Nathaniel Deutsch, and Ethan Katz were thoughtful interlocutors in a variety of settings. Neryvia Pillay Bell was indispensable down the stretch. And Larry Schehr, somewhere, is smiling.

Notes

INTRODUCTION

1. Aziz Zemouri and Jean-Michel Décugis, "Une piste néonazie," *Le Point*, 19 March 2012, web.

2. "Transcription des conversations entre Mohammed Merah et les négociateurs," *Libération*, 17 July 2012, web. All translations are my own throughout, except when I cite existing translations.

3. Zemouri and Décugis, "Une piste néonazie"; "Toulouse: Que sait-on du tueur à scooter?" *Sud-Ouest*, 20 March 2012, web.

4. "Nicolas Sarkozy suspend sa participation à la campagne," *Le Point*, 19 March 2012, web.

5. For a bibliography on the debates surrounding the new antisemitism, see Chapter 5, note 3.

6. David Theo Goldberg, "The Comparative and the Relational: Meditations on Racial Method," in *A Companion to Comparative Literature*, ed. Ali Behdad and Dominic Thomas (New York: Wiley-Blackwell, 2011), 360.

7. Michael Rothberg, *Multidirectional Memory: Remembering the Holocaust in the Age of Decolonization* (Stanford: Stanford University Press, 2009), 6–7.

8. Christian S. Davis, *Colonialism, Antisemitism, and Germans of Jewish Descent in Imperial Germany* (Ann Arbor: University of Michigan Press, 2012), 107.

9. Davis, *Colonialism*, 106.

10. Here, for instance, is Enzo Traverso, wary of giving any impression that the Holocaust "'invented' antisemitism, by conferring the appearance of a coherent, cumulative, and linear process upon a body of discourse and practices that, before Nazism, had been perceived in the various European

countries as discordant, heterogeneous, and in many cases decidedly archaic" (Traverso, *The Origins of Nazi Violence*, trans. Janet Lloyd [New York: The New Press, 2003], 6). See also David Nirenberg, *Communities of Violence: Persecution of Minorities in the Middle Ages* (Princeton: Princeton University Press, 1996), 4–5 and Pierre-André Taguieff, *La Judéophobie des modernes: Des Lumières au Jihad mondial* (Paris: Odile Jacob, 2008), 176.

11. The expression is Marc Angenot's (Angenot, *Ce que l'on dit des Juifs en 1889: Antisémitisme et discours social* [Saint-Denis: Presses Universitaires de Vincennes, 1989], 135). Writing in a similar vein about French colonial Algeria, David Carroll argues that "throughout the Third Republic, colonialist racism and the anti-Semitism that would later form a fundamental component of French fascism coexisted with and even mutually supported one another. . . . Colonialism relied on both colonialist racism and anti-Semitism to ensure that 'the Other' would remain both other and subservient, with each racism acting in collusion with the other to perpetuate and justify the oppression at the very heart of colonialism" (Carroll, "Fascism, Colonialism, and 'Race': The Reality of a Fiction," in *Fascism and Neofascism: Critical Writings on the Radical Right in Europe*, ed. Angelica Fenner and Eric D. Weitz [New York: Palgrave Macmillan, 2004], 147). For another affirmation of the general, reciprocal relationship between these two racisms, see Herrick Chapman and Laura Frader, "Introduction: Race in France," in *Race in France: Interdisciplinary Perspectives on the Politics of Difference*, ed. Herrick Chapman and Laura Frader (New York: Berghahn, 2004), 5.

12. Étienne Balibar and Immanuel Wallerstein, *Race, Nation, Class: Ambiguous Identities*, trans. Chris Turner (New York: Verso, 1991), 45.

13. Balibar and Wallerstein, *Race, Nation, Class*, 45.

14. See the chapter titled "The Spatial Fix: Hegel, Von Thünen and Marx," in David Harvey, *Spaces of Capital: Towards a Critical Geography* (New York: Routledge, 2001), 284–311.

15. See, for example, Jonathan Boyarin, *The Unconverted Self: Jews, Indians, and the Identity of Christian Europe* (Chicago: University of Chicago Press, 2009); Gil Anidjar, *The Jew, the Arab: A History of the Enemy* (Stanford: Stanford University Press, 2003); Anouar Majid, *We Are All Moors: Ending Centuries of Crusades Against Muslims and Other Minorities* (Minneapolis: University of Minnesota Press, 2009); and Tudor Parfitt, "The Use of the Jew in Colonial Discourse," in *Orientalism and the Jews*, ed. Ivan Davidson Kalmar and Derek J. Penslar (Waltham, MA: Brandeis University Press, 2005), 51–67. And this kind of analysis need not always be centered on Europe: Amir Mufti, in an interesting twist, reads the Jewish question in relation to minoritization of Muslims by Hindus in India (Mufti, *Enlightenment in the Colony: The Jewish Question and the Crisis of Postcolonial Culture* [Princeton: Princeton University Press, 2007]).

16. Parfitt, "The Use of the Jew in Colonial Discourse," 51.

17. Claire Jean Kim, "The Racial Triangulation of Asian Americans," *Politics and Society* 27.1 (1999): 106.

18. Edward W. Soja, *Postmodern Geographies: The Reassertion of Space in Critical Social Theory* (London: Verso, 1989), 16.

19. On this, see Chapter 1.

20. Ivan Davidson Kalmar and Derek J. Penslar, "Orientalism and the Jews: An Introduction," in *Orientalism and the Jews*, ed. Ivan Davidson Kalmar and Derek J. Penslar, xxxii (Waltham, MA: Brandeis University Press, 2005).

21. Stephen Wilson counts 55 antisemitic riots in 1898 in metropolitan France. For his detailed account of those disturbances, see Wilson, *Ideology and Experience: Antisemitism in France at the Time of the Dreyfus Affair* (Oxford: Littman Library of Jewish Civilization, 2007), 106–24.

22. On the Fashoda Affair's implications for French antisemitism, see Chapters 3 and 4.

23. Pierre Birnbaum, *Le Moment antisémite: Un tour de la France en 1898* (Paris: Fayard, 1998).

24. Pierre Birnbaum and Lisa Moses Leff both provide brief but illuminating accounts of how the 1870 Crémieux decree, which made French citizens of all Algerian Jews, fed antisemitic sentiment in France and Algeria (Birnbaum, *"La France aux Français": Histoire des haines nationalistes* [Paris: Seuil, 2006], 259–81; Leff, *Sacred Bonds of Solidarity: The Rise of Jewish Internationalism in Nineteenth-Century France* [Stanford: Stanford University Press, 2006], 207–28). And Julie Kalman has offered nuanced accounts of how, in the decades before the late nineteenth-century emergence of antisemitism as a full-blown ideology, French representations of "Oriental" Jews abroad produced fluid discourses—often "both philosemitic and antisemitic at the same time"—designed to navigate "the contested terrain of Frenchness" as capitalism, nationalism, and other forces remade French society (Kalman, *Orientalizing the Jew: Religion, Culture and Imperialism in Nineteenth-Century France* [Bloomington: Indiana University Press, 2017], 7, 9; see also Kalman, *Rethinking Antisemitism in Nineteenth-Century France* [Cambridge: Cambridge University Press, 2010], 90–127). Typically, though, scholars of French antisemitism have been little inclined to ascribe to the imperial periphery developments of central ideological importance in the metropole. Michel Winock, to cite but one example, compiles a varied list of factors contributing to the surge of antisemitism in the 1880s—including the arrival in France of Jews fleeing pogroms in Russia and eastern Europe, the inflammation of reactionary sentiment by the Third Republic's intervention in domains like divorce and education, and the 1882 crash of the Union Générale bank—but makes no mention of the impact on metropolitan antisemitism of the increasing population of indigenous Jews in France's growing North African colonial empire (Winock, *La France et les Juifs de 1789 à nos jours* [Paris: Seuil, 2004], 85–86). Historians who study French imperialism during the Vichy years have had more occasion to document the intersections between French antisemitism and empire. But such work tends to treat official Vichy antisemitism overseas as "the projection of metropolitan demonizations onto the colonies," to use Eric Jennings's formulation, rather than consider empire's earlier role in constituting metropolitan antisemitism itself (Jennings, *Vichy in the Tropics: Pétain's National Revolution in Madagascar, Guadeloupe, and Indochina, 1940–44* [Stanford: Stanford University

Press, 2001], 47). This constitutive role is especially worth revisiting, I think, now that groundbreaking new work by historiographers like Ethan Katz, Joshua Schreier, and Sarah Abrevaya Stein has approached colonial North Africa as a revealing battleground in the complex, sometimes antisemitic extension of French imperial governance over indigenous North African Jews (Katz, *The Burdens of Brotherhood: Jews and Muslims from North Africa to France* [Cambridge, MA: Harvard University Press, 2015]; Schreier, *Arabs of the Jewish Faith: The Civilizing Mission in Colonial Algeria* [New Brunswick, NJ: Rutgers University Press, 2010]; Stein, *Saharan Jews and the Fate of French Algeria* [Chicago: University of Chicago Press, 2014]). For rich collections of essays similarly evincing the colonial turn in Jewish studies and historiography, see also Kalmar and Penslar, eds., *Orientalism and the Jews* and Ethan B. Katz, Lisa Moses Leff, and Maud S. Mandel, eds., *Colonialism and the Jews* (Bloomington: Indiana University Press, 2017).

25. Hannah Arendt, *The Origins of Totalitarianism* (San Diego: Harcourt, 1976), 89.

26. Pierre-André Taguieff, *Rising from the Muck: The New Anti-Semitism in Europe*, trans. Patrick Camiller (Chicago: Dee, 2004), 12. Finkielkraut, for his part, distinguishes in contemporary French antisemitic attacks a "violence of Arab Muslim origin" (Alain Finkielkraut, *Au nom de l'Autre: Réflexions sur l'antisémitisme qui vient* [Paris: Gallimard, 2003], 34–35).

27. Marie Lemonnier, "Juifs et musulmans, frères ennemis?" *Le Nouvel Observateur*, 5 July 2012, 80–81.

28. Nicolas Weill, *La République et les antisémites* (Paris: Grasset, 2004), 62. Of course, it is also possible to inscribe the new antisemitism more specifically within the history of an "old," properly European antisemitism. As those who have chronicled it are the first to acknowledge, the new antisemitism borrows readily from an archive of antisemitic tropes, like the idea of a world Jewish conspiracy, long ensconced in the European imaginary. Merah's new antisemitism and the old antisemitism of the neo-Nazis with whom his crimes were first connected are therefore not without their historical and ideological points of overlap. Indeed, the interpenetration of new and old antisemitisms in France is such that some have questioned whether it is productive to speak of a "new" antisemitism at all (Nonna Mayer, "Nouvelle judéophobie ou vieil antisémitisme?" *Raisons politiques* 4.16 [2004]: 96; Weill, *La République et les antisémites*, 59–62). For a bibliography about the debate surrounding the new antisemitism, see Chapter 5, in which I will have occasion to revisit the question at more length.

29. Here is the historian and leftist politician Esther Benbassa, interviewed in the issue of the *Nouvel Observateur* mentioned previously: "By climbing the socioeconomic ladder, young people of immigrant descent will abandon certain prejudices and lose the legitimate frustration that renders them impatient and makes some of them aggressive toward Jews" (Benbassa, "La Parole s'est libérée," *Le Nouvel Observateur*, 5 July 2012, 79).

30. Taguieff, *Rising from the Muck*, 104.

31. Taguieff, *Rising from the Muck*, 91.

32. Nacira Guénif-Souilamas, "Jews and Arabs in Postcolonial France: A Situated Account of a Long Painful Story of Intimacy," in *Israeli-Palestinian Conflict in the Francophone World*, ed. Nathalie Debrauwere-Miller (New York: Routledge, 2010), 197.

33. Shmuel Trigano, *La Démission de la République: Juifs et Musulmans en France* (Paris: Presses Universitaires de France, 2003), 15. Emmanuel Brenner, for his part, flatly declares that France's Muslims are still behaving exactly like they are supposed to have behaved nearly one hundred fifty years ago: "Everything is happening today in France as if the colonial situation had never ended. . . . Everything is happening as if the Crémieux decree of 1870, experienced as a trauma by Algeria's Muslim population, was never overcome. As if French Jews' place in contemporary French society, their high standing, and their excellent integration into the nation reopened this old wound from the colonial Maghreb" (Brenner, *"France, prends garde de perdre ton âme . . .": Fracture sociale et antisémitisme dans la République* [Paris: Mille et une nuits, 2004], 125–26).

34. Lemonnier, "Juifs et musulmans, frères ennemis?" 81.

35. Jacques Taïeb, "Tumulte autour d'un décret: Le décret Crémieux ou la première logique colonial," *Les nouveaux cahiers* 123 (1995/96): 69 –79. See also Nancy Wood, *Vectors of Memory: Legacies of Trauma in Postwar Europe* (Oxford: Berg, 1999), 170–71. For a brief account of the extent to which, before 1870, Algerian Jews were already subject to French law, see André Chouraqui, *Histoire des Juifs en Afrique du Nord, tome 2: Le Retour en Orient* (Paris: Rocher, 1998), 19.

36. See note 24. I will return to this in Chapter 2.

37. Édouard Drumont, *La France juive: Essai d'histoire contemporaine* (Paris: Marpon et Flammarion, 1886), 2:24, 22.

38. For one of the more detailed refutations of the notion that the Crémieux decree caused the revolt, see Richard Ayoun, "Le Décret Crémieux et l'insurrection de 1871 en Algérie," *Revue d'histoire moderne et contemporaine* 35.1 (1988): 61–87. I provide a more extensive bibliography in Chapter 2.

39. Here, for example, is Jeffrey Mehlman, writing in 2010: "And so the Crémieux law was passed, granting French citizenship in 1870 to Jews but not Arabs, and the result was widespread rioting throughout Algeria" (Mehlman, "A New Judeocentrism? On a Recent Trend in French Thought," in *Israeli-Palestinian Conflict in the Francophone World*, ed. Nathalie Debrauwere-Miller [New York: Routledge, 2010], 214).

40. Ian Hacking, *Historical Ontology* (Cambridge, MA: Harvard University Press, 2002), 1–26.

41. On the Jews' *dhimmi* status, see Michel Abitbol, *Le Passé d'une discorde: Juifs et Arabes du VIIe siècle à nos jours* (Paris: Perrin, 2003), 33–39.

42. Ayoun, "Le Décret Crémieux et l'insurrection de 1871 en Algérie," 71.

43. Nacira Guénif-Souilamas, "Des opprimés se sont mués en oppresseurs de la pire espèce," *Le Monde*, 13 July 2004.

44. Michel Wieviorka, *The Lure of Anti-Semitism: Hatred of Jews in Present-Day France*, trans. Kristin Couper Lobel and Anna Declerck (Leiden: Brill, 2007), 143.

45. Finkielkraut, *Au nom de l'Autre*, 11. "Old Demons, New Debates: Anti-Semitism in the West" is the full name of the conference organized in New York by the YIVO Institute for Jewish Research.

46. Guénif-Souilamas argues that in postcolonial France antisemitism has been "outsourced to the new, visibly different French, Arabs, Muslims, and blacks" and "plays as the substitute fuel to a historical Christian blend of anti-Semitism conveniently cut from its European roots" (Guénif-Souilamas, "Jews and Arabs in Postcolonial France," 195). See also Weill, *La République et les antisémites*, 61–62.

47. Despite claims like Emmanuel Brenner's that most Algerian Muslims "rejoiced" at the denaturalization of Algerian Jews in 1940—a result predicted by Vichy authorities themselves, who assumed Muslim discontent as a pretext for abrogating the Crémieux decree—many Algerian Muslim leaders in fact felt otherwise (Brenner, *"France, prends garde de perdre ton âme,"* 124). A 1942 letter from a group including Ali Boumendjel, a leader of the Algerian national movement, and chief Muslim cleric Sheik el-Okbi assured the Algerian Jewish community of Algerian Muslims' conviction that "it would be ill-judged of them to rejoice about the special measures taken against Algerian Jews . . . when they themselves are struck daily by racism" (quoted in Abitbol, *Le Passé*, 368–69). On Algerian Muslims' solidarity with Jews after the revocation of the Crémieux decree, see also Katz, *The Burdens of Brotherhood*, 146–47.

48. Harvey, *Spaces of Capital*, 306.

49. Neil Smith, *Uneven Development: Nature, Capital, and the Production of Space*, 3rd ed. (Athens: University of Georgia Press, 2008), 119–20.

50. On all this, see especially Smith, *Uneven Development*, chaps. 3, 4, 5.

51. Max Horkheimer and Theodor Adorno are representative in this respect when they explain that the "diversion" of antisemitism is "an obvious asset to the ruling clique" (Horkheimer and Adorno, *Dialectic of Enlightenment*, trans. John Cumming [New York: Continuum, 1995], 170).

52. Smith, *Uneven Development*, 119–20.

53. Andrew Herod, *Scale* (New York: Routledge, 2011), 16.

54. Jean-Paul Sartre, *Anti-Semite and Jew*, trans. George J. Becker (New York: Schocken, 1995), 149.

55. Quoted in Frantz Fanon, *Black Skin, White Masks*, trans. Richard Philcox (New York: Grove, 2008), 67–68. The italics are Fanon's.

56. Fanon, *Black Skin, White Masks*, 67–68.

57. Sartre, *Anti-Semite and Jew*, 35. Engels is quoted in Robert Wistrich, *Laboratory for World Destruction: Germans and Jews in Central Europe* (Lincoln: University of Nebraska Press, 2007), 85.

58. Balibar and Wallerstein, *Race, Nation, Class*, 33. I would inscribe myself here within the burgeoning reflection on "racial capitalism," which understands the production of difference—racial or otherwise—as intrinsic to the functioning of capital since its inception. For seminal developments of the notion, see especially W. E. B. Du Bois, *Black Reconstruction in America, 1860–1880* (New York: Free Press, 1998) and Cedric J. Robinson, *Black Marxism: The Making of the Black Radical Tradition* (Chapel Hill: University

of North Carolina Press, 2000). For a useful history of racial capitalism as an idea, see Lisa Lowe, *The Intimacies of Four Continents* (Durham: Duke University Press, 2015), 148–70.

59. Quoted in Fanon, *Black Skin, White Masks*, 68.

60. Fanon, *Black Skin, White Masks*, 138, 143.

61. Fanon, *Black Skin, White Masks*, 95. Rothberg is right, in this regard, to note that Fanon overlooks historical associations of Jews with blackness, as well as their sexualization and biologization by European racial discourse (Rothberg, *Multidirectional Memory*, 94). On the racialization and primitivization of Jews as "black," see Sander Gilman, *Freud, Race, and Gender* (Princeton: Princeton University Press, 1993), 19–22 and Taguieff, *La Judéophobie des modernes*, 194–202.

62. Sartre, *Anti-Semite and Jew*, 41.

63. Fanon, *Black Skin, White Masks*, 157.

64. Fanon, *Black Skin, White Masks*, 138, 140.

65. Bryan Cheyette, "Frantz Fanon and the Black-Jewish Imaginary," in *Frantz Fanon's "Black Skin, White Masks": New Interdisciplinary Essays*, ed. Max Silverman (Manchester: Manchester University Press, 2005), 81.

66. This is what happens in those materialist analyses less willing than Sartre to underplay the historical association of Jews with money. Michel Wieviorka describes the resulting difficulty, to which he attributes the age-old question of whether antisemitism is a racism, as follows: "It is true that certain sociological approaches, particularly of Hegelian or Marxist inspiration like that of Oliver C. Cox, consider the social functions of racism and antisemitism to be so different that it is necessary to carefully distinguish between the two phenomena: for these approaches, antisemitism often targets the Jew as symbol of power, capital, or money, whereas racism inferiorizes the already socially disadvantaged Blacks" (Wieviorka, *Le Racisme, une introduction* [Paris: La Découverte, 1998], 51–52). Among those who differentiate between antisemitism and other racisms on these grounds is Moishe Postone: "It is not only the degree, but also the quality of power attributed to the Jews which distinguishes anti-Semitism from other forms of racism" (Postone, "Anti-Semitism and National Socialism: Notes on the German Reaction to 'Holocaust,'" *New German Critique* 19 [1980]: 106).

67. Shu-Mei Shih, "Comparative Racialization: An Introduction," *PMLA* 123.5 (2008): 1349–50.

68. Sartre, *Anti-Semite and Jew*, 23 (original emphasis).

69. Fanon, *Black Skin, White Masks*, 142.

70. Fanon, *Black Skin, White Masks*, 138.

71. Sartre, *Anti-Semite and Jew*, 23–24.

72. Sartre, *Anti-Semite and Jew*, 25.

73. Arthur Hertzberg, *The French Enlightenment and the Jews* (New York: Columbia University Press, 1968), 303, 305.

74. One can take my argument here to describe a key entry, prompted by the imperial emergence of the modern world system, in the history of what David Nirenberg calls "the labor done by Judaism" as "a set of ideas and attributes with which non-Jews can make sense of and criticize their

world" (Nirenberg, *Anti-Judaism: The Western Tradition* [New York: Norton, 2013]), 2–3).

75. Weill, *La République et les antisémites*, 45.

76. See note 66 for Wieviorka's version of the question, to which he gives a cautiously affirmative response: "The debate remains open, but the thesis that antisemitism belongs to the larger family of racism seems, under examination, stronger than the opposite thesis" (Wieviorka, *Le Racisme, une introduction*, 52). Here, by contrast, is Poliakov, author of the magisterial *Histoire de l'antisémitisme*, answering unequivocally in the negative: "And since the subject is antisemitism, I will conclude on a final terminological inaccuracy, its inclusion among 'racisms.' The latter's origins date back only to the eighteenth century, while the former dates back to time immemorial" (Léon Poliakov, "L'antisémitisme est-il un racisme?" in *Racisme et modernité*, ed. Michel Wieviorka [Paris: La Découverte, 1993], 84).

CHAPTER 1

1. Bernard Wasserstein, "Blame the Victim—Hannah Arendt Among the Nazis: The Historian and Her Sources," *Times Literary Supplement*, 9 October 2009.

2. See note 48 below.

3. Étienne Balibar and Immanuel Wallerstein, *Race, Nation, Class: Ambiguous Identities*, trans. Chris Turner (London: Verso, 1991), 49.

4. A premise of Arendt's boomerang thesis is that overseas imperialism provided impetus for what she calls the "continental imperialism" espoused first by the "pan-movements" (Pan-Slavism, Pan-Germanism) and then the Nazis (Arendt, *The Origins of Totalitarianism* [San Diego: Harcourt, 1976], 222; subsequent references to *Origins* in this chapter will be made parenthetically in the text using the abbreviation *OT*). Unless otherwise indicated, I will be using the terms "imperialism" and "empire" here to refer to overseas imperialism.

5. See note 52 below.

6. The presence of Jews like Alfred Beit and Barney Barnato among the "Randlords" who controlled the South African diamond and gold syndicates stirred suspicions that Jews were pulling England into war to protect their wealth. "Beit and Eckstein, Barnato and Oppenheim, Steinkopf and Levi," sneered the left-wing weekly newspaper *Justice* in 1899, "these are the trueborn Britons who are egging us common Englishmen into the war with the Transvaal" (quoted in Claire Hirshfield, "The Anglo-Boer War and the Issue of Jewish Culpability," *Journal of Contemporary History* 15.4 [1980]: 622). On this chapter in the history of British antisemitism, see also Bryan Cheyette, *Constructions of "the Jew" in English Literature and Society: Racial Representations, 1875–1945* (Cambridge: Cambridge University Press, 1993), 55–93, 150–205; Colin Holmes, *Anti-Semitism in British Society, 1876–1939* (New York: Holmes and Meier, 1979), 66–70; and Albert S. Lindemann,

Esau's Tears: Modern Anti-Semitism and the Rise of the Jews (Cambridge: Cambridge University Press, 1997), 357–63.

7. Tocqueville makes this argument in book 2, chapter 1 ("Why Feudal Rights Had Become More Hated Among the People of France than Anywhere Else") of *The Ancien Régime and the Revolution* (Alexis de Tocqueville, *The Ancien Régime and the Revolution*, 1856, trans. and ed. Gerald Bevan [London: Penguin, 2008], 36–45).

8. Arendt does note that the influence and "international connections" of Jewish financiers in South Africa "naturally stimulated the general popular delusions concerning Jewish political power all over the world" (*OT*, 202).

9. Ron H. Feldman and Jerome Kohn date the article to 1937 or 1938. Arendt writes that "the Jew, as pariah, offered a caricature of the bourgeois citizen. For a bourgeoisie lacking in self-confidence, no wound cut deeper than to hear its traits called Jewish. The bourgeoisie understood that antisemitism was the way to cast off this odium. In the end all that is left of bourgeois traits is that they are 'Jewish.' In the end only Jews are crassly materialistic, unpatriotic, revolutionary, destructive, speculative, and deceitful, living only for the moment and lacking any historical ties to the nation" (Arendt, *The Jewish Writings*, ed. Ron H. Feldman and Jerome Kohn [New York: Schocken, 2007], 108–9).

10. Pierre Birnbaum calls these Jews "the colonizers of the Republic," noting their decorated service in colonial wars, their repeated defense of colonial policies in the press, and their quickness to join the *groupe colonial* founded in the National Assembly in 1891 (Birnbaum, *Les Fous de la République: Histoire politique des Juifs d'État de Gambetta à Vichy* [Paris: Fayard, 1992], 260–69). On the enthusiasm of French Jews for the colonial *mission civilisatrice*, as well as their ideological contribution to it, see Paula Hyman, *The Jews of Modern France* (Berkeley: University of California Press, 1998), 81–83 and Lisa Moses Leff, *Sacred Bonds of Solidarity: The Rise of Jewish Internationalism in Nineteenth-Century France* (Stanford: Stanford University Press, 2006), 117–56.

11. Arendt appears not to equate political engagement with real or perceived influence: "Under the Third Republic, Jews . . . had all but vanished from important positions (though not from the political scene)" (*OT*, 4–5).

12. Arendt cites the increased autonomy of pre-imperial states from Jewish finance as states found their footing, became credible, and inspired allegiance: "By the middle of the last century some states had won enough confidence to get along without Jewish backing and financing of government loans. The nationals' growing consciousness, moreover, that their private destinies were becoming more and more dependent upon those of their countries made them ready to grant the governments more of the necessary credit" (*OT*, 18–19).

13. Arendt consistently scoffed at the notion that Jews could have engaged in large-scale political conspiracy or fomented wars of profit, considering them too politically naïve and neutral for such business. Of the Rothschilds, the great international Jewish banking family and bugaboo of antisemitic conspiracy theorists everywhere, she writes: "The truth of that matter was that the Rothschilds had as little political idea as other Jewish bankers of what they

wanted to carry out in France, to say nothing of a well-defined purpose which would even remotely suggest a war. On the contrary, like their fellow Jews they never allied themselves with any specific government, but rather with governments, with authority as such" (*OT*, 25).

14. Quoted in Wasserstein, "Blame the Victim," 14. Laqueur's original remark appears in Walter Laqueur, "The Arendt Cult: Hannah Arendt as Political Commentator," *Journal of Contemporary History* 33.4 (1998): 492.

15. I am paraphrasing George Kateb, who ventures that Arendt "is too generous" and "perhaps gives too much of herself" in her attempts in *Origins* to imagine the (racist) impressions of Europeans arriving in Africa. See Kateb, *Hannah Arendt: Politics, Conscience, Evil* (Totowa, NJ: Rowman and Allanheld, 1983), 62–63. On the debate surrounding Arendt's representations in *Origins* of black Africans, see note 48 below.

16. J. A. Hobson, *Imperialism: A Study*, 1905, 2nd ed. (New York: Cosimo, 2005), 361.

17. For the sake of clarity, I have generally reproduced here Arendt's terminological distinction between "imperialism," by which she means a mode of "expansion for expansion's sake" whose beginnings she dates to 1884 (the year of the Berlin Conference that formalized the Scramble for Africa), and an earlier "colonialism," which she believed had not exhibited that tendency. See, on this, *OT*, xvii.

18. J. A. Hobson, "Capitalism and Imperialism in South Africa," *Contemporary Review* 77 (1900): 5.

19. J. A. Hobson, *The War in South Africa: Its Causes and Effects* (London: James Nisbet, 1900), 189–90.

20. Hobson, "Capitalism and Imperialism in South Africa," 5–6.

21. On the lives of Jewish "Randlords" like Alfred Beit and Barney Barnato, see Geoffrey Wheatcroft, *The Randlords: The Exploits and Exploitations of South Africa's Mining Magnates* (New York: Atheneum, 1986).

22. Most recently and extensively, see Joshua Schreier, *Arabs of the Jewish Faith: The Civilizing Mission in Colonial Algeria* (New Brunswick, NJ: Rutgers University Press, 2010) and Sarah Abrevaya Stein, *Saharan Jews and the Fate of French Algeria* (Chicago: University of Chicago Press, 2014). See also Leff, *Sacred Bonds of Solidarity*, 117–56.

23. Léon Poliakov, *La Causalité diabolique* (Paris: Calmann-Lévy, 2006), 235–37.

24. Arendt repeated the characterization in *Men in Dark Times*: "only Nietzsche, as far as I know, has ever pointed out . . . that the position and functions of the Jewish people in Europe predestined them to become the 'good Europeans' *par excellence*. The Jewish middle classes of Paris and London, Berlin and Vienna, Warsaw and Moscow, were in fact neither cosmopolitan nor international, though the intellectuals among them thought of themselves in these terms. They were European, *something that could be said of no other group*" (Hannah Arendt, *Men in Dark Times* [San Diego: Harcourt Brace, 1968], 42; emphasis added).

25. Marcel Stoetzler, "Anti-Semitism, the Bourgeoisie, and the Self-Destruction of the Nation-State," in *Hannah Arendt and the Uses of History:*

Imperialism, Nation, Race, and Genocide, ed. Richard H. King and Dan Stone (New York: Berghahn, 2008), 138–39 (original emphasis).

26. Hannah Arendt, *The Human Condition*, 2nd ed. (Chicago: University of Chicago Press, 1998), 52. Subsequent references will be made parenthetically in the text using the abbreviation *HC*.

27. Though Arendt believed that nationalism could exceed itself by making common cause with race-thinking—resulting in, as she put it, "the confusion of imperialism with nationalism" (*OT*, 153)—she generally treated racism and nationalism as divergent phenomena, since "racism deliberately cut across all national boundaries" (*OT*, 161). Arendt differs, in this respect, from Étienne Balibar, who considers racism and nationalism fundamentally co-constitutive (Balibar and Wallerstein, *Race, Nation, Class*, 37–67). Arendt's position more closely parallels that of Benedict Anderson, who maintains that "the dreams of racism actually have their origins in the ideologies of *class*, rather than those of nation." Unlike Arendt, however, Anderson emphasizes racism's historical role as a subnational instrument of class domination rather than as a catalyst of supranational political movements (Anderson, *Imagined Communities: Reflections on the Origin and Spread of Nationalism* [London: Verso, 2006], 149–50; original emphasis).

28. Seyla Benhabib, *The Reluctant Modernism of Hannah Arendt*, 2nd ed. (Lanham, MD: Rowman and Littlefield, 2003), 64–65.

29. Margaret Canovan, *Hannah Arendt: A Reinterpretation of Her Political Thought* (Cambridge: Cambridge University Press, 1992), 28–29.

30. See Mildred Bakan, "Hannah Arendt's Concepts of Labor and Work," in *Hannah Arendt: The Recovery of the Public World*, ed. Melvyn A. Hill (New York: St. Martin's, 1979), 49–65 and Bikhu Parekh, "Hannah Arendt's Critique of Marx," in *Hannah Arendt: The Recovery of the Public World*, ed. Melvyn A. Hill (New York: St. Martin's, 1979), 67–100. For more forgiving readings of Arendt's engagement with Marx, see Canovan, *Hannah Arendt*, 63–98 and Jennifer Ring, "On Needing Both Marx and Arendt: Alienation and the Flight from Inwardness," *Political Theory* 17.3 (1989): 432–48.

31. Benhabib, *Reluctant Modernism*, 137. For other feminist readings of Arendt along these lines, see Mary G. Dietz, "Feminist Receptions of Hannah Arendt," in *Feminist Interpretations of Hannah Arendt*, ed. Bonnie Honig (University Park: Pennsylvania State University Press, 1995), 17–50; Dietz, "Hannah Arendt and Feminist Politics," in *Feminist Interpretations and Political Theory*, ed. Mary Lyndon Shanley and Carole Pateman (University Park: Pennsylvania State University Press, 1991), 232–52; Hanna Fenichel Pitkin, "Conformism, Housekeeping, and the Attack of the Blob: The Origins of Hannah Arendt's Concept of the Social," in *Feminist Interpretations of Hannah Arendt*, ed. Bonnie Honig (University Park: Pennsylvania State University Press, 1995), 51–81; Pitkin, "Justice: On Relating Private and Public," *Political Theory* 9.3 (1981): 327–52; and Adrienne Rich, *On Lies, Secrets, and Silence: Selected Prose, 1966–1978* (New York: W. W. Norton, 1979), 203–14.

32. Rich, *On Lies*, 205.

33. Arendt, *Men in Dark Times*, 13–14.

34. European Jewish cohesion conversely depended, in Arendt's estimation, a bit too precariously on a comity of nations already eroding by the end of the nineteenth century. "This breakdown of European solidarity," she observes bitterly, "was at once reflected in the breakdown of Jewish solidarity all over Europe. When the persecution of the German Jews began, Jews of other European countries discovered that German Jews constituted an exception whose fate could bear no resemblance to their own" (*OT*, 22). Rather than interrogate the inherent tenuousness of the arrangement itself, however, Arendt consistently finds reasons for its implosion elsewhere (imperialism, antisemitism, totalitarianism, etc.).

35. On Schmitt's influence on members of the Frankfurt School, see Ellen Kennedy, "Carl Schmitt and the Frankfurt School," *Telos* 71 (1987): 37–66.

36. Carl Schmitt, *The* Nomos *of the Earth in the International Law of the* Jus Publicum Europaeum, trans. G. L. Ulmen (New York: Telos, 2006), 49. Subsequent references will be made parenthetically in the text.

37. As Patricia Owens has justly observed, Arendt thought of "territory" as something very different from the violently appropriated land on which Schmitt considered the *nomos* to have been founded. Owens points to a passage in Arendt's *Eichmann in Jerusalem: A Report on the Banality of Evil*, which I reproduce here: "'territory,' as the law understands it, is a political and a legal concept, and not merely a geographical form. It relates not so much, and not primarily, to a piece of land as to the space between individuals in a group, whose members are bound to, and at the same time separated and protected from, each other by all kinds of relationships. . . . Such relationships become spatially manifest insofar as they themselves constitute the space wherein the different members of a group relate to and have intercourse with each other." Arendt's idea of territory, it is clear, resembles her notion of the "common world" of things, institutions, and culture that gather and relate members of a polity. See Owens, "The Return of Realism? War and Changing Concepts of the Political," in *The Changing Character of War*, ed. Hew Strachan and Sybille Scheipers (Oxford: Oxford University Press, 2011), 495–96.

38. See note 24.

39. For Schmitt's definition of the state of exception, see the first chapter of his *Political Theology* (Carl Schmitt, *Political Theology: Four Chapters on the Concept of Sovereignty*, trans. George Schwab [Chicago: University of Chicago Press, 2005], 5–15).

40. Giorgio Agamben, *Homo Sacer: Sovereign Power and Bare Life*, trans. Daniel Heller-Roazen (Stanford: Stanford University Press, 1998), 19.

41. Agamben, *Homo Sacer*, 170.

42. Arendt writes in *Men in Dark Times* that, in the case of the Jews, "we can speak of real worldlessness. And worldlessness, alas, is always a form of barbarism" (13).

43. I take the phrase from Wasserstein's article, the most significant recent volley in the ongoing accusation that Arendt lacked "love of the Jewish people," as Gershom Scholem famously put it in a letter to Arendt following the publication of *Eichmann in Jerusalem* (Wasserstein, "Blame the Victim"; Scholem, "*Eichmann in Jerusalem*: An Exchange of Letters Between Gershom

Scholem and Hannah Arendt," in *The Jew as Pariah: Jewish Identity and Politics in the Modern Age* by Hannah Arendt, ed. Ron H. Feldman [New York: Grove, 1978], 241). For a measured account of the Eichmann controversy, see Elisabeth Young-Bruehl, *Hannah Arendt: For Love of the World* (New Haven: Yale University Press, 2004), 347–78.

44. Zygmunt Bauman, *Life in Fragments: Essays in Postmodern Morality* (Oxford: Blackwell, 1995), 208, 213.

45. George Mosse, *The Crisis of German Ideology: Intellectual Origins of the Third Reich* (New York: Howard Fertig, 1964), 3–7.

46. Zygmunt Bauman, *Modernity and Ambivalence* (Cambridge: Polity, 1991), 55.

47. Jacques Derrida, *Specters of Marx: The State of the Debt, the Work of Mourning and the New International*, trans. Peggy Kamuf (New York: Routledge, 1994), 63.

48. For a useful summary of this debate, see Richard H. King and Dan Stone, introduction to *Hannah Arendt and the Uses of History: Imperialism, Nation, Race, and Genocide*, ed. Richard H. King and Dan Stone (New York: Berghahn, 2008), 9–11. Critiques of Arendt's description of black Africans include Robert Bernasconi, "When the Real Crime Began: Hannah Arendt's *The Origins of Totalitarianism* and the Dignity of the Western Philosophical Tradition," in *Hannah Arendt and the Uses of History: Imperialism, Nation, Race, and Genocide*, ed. Richard H. King and Dan Stone (New York: Berghahn, 2008), 61–62; Shiraz Dossa, "Human Status and Politics: Hannah Arendt on the Holocaust," *Canadian Journal of Political Science* 13.2 (1980): 318–23; Kathryn T. Gines, "Race Thinking and Racism in Hannah Arendt's *The Origins of Totalitarianism*," in *Hannah Arendt and the Uses of History: Imperialism, Nation, Race, and Genocide*, ed. Richard H. King and Dan Stone (New York: Berghahn, 2008), 38–53; Norma Claire Moruzzi, *Speaking Through the Mask: Hannah Arendt and the Politics of Social Identity* (Ithaca, NY: Cornell University Press, 2000), 96–104; Anne Norton, "Heart of Darkness: Africa and African Americans in the Writings of Hannah Arendt," in *Feminist Interpretations of Hannah Arendt*, ed. Bonnie Honig (University Park: Pennsylvania State University Press, 1995), 252–53; William Pietz, "The 'Post-Colonialism' of Cold War Discourse," *Social Text* 19–20 (1988): 66–69; Gail Presbey, "Critic of Boers or Africans? Arendt's Treatment of South Africa in *The Origins of Totalitarianism*," in *Postcolonial African Philosophy: A Critical Reader*, ed. Emmanuel Chukwudi Eze (Oxford: Blackwell, 1997), 162–80; and Michael Rothberg, *Multidirectional Memory: Remembering the Holocaust in the Age of Decolonization* (Stanford: Stanford University Press, 2009), 33–65. For defenses of Arendt on this count, see Benhabib, *Reluctant Modernism*, 83–86; Canovan, *Hannah Arendt*, 37–38; and Kateb, *Hannah Arendt*, 62–63.

49. Rothberg, *Multidirectional Memory*, 60, 64.

50. Jerome Kohn has made the same observation. See Kohn, "Arendt's Concept and Description of Totalitarianism," *Social Research* 69.2 (2002): 637.

51. Arendt returned to Luxemburg's *The Accumulation of Capital* in her essay on Luxemburg in *Men in Dark Times*. Arendt's summary merits

reproducing at length: "The central thesis of this 'curious work of genius' is simple enough. Since capitalism didn't show any signs of collapse 'under the weight of its economic contradictions,' [Luxemburg] began to look for an outside cause to explain its continued existence and growth. She found it in the so-called third man theory, that is, in the fact that the process of growth was not merely the consequence of innate laws ruling capitalist production but of the continued existence of pre-capitalist sectors in the country which 'capitalism' captured and brought into its sphere of influence. Once this process had spread to the whole national territory, capitalists were forced to look to other parts of the earth, to pre-capitalist lands, to draw them into the process of capital accumulation, which, as it were, fed on whatever was outside itself. In other words, Marx's 'original accumulation of capital' was not, like original sin, a single event, a unique deed of expropriation by the nascent bourgeoisie, setting off a process of accumulation that would then follow 'with iron necessity' its own inherent law up to the final collapse. On the contrary, expropriation had to be repeated time and again to keep the system in motion. Hence, capitalism was not a closed system that generated its own contradictions and was 'pregnant with revolution'; it fed on outside factors, and its *automatic* collapse could occur, if at all, only when the whole surface of the earth was conquered and had been devoured" (Arendt, *Men in Dark Times*, 39–40; original emphasis).

52. See, for example, Benhabib, *Reluctant Modernism*, 76; Margaret Canovan, *The Political Thought of Hannah Arendt* (New York: Harcourt Brace Jovanovich, 1974), 72; and Pascal Grosse, "From Colonialism to National Socialism to Postcolonialism: Hannah Arendt's *Origins of Totalitarianism*," *Postcolonial Studies* 9.1 (2006): 38–39.

53. For an overview of work in this vein, see Ann Laura Stoler and Frederick Cooper, "Between Metropole and Colony: Rethinking a Research Agenda," in *Tensions of Empire: Colonial Cultures in a Bourgeois World*, ed. Ann Laura Stoler and Frederick Cooper (Berkeley: University of California Press, 1997), 1–56.

54. See, for instance, Jürgen Zimmerer, "The Birth of the *Ostland* out of the Spirit of Colonialism: A Postcolonial Perspective on the Nazi Policy of Conquest and Extermination," in *Colonialism and Genocide*, ed. A. Dirk Moses and Dan Stone (London: Routledge, 2007), 101–23 and Zimmerer, "Colonialism and the Holocaust: Towards an Archeology of Genocide," in *Genocide and Settler Society: Frontier Violence and Stolen Indigenous Children in Australian History*, ed. A. Dirk Moses (New York: Berghahn, 2004), 49–76. For a comprehensive summary of the debates surrounding the continuity thesis, see Volker Langbehn and Mohammad Salama, "Introduction: Reconfiguring German Colonialism," in *German Colonialism: Race, the Holocaust, and Postwar Germany*, ed. Volker Langbehn and Mohammad Salama (New York: Columbia University Press, 2011), ix–xxxi, as well as various essays contained in the same collection.

55. Arendt even goes so far as to contend that overseas imperialism "succeeded in giving a new lease on life to the antiquated institutions of the nation-state" because, at least for a time, it "spirited away all troubles" (*OT*, 225, 147).

56. A. Dirk Moses, "Hannah Arendt, Imperialisms, and the Holocaust," in *German Colonialism: Race, the Holocaust, and Postwar Germany*, ed. Volker Langbehn and Mohammad Salama (New York: Columbia University Press, 2011), 75.

57. See note 52.

58. Quoted in Hannah Arendt, *Essays in Understanding, 1930–1954*, ed. Jerome Kohn (New York: Harcourt Brace, 1994), 405.

59. Arendt, *Essays*, 405. Arendt reiterated her stance the following year in a lecture at the New School: "The elements of totalitarianism form its origins if by origins we do not understand 'causes.' Causality, i.e., the factor of determination of a process of events in which always one event causes and can be explained by another is probably an altogether alien and falsifying category in the realm of the historical and political sciences. Elements by themselves probably never cause anything. They become origins of events if and when they crystallize into fixed and definite forms. Then, and only then, can we trace their history backwards. The event illuminates its own past, but it can never be deduced from it" (quoted in Young-Bruehl, *Hannah Arendt*, 203).

60. Rothberg, *Multidirectional Memory*, 55–56.

61. Benhabib, *Reluctant Modernism*, 91–95. See also Seyla Benhabib, "Hannah Arendt and the Redemptive Power of Narrative," *Social Research* 57.1 (1990): 186–93.

62. Grosse, "From Colonialism to National Socialism," 36.

63. Aimé Césaire, *Discourse on Colonialism*, trans. Joan Pinkham (New York: Monthly Review, 2000), 36.

64. Du Bois writes: "There was no Nazi atrocity—concentration camps, wholesale maiming and murder, defilement of women or ghastly blasphemy of childhood—which the Christian civilization of Europe had not long been practicing against colored folk in all parts of the world in the name of and for the defense of a Superior Race born to rule the world" (W. E. B. Du Bois, *The World and Africa* [New York: Viking, 1947], 23). Memmi, echoing the sentiment, proclaims that "every colonial nation carries the seeds of fascist temptation in its bosom" (Albert Memmi, *The Colonizer and the Colonized*, trans. Howard Greenfeld [Boston: Beacon, 1991], 62).

CHAPTER 2

1. Guy de Maupassant, *Bel-Ami* (Paris: Gallimard, 1973), 52. Subsequent citations of the novel will be made parenthetically in the text.

2. For a concise history of southern French Jewry, see Esther Benbassa, *The Jews of France: A History from Antiquity to the Present*, trans. M. B. DeBevoise (Princeton: Princeton University Press, 1999), 41–57. That Walter hails from the Midi stands out all the more given the Alsatian origins of Arthur Meyer, director of the *Le Gaulois* newspaper for which Maupassant worked and in whom many have seen a model for Walter (Odette Carrasco, *Arthur Meyer, Directeur du "Gaulois": Un patron de presse juif, royaliste et*

antidreyfusard [Paris: Imago, 2003], 13; Louis Forestier, introduction to *Bel-Ami*, by Guy de Maupassant, in *Romans*, ed. Louis Forestier, Bibliothèque de la Pléiade [Paris: Gallimard, 1987], 1332–33).

3. Fredric Jameson, "Modernism and Imperialism," in *Nationalism, Colonialism, and Literature*, by Terry Eagleton, Fredric Jameson, and Edward W. Said (Minneapolis: University of Minnesota Press, 1990), 48.

4. Louis Noir, *La Banque juive* (Paris: Ducher, 1888), 83. Isaac is given the stock description reserved for bankers in literature of the sort: miserly, unctuous, and indelicate, he is "capable of every theft that does not land one in court" (82). See Chapter 3 for Noir's enthusiastic paean to the virulently antisemitic Marquis de Morès, killed in Tunisia in 1896 while on a personal quest to expel the British from Egypt.

5. Robert de Bonnières, *Les Monach, roman parisien* (Paris: Ollendorff, 1885), 35, 43.

6. I have here in mind, again, Neil Smith's notion about capital's "contradictory tendencies toward differentiation and equalization" (Smith, *Uneven Development: Nature, Capital, and the Production of Space*, 3rd ed. [Athens: University of Georgia Press, 2008], 189).

7. Jameson, "Modernism and Imperialism," 49–50.

8. "The black woman comes to the white man, never the white woman to the black man; the Jew's daughter aspires to the gentleman's hand, but never would the gentleman's daughter debase herself with a Jew" (quoted in Pierre-André Taguieff, *La Judéophobie des modernes: Des Lumières au Jihad mondial* [Paris: Odile Jacob, 2008], 195).

9. Alphonse Toussenel, *Les Juifs, rois de l'époque: Histoire de la féodalité financière* (Paris: Librairie de l'école sociétaire, 1845), 167.

10. Édouard Drumont, *La France juive: Essai d'histoire contemporaine* (Paris: Marpon et Flammarion, 1886), 1:24 (original emphasis). In its first year alone, *La France juive* sold over 65,000 copies. On the book's publication history and stunning success, see Michel Winock, *Nationalisme, antisémitisme et fascisme en France* (Paris: Seuil, 2004), 116–18.

11. Bryan Cheyette, *Constructions of "the Jew" in English Literature and Society: Racial Representations, 1875–1945* (Cambridge: Cambridge University Press, 1993), 177.

12. The subsequent novels are *Mr. Clutterbuck's Election* (1908), *A Change in the Cabinet* (1909), and *Pongo and the Bull* (1910). For an incisive reading of the series, as well as of Belloc's antisemitic nonfiction, see Cheyette, *Constructions*, 150–79.

13. Jean-Louis Bory, preface to *Bel-Ami*, by Guy de Maupassant (Paris: Gallimard, 1973), 15–16.

14. See, for instance, what Cheyette rightfully describes as the "outrageous claim" by A. N. Wilson's 1984 Belloc biography that "Mr. Barnett is a recognizable type; perhaps cruder than his Rothschild or Oppenheimer Edwardian originals, infinitely less so than his modern equivalents, like 'Lord' [*sic*] Kagan or Sir James Goldsmith" (quoted in Cheyette, *Constructions*, 162n13).

15. Hilaire Belloc, *The Jews* (Boston: Houghton Mifflin, 1922), 50.

16. Here is Arendt: "As soon as the gold and diamond industries reached the stage of imperialist development where absentee shareholders demand their governments' political protection, it turned out that the Jews could not hold their important economic position" (Hannah Arendt, *The Origins of Totalitarianism* [San Diego: Harcourt, 1976], 202).

17. Arendt, *Origins*, 50. Arendt elsewhere makes the same point thusly: "Nineteenth-century antisemitism, at any rate, reached its climax in France and was defeated because it remained a national domestic issue without contact with imperialist trends, which did not exist there" (Arendt, *Origins*, 79).

18. The moderate republicans like Gambetta and Ferry who dominated the first twenty years of the Third Republic were known as Opportunists, so named because they favored the gradual implementation, at the "opportune moment," of reforms demanded by more radical republicans.

19. Neither, it should be added, does this preclude that French authorities in colonies with significant Jewish populations might occasionally impose policies reflecting antisemitic sentiment among French colonists and metropolitans, as Sarah Abrevaya Stein has recently argued was the case. Stein demonstrates in particular how military authorities were sometimes inspired, at the end of the century, to take out their anti-Dreyfusard frustrations on the Jews of the Algerian Sahara, though she is careful to add that this never constituted a systematic policy (Stein, *Saharan Jews and the Fate of French Algeria* [Chicago: University of Chicago Press, 2014], 66–74).

20. See Raoul Girardet, *L'Idée coloniale en France, 1871–1962* (Paris: La Table Ronde, 1972), 57–58, 62–64 and Wolfgang Schivelbusch, *The Culture of Defeat*, trans. Jefferson Chase (New York: Picador, 2003), 180–81.

21. Quoted in Girardet, *L'Idée coloniale*, 63.

22. Henri Rochefort, "L'Adhésion des puissances," *L'Intransigeant*, 25 April 1881, 1.

23. Harvey in turn locates Marx's inspiration for the spatial fix in Hegel and the German economist Johann Heinrich von Thünen (David Harvey, *Spaces of Capital: Towards a Critical Geography* [New York: Routledge, 2001], 288–95).

24. Arendt, *Origins*, 204, 206.

25. Michel Winock, *La France et les Juifs de 1789 à nos jours* (Paris: Seuil, 2004), 85.

26. Winock, *Nationalisme, antisémitisme et fascisme*, 119.

27. Grégoire Kauffmann, *Edouard Drumont* (Paris: Perrin, 2008), 25–26, 58–60. For biographical information on Drumont, see also Frederick Busi, *The Pope of Antisemitism: The Career and Legacy of Edouard-Adolphe Drumont* (Lanham, MD: University Press of America, 1986).

28. Drumont, *La France juive*, 2:65; Kauffmann, *Edouard Drumont*, 89.

29. Drumont, *La France juive*, 2:59.

30. Drumont, *La France juive*, 1:139.

31. An Alliance Anti-Israélite Universelle was in fact founded in Bucharest in 1886, with Drumont as president, but never came to much. The Ligue Antisémitique Nationale de France was more active but not very long-lived,

folding in 1890 (Robert F. Byrnes, *Antisemitism in Modern France* [New Brunswick, NJ: Rutgers University Press, 1950], 233–34).

32. For a representative denunciation of the Tonkin expedition, see Drumont, *La France juive*, 1:498–518.

33. Aron Rodrigue, *French Jews, Turkish Jews: The Alliance israélite universelle and the Politics of Jewish Schooling in Turkey, 1860–1925* (Bloomington: Indiana University Press, 1990), 8.

34. On the relationship between Jewish internationalism and French imperial policy, see Pierre Birnbaum, *Les Fous de la République: Histoire politique des Juifs d'État de Gambetta à Vichy* (Paris: Fayard, 1992), 260–69; Paula Hyman, *The Jews of Modern France* (Berkeley: University of California Press, 1998), 81–83; and Lisa Moses Leff, *Sacred Bonds of Solidarity: The Rise of Jewish Internationalism in Nineteenth-Century France* (Stanford: Stanford University Press, 2006), 117–56.

35. I am indebted to Rodrigue's *French Jews, Turkish Jews* for the account of the Damascus affair that follows. See also Jonathan Frankel, *The Damascus Affair: "Ritual" Murder, Politics, and the Jews in 1840* (Cambridge: Cambridge University Press, 1997).

36. Rodrigue, *French Jews, Turkish Jews*, xii.

37. Rodrigue, *French Jews, Turkish Jews*, xii. The Alliance's special influence over Oriental and Sephardic Jewry was not the exclusive product of French imperial expansion. As Rodrigue points out, Russia's resistance to Western intervention within its sphere of influence made it difficult for the Alliance to gain a foothold among the Ashkenazi Jews of eastern Europe (Rodrigue, *French Jews, Turkish Jews*, 24).

38. Toussenel, *Les Juifs, rois de l'époque*, 65. Toussenel mentions the Algerian scandals of the 1830s and 1840s that rocked France in his day but cites them only as evidence of a generalized French malaise, rather than as the direct work of Jews (Toussenel, *Les Juifs, rois de l'époque*, 2).

39. See note 34.

40. Quoted in Winock, *La France et les Juifs*, 70.

41. Michel Abitbol, *Le Passé d'une discorde: Juifs et Arabes du VIIe siècle à nos jours* (Paris: Perrin, 2003), 296. By the 1890s, Jews would represent 15 percent of the French Algerian electorate in the administrative *départements* of Algiers, Constantine, and Oran (Leff, *Sacred Bonds of Solidarity*, 208–9).

42. Drumont, *La France juive*, 2:11.

43. Drumont, *La France juive*, 2:67.

44. Drumont, *La France juive*, page "e."

45. Georges Meynié, *L'Algérie juive* (Paris: Savine, 1887), 248–49.

46. Meynié, *L'Algérie juive*, 144.

47. Meynié, *L'Algérie juive*, 243.

48. Meynié, *L'Algérie juive*, 141.

49. Drumont, *La France juive*, 2:48.

50. Drumont, *La France juive*, 2:48–54.

51. Charles-Robert Ageron, *Les Algériens musulmans et la France, 1871–1919* (Paris: PUF, 1968), 1:584.

52. Ageron, *Les Algériens musulmans*, 1:585.

53. Drumont, *La France juive*, 2:49.

54. Ageron, *Les Algériens musulmans*, 1:586.

55. Ageron, *Les Algériens musulmans*, 1:585.

56. Denise Bouche, *Histoire de la colonisation française* (Paris: Fayard, 1991), 59.

57. Henri Rochefort, "Le Secret de l'affaire tunisienne," *L'Intransigeant*, 27 September 1881, 1.

58. Winock, *La France et les Juifs*, 98.

59. Rochefort, "Le Secret de l'affaire tunisienne." Despite Rochefort's insinuation to the contrary, neither Jecker nor the Tunisian banker in question was in fact Jewish.

60. Henri Rochefort, *Les Aventures de ma vie* (Paris: Dupont, 1896), 3:169, 174.

61. Rochefort, *Les Aventures de ma vie*, 2:250.

62. Henri Rochefort, "Le Dessous des cartes," *L'Intransigeant*, 3 July 1881, 1.

63. Camille Pelletan, "Lettres de Tunis," *La Justice*, 27 October 1881, 1.

64. Camille Pelletan, "La Question tunisienne," *La Justice*, 31 October 1881, 1.

65. Camille Pelletan, "La Question tunisienne," *La Justice*, 2 November 1881, 1.

66. Transcript of Rochefort libel suit, *L'Intransigeant*, 15 December 1881, 1–2.

67. Pelletan, "La Question tunisienne," 2 November 1881. The Société Callas had supposedly proposed the Crédit Foncier.

68. Jean Ganiage, *Les Origines du Protectorat français en Tunisie, 1861–1881* (Paris: PUF, 1959), 688.

69. Pelletan, "La Question tunisienne," 2 November 1881.

70. Speech in the Chamber of Deputies, as recorded in "Discours de M. Clemenceau," *La Justice*, 9 November 1881.

71. Auguste Chirac, *Les Rois de la République: Histoire des juiveries*, 1883 (Paris: Éditions du Trident, 1987), 278.

72. Auguste Chirac, *L'Agiotage de 1870 à 1884* (Paris: La Revue Socialiste, 1886), 97–98.

73. The dedication reads as follows: "In memory of Léon Gambetta. I dedicate this book to the memory of the great citizen whose patriotic work was disrupted and political career obviously cut short by *the coalition of Jewries*" (Chirac, *Les Rois de la République* title page; original emphasis).

74. Forestier, introduction to *Bel-Ami*, 1332.

75. Birnbaum, *Les Fous de la République*, 264.

76. On Maupassant's real-life sources of inspiration surrounding the Tunisian affair, see Forestier, introduction to *Bel-Ami*, 1326–29; Armand Lanoux, *Maupassant le Bel-Ami* (Paris: Grasset, 1979), 217–20; and André Vial, *Guy de Maupassant et l'art du roman* (Paris: Nizet, 1954), 317–29. As Lanoux notes, Maupassant referenced the Tunisian affair as a journalist before he dramatized it as a novelist.

77. Drumont, *La France juive*, 1:478.

78. Drumont, *La France juive*, 1:476.

79. Drumont, *La France juive*, 1:478–82. Ben Ismaïl's legally fraught transaction indeed occurred, though Drumont's antisemitic take on the question obviously adds certain embellishments.

80. On antisemitism and the French left, see Marc Crapez, *L'Antisémitisme de gauche au XIXe siècle* (Paris: Berg International, 2002) and Zeev Sternhell, *La Droite révolutionnaire, 1885–1914: Les origines françaises du fascisme* (Paris: Fayard, 2000), 189–223.

81. The crash of the Union Générale bank, whose famous collapse in 1882 ruined countless small French investors and rattled public confidence in the stock market for years to come, was widely (though inaccurately) attributed to financial manipulations by the Jewish Rothschild banking family. On the contribution of the crash to antisemitism, see, for instance, Jacob Katz, *From Prejudice to Destruction: Anti-Semitism, 1700–1933* (Cambridge, MA: Harvard University Press, 1980), 293–94; Léon Poliakov, *Histoire de l'antisémitisme. 2: L'âge de la science* (Paris: Calmann-Lévy, 1981), 290; and Stephen Wilson, *Ideology and Experience: Antisemitism in France at the Time of the Dreyfus Affair* (Oxford: Littman Library of Jewish Civilization, 2007), 248–49.

82. Drumont would take up the Union Générale question the same year in *La France juive devant l'opinion* (1886). Drumont's initial reluctance to address the Union Générale scandal may be explained by the explicitly Catholic, antisemitic mission given the Union by its founder, Eugène Bontoux. I return to Bontoux and the Union Générale crash in Chapter 5.

83. Chirac, *Les Rois de la République*, 35 (original emphasis).

84. Chirac, *Les Rois de la République*, 35, 43.

85. See, in particular, his *Histoire générale et système comparé des langues sémitiques* (1855), to which Edward Said refers as "a virtual encyclopedia of race prejudice" (Said, *Orientalism* [New York: Vintage, 1979], 361n26).

86. As I pointed out earlier, Madame Mussali was not in fact Jewish. For reasons that will shortly become clear, Drumont found it expeditious to collapse Roustan's entourage of Jews and para-Jews into one, female body.

87. Albert S. Lindemann, *Esau's Tears: Modern Anti-Semitism and the Rise of the Jews* (Cambridge: Cambridge University Press, 1997), 223–24; Winock, *Nationalisme, antisémitisme et fascisme*, 118.

88. Drumont, *La France juive*, 1:476.

89. The trope of the corpulent Oriental Jewess has been attributed to the thin conceptual line separating the carnality associated with the "beautiful Jewess"—a stock representation in nineteenth-century European culture—from that imputed to the male Jew by virtue of his supposed rapacity. Once married, writes Julie Kalman, the Jew and Jewess became "linked in their physicality, and it was his that prevailed" (Kalman, *Rethinking Antisemitism in Nineteenth-Century France* [Cambridge: Cambridge University Press, 2010], 96). Kalman cites Swiss-born Parisian writer and traveler Charles Didier, who felt "repulsion and disgust" at the thought of the ugly Jew's possession of his beautiful bride, and so depicted the rapid physical degradation undergone by the Oriental Jewish woman's body after marriage: "as a rule she

is married at fourteen; at fifteen, she is a mother and a wet-nurse; at twenty, she is withered; she is stout at twenty-five" (quoted in Kalman, *Rethinking Antisemitism*, 96–97).

90. The figure is from 1889 (Leff, *Sacred Bonds of Solidarity*, 209).

91. By the end of the 1890s, there were one-sixth as many Jews in Algeria as French colonists (Wilson, *Ideology and Experience*, 231).

92. Drumont, *La France juive*, 2:13.

93. Drumont, *La France juive*, 1:483n1.

94. Drumont, *La France juive*, 1:484 (original emphasis).

95. Drumont, *La France juive*, 2:14.

96. Drumont, *La France juive*, 2:24.

97. Drumont, *La France juive*, 2:22.

98. Pierre Birnbaum, *"La France aux Français": Histoire des haines nationalistes* (Paris: Seuil, 2006), 268–71.

99. "To those who know these proud and warlike indigenous races," wrote Prébois of Algerian Arabs, "it is obvious that their pride was wounded to see themselves risk subordination to the Jews" (quoted in Drumont, *La France juive*, 2:21). Michel Winock has debunked this attribution of the insurrection to the Crémieux decree, a causality first expounded by Algerian military officials and colonists and later embraced by Drumont and metropolitan antisemites in the 1880s and 1890s. Winock points to the far more important role played by long-simmering Arab resentment and to the opportunity presented by France's military disarray in the wake of the 1870 defeat at Sedan (Winock, *La France et les Juifs*, 75–81). Other contemporary refutations of the Crémieux myth can be found in Richard Ayoun, "Le Décret Crémieux et l'insurrection de 1871 en Algérie," *Revue d'histoire moderne et contemporaine* 35.1 (1988): 61–87 and Patricia Lorcin, *Imperial Identities: Stereotyping, Prejudice and Race in Colonial Algeria* (London: I. B. Tauris, 1999), 174. As early as 1897, Louis Forest concluded that if "Algerian Jews had not been naturalized on October 24, 1870, the insurrection would nevertheless have occurred at the same time, in the same place, and with the same force and intensity" (Forest, *La Naturalisation des juifs algériens et l'insurrection de 1871, étude historique* [Paris: Société française d'imprimerie et de librairie, 1897], 55). The Crémieux myth, as I have been calling it, was propagated early on by disgruntled members of the Algerian colonial military, whose anti-Crémieux sentiment Arendt associates with resentment against the transfer of power to a civil administration in 1870–71 (Hannah Arendt, "Why the Crémieux Decree Was Abrogated," *Contemporary Jewish Record* 6.2 [1943]: 117–18). We have seen already, too, how French colonists were dismayed to find themselves in electoral competition with Jews, whose citizenship they were quick to blame for the uprising. On the early elaboration of the myth by French military officials and colonists, see Leff, *Sacred Bonds of Solidarity*, 207–11.

100. Drumont, *La France juive*, 2:27n1.

101. Drumont, *La France juive*, 2:25. For more on the relationship between antisemitism and philo-Arabism, see the chapter titled "Le noble catholique, le fier Arabe et le juif pervers," in Birnbaum, *"La France aux Français."* See also Winock, *La France et les Juifs*, 79–80.

102. On Maupassant's Algerian travels, see Denise Brahimi's introduction to Guy de Maupassant, *Maupassant au Maghreb*, ed. Denise Brahimi (Paris: Le Sycomore, 1982) and Lanoux, *Maupassant le Bel-Ami*, 149–55.

103. Guy de Maupassant, *Au soleil*, in *Maupassant au Maghreb*, ed. Denise Brahimi (Paris: Le Sycomore, 1982), 182.

104. Quoted in Drumont, *La France juive*, 2:15.

105. Maupassant, *Au soleil*, 182.

106. Drumont, *La France juive*, 1:xii.

107. Maupassant, *Au soleil*, 183.

108. Quoted in Drumont, *La France juive*, 2:15.

109. Drumont, *La France juive*, 2:17. André Vial is sufficiently confident that Maupassant read Chirac's *Les Rois de la République* (1883), in which Chirac implicates d'Erlanger in the Tunisian affair, to draw parallels between Chirac's wild speculations and the plot of *Bel-Ami* (Vial, *Guy de Maupassant*, 322).

110. Édouard Drumont, *Le Secret de Fourmies* (Paris: Savine, 1892), 100.

111. In an article about Algerian Jews and the Crémieux decree, *La Libre parole* cites Jules Rateau from *L'Echo de Paris*, who points out how "one must not forget that the province of Constantine borders on Tunisia, from where the Jews who swarm there can reach Algeria with the greatest ease, especially since the establishment of our protectorate" (quoted in "Les Juifs d'Algérie," *La Libre parole*, 3 January 1896, 1 [author obscured]).

112. Noir, *La Banque juive*, 83, 95. Isaac's cousin Jonathan-ben-Joseph drives home the point by showing up in Paris from Algiers wearing "the dirty, worn, and stinking outfit of a Tunisian Jew" (207).

113. Guy de Maupassant, *Chroniques*, ed. Gérard Delaisement (Paris: Rive Droite, 2003), 2:966.

114. Jameson, "Modernism and Imperialism."

115. Jameson, "Modernism and Imperialism," 49.

116. Jameson, "Modernism and Imperialism," 50.

117. Moishe Postone, "Anti-Semitism and National Socialism: Notes on the German Reaction to 'Holocaust,'" *New German Critique* 19 (1980): 107.

118. Peter Brooks, *Reading for the Plot: Design and Intention in Narrative* (Cambridge, MA: Harvard University Press, 2006), 12.

119. As Jameson puts it elsewhere, the representation of conspiracy constitutes "an attempt . . . to think a system so vast that it cannot be encompassed by the natural and historically developed categories of perception with which human beings normally orient themselves" (Fredric Jameson, *The Geopolitical Aesthetic: Cinema and Space in the World System* [Bloomington: Indiana University Press, 1992], 1–2).

120. Here is Maupassant's own tableau of Algiers published in *Le Gaulois* on 17 July 1881: "From the tip of the jetty the view of the city is marvelous. One sees with ecstasy the dazzling cascade of houses tumbling down over each other from the top of the mountain all the way to the sea" (Maupassant, *Chroniques*, 1:241).

121. Maupassant, *Chroniques*, 1:246.

122. Gerald Prince reads *Bel-Ami* as a novel about how narrative is "the novelist's ultimate enemy" because, among other things, it only "supplies a simulacrum of reality" (Prince, "Bel-Ami and Narrative as Antagonist," *French Forum* 11.2 [1986]: 220–21). But Maupassant still understands some narrative simulacra—like the novel he has written—to hew closer to the spirit of reality than others.

123. Nicholas White, *The Family in Crisis in Late Nineteenth-Century French Fiction* (Cambridge: Cambridge University Press, 2006), 88–89.

124. Maupassant, *Au soleil*, 182.

125. In a didactic pause from the narrative, Maurceley confidently maintains that Muslims had been ready to defend France in the Franco-Prussian War: "But a Jew came along who changed this devotion into anger. And soon the entire Algerian territory took up arms against us. . . . Indeed, the Crémieux law sprang like a bad dream from the confusion of things metropolitan—odious law that gave the Jews the rights of French citizenship over the whole of the colony. The Bach'agha at first did not want to believe in the promulgation of this law, but when doubt was no longer possible, his indignation drove him to rebellion" (Baude de Maurceley, *Amour et gloire, roman franco-saharien* [Paris: Garnier Frères, 1897], 37–38).

126. Paul de Garros, *La Revanche de l'honneur* (Limoges: Barbou, 1898), 45, 47. Further page references are to this edition and will be made parenthetically in the text.

127. Girardet, *L'Idée coloniale*, 65.

128. Paul de Garros was born Paul-Edmond Mathieu de Garros in 1867 at the Château de Rousson, near Châteauneuf-sur-Cher in central France (Archives Biographiques Françaises, Bibliothèque Nationale de France [I 199–200, 719]). Pierre is at first the portrait of aristocratic hebetude. When the reader encounters him, he has been "exempted from military service" and consequentially "had abandoned himself to that country lethargy, that dissipated and feeble life which kills energy and saps the spirit, without remembering that, even when rich, one remains duty-bound to be useful" (12).

129. On this distinction by modern antisemitism between supposedly different kinds of capital, see Postone, "Anti-Semitism and National Socialism," 108–12.

CHAPTER 3

1. On the Fashoda Affair, see Charles-Robert Ageron, *France coloniale ou parti colonial?* (Paris: PUF, 1978), 165–87; Edward Berenson, *Heroes of Empire: Five Charismatic Men and the Conquest of Africa* (Berkeley: University of California Press, 2011), 166–96; David Levering Lewis, *The Race to Fashoda: European Colonialism and African Resistance in the Scramble for Africa* (New York: Weidenfeld and Nicholson, 1987); and Marc Michel, *La Mission Marchand, 1895–99* (Paris: Mouton, 1972).

2. Terje Tvedt argues, for instance, that Fashoda was too far north of the Nile headwaters to be of any use in damming the river and that at least some French authors were aware of this (Tvedt, *The River Nile in the Age of the British: Political Ecology and the Quest for Economic Power* [London: I. B. Taurus, 2004], 46–47).

3. In 1894, Marchand, along with two other future members of the second Fashoda expedition, had fought under Monteil in the Ivory Coast against the Mandinka leader Samori Turé.

4. H. Vernier, "La Capitulation de la France—L'Abandon de Fachoda," *La Libre parole*, 5 November 1898, 1.

5. Berenson, *Heroes of Empire*, 195.

6. "Everyone knows anyway," fulminated Drumont in 1892, "that it is in Alphonse de Rothschild's very office that was prepared the agreement between the Khedive and Disraeli, which, by giving England ownership of the majority of Suez stock shares, prepared her domination in Egypt" (Édouard Drumont, "Sem, Cham et Japhet," *La Libre parole*, 21 October 1892, 1). Morès likewise incriminated the French Rothschild brother, Alphonse, in the transaction: "We would next mention the delivery of Suez to the English. The transfer of shares was done in Rothschild's office and with his help. How much did he profit from delivering to the English the fruit of French labor and Egypt?" (Marquis de Morès, *Rothschild, Ravachol & Cie* [Paris: Hayard, 1892], 43). Both were wrong. Lionel de Rothschild, of the powerful Jewish banking family's British arm, communicated to British prime minister Benjamin Disraeli the willingness of the indebted Egyptian Khedive to sell Egypt's shares in the canal. Eager to pull off such a financial coup against the French, Disraeli asked Lionel to finance the purchase on Britain's behalf, and Lionel assented. It seems, however, that in a break with firm tradition, Lionel had in fact withheld news of the deal from his brother in Paris. Stanley Weintraub even relates that Disraeli would later explain to the Prince of Wales that the London Rothschilds "could not appeal to their strongest ally, their own family in Paris, for Baron Alphonse is *si francese* that he would have betrayed the whole scheme instantly" (Weintraub, *Disraeli: A Biography* [New York: Truman Talley, 1993], 541–45).

7. See *La Libre parole*, 19 June, 22 June, 26 June, 14 July, and 20 July 1896, as well as *Le Figaro*, 19 June 1896.

8. Édouard Drumont, "Anniversaire de Morès—Discours d'Edouard Drumont," *La Libre parole*, 20 July 1899, 1. Drumont had already said as much a few months earlier: "It was likewise said that the expedition in which Morès would find a glorious death was chimerical and crazy. Marchand's expedition proved that, on the contrary, [Morès's expedition] was full of grandeur and could have produced great results" (Drumont, "Le Monument de Morès," *La Libre parole*, 14 April 1899, 1).

9. Maurice Barrès, *Scènes et doctrines du nationalisme*, 1902 (Paris: Trident, 1987), 238, 259.

10. "The Marquis de Morès was a veritable romance hero [*héros de roman*]," trumpeted one hastily produced pamphlet by the prolific dime novelist Louis Noir (Noir, *Le Massacre de l'expédition du Marquis de Morès* [Paris: Fayard,

1896], 2). Noir's insistence on Morès's soldierly qualities codes the Marquis in the terms conveyed by *roman* in its historical sense, as knightly romance, and according to which other commentators understood Morès to have lived his life. Readers might also have seen in Morès one of Noir's own popular colonial adventure heroes. Morès's suspension here somewhere between the premodern romance and modern novel echoes the extent to which, as we will see, he was understood by many to have bridged epochs.

11. See, for example, *La Libre parole illustrée*, 22 August, 5 September, 19 September, 26 September, and 7 November 1896.

12. Paul Rudd, *La Libre parole illustrée*, 22 August 1896, 3.

13. Morès was apparently an avid rereader of *La Chevalerie*, Léon Gautier's popular 1884 account of feudal chivalric practices in France (Robert F. Byrnes, *Antisemitism in Modern France* [New Brunswick, NJ: Rutgers University Press, 1950], 238–39). I will return in some detail to this point further on, as well as to Morès's para-socialist schemes. Meanwhile, it bears remarking that in 1872 Gautier also published a translation and critical study of the *Chanson de Roland*, the text through which so many of Morès's mourners would filter their patriotic grief. For present-day discussions of Morès, all of which I rely on here, see Byrnes, *Antisemitism in Modern France*, 225–50; Donald Dresden, *The Marquis de Morès: Emperor of the Badlands* (Norman: University of Oklahoma Press, 1970); Jerome Tweton, *The Marquis de Morès: Dakota Capitalist, French Nationalist* (Fargo: North Dakota Institute for Regional Studies, 1972); and Michel Winock, *Nationalisme, antisémitisme et fascisme en France* (Paris: Seuil, 2004), 135–37. I will be drawing as well on a number of laudatory biographies penned by his friends and contemporaries to satisfy an evidently brisk market for details about the late Marquis. These include Jules Delahaye, *Les Assassins et les vengeurs de Morès*, 3 vols. (Paris: Retaux, 1905–7); Charles Droulers, *Le Marquis de Morès, 1858–96* (Paris: Plon, 1932); Félicien Pascal, *L'Assassinat de Morès: Un crime d'état* (Paris: Hardy et Bernard, 1902); and Auguste Pavy, *L'Expédition de Morès* (Paris: André, 1897).

14. See Tweton, *The Marquis de Morès*, 185.

15. See Michael N. Barnett, *Empire of Humanity: A History of Humanitarianism* (Ithaca, NY: Cornell University Press, 2011), 67.

16. "Morès had the same faith as Gordon, a virile and simple faith, immune to all superstitious tendencies and even to a certain sentimentalism that is the poetry of Religion, a sort of communion with the Son of God dying willingly for man's salvation, with Christ who, as Carlyle put it, 'was the greatest of all heroes'" (Édouard Drumont, "Morès," *La Libre parole*, 22 June 1896, 1). A decade earlier, Drumont had opened the section of *La France juive* dedicated to Adolphe Crémieux with an account of a meeting in Egypt between Gordon and Joseph Reinach, Gambetta's Jewish chief of staff. Drumont contrasts Gordon, the "apostle-soldier" and "Christian hero," with Jewish and para-Jewish makers of colonial policy like Gambetta and England's own Disraeli, whom Gordon, to Drumont's great approval, collectively refers to as "mountebanks" (charlatans) (Drumont, *La France juive: Essai d'histoire contemporaine* [Paris: Marpon et Flammarion, 1886], 2:3).

17. Herman Lebovics writes of the desire by Baudelaire, Rimbaud, and others in the nineteenth-century aesthetic avant-garde to "escape history" and "escape the tyranny of the new market society" by seeking adventure in supposedly timeless imperial spaces. For Lebovics, these artists' escapism was at once a reaction against material modernity and a crucial impulse in the modernist cult of newness they forged (Lebovics, *Imperialism and the Corruption of Democracies* [Durham: Duke University Press, 2006], 62, 85). On Flaubert's disappointed escape from modernity in Egypt, see Ali Behdad, *Belated Travelers: Orientalism in the Age of Colonial Dissolution* (Durham: Duke University Press, 1994), 53–72 and Richard Terdiman, *Discourse/Counter-discourse: The Theory and Practice of Symbolic Resistance in Nineteenth-Century France* (Ithaca, NY: Cornell University Press, 1985), 227–57.

18. Ann Laura Stoler, *Race and the Education of Desire: Foucault's "History of Sexuality" and the Colonial Order of Things* (Durham: Duke University Press, 1995), 15.

19. Madeleine Dobie, *Foreign Bodies: Gender, Language, and Culture in French Orientalism* (Stanford: Stanford University Press, 2004), 159.

20. Édouard Drumont, "Discours d'Édouard Drumont," *La Libre parole*, 20 July 1896, 1.

21. Tzvetan Todorov, *On Human Diversity: Nationalism, Racism, and Exoticism in French Thought*, trans. Catherine Porter (Cambridge, MA: Harvard University Press, 1993), 248.

22. Quoted in Todorov, *On Human Diversity*, 59.

23. On Morès's relations to socialism, see Byrnes, *Antisemitism in Modern France*, 240–41, 243–45 and Tweton, *The Marquis de Morès*, 131–32.

24. One of Morès's many antisemitic crusades, against a Jewish meat supplier to the army, helped make him a popular figure among butchers. Having gone undercover to gather evidence, Morès publicly accused the company of conspiring to poison soldiers in the pursuit of financial gain (Tweton, *The Marquis de Morès*, 142). Such kinds of army-supply charges were a recurring antisemitic theme, conveniently combining as they did allegations of Jewish treason with the stock motif of unbounded Jewish avarice. Morès had read about a similar supposed scheme in Drumont's *La France juive*, in which Drumont denounced the Jew Chemla for provisioning soldiers in France's 1881 conquest of Tunisia with insalubrious fare (see Chapter 2).

25. Barrès, *Scènes et doctrines*, 231; Byrnes, *Antisemitism in Modern France*, 226.

26. Marquis de Morès, "Lettre ouverte à M. Casimir-Perier, Président de la République française," *Lettres au peuple*, 11 January 1894. Of course, Morès remained less interested in justice as an end than as a means, going on in the same letter to emphasize the pacificatory and strategic advantages to be gained by better treatment of Algerian Arabs. No longer "driven to rebellion" by spoliation at the hands of Jews, he explains, these Arabs will serve the cause of further French penetration into Africa.

27. Jean Drault, "Morès.—Sa vie.—Son œuvre," *La Libre parole*, 19 July 1896, 2.

28. For thick descriptions of Algerian antisemitism in the fin de siècle, see Geneviève Dermenjian, *La Crise anti-juive oranaise, 1895–1905* (Paris: L'Harmattan, 1986) and Stephen Wilson, *Ideology and Experience: Antisemitism in France at the Time of the Dreyfus Affair* (Oxford: Littman Library of Jewish Civilization, 2007), especially chaps. 9 and 12.

29. Delahaye, *Les Assassins et les vengeurs de Morès*, 1:77.

30. For the most detailed contemporaneous account of Morès's sprawling African agenda, see Delahaye, *Les Assassins et les vengeurs de Morès*, 1:49–156. See also Byrnes, *Antisemitism in Modern France*, 247 and Tweton, *The Marquis de Morès*, 187–90.

31. Winock, *Nationalisme, antisémitisme et fascisme*, 135.

32. "L'Exemple du mort," *Le Figaro*, 19 June 1896, 1.

33. On Morès's falling out with French officials in Tunisia, see Tweton, *The Marquis de Morès*, 196.

34. For concise accounts of Dupleix's and Lally's ill-fated Indian careers, see Barnett Singer and John Langdon, *Cultured Force: Makers and Defenders of the French Colonial Empire* (Madison: University of Wisconsin Press, 2004), 25–33.

35. Jean Hess, "Le Massacre de la mission Morès," *Le Figaro*, 19 June 1896, 2.

36. Drault, "Morès.—Sa vie.—Son œuvre," 2.

37. Léoville, "La Mort du Marquis de Morès," *La Libre parole illustrée*, 27 June 1896, 2.

38. Byrnes, *Antisemitism in Modern France*, 238–39; Léon Gautier, *La Chevalerie* (Paris: Delagrave, 1890), 126, 130.

39. David Carroll, *French Literary Fascism: Nationalism, Anti-Semitism, and the Ideology of Culture* (Princeton: Princeton University Press, 1995), 6–7, 171–80. Lacoue-Labarthe offers the following succinct formulation: "Racism—antisemitism especially—is, more than anything, fundamentally an aestheticism" (Philippe Lacoue-Labarthe, *La Fiction du politique: Heidegger, l'art et la politique* [Paris: Bourgois, 1998], 109–10).

40. Gautier, *La Chevalerie*, 126.

41. Tweton, *The Marquis de Morès*, 208–9.

42. Tweton, *The Marquis de Morès*, 205.

43. Barrès, *Scènes et doctrines*, 230–31.

44. Barrès, *Scènes et doctrines*, 231.

45. Zeev Sternhell, *Maurice Barrès et le nationalisme français* (Paris: Fayard, 2000), 380–81.

46. Maurice Barrès, "Morès," *Le Figaro*, 19 June 1896, 1.

47. Drumont, "Discours d'Édouard Drumont," 1.

48. Drumont, "Morès," 1.

49. Barrès, *Scènes et doctrines*, 231.

50. Benedict Anderson, *Imagined Communities: Reflections on the Origin and Spread of Nationalism* (London: Verso, 2006), 24.

51. Anderson, *Imagined Communities*, 23–24.

52. Ian Baucom, *Out of Place: Englishness, Empire, and the Locations of Identity* (Princeton: Princeton University Press, 1999), 52–54.

53. Anderson, *Imagined Communities*, 24–25.

54. Homi K. Bhabha, *The Location of Culture* (London: Routledge, 1994), 228.

55. Bhabha, *The Location of Culture*, 229; Walter Benjamin, *Illuminations*, ed. Hannah Arendt, trans. Harry Zohn (New York: Schocken, 1968), 261. Bhabha makes the point explicitly, arguing that "we are now confronted with what Walter Benjamin describes as the blasting of a monadic moment from the homogeneous course of history, 'establishing a conception of the present as the "time of the now"'" (Bhabha, *The Location of Culture*, 6).

56. Benjamin, *Illuminations*, 261.

57. Bhabha, *The Location of Culture*, 233.

58. Baucom, *Out of Place*, 54.

59. Anderson, *Imagined Communities*, 24; Benjamin, *Illuminations*, 263.

60. Barrès, *Scènes et doctrines*, 231.

61. Johannes Fabian, *Time and the Other: How Anthropology Makes Its Object* (New York: Columbia University Press, 2002). For the arguments I am summarizing here, see the pivotal first chapter, "Time and the Emerging Other," especially pages 2–17.

62. Sternhell, *Maurice Barrès*, 284.

63. See Maurice Barrès, *La Terre et les Morts: Sur quelles réalités fonder la conscience française* (Paris: Ligue de la Patrie française, 1899).

64. Barrès, *Scènes et doctrines*, 234.

65. On the profound importance of Taine for Barrèsian nationalism, see Sternhell, *Maurice Barrès*, 324–26.

66. Hippolyte Taine, *Histoire de la littérature anglaise* (Paris: Hachette, 1863–64), 1:xlvii.

67. Barrès, *Scènes et doctrines*, 237.

68. Barrès, *Scènes et doctrines*, 237.

69. Taine, *Histoire de la littérature anglaise*, 1:xxviii–xxix.

70. Barrès, "Morès," 1; Drumont, "Morès," 1.

71. Barrès, *Scènes et doctrines*, 237.

72. Barrès was familiar with Carlyle's work and referenced him often (Sternhell, *Maurice Barrès*, 310n1).

73. On Barrès's Boulangism, see Sternhell, *Maurice Barrès*, 185–95.

74. Barrès, *Scènes et doctrines*, 236.

75. Paul Ricoeur, *Time and Narrative*, trans. Kathleen McLaughlin and David Pellauer, 3 vols. (Chicago: University of Chicago Press, 1984).

76. Anderson, *Imagined Communities*, 24–25.

77. Anderson's appended chapter titled "Memory and Forgetting" in the second edition of *Imagined Communities* tackles the subject of memory, of course, but only from the perspective of the national collectivity rather than of individual subjective experience.

78. On the importance of Barrès, for instance, to Pierre Drieu La Rochelle's fascist writing and thought in the 1930s, see Winock, *Nationalisme, antisémitisme et fascisme*, 335. Morès's legend, too, was still going strong in the 1930s among those of a certain political disposition. In 1934 the novelist, playwright, and poet Pierre Frondaie updated the *héros de roman* ("romance

hero") trope for the moving picture era, lauding Morès as one of those "predestined to the cinema" who dared actually to do what Hollywood's leading men could only ape. Hitler later receives a nod from Frondaie for having at least managed to slow the Jewish "train of iron and gold" that Morès had tried to derail (Pierre Frondaie, *L'Assassinat du Marquis de Morès* [Paris: Éditions Émile-Paul Frères, 1934], 12–13, 92).

79. On the corresponding French debate about colonial "assimilation" versus "association," see Raymond Betts, *Assimilation and Association in French Colonial Theory, 1890–1914* (Lincoln: University of Nebraska Press, 2005).

80. On this "Kabyle Myth," see Patricia Lorcin, *Imperial Identities: Stereotyping, Prejudice and Race in Colonial Algeria* (London: I. B. Tauris, 1999), especially pages 146–69.

81. Anne McClintock, *Imperial Leather: Race, Gender and Sexuality in the Colonial Conquest* (New York: Routledge, 1995).

82. Barrès, *Scènes et doctrines*, 235.

83. Drault, "Morès.—Sa vie.—Son œuvre," 2.

84. Benjamin Claude Brower, *A Desert Named Peace: The Violence of France's Empire in the Algerian Sahara, 1844–1902* (New York: Columbia University Press, 2009), 229.

85. Benjamin Brower offers that "the Tuareg were the perfect 'antidote' to the emerging forms of modernity in Europe" despised by the "elitist" Duveyrier (Brower, *A Desert Named Peace*, 236).

86. On the treaty, see Dresden, *The Marquis de Morès*, 233. On Polignac's influence over Morès, see Byrnes, *Antisemitism in Modern France*, 247 and Tweton, *The Marquis de Morès*, 186–88. Morès likely shared Polignac's admiration for Duveyrier, whose "rare energy" and "remarkable qualities" Polignac applauded (Ludovic de Polignac, "A Propos du traité de Ghadamès," *Le Temps*, 16 June 1893, 2).

87. Brower, *A Desert Named Peace*, 232.

88. Delahaye, *Les Assassins et les vengeurs de Morès*, 1:91.

89. Barrès, *Scènes et doctrines*, 244.

90. Morès was inspired by Polignac's book-length call for such an alliance. See Ludovic de Polignac, *France et Islam* (Algiers: Remordet, 1893).

91. Drumont, *Les Héros et les pitres*, 7.

92. Drumont, *Les Héros et les pitres*, 7.

93. Berenson, *Heroes of Empire*, 195.

94. Raoul Girardet, *L'Idée coloniale en France de 1871 à 1962* (Paris: Hachette, 2007), 150–52.

95. Quoted in Girardet, *L'Idée coloniale*, 151.

96. Barrès, *Scènes et doctrines*, 232.

97. Barrès, *Scènes et doctrines*, 232.

98. Quoted in Girardet, *L'Idée coloniale*, 86.

99. Fabian, *Time and the Other*, 17.

100. McClintock, *Imperial Leather*, 40; Walter Mignolo, "Globalization, Civilization Processes, and the Relocation of Languages and Cultures," in *The Cultures of Globalization*, ed. Fredric Jameson and Masao Miyoshi (Durham: Duke University Press, 1998), 36.

101. Dipesh Chakrabarty, *Provincializing Europe: Postcolonial Thought and Historical Difference* (Princeton: Princeton University Press, 2008), 23.

102. Benjamin, *Illuminations*, 256.

103. Benjamin, *Illuminations*, 257.

104. Bhabha, *The Location of Culture*, 314.

105. Here we can better understand why Bhabha, though occasionally citing the messianic alternative to homogeneous time offered in the "Theses" by Benjamin himself, tends nevertheless to privilege the Benjamin of "The Storyteller" and "The Task of the Translator" when interrogating homogeneous temporality. These latter essays better lend themselves to Bhabha's Derridean emphasis on the deferral of meaning produced when, in language, signs exert a constant retroactive force on those that precede them. Wielding poststructuralist tools not at Benjamin's disposal, Bhabha seems instinctively to distance himself from the threat that Benjamin's messianic model, like homogeneous time, merely reimagines an organizing logos. See, especially, the essay "Dissemination," in Bhabha, *The Location of Culture.*

106. Benjamin, *Illuminations*, 264.

107. Fredric Jameson, "Marx's Purloined Letter," in *Ghostly Demarcations: A Symposium on Jacques Derrida's "Specters of Marx,"* ed. Michael Sprinker (London: Verso, 2008), 62.

108. Jacques Derrida, "Marx & Sons," in *Ghostly Demarcations: A Symposium on Jacques Derrida's "Specters of Marx,"* ed. Michael Sprinker (London: Verso, 2008), 254.

109. Derrida, "Marx & Sons," 253; Jacques Derrida, *Specters of Marx: The State of the Debt, the Work of Mourning and the New International*, trans. Peggy Kamuf (New York: Routledge, 1994), 212.

110. Benjamin, *Illuminations*, 254 (original emphasis).

111. Anderson, *Imagined Communities*, 24.

112. Derrida, "Marx & Sons," 254–55.

113. Maurice Barrès, *De Hegel aux cantines du Nord* (Paris: Sansot, 1904), 22.

CHAPTER 4

1. I borrow the phrase "degeneration theory" from J. Edward Chamberlin, ed., *Degeneration: The Dark Side of Progress* (New York: Columbia University Press, 1985). For intellectual and cultural histories of degeneration in France, see Robert A. Nye, *Crime, Madness and Politics in Modern France: The Medical Concept of National Decline* (Princeton: Princeton University Press, 1984) and chapters 2–4 of Daniel Pick, *Faces of Degeneration: A European Disorder c. 1848–1918* (Cambridge: Cambridge University Press, 1989).

2. Robert F. Byrnes, *Antisemitism in Modern France* (New Brunswick, NJ: Rutgers University Press, 1950), 238–41.

3. Drumont, in a representative vein, describes a growing Jewish propensity for mental and physical aberration: "Sudden death is, however, more

common among the Jews than suicide, which is nevertheless increasing to an astonishing extent that reflects the spread among them of neurosis" (Édouard Drumont, *La France juive: Essai d'histoire contemporaine* [Paris: Marpon et Flammarion, 1886], 1:122). On the pathologization of Jews, see Sander Gilman, *The Jew's Body* (New York: Routledge, 1991).

4. Drumont, *La France juive*, 2:576.

5. Maurice Barrès, *La Terre et les Morts: Sur quelles réalités fonder la conscience française* (Paris: Ligue de la Patrie française, 1899), 25–26.

6. Melchior de Vogüé, "Réponse de M. le vicomte de Vogüé au discours de M. Maurice Barrès," speech, Palais de L'Insitut, Paris, 17 January 1907. The speech is available on the website of the Académie Française.

7. On the alignment of the French right with the project of empire beginning in the late 1890s, see Charles-Robert Ageron, *L'anticolonialisme en France de 1871 à 1914* (Paris: PUF, 1973), 20 and Raoul Girardet, *L'Idée coloniale en France de 1871 à 1962* (Paris: Hachette, 2007), 150–56.

8. On the relationship between antisemitism and Boulangism, see Byrnes, *Antisemitism in Modern France*, 232–37.

9. Édouard Drumont, "Le Général Dodds," *La Libre parole*, 15 May 1893, 1.

10. Lucien Pemjean, "Supplément illustré," *La Libre parole*, 29 May 1899.

11. For a detailed account of how Marchand disappointed the hopes placed in him by the French right, see Edward Berenson, *Heroes of Empire: Five Charismatic Men and the Conquest of Africa* (Berkeley: University of California Press, 2011), 166–96.

12. Scholars of French colonialism have often cited *Les Morts qui parlent* for the role its discourse of colonial regeneration played in wooing reactionaries to the cause of empire. See Berenson, *Heroes of Empire*, 250–52; Girardet, *L'Idée coloniale*, 154–56; and Martine Astier Loutfi, *Littérature et colonialisme: L'expansion coloniale vue dans la littérature romanesque française, 1871–1914* (Paris: Mouton, 1971), 84–88.

13. From the colonial Algerian officer Hector Servadac, at odds throughout Jules Verne's 1877 *Hector Servadac* with the avaricious Jew Isa[a]c Hakhabut, to the former colonial Algerian officer Général Comte Martin d'Epagnes, the only character in Robert de Bonnières 1885 *Les Monach* to successfully face down the conniving Jewish Monach family, fictional soldiers with imperial connections confronted Jewish foes in late-century French literature with some frequency. This is doubtless an artifact, at least in part, of the denunciation by some in France's military of the Crémieux decree that in 1870 extended French citizenship to all Algerian Jews. On the Crémieux decree, as well as on *Les Monach*, see Chapter 2.

14. Archives Biographiques Françaises, Bibliothèque Nationale de France (I 1035, II 635, III 454).

15. Quoted in Byrnes, *Antisemitism in Modern France*, 131.

16. Melchior de Vogüé, *Les Morts qui parlent* (Paris: Plon, 1899), 225, 227. Subsequent citations of *Les Morts qui parlent* will be made parenthetically in the text. On Vogüé's relationship with Lyautey, see Berenson, *Heroes of Empire*, 250–51 and Loutfi, *Littérature et colonialisme*, 88n65.

17. For a concise history of French antiparliamentarianism, see Michel Winock, *La France politique, XIXe–XXe siècle* (Paris: Seuil, 2003), 205–25.

18. Beginning in 1897 with *Les Déracinés*, Barrès's novelistic trilogy *Le Roman de l'énergie nationale* (1897–1902) expounded his doctrine of an innate national energy born of an attachment to tradition and channeled through patriotic fervor.

19. See Michel Serres, *Feux et signaux de brume, Zola* (Paris: Grasset, 1975).

20. Melchior de Vogüé, *Spectacles contemporains* (Paris: Colin, 1891), 343.

21. Quoted in Loutfi, *Littérature et colonialisme*, 88.

22. On this, see Pascal Ory and Jean-François Sirinelli, *Les Intellectuels en France: De l'affaire Dreyfus à nos jours* (Paris: Perrin, 2004), 59–60. *Les Morts qui parlent* is dedicated to Brunetière.

23. Melchior de Vogüé, *Heures d'histoire* (Paris: Colin, 1893), 324, 330.

24. Melchior de Vogüé, preamble to *Un siècle, mouvement du monde de 1800 à 1900*, ed. Ludovico Péchenard (Paris: Oudin, 1900), xix, xx–xxi.

25. Ory and Sirinelli, *Les Intellectuels en France*, 59.

26. Vogüé, preamble, xxi, xxii.

27. Gellion-Danglar's *Les Sémites et le sémitisme, aux points de vue ethnographique, religieux et politique* (1882), Tridon's *Du molochisme juif* (1884), and Regnard's *Aryens et Sémites: Le bilan du judaïsme et du christianisme* (1890) typify the atheist, antisemitic production of a socialist and revolutionary left—among whose antisemitic practitioners may also be counted Pierre-Joseph Proudhon, Charles Fourier, Alphonse Toussenel, and Auguste Chirac—that contributed to modern French antisemitism's racialist, essentializing turn. See Marc Crapez, *L'Antisémitisme de gauche au XIXe siècle* (Paris: Berg International, 2002); Léon Poliakov, *Histoire de l'antisémitisme. 2: L'âge de la science* (Paris: Calmann-Lévy, 1981), 286–87; Zeev Sternhell, *La Droite révolutionnaire, 1885–1914: Les origines françaises du fascisme* (Paris: Fayard, 2000), 189–223; and Michel Winock, *Nationalisme, antisémitisme et fascisme en France* (Paris: Seuil, 2004), 122–25.

28. Ernest Renan, *La Réforme intellectuelle et morale*, *Oeuvres completes* (Paris: Calmann-Lévy, 1947–61), 1:390.

29. Henri de Boulainvilliers, *Essais sur la noblesse de France, contenans une dissertation sur son origine et abaissement* (Amsterdam, 1732).

30. Renan, *La Réforme*, 1:390–91.

31. Benedict Anderson, *Imagined Communities: Reflections on the Origin and Spread of Nationalism* (London: Verso, 2006), 150; Hannah Arendt, *The Origins of Totalitarianism* (San Diego: Harcourt, 1976), 162.

32. Renan, *La Réforme*, 1:391.

33. Auguste Comte, *Système de politique positive, ou, Traité de sociologie instituant la religion de l'humanité* (Paris: Mathias, 1851–54), 2:185.

34. Charles Maurras, *L'Avenir de l'intelligence* (Paris: Flammarion, 1927), 133.

35. I borrow the translation from Michael Sutton's careful study on Maurras (Sutton, *Nationalism, Positivism and Catholicism: The Politics of Charles Maurras and French Catholics, 1890–1914* [Cambridge: Cambridge University Press, 1982], 85).

36. Here is Maurras on Judaism and the Revolution: "it is in the Law and the Prophets, interpreted literally and unspiritually, that are to be found the

first expressions in antiquity of the individualism, egalitarianism, humanitarianism and social and political idealism that were to mark 1789" (quoted in Sutton, *Nationalism*, 38).

37. Renan, *La Réforme*, 1:384.

38. Maurras warned that the Third Republic had no real way to defend its colonial empire, leaving France vulnerable to British demands: "one must admit that we acquired much without anticipating that it would be necessary to stand guard over our possessions . . . all of British policy will thus one day be summarizable in terms a seven-year-old would easily understand:—*You will do as we please, or we will take your colonial empire*" (Charles Maurras, *Kiel et Tanger, 1895–1905: La République française devant l'Europe* [Paris: Nouvelle librairie nationale, 1921], 120–21).

39. Vogüé, *Spectacles contemporains*, 365–66.

40. Ernst Nolte, *Three Faces of Fascism: Action Française, Italian Fascism, National Socialism*, trans. Leila Vennewitz (New York: Holt, Rinehart and Winston, 1966); Sternhell, *La Droite révolutionnaire*, 349–96.

41. Max Horkheimer and Theodor W. Adorno, *Dialectic of Enlightenment*, trans. John Cumming (New York: Continuum, 1995), 179–85.

42. I am in agreement here with Anson Rabinbach, who writes about Horkheimer and Adorno's thesis of antisemitic mimetic regression that "it is ultimately not clear whether this version of primal anti-Semitism can usefully distinguish modern racism, Christian Jew-hatred (ancient or primordial), anti-Judaism, or whether—in the end—it has anything to do with the Jews at all (Rabinbach, "Why Were the Jews Sacrificed? The Place of Anti-Semitism in *Dialectic of Enlightenment*," *New German Critique* 81 [2000]: 61).

43. For a seminal such use of Freud, see Homi Bhabha's essay "The Other Question: Stereotype, Discrimination, and the Discourse of Colonialism," in *The Location of Culture* (New York: Routledge, 1994), 94–120.

44. Horkheimer and Adorno, *Dialectic*, 180.

45. Horkheimer and Adorno, *Dialectic*, 27.

46. Horkheimer and Adorno, *Dialectic*, 187, 185.

47. Horkheimer and Adorno, *Dialectic*, 184.

48. Horkheimer and Adorno, *Dialectic*, 186.

49. Horkheimer and Adorno, *Dialectic*, 186.

50. Jonathan Judaken, "Between Philosemitism and Antisemitism: The Frankfurt School's Anti-Antisemitism," in *Antisemitism and Philosemitism in the Twentieth and Twenty-First Centuries: Representing Jews, Jewishness, and Modern Culture*, ed. Phyllis Lassner and Lara Trubowitz (Newark: University of Delaware Press, 2008), 39.

51. Max Horkheimer and Theodor W. Adorno, *Dialectic of Enlightenment: Philosophical Fragments*, trans. Edmund Jephcott, ed. Gunzelin Schmid Noerr (Stanford: Stanford University Press, 2002), 189.

52. Pick, *Faces of Degeneration*, 229, 101.

53. Zygmunt Bauman, *Modernity and the Holocaust* (Ithaca, NY: Cornell University Press, 2000), 66.

54. On the link between Boulainvilliers and later French race-thinking of the sort pioneered by Gobineau, see Arendt, *Origins*, 171–73.

55. "From the very day when the conquest is accomplished and the fusion begins," writes Gobineau, "there appears a noticeable change of quality in the blood of the masters" (Arthur de Gobineau, *The Inequality of the Human Races*, trans. Adrian Collins [New York: Fertig, 1999], 31).

56. Horkheimer and Adorno, *Dialectic*, 181.

57. See, especially, Renan's 1855 *Histoire générale et système comparé des langues sémitiques*. On the differences between Aryans and Semites popularized by Renan, see Maurice Olender, *The Languages of Paradise: Race, Religion, and Philology in the Nineteenth Century*, trans. Arthur Goldhammer (Cambridge, MA: Harvard University Press, 2008), 51–81.

58. Once a people "pass into the state of a nation," maintains Gobineau, "one or other of two destinies is inevitable. It will either conquer or be conquered" (Gobineau, *Inequality*, 30).

59. Using the example of Algeria, colonized by the French in 1830, to illustrate his doctrine that "civilization is incommunicable," Gobineau cites the failure of "French goodwill and conciliation in the ancient kingdom of Algiers at the present day" (Gobineau, *Inequality*, 171).

60. Melchior de Vogüé, *Le Maître de la mer* (Paris: Plon-Nourrit, 1903), 80. Pierre is, again, himself also quite clearly meant to evoke Marchand. The story Pierre tells Jacques about a battle with "Samory" references the very real Samori Turé, the Mandinka leader with whom French colonial forces clashed in West Africa in the late nineteenth century (221). Among those involved was Marchand, who fought against Samori in 1894 and whose 1898 exploits at Fashoda remained fresh in the minds of readers of a novel published in 1899. Vogüé, however, was not content merely to cast Pierre in the image of history. Marchand having disappointed the expectations of a French right that, around the time Vogüé was writing his novel, had hoped Marchand would return to lead a triumphant revolution against the Dreyfusards (see note 11), Vogüé reinvests his fictional Marchand figure with the impact Marchand himself had failed to have. Vogüé also recasts history in the climactic duel between Elzéar and Pierre, which subtly references another famous episode in antisemitism's late nineteenth-century intersection with imperialist ambition. Recall from the preceding chapter that in the early days of the Dreyfus Affair, the Marquis de Morès had frivolously dueled with a Jewish officer, Mayer, dealing him a mortal blow to the lung. Mayer's death sparked a public backlash against Morès so strong that for a time Drumont was forced to temper his anti-Dreyfusard attacks in *La Libre parole*. Though Morès recovered from this public relations debacle, he had demonstrated a pattern of behavior whose accumulated disgraces would eventually contribute to his departure for Africa. Like Morès's victim Mayer, *Les Morts qui parlent*'s Elzéar dies of a punctured lung (327). But unlike Morès, Elzéar's aggressor Pierre departs for Africa in triumph. Thus does the novel rescript one of the more unsavory aspects of Morès's life, investing the infamous duel after the fact with ideological portent.

61. Neil Smith, *Uneven Development: Nature, Capital, and the Production of Space*, 3rd ed. (Athens: University of Georgia Press, 2008), 229.

62. For Étienne Balibar's gloss of Fichte's eighteenth-century reflection on the "internal frontiers" essential to the nation, see Balibar, *Masses, Classes,*

Ideas: Studies on Politics and Philosophy Before and After Marx, trans. James Swenson (London: Routledge, 1994), 61–87. I use the expression here to mean, as Ann Stoler has put it, that "the purity of the community is prone to penetration on its interior and exterior borders" (Stoler, "Sexual Affronts and Racial Frontiers: European Identities and the Cultural Politics of Exclusion in Colonial Southeast Asia," in *Tensions of Empire: Colonial Cultures in a Bourgeois World*, ed. Ann Laura Stoler and Frederick Cooper [Berkeley: University of California Press, 1997], 198–237). See also her elegant deployment of the idea throughout Stoler, *Race and the Education of Desire: Foucault's "History of Sexuality" and the Colonial Order of Things* (Durham: Duke University Press, 1995).

63. Michel Foucault, *"Society Must Be Defended": Lectures at the Collège de France, 1975–76*, ed. Mauro Bertani and Alessandro Fontana, trans. David Macey (New York: Picador, 2003), 49–51.

64. Foucault, *"Society Must Be Defended,"* 103.

65. Stoler, *Race and the Education of Desire*, 133. Stoler places into her Foucauldian frame ideas about the Crémieux decree's continental effects borrowed from chapters 9 and 12 of Stephen Wilson, *Ideology and Experience: Antisemitism in France at the Time of the Dreyfus Affair* (Oxford: Littman Library of Jewish Civilization, 2007).

66. See notes 7 and 12.

CHAPTER 5

1. Joseph Bamat, "Hollande Says Terrorist Cells in France Will Be Eliminated," *France 24*, 10 November 2012, web. I have translated Hollande's remark from the embedded interview.

2. Bamat, "Hollande Says Terrorist Cells in France Will Be Eliminated."

3. In the European context, French commentators have been particularly active in elaborating this idea of a "new antisemitism." Representative publications include Emmanuel Brenner, *"France, prends garde de perdre ton âme . . .": Fracture sociale et antisémitisme dans la République* (Paris: Mille et une nuits, 2004); Raphaël Draï, *Sous le signe de Sion: L'Antisémitisme nouveau est arrivé* (Paris: Michalon, 2001); Alain Finkielkraut, *Au nom de l'Autre: Réflexions sur l'antisémitisme qui vient* (Paris: Gallimard, 2003); Pierre-André Taguieff, *Rising from the Muck: The New Anti-Semitism in Europe*, trans. Patrick Camiller (Chicago: Dee, 2004); and Shmuel Trigano, *La Démission de la République: Juifs et Musulmans en France* (Paris: Presses Universitaires de France, 2003).

4. Nonna Mayer, "Nouvelle judéophobie ou vieil antisémitisme?" *Raisons politiques* 4.16 (2004): 96; Nicolas Weill, *La République et les antisémites* (Paris: Grasset, 2004), 33–35, 58–62. Mayer's and Weill's studies count among a number of skeptical responses to the alarm sounded in France during the early 2000s over a mounting "new antisemitism." These often understand analysts to have disproportionately and simplistically insisted on the threat

of Muslim antisemitism, and include Étienne Balibar, "Un nouvel antisémitisme?" in *Antisémitisme: L'Intolérable chantage: Israël-Palestine, une affaire française* (Paris: La Découverte, 2003), 89–96; Vincent Geisser, *La Nouvelle islamophobie* (Paris: La Découverte, 2003), 77–93; Ivan Segré, *La Réaction philosémite, ou, La Trahison des clercs* (Paris: Lignes, 2009); Guillaume Weill-Raynal, *Une haine imaginaire?: Contre-enquête sur le "nouvel antisémitisme"* (Paris: Colin, 2005); and Michel Wieviorka, *L'Antisémitisme est-il de retour?* (Paris: Larousse, 2008). The polemic has also raged elsewhere, producing a mushrooming bibliography too large to reproduce here. Representative Anglophone interventions propounding the existence of a global new antisemitism include Phyllis Chesler, *The New Anti-Semitism: The Current Crisis and What We Must Do About It* (San Francisco: Jossey-Bass, 2005); Abraham Foxman, *Never Again? The Threat of the New Anti-Semitism* (New York: Harper Collins, 2003); and Walter Laqueur, *The Changing Face of Anti-Semitism: From Ancient Times to the Present Day* (Oxford: Oxford University Press, 2006), 1–20. For tart rebuttals, see Norman G. Finkelstein, *Beyond Chutzpah: On the Misuse of Anti-Semitism and the Abuse of History*, updated ed. (Berkeley: University of California Press, 2008), 21–85 and Brian Klug, "The Myth of the New Anti-Semitism," *The Nation*, 2 February 2004, 23–29. Doubters often take issue with a tendency among those describing the new antisemitism to conflate antisemitism and anti-Zionism.

5. Julia Kristeva, *Powers of Horror: An Essay on Abjection*, trans. Leon S. Roudiez (New York: Columbia University Press, 1982), 185.

6. Zygmunt Bauman, *Life in Fragments: Essays in Postmodern Morality* (Oxford: Blackwell, 1995), 208, 213.

7. Giorgio Agamben, *Homo Sacer: Sovereign Power and Bare Life*, trans. Daniel Heller-Roazen (Stanford: Stanford University Press, 1998), 19, 166–80.

8. Jean-François Lyotard, *Heidegger and "the jews,"* trans. Andreas Mitchell and Mark Roberts (Minneapolis: University of Minnesota Press, 1990), 11–23.

9. Moshe Ma'oz, introduction to *Muslim Attitudes to Jews and Israel: The Ambivalences of Rejection, Antagonism, Intolerance, and Cooperation*, ed. Moshe Ma'oz (Portland: Sussex Academic Press, 2010), 24. See also Diana Knight, "Muslims Are the New Jews," *The Sunday Times*, 15 October 2006. Esther Benbassa, the eminent French scholar of Jewish history, puts it succinctly: "This time, the Other is the Muslim Arab, who replaces the Jew of yesteryear" (Benbassa, "Xenophobia, Anti-Semitism, and Racism: Europe's Recurring Evils?" trans. Paul A. Silverstein, in *Anti-Semitism and Islamophobia: Hatreds Old and New in Europe*, ed. Matti Bunzl [Chicago: Prickly Paradigm Press, 2007], 88). Enzo Traverso seconds the notion: "In contemporary Europe . . . Islamophobia plays the role for the new racism that anti-Semitism had in the past" (Traverso, *The End of Jewish Modernity*, trans. David Fernbach [London: Pluto, 2016], 94).

10. Jean-Claude Milner, *Les Penchants criminels de l'Europe démocratique* (Paris: Verdier, 2003), 89.

11. Slavoj Žižek, *The Parallax View* (Cambridge, MA: MIT Press, 2009), 254.

12. Žižek, *The Parallax View*, 257.

13. See note 3.

14. In France, Michel Wieviorka has offered some of the most careful documentation of contemporary Muslim antisemitism, parsing the phenomenon in nuanced detail without according it the disproportionate attention it often receives in accounts of the "new antisemitism." See Wieviorka, *L'Antisémitisme*, 81–96 and Wieviorka, *The Lure of Anti-Semitism: Hatred of Jews in Present-Day France*, trans. Kristin Couper Lobel and Anna Declerck (Leiden: Brill, 2007), 93–158.

15. Balibar, "Un nouvel antisémitisme?" 93, 96.

16. Brian Klug, "A Contradiction in the 'New Europe,'" in *Anti-Semitism and Islamophobia: Hatreds Old and New in Europe*, ed. Matti Bunzl (Chicago: Prickly Paradigm Press, 2007), 55.

17. Finkielkraut, *Au nom de l'Autre*, 16.

18. Gil Anidjar, *The Jew, the Arab: A History of the Enemy* (Stanford: Stanford University Press, 2003). See, as well, Jonathan Boyarin, *The Unconverted Self: Jews, Indians, and the Identity of Christian Europe* (Chicago: University of Chicago Press, 2009), 37–53 and Anouar Majid, *We Are All Moors: Ending Centuries of Crusades Against Muslims and Other Minorities* (Minneapolis: University of Minnesota Press, 2009), 87–122. Ethan B. Katz, writing about the specifically French context, reminds us conversely that Jewish-Muslim relations themselves cannot be understood in isolation from their "triangular" mediation by the French colonizing power. World War II–era Muslim antisemitism, for instance, developed alongside the anti-Jewish policies of the Vichy government and Nazi occupiers with which some North African Muslims collaborated (Katz, *The Burdens of Brotherhood: Jews and Muslims from North Africa to France* [Cambridge, MA: Harvard University Press, 2015], 5, 125–41). I would distinguish here between the *construct* of Muslim antisemitism—with whose role in various European discourses I will be chiefly concerned—and the actual, complex phenomenon that is Muslim antisemitism itself. For a careful history of the relationship between Jewish and Muslim communities in France, see also Maud S. Mandel, *Muslims and Jews in France: History of a Conflict* (Princeton: Princeton University Press, 2014).

19. Mary Louise Pratt, *Imperial Eyes: Travel Writing and Transculturation*, 2nd ed. (New York: Routledge, 2008), 15–36.

20. Neil Smith, *Uneven Development: Nature, Capital, and the Production of Space*, 3rd ed. (Athens: University of Georgia Press, 2008), 229.

21. Smith, *Uneven Development*, 119–20.

22. Smith, *Uneven Development*, 229–30.

23. Neil Brenner, "The Limits to Scale? Methodological Reflections on Scalar Structuration," *Progress in Human Geography* 25.4 (2001): 600 (original emphasis).

24. Smith, *Uneven Development*, 111–13, 121–22, 126–28, 148–49.

25. Karl Marx, "On the Jewish Question," in *Early Writings*, trans. Rodney Livingstone and Gregor Benton (London: Penguin, 1992), 236. Subsequent references to Marx's essay will be made parenthetically in the text.

26. Bernard Lewis, *Semites and Anti-Semites: An Inquiry into Conflict and Prejudice* (New York: Norton, 1999), 112.

27. Wendy Brown offers a useful summary of the debate surrounding Marx's antisemitism in "On the Jewish Question" (Brown, "Rights and Identity in Late Modernity: Revisiting the 'Jewish Question,'" in *Identities, Politics, and Rights*, ed. Austin Sarat and Thomas R. Kearns [Ann Arbor: University of Michigan Press, 1995], 91–92). For a bibliographic overview of the enormous literature on the debate, see Roland Boer, *Criticism of Earth: On Marx, Engels, and Theology* (Leiden: Brill, 2012), 91n55.

28. "One of the functions of racism," writes Sartre, "is to compensate the latent universalism of bourgeois liberalism: since all human beings have the same rights, the Algerian will be made subhuman" (Jean-Paul Sartre, *Colonialism and Neocolonialism*, trans. Azzedine Haddour, Steve Brewer, and Terry McWilliams [New York: Routledge, 2006], 51).

29. David Theo Goldberg, "The Comparative and the Relational: Meditations on Racial Method," in *A Companion to Comparative Literature*, ed. Ali Behdad and Dominic Thomas (New York: Wiley-Blackwell, 2011), 360. See my discussion of this in the Introduction.

30. See, for example, Susannah Heschel, *Abraham Geiger and the Jewish Jesus* (Chicago: University of Chicago Press, 1998), 21–22. Heschel advances that Christianity's theological appropriation then expurgation of Judaism furnished a template for Europe's more outward-directed patterns of Orientalist domination. See also Ivan Davidson Kalmar and Derek J. Penslar, "Orientalism and the Jews: An Introduction," in *Orientalism and the Jews*, ed. Ivan Davidson Kalmar and Derek J. Penslar (Waltham, MA: Brandeis University Press, 2005), xiii–xl.

31. Note that I am counting all European Muslims as members of a "postcolonial" minority, whether they are actually descended from colonized peoples or represent the outcome of migrations unrelated to colonial empire. Here I follow Paul Gilroy, who has argued in the British context that while "later groups of immigrants may not . . . be connected to the history of empire and colony in any way whatsoever," they still "experience the misfortune of being caught up in a pattern of hostility and conflict that belongs emphatically to its lingering aftermath" (Gilroy, *Postcolonial Melancholia* [New York: Columbia University Press, 2005], 101).

Some further observations about Gilroy are in order, given his efforts in the same volume to think British wartime and colonial memories together. If, for Gilroy, the former colonizer's lingering "postimperial melancholia" involves a malaise over colonial crimes, so too, in his nuanced telling, does it contain nostalgia for an imagined metropolitan cultural idyll lost to the demographic upheavals of decolonization. Displaced and acted out as xenophobic racism, this neurotic cocktail of shame and longing means that still-malignant imperial features of the body politic go widely undiagnosed. Gilroy locates a symptom of such postcolonial failure in Britain's undiminished mythologizing of its triumph over radical Nazi evil. That victory's simplicity of purpose, he advances, is obsessively revisited as a psychic escape from the apparent complexities of postcolonial diversity (Gilroy, *Postcolonial Melancholia*, 87–101). One might argue something similar about the new Europe, whose inclusionary identity trades so heavily on continental Jewry's rapid postwar (re)assimilation as to distract from the vexed European integration of various postcolonial minorities. The difference, however, at least with regard to Muslims, is that this psychosocial operation does not simply avoid the complicated question of European Islam in favor of an idealized Judeo-European harmony. Rather, European Muslims are themselves now furnishing the stage, in their increasingly assumed antisemitism, on which Europe performs its defining tolerance of Jews. Instead of simply reaching for the comforts of a romanticized past over the challenges of a postcolonial present, as Gilroy understands Britain to have done, Europe is now retrofitting elements of the postcolonial present to the purposes of an anti-Nazi raison d'être otherwise receding quickly into the past.

32. Matti Bunzl, "Anti-Semitism and Islamophobia," in *Anti-Semitism and Islamophobia: Hatreds Old and New in Europe*, ed. Matti Bunzl (Chicago: Prickly Paradigm Press, 2007), 13.

33. Albert S. Lindemann, *Esau's Tears: Modern Anti-Semitism and the Rise of the Jews* (Cambridge: Cambridge University Press, 1997), 209.

34. Émile Zola, *La Débâcle*, in *Les Rougon-Macquart*, ed. Henri Mitterand, Bibliothèque de la Pléiade (Paris: Gallimard, 1967), 5:742–43.

35. Theodor Adorno, *The Stars Down to Earth and Other Essays on the Irrational in Culture*, ed. Stephen Crook (London: Routledge, 1994), 147.

36. Émile Zola, "Lettre à la France," in *Œuvres complètes*, ed. Henri Mitterand (Paris: Nouveau Monde, 2008), 18:436.

37. Émile Zola, *Vérité*, in *Œuvres complètes*, ed. Henri Mitterand (Paris: Nouveau Monde, 2009), 20:68–69.

38. Émile Zola, "Pour les juifs," in *Œuvres complètes*, ed. Henri Mitterand (Paris: Nouveau Monde, 2008), 17:428.

39. Émile Zola, *L'Argent*, in *Les Rougon-Macquart*, ed. Henri Mitterand, Bibliothèque de la Pléiade (Paris: Gallimard, 1967), 5:398. Subsequent references to the novel will be made parenthetically in the text. In places I have adhered closely to Valerie Minogue's excellent recent translation of the novel (Émile Zola, *Money*, trans. Valerie Minogue [Oxford: Oxford University Press, 2014]).

40. Henri Mitterand, introduction to *L'Argent*, by Émile Zola, in *Les Rougon-Macquart*, ed. Henri Mitterand, Bibliothèque de la Pléiade (Paris: Gallimard, 1967), 5:1272.

41. See, for example, Jacob Katz, *From Prejudice to Destruction: Anti-Semitism, 1700–1933* (Cambridge, MA: Harvard University Press, 1980), 293–94; Léon Poliakov, *Histoire de l'antisémitisme. 2: L'âge de la science* (Paris: Calmann-Lévy, 1981), 290; and Stephen Wilson, *Ideology and Experience: Antisemitism in France at the Time of the Dreyfus Affair* (Oxford: Littman Library of Jewish Civilization, 2007), 248–49.

42. Mitterand, introduction to *L'Argent*, 1242.

43. Émile Zola, "Lettre à la jeunesse," in *Œuvres complètes*, ed. Henri Mitterand (Paris: Nouveau Monde, 2008), 18:428.

44. Richard Grant, "The Jewish Question in Zola's *L'Argent*," *PMLA* 70.5 (December 1955): 961; Mitterand, introduction to *L'Argent*, 1259.

45. Quoted in Grant, "The Jewish Question," 960.

46. Grant, "The Jewish Question," 960.

47. Mitterand, introduction to *L'Argent*, 1258–59.

48. Quoted in Mitterand, introduction to *L'Argent*, 1259.

49. Vogüé's 1899 novel *Les Morts qui parlent*, with its conquering colonial heroes come home from Africa, is paradigmatic in this respect (see Chapter 4).

50. Quoted in Mitterand, introduction to *L'Argent*, 1244.

51. Quoted in Mitterand, introduction to *L'Argent*, 1251.

52. Raymond Schwab, *La Renaissance orientale* (New York: AMS, 1977).

53. Émile Zola, *La Curée*, in *Les Rougon-Macquart*, ed. Henri Mitterand, Bibliothèque de la Pléiade (Paris: Gallimard, 1960), 1:396, 418.

54. Zola, *Vérité*, 250.

55. The best-known literary rendition of this figure is Walter, the Jewish newspaper owner whose corrupt hand in France's fictional invasion of Morocco provides Guy de Maupassant's 1885 novel *Bel-Ami* its background scandal (see Chapter 2).

56. Zola, *Vérité*, 250 (emphasis added).

57. Émile Zola, *Paris*, in *Œuvres complètes*, ed. Henri Mitterand (Paris: Nouveau Monde, 2008), 17:38.

58. Zola, "Pour les juifs," 428.

59. Zola, "Pour les juifs," 429.

60. Mitterand, introduction to *L'Argent*, 1237–38.

61. Zola, *Vérité*, 232. Likewise in Zola's universe can the Jew become an antisemite, something Baron Nathan demonstrates in *Vérité* by cravenly embracing the antisemitism of his Gentile aristocratic protectors.

62. Émile Zola, "Pour *Justice*," in *Œuvres complètes*, ed. Henri Mitterand (Paris: Nouveau Monde, 2009), 20:398–99.

63. Zola, "Pour les juifs," 429.

64. On this disappearance of the Jews envisioned by Zola, see Maurice Samuels, *The Right to Difference: French Universalism and the Jews* (Chicago: University of Chicago Press, 2016), 95–116.

65. Zola, "Pour les juifs," 427.

66. Zola, "Pour *Justice*," 397–98.

67. Zola, *Paris*, 134.

68. Saccard's Catholic investors imbue the imagined windfall with biblical grandiosity, envisioning a reprise of the Old Testament miracle granted the prophet Elijah when, from the top of Mount Carmel, he prayed successfully for the rain that ended three years of drought and famine in the kingdom of Israel (1 Kings 18): "As for the Carmel silver mines, they were greeted with a religious shudder . . . all dreamed of Carmel, of this miraculous shower of money raining down from the holy places in a halo of glory" (169).

69. André Wurmser, preface to *L'Argent*, by Émile Zola (Paris: Gallimard, 1980), 31.

70. Giulio M. Gallarotti, "The Scramble for Gold: Monetary Regimes Transformation in the 1870s," in *Monetary Regimes in Transition*, ed. Michael D. Bordo and Forrest Capie (Cambridge: Cambridge University Press, 1993), 18.

71. H. W. Brands, *The Reckless Decade: America in the 1890s* (Chicago: University of Chicago Press, 2002), 203. Silver's inflationary influence, it was

thought, would make life easier for indebted farmers and laborers by making debts easier to repay as inflation drove incomes higher (200–201).

72. Emily Apter, "Speculation and Economic Xenophobia as Literary World Systems: The Nineteenth-Century Business Novel," in *French Global: A New Approach to Literary History*, ed. Christie Macdonald and Susan Rubin Suleiman (New York: Columbia University Press, 2010), 401.

73. See, especially, Max Horkheimer and Theodor Adorno, who remark on the ideological convenience to the bourgeoisie of blaming Jews for the "economic injustice of the whole class." "Bourgeois anti-Semitism," they declare, "has a specific economic reason: the concealment of domination in production" (Horkheimer and Adorno, *Dialectic of Enlightenment*, trans. John Cumming [New York: Continuum, 1995], 173–74). Hannah Arendt, in her first extended rumination on antisemitism, offers a more psychologizing take on the bourgeois deflection of guilt, proposing that the early nineteenth-century German bourgeoisie redirected blame to the Jews for speculative and materialistic behavior held against it by aristocrats (see Chapter 1, note 9). Arendt's definitive later statement on antisemitism in *The Origins of Totalitarianism* likewise approaches antisemitism as a sociopsychological by-product of the bourgeoisie's ascent, though now she deemphasizes that class's intentional scapegoating of the Jew. Instead, she explains modern antisemitism as what happened when the bourgeoisie's investment in the state rendered Jewish finance superfluous and thus suspect. For a discussion of what I call this "displacement thesis," see Chapter 1.

74. Georg Lukács, *Writer and Critic and Other Essays*, trans. Arthur Kahn (Lincoln: Authors Guild, 2005), 122–23.

75. Zola's anti-antisemitism and anti-anticapitalism clearly go hand in hand. Together they represent the complementary impulses of his plan, in *L'Argent*, to show "the power of money above even this question of the Jews, which in my opinion shrinks everything" (quoted in Mitterand, introduction to *L'Argent*, 5:1244). Conversely, Zola's anti-anticapitalism likely also contributed to *L'Argent*'s hackneyed antisemitic representations of Jewish greed. The cultural expectations surrounding the banking novel genre—more dominated than ever, since the Union Générale affair, by Jewish conspiracy narratives like *L'Amour de l'Argent* (1882) and *La Comtesse Shylock* (1885)—fairly demanded that Zola concede some measure of Jewish financial malignance, lest he appear a stooge of capital. Zola predicted that his embrace of finance's fecund potential would rattle some cages, telling a journalist about his forthcoming novel that "I will be an apologist for money, despite the future attacks this will certainly invite" (quoted in Mitterand, introduction to *L'Argent*, 1237). A healthy dose of Rothschild-baiting could at least inoculate him against charges of total naïveté.

76. Quoted in Zachary Karabell, *Parting the Desert: The Creation of the Suez Canal* (New York: Vintage, 2003), 144.

77. Edward Said, *Orientalism* (New York: Vintage, 1979), 169.

78. On the Egyptian corvée labor used to build the canal, see Karabell, *Parting the Desert*, 169–79.

79. Émile Zola, *Son Excellence Eugène Rougon*, in *Les Rougon-Macquart*, ed. Henri Mitterand, Bibliothèque de la Pléiade (Paris: Gallimard, 1961),

2:45–46. The character behind the scheme, Marsy, is patterned after the real-life Duc de Morny, Emperor Napoleon III's wealthy and unscrupulous brother-in-law, who for a time machinated to seize control of the Canal Company from Lesseps. The fictional canal project's two-year dormancy appears to reference the fact that, nearly two years after the 1858 investment subscription, none of the Suez Canal had yet been dug (Karabell, *Parting the Desert*, 164, 195).

80. Émile Zola, *Fécondité*, in *Œuvres complètes*, ed. Henri Mitterand (Paris: Nouveau Monde, 2008), 18:388–91.

81. Martin Steins, "Zola colonialiste," *Revue des langues vivantes* 41 (1975): 19.

82. David Baguley, *Fécondité d'Émile Zola: Roman à thèse, évangile, mythe* (Toronto: University of Toronto Press, 1973), 229. On the Fashoda Affair, see my comments in Chapters 3 and 4.

83. Zola, *Fécondité*, 391.

84. Baguley, *Fécondité*, 28–55.

85. To cite but one of the more sustained and detailed examples, see Anne McClintock, *Imperial Leather: Race, Gender and Sexuality in the Colonial Contest* (New York: Routledge, 1995).

86. Zola, *Fécondité*, 392, 396.

87. For a still useful overview of this question, see Ann Laura Stoler and Frederick Cooper, "Between Metropole and Colony: Rethinking a Research Agenda," in *Tensions of Empire: Colonial Cultures in a Bourgeois World*, ed. Ann Laura Stoler and Frederick Cooper (Berkeley: University of California Press, 1997), 1–56.

88. Examples include Patricia Lorcin, *Imperial Identities: Stereotyping, Prejudice and Race in Colonial Algeria* (London: I. B. Tauris, 1999); Paul Rabinow, *French Modern: Norms and Forms of the Social Environment* (Chicago: University of Chicago Press, 1995); and Gwendolyn Wright, *The Politics of Design in French Colonial Urbanism* (Chicago: University of Chicago Press, 1991).

89. See, for instance, Richard H. King and Dan Stone, eds., *Hannah Arendt and the Uses of History: Imperialism, Nation, Race, and Genocide* (New York: Berghahn, 2008).

90. Hannah Arendt writes bitingly about the colonizing powers' "confusion of imperialism with nationalism" (Arendt, *The Origins of Totalitarianism* [San Diego: Harcourt, 1976], 153).

91. Friedrich Nietzsche, *The Antichrist*, *The Portable Nietzsche*, ed. and trans. Walter Kaufmann (New York: Penguin, 1968), 656.

92. In his well-known series of articles about India published by the *New York Tribune* in 1853, Marx noted the "sickening" and "devastating" effects of British colonialism on the subcontinent (Karl Marx and Frederick Engels, *On Colonialism: Articles from the "New York Tribune" and Other Writings* [New York: International Publishers, 1972], 40, 86).

93. Friedrich Nietzsche, *Selected Letters of Friedrich Nietzsche*, ed. and trans. Christopher Middleton (Indianapolis: Hackett, 1996), 346.

94. Friedrich Nietzsche, *Human, All-Too-Human*, *The Portable Nietzsche*, ed. and trans. Walter Kaufmann (New York: Penguin, 1968), 62.

95. For concise historical accounts of German antisemitism during this period, all of which I am drawing from here, see Katz, *From Prejudice to Destruction*, 260–72; Lindemann, *Esau's Tears*, 103–57; and Léon Poliakov, *The History of Anti-Semitism*, vol. 4, *Suicidal Europe, 1870–1933*, trans. George Klin (Philadelphia: University of Pennsylvania Press, 2003), 3–30.

96. Quoted in Yirmiyahu Yovel, *Dark Riddle: Hegel, Nietzsche, and the Jews* (Cambridge: Polity, 1998), 126.

97. Quoted in Yovel, *Dark Riddle*, 126.

98. Quoted in Yovel, *Dark Riddle*, 126.

99. Quoted in Yovel, *Dark Riddle*, 128.

100. This said, Nietzsche's claim not to have any Jewish friends can be taken with a grain of salt. Yovel argues, plausibly enough, that Nietzsche only intends to mock the classic refuge of the disingenuous antisemite who maintains that "many of my best friends are Jewish" (Yovel, *Dark Riddle*, 128).

101. Nietzsche, *Human, All-Too-Human*, 62.

102. "Nietzsche is thus not a philo-Semite but rather an anti-anti-Semite," remarks Sander Gilman (Gilman, "Heine, Nietzsche and the Idea of the Jew," in *Nietzsche and Jewish Culture*, ed. Jacob Golomb [New York: Routledge, 1997], 79). See also Robert C. Holub, "Nietzsche and the Jewish Question," *New German Critique* 22.3 (1995): 108.

103. Holub, "Nietzsche and the Jewish Question," 103.

104. Friedrich Nietzsche, *Beyond Good and Evil*, *Basic Writings of Nietzsche*, ed. and trans. Walter Kaufmann (New York: Modern Library, 2000), 377.

105. Nietzsche, *The Antichrist*, 622 (original emphasis).

106. Nietzsche, *The Antichrist*, 595.

107. Friedrich Nietzsche, *On the Genealogy of Morals*, *Basic Writings of Nietzsche*, ed. and trans. Walter Kaufmann (New York: Modern Library, 2000), 488.

108. Nietzsche, *The Antichrist*, 594.

109. Friedrich Nietzsche, *Daybreak: Thoughts on the Prejudices of Morality*, ed. Maudemarie Clark and Brian Leiter, trans. R. J. Hollingdale (Cambridge: Cambridge University Press, 1997), 205–6 (original emphasis).

110. Hubert Cancik, "'Mongols, Semites and the Pure-Bred Greeks': Nietzsche's Handling of the Racial Doctrines of His Time," in *Nietzsche and Jewish Culture*, ed. Jacob Golomb (New York: Routledge, 1997), 66; Daniel W. Conway, "*Ecce Caesar*: Nietzsche's Imperial Aspirations," in *Nietzsche, Godfather of Fascism?: On the Uses and Abuses of a Philosophy*, ed. Jacob Golomb and Robert S. Wistrich (Princeton: Princeton University Press, 2002), 185.

111. The most influential exponent of this view was the great Nietzsche scholar and translator Walter Kaufmann, who argued that Nietzsche in fact considered Christianity the "miscarriage" of Judaism (Walter Kaufmann, *Nietzsche: Philosopher, Psychologist, Antichrist*, 4th ed. [Princeton: Princeton University Press, 1974], 299). On Nietzsche's tripartite distinction among ancient, priestly, and contemporary Jews, see Michael F. Duffy and Willard Mittelman, "Nietzsche's Attitudes Toward the Jews," *Journal of the History*

of Ideas 49.2 (1988): 301–17. On Nietzsche and the Jews more generally, see the comprehensive bibliography assembled by Gilman (Gilman, "Heine, Nietzsche and the Idea of the Jew," 97–98n3).

112. Duffy and Mittelman, "Nietzsche's Attitudes Toward the Jews," 303–4; Howard Eiland, "Nietzsche's Jew," *Salmagundi* 66 (Winter–Spring 1985): 105. Gilman goes so far as to suggest that Nietzsche's lifelong concern about falling prey to his father's insanity aligned him psychically with the picture of Jewish madness and degeneracy fantasized by antisemites (Gilman, "Heine, Nietzsche and the Idea of the Jew," 97–98).

113. Here is a representative example, in which Nietzsche associates Christianity with democracy: "*such* men [Christians] have so far held sway over the fate of Europe, with their 'equal before God,' until finally a smaller, almost ridiculous type, a herd animal, something eager to please, sickly, and mediocre has been bred, the European of today" (Nietzsche, *Beyond Good and Evil*, 266 [original emphasis]). See also the section titled "The Herd" in Friedrich Nietzsche, *The Will to Power*, ed. Walter Kaufmann, trans. Walter Kaufmann and R. J. Hollingdale (New York: Vintage, 1968), 156–62.

114. Nietzsche, *Beyond Good and Evil*, 378.

115. Nietzsche, *Beyond Good and Evil*, 378–79.

116. Nietzsche, *Human, All-Too-Human*, 62.

117. Nietzsche, *On the Genealogy of Morals*, 489.

118. Nietzsche, *Beyond Good and Evil*, 378.

119. Nietzsche, *On the Genealogy of Morals*, 560.

120. Nietzsche, *The Antichrist*, 593 (original emphasis).

121. Quoted in Kaufmann, *Nietzsche*, 44.

122. Nietzsche, *Beyond Good and Evil*, 374. Here is the definition that Nietzsche elsewhere gives of the famous "will to power": "The victorious concept 'force,' by means of which our physicists have created God and the world, still needs to be completed: an inner will must be ascribed to it, which I designate as 'will to power,' i.e., as an insatiable desire to manifest power; or as the employment and exercise of power, as a creative drive, etc." (Nietzsche, *The Will to Power*, 332–33).

123. Nietzsche, *Beyond Good and Evil*, 378.

124. Nietzsche, *On the Genealogy of Morals*, 469 (original emphasis).

125. Nietzsche, *On the Genealogy of Morals*, 520–21, 524.

126. Nietzsche, *Beyond Good and Evil*, 533.

127. Nietzsche, *Beyond Good and Evil*, 375.

128. Nietzsche, *On the Genealogy of Morals*, 594.

129. Nietzsche, *On the Genealogy of Morals*, 469.

130. Nietzsche, *On the Genealogy of Morals*, 488–89.

131. Nietzsche, *On the Genealogy of Morals*, 488 (original emphasis).

132. On this, see Daniel Conway, *Nietzsche's Dangerous Game: Philosophy in the Twilight of the Idols* (Cambridge: Cambridge University Press, 1997), 199.

133. Nietzsche, *On the Genealogy of Morals*, 476–77.

134. Nietzsche, *The Will to Power*, 73.

135. Nietzsche, *The Antichrist*, 552 (original emphasis). Both remarks preface stinging rebukes of Rousseau, whose famed precept of natural equality Nietzsche dismisses as an invention in the craven service of democratic ideals. On Nietzsche's rejection of Rousseau, see Kauffman, *Nietzsche*, 167–70.

136. Eva M. Knodt, "The Janus Face of Decadence: Nietzsche's Genealogy and the Rhetoric of Anti-Semitism," *German Quarterly* 66.2 (1993): 164.

137. Nietzsche, *On the Genealogy of Morals*, 521.

138. Eiland, "Nietzsche's Jew," 116.

139. Gilles Deleuze, *Nietzsche and Philosophy*, trans. Hugh Tomlinson (New York: Columbia University Press, 2006), 195.

140. Nietzsche, *On the Genealogy of Morals*, 522.

141. Nietzsche, *On the Genealogy of Morals*, 522.

142. Nietzsche, *Beyond Good and Evil*, 393 (original emphasis).

143. Nietzsche, *On the Genealogy of Morals*, 476.

144. Nietzsche, *Beyond Good and Evil*, 393.

145. Nietzsche, *On the Genealogy of Morals*, 522.

146. Friedrich Nietzsche, *Untimely Meditations*, ed. Daniel Breazale, trans. R. J. Hollingdale (Cambridge: Cambridge University Press, 1997), 122.

147. Nietzsche, *On the Genealogy of Morals*, 477.

148. Nietzsche, *The Will to Power*, 504.

149. Nietzsche, *Beyond Good and Evil*, 366–67 (original emphasis).

150. Nietzsche, *On the Genealogy of Morals*, 523.

151. Nietzsche, *On the Genealogy of Morals*, 562–63 (original emphasis).

152. Nietzsche, *Beyond Good and Evil*, 366.

153. Nietzsche, *Beyond Good and Evil*, 366.

154. Conway, "*Ecce Caesar*," 179.

155. Nietzsche, *Daybreak*, 206–7 (original emphasis).

156. Nietzsche, *Daybreak*, 207.

157. Nietzsche, *The Will to Power*, 487.

158. Timothy Brennan considers this kind of pronouncement emblematic of a European right finding it increasingly ideologically expedient to place "the new politically active laborers . . . alongside the 'barbarians' of the global periphery" (Brennan, "Borrowed Light: Nietzsche and the Colonies," in *German Colonialism: Race, the Holocaust, and Postwar Germany*, ed. Volker Langbehn and Mohammad Salama [New York: Columbia University Press, 2011], 6).

159. Horkheimer and Adorno, *Dialectic*, 100.

160. Brennan, "Borrowed Light," 5; Conway, "*Ecce Caesar*," 175–76; Robert C. Holub, "Nietzsche's Colonialist Imagination: Nueva Germania, Good Europeanism, and Great Politics," in *The Imperialist Imagination: German Colonialism and Its Legacy*, ed. Sara Friedrichsmeyer, Sara Lennox, and Susanne Zantop (Ann Arbor: University of Michigan Press, 1999), 45.

161. Holub revisits the usual assumption by scholars that Nietzsche rejected the enterprise out of hand. Nietzsche, he argues, "was not as ill-disposed toward the Paraguayan settlement as one might have anticipated," citing among other sources a letter in which Nietzsche admits to seeing "a great deal that is reasonable in the entire matter" (Holub, "Nietzsche's Colonialist Imagination,"

36–37). Nietzsche found nothing reasonable, however, about Förster himself, writing to his mother in 1887 that despite "cheering" news from Paraguay he had still not "the slightest wish to settle in the vicinity of my anti-Semitic brother-in-law" (Nietzsche, *Selected Letters*, 271–72). On Förster's vision of colonies "as isolated breeding grounds for purebred Aryans," see Christian S. Davis, *Colonialism, Antisemitism, and Germans of Jewish Descent in Imperial Germany* (Ann Arbor: University of Michigan Press, 2012), 45–46.

162. Quoted in Holub, "Nietzsche's Colonialist Imagination," 43.

163. Nietzsche, *The Will to Power*, 459.

164. Friedrich Nietzsche, *The Gay Science*, ed. and trans. Walter Kaufmann (New York: Vintage, 1974), 318.

165. Benedict Anderson, *Imagined Communities: Reflections on the Origin and Spread of Nationalism* (New York: Verso, 2006), 150.

166. The second and third essays of the *Genealogy of Morals*, for example, are in large part directed at Dühring. On this, see Weaver Santaniello, *Nietzsche, God, and the Jews: His Critique of Judeo-Christianity in Relation to the Nazi Myth* (Albany: State University of New York Press, 1994), 100–103.

167. Note that not all German antisemites were colonialist. Some decried official German colonialism as the corrupt instrument of big business; others fretted about the potential of colonialism to produce race-mixing (Davis, *Antisemitism*, 47). Note as well the long German tradition of conceiving colonial spaces as a possible destination for unwanted Jews rather than as a place to escape them. The eighteenth-century German Orientalist Johann David Michaelis thought Jews might best be employed as slave labor in West Indian sugar plantations (Jonathan M. Hess, *Germans, Jews and the Claims of Modernity* [New Haven: Yale University Press, 2002], 79–89). A century later the virulent German antisemite Paul de Lagarde proposed evacuating German Jews to the island of Madagascar—a deportation plan revived in the 1920s by the Poles, greeted with some enthusiasm the following decade by the French, and eventually given serious consideration by the Nazis (David Cymet, *History vs. Apologetics: The Holocaust, the Third Reich, and the Catholic Church* [Plymouth: Lexington, 2010], 125–28).

168. Quoted in Kaufmann, *Nietzsche*, 44.

169. Nietzsche, *On the Genealogy of Morals*, 594.

170. Nietzsche, *Daybreak*, 205–6.

171. Nietzsche, *On the Genealogy of Morals*, 562.

172. Sarah Kofman proposes that Nietzsche sees in the Jews only an eventual "model" for the Overman, rather than potential Overmen themselves, because they are destined never quite to appreciate their intrinsic will to power as a people. Standing upright, finally, before a God they have too long groveled beneath, they will nevertheless understand this newfound strength to emanate from the heavens, instead of appreciating that this strength had only ever been "borrowed" by an imaginary God in whom the Hebrews once concentrated their deep spiritual reserves (Kofman, *Le Mépris des Juifs: Nietzsche, les Juifs, l'antisémitisme* [Paris: Galilée, 1994], 47–50). Such a continued projection or transference, I would add, is precisely what suits them to stewardship

of the future Europe, since for Nietzsche the European herd will hopefully be similarly content to locate the source of its residual life instinct in a distant proxy—the domination of colonial subalterns—safely externalized and abstracted from the herd itself.

173. Étienne Balibar and Immanuel Wallerstein, *Race, Nation, Class: Ambiguous Identities*, trans. Chris Turner (New York: Verso, 1991), 62.

174. By "grand politics," I mean Nietzsche's goal of a sweeping revaluation unconcerned with the petty political squabbles of the state. The model for this is, again, the Jews and their "truly *grand* politics of revenge" (Nietzsche, *On the Genealogy of Morals*, 471 [original emphasis]).

175. Anidjar, *The Jew, the Arab*, 48.

176. Taguieff, *Rising from the Muck*, 109.

177. Michael Rothberg, *Multidirectional Memory: Remembering the Holocaust in the Age of Decolonization* (Stanford: Stanford University Press, 2009), 22.

178. Henri Mitterand, *Zola, tome 3: L'Honneur, 1893–1902* (Paris: Fayard, 2002), 779–81.

179. Balibar and Wallerstein, *Race, Nation, Class*, 53–54.

180. Zola, *Fécondité*, 391.

181. Émile Zola, "À propos de l'antisémitisme," in *Œuvres complètes*, ed. Henri Mitterand (Paris: Nouveau Monde, 2008), 18:592.

182. Louis Bertrand, "Nietzsche et la Méditerranée," *Revue des deux mondes* 25 (1915): 181.

183. Bertrand, "Nietzsche et la Méditerranée," 182.

184. Louis Bertrand, *Le Sang des races* (Paris: Ollendorff, 1920), 25. Seth Graebner, in his discussion of *Le Sang des races*, has noted what he calls this "primal scene of group solidarity" opposing Latins and Jews (Graebner, *History's Place: Nostalgia and the City in French Algerian Literature* [Lanham, MD: Lexington, 2007], 38).

185. Sarah Hammerschlag, *The Figural Jew: Politics and Identity in Postwar French Thought* (Chicago: University of Chicago Press, 2010), 40n64.

186. Quoted in Michel Abitbol, *Le Passé d'une discorde: Juifs et Arabes du VIIe siècle à nos jours* (Paris: Perrin, 2003), 291. Drumont had ridden the 1898 wave of Algerian antisemitic sentiment to electoral success. His political career would prove undistinguished. In September of the same year, with the Drumont-led anti-Dreyfusards reeling from August revelations about the army's framing of Dreyfus, Drumont reminisced about Algeria as if recalling a battle won in a losing war: "It is a pleasure, too, before the disgusting spectacle we are witnessing, to think back upon the glorious days of our electoral campaign, those good times when a whole people pulsated with the same patriotic feeling, and everyone applauded the idea we represented with cheers, flowers, and songs" (Édouard Drumont, "France et Algérie," *La Libre parole*, 23 September 1898, 1). Drumont likely saw his Algerian adventure for what it was: the consolation prize for nearly a decade and a half of antisemitic agitation that, while periodically successful, was by this point losing ground. On Drumont's Algerian political forays, see Grégoire Kauffmann, *Edouard Drumont* (Paris: Perrin, 2008), 356–69, 407–15.

187. On organized French antisemitism's decline at the turn of the century, see Michel Winock, *La France et les Juifs de 1789 à nos jours* (Paris: Seuil, 2004), 165–67. For a detailed account of antisemitism's waning political fortunes in Algeria around this time, see Geneviève Dermenjian, *La Crise anti-juive oranaise, 1895–1905* (Paris: L'Harmattan, 1986), 181–233.

188. Louis Bertrand, *La Cina* (Paris: Ollendorff, 1901), 31, 53. Subsequent references to the novel will be made parenthetically in the text.

189. Robert Randau, *Les Colons: Roman de la patrie algérienne* (Paris: Sansot, 1907), 286.

190. To the "Semitic race," within which he situated both Hebrews and Muslims, Renan attributed the simple-minded obduracy of a monotheism "devoid of all flexibility" (quoted in Maurice Olender, *The Languages of Paradise: Race, Religion, and Philology in the Nineteenth Century*, trans. Arthur Goldhammer [Cambridge, MA: Harvard University Press, 2008], 56–57).

191. Bertrand's 1936 pamphlet *Hitler*, admiring of its subject and merciless toward the Jews, certainly suggests nothing philo-Semitic about his earlier anti-antisemitism.

192. Jonathan Judaken, *Jean-Paul Sartre and the Jewish Question: Anti-Antisemitism and the Politics of the French Intellectual* (Lincoln: University of Nebraska Press, 2006), 18–21. See also Jonathan Judaken, "Between Philosemitism and Antisemitism: The Frankfurt School's Anti-Antisemitism," in *Antisemitism and Philosemitism in the Twentieth and Twenty-First Centuries: Representing Jews, Jewishness, and Modern Culture*, ed. Phyllis Lassner and Lara Trubowitz (Newark: University of Delaware Press, 2008), 23–46. Judaken uses the term "anti-antisemitism" to designate efforts undertaken by "leftist, 'progressive' intellectuals like Sartre who have intervened on behalf of Jews" (Judaken, *Jean-Paul Sartre*, 19–20). I use the term significantly more expansively to include those who, like Nietzsche, are hardly leftist thinkers but either self-identify as "anti-antisemites" (which Nietzsche did—see note 121) or mount explicit enough attacks on antisemitism to reasonably warrant the label.

193. For extended considerations of Bertrand's politics, influence, and influences, see Peter Dunwoodie, *Writing French Algeria* (Oxford: Clarendon, 1998), 83–108; Graebner, *History's Place*, 27–69; and Lorcin, *Imperial Identities*, 196–213.

194. See Jonathan G. Katz, "The 1907 Mauchamp Affair and the French Civilizing Mission in Morocco," *Journal of North African Studies* 6.1 (2001): 143–66.

195. André Chouraqui, *Histoire des Juifs en Afrique du Nord, tome 2: Le Retour en Orient* (Paris: Rocher, 1998), 45.

196. Hippolyte Prague, "La Question du Maroc et les Juifs," *Archives Israélites*, 8 August 1907, 250.

197. Prague, "La Question du Maroc," 249–50.

198. Abitbol, *Le Passé*, 237; Lewis, *Semites and Anti-Semites*, 133.

199. Abitbol, *Le Passé*, 33–39; Lewis, *Semites and Anti-Semites*, 123.

200. Abitbol, *Le Passé*, 231.

201. Wieviorka, *The Lure of Anti-Semitism*, 144.

202. Taguieff, *Rising from the Muck*, 67–69, 121.

203. Taguieff, *Rising from the Muck*, 121. For Nietzsche's rejection of Christian martyrdom, see Nietzsche, *The Antichrist*, 636–38.

204. Taguieff, *Rising from the Muck*, 121.

205. Taguieff, *Rising from the Muck*, 68, 91.

206. Finkielkraut, *Au nom de l'Autre*, 26–27.

207. See note 217 below.

208. Finkielkraut, *Au nom de l'Autre*, 22.

209. Finkielkraut, *Au nom de l'Autre*, 14.

210. Finkielkraut, *Au nom de l'Autre*, 20 (original emphasis).

211. Arendt elaborates this distinction most fully in *The Human Condition*. See my discussion in Chapter 1.

212. See, once more, Chapter 1.

213. Bunzl, "Anti-Semitism and Islamophobia," 13.

214. Arendt, *Origins*, 23.

215. See note 173.

216. Prague, "La Question du Maroc," 250.

217. Finkielkraut, *Au nom de l'Autre*, 16. Here is Finkielkraut on democratic, post-Nazi Europe: "What unites today's Europe is the disavowal of war, of hegemonism, of antisemitism, and, step by step, of all the catastrophes it has fomented, all the forms of intolerance or inequality it has implemented" (Finkielkraut, *Au nom de l'Autre*, 16).

218. Émile Cahen, "Chronique," *Archives Israélites*, 28 March 1907, 101–2. Cahen singles out the antisemitic journalist Henri Rochefort, who had made a name for himself arguing that Jewish motives lay behind France's 1881 invasion of Tunisia and who was now similarly holding forth about Morocco. "As for such violent hatred directed by the Muslims at our coreligionists," writes Cahen, "it is far from being as extensive as our good anti-Jewish agitators would maintain, since in Turkey, for example, the Israelites' lot has never been unpleasant, and the viceroy of Egypt, in a recent interview with an editor of the *Temps*, has not been afraid to assert his liberalism quite vigorously" (101). On Rochefort's role in the Tunisian affair, see Chapter 2.

Bibliography

Abitbol, Michel. *Le Passé d'une discorde: Juifs et Arabes du VIIe siècle à nos jours*. Paris: Perrin, 2003.

Adorno, Theodor. *The Stars Down to Earth and Other Essays on the Irrational in Culture*. Edited by Stephen Crook. London: Routledge, 1994.

Agamben, Giorgio. *Homo Sacer: Sovereign Power and Bare Life*. Translated by Daniel Heller-Roazen. Stanford: Stanford University Press, 1998.

Ageron, Charles-Robert. *Les Algériens musulmans et la France, 1871–1919*. 2 vols. Paris: PUF, 1968.

———. *L'anticolonialisme en France de 1871 à 1914*. Paris: PUF, 1973.

———. *France coloniale ou parti colonial?* Paris: PUF, 1978.

Anderson, Benedict. *Imagined Communities: Reflections on the Origin and Spread of Nationalism*. London: Verso, 2006.

Angenot, Marc. *Ce que l'on dit des Juifs en 1889: Antisémitisme et discours social*. Saint-Denis: Presses Universitaires de Vincennes, 1989.

Anidjar, Gil. *The Jew, the Arab: A History of the Enemy*. Stanford: Stanford University Press, 2003.

Apter, Emily. "Speculation and Economic Xenophobia as Literary World Systems: The Nineteenth-Century Business Novel." In *French Global: A New Approach to Literary History*, edited by Christie Macdonald and Susan Rubin Suleiman, 388–403. New York: Columbia University Press, 2010.

Arendt, Hannah. *Essays in Understanding, 1930–1954*. Edited by Jerome Kohn. New York: Harcourt Brace, 1994.

———. *The Human Condition*. 2nd ed. Chicago: University of Chicago Press, 1998.

———. *The Jewish Writings*. Edited by Ron H. Feldman and Jerome Kohn. New York: Schocken, 2007.

———. *Men in Dark Times*. San Diego: Harcourt Brace, 1968.
———. *The Origins of Totalitarianism*. San Diego: Harcourt, 1976.
———. "Why the Crémieux Decree Was Abrogated." *Contemporary Jewish Record* 6.2 (1943): 115–24.
Ayoun, Richard. "Le Décret Crémieux et l'insurrection de 1871 en Algérie." *Revue d'histoire moderne et contemporaine* 35.1 (1988): 61–87.
Baguley, David. *Fécondité d'Émile Zola: Roman à thèse, évangile, mythe*. Toronto: University of Toronto Press, 1973.
Bakan, Mildred. "Hannah Arendt's Concepts of Labor and Work." In *Hannah Arendt: The Recovery of the Public World*, edited by Melvyn A. Hill, 49–65. New York: St. Martin's, 1979.
Balibar, Étienne. *Masses, Classes, Ideas: Studies on Politics and Philosophy Before and After Marx*. Translated by James Swenson. London: Routledge, 1994.
———. "Un nouvel antisémitisme?" In *Antisémitisme: L'Intolérable chantage: Israël-Palestine, une affaire française*, 89–96. Paris: La Découverte, 2003.
Balibar, Étienne, and Immanuel Wallerstein. *Race, Nation, Class: Ambiguous Identities*. Translated by Chris Turner. New York: Verso, 1991.
Bamat, Joseph. "Hollande Says Terrorist Cells in France Will Be Eliminated." *France 24*, 10 November 2012. Web.
Barnett, Michael N. *Empire of Humanity: A History of Humanitarianism*. Ithaca, NY: Cornell University Press, 2011.
Barrès, Maurice. *De Hegel aux cantines du Nord*. Paris: Sansot, 1904.
———. "Morès." *Le Figaro*, 19 June 1896.
———. *Scènes et doctrines du nationalisme*. Paris: Trident, 1987. First published 1902 by Félix Juven.
———. *La Terre et les Morts: Sur quelles réalités fonder la conscience française*. Paris: Ligue de la Patrie française, 1899.
Baucom, Ian. *Out of Place: Englishness, Empire, and the Locations of Identity*. Princeton: Princeton University Press, 1999.
Bauman, Zygmunt. *Life in Fragments: Essays in Postmodern Morality*. Oxford: Blackwell, 1995.
———. *Modernity and Ambivalence*. Cambridge: Polity, 1991.
———. *Modernity and the Holocaust*. Ithaca, NY: Cornell University Press, 2000.
Behdad, Ali. *Belated Travelers: Orientalism in the Age of Colonial Dissolution*. Durham: Duke University Press, 1994.
Belloc, Hilaire. *The Jews*. Boston: Houghton Mifflin, 1922.
Benbassa, Esther. *The Jews of France: A History from Antiquity to the Present*. Translated by M. B. DeBevoise. Princeton: Princeton University Press, 1999.
———. "La Parole s'est libérée." *Le Nouvel Observateur*, 5 July 2012.
———. "Xenophobia, Anti-Semitism, and Racism: Europe's Recurring Evils?" Translated by Paul A. Silverstein. In *Anti-Semitism and Islamophobia: Hatreds Old and New in Europe*, edited by Matti Bunzl, 77–89. Chicago: Prickly Paradigm Press, 2007.

Benhabib, Seyla. "Hannah Arendt and the Redemptive Power of Narrative." *Social Research* 57.1 (1990): 167–93.

———. *The Reluctant Modernism of Hannah Arendt.* 2nd ed. Lanham, MD: Rowman and Littlefield, 2003.

Benjamin, Walter. *Illuminations.* Edited by Hannah Arendt. Translated by Harry Zohn. New York: Schocken, 1968.

Berenson, Edward. *Heroes of Empire: Five Charismatic Men and the Conquest of Africa.* Berkeley: University of California Press, 2011.

Bernasconi, Robert. "When the Real Crime Began: Hannah Arendt's *The Origins of Totalitarianism* and the Dignity of the Western Philosophical Tradition." In *Hannah Arendt and the Uses of History: Imperialism, Nation, Race, and Genocide*, edited by Richard H. King and Dan Stone, 54–67. New York: Berghahn, 2008.

Bertrand, Louis. *La Cina.* Paris: Ollendorff, 1901.

———. "Nietzsche et la Méditerranée." *Revue des deux mondes* 25 (1915): 175–86.

———. *Le Sang des races.* Paris: Ollendorff, 1920.

Betts, Raymond. *Assimilation and Association in French Colonial Theory, 1890–1914.* Lincoln: University of Nebraska Press, 2005.

Bhabha, Homi K. *The Location of Culture.* London: Routledge, 1994.

Birnbaum, Pierre. *Les Fous de la République: Histoire politique des Juifs d'État de Gambetta à Vichy.* Paris: Fayard, 1992.

———.*"La France aux Français": Histoire des haines nationalistes.* Paris: Seuil, 2006.

———. *Le Moment antisémite: Un tour de la France en 1898.* Paris: Fayard, 1998.

Boer, Roland. *Criticism of Earth: On Marx, Engels, and Theology.* Leiden: Brill, 2012.

Bonnières, Robert de. *Les Monach, roman parisien.* Paris: Ollendorff, 1885.

Bory, Jean-Louis. Preface to *Bel-Ami*, by Guy de Maupassant, 8–26. Paris: Gallimard, 1973.

Bouche, Denise. *Histoire de la colonisation française.* Paris: Fayard, 1991.

Boulainvilliers, Henri de. *Essais sur la noblesse de France, contenans une dissertation sur son origine et abaissement.* Amsterdam, 1732.

Boyarin, Jonathan. *The Unconverted Self: Jews, Indians, and the Identity of Christian Europe.* Chicago: University of Chicago Press, 2009.

Brahimi, Denise. Introduction to *Maupassant au Maghreb*, by Guy de Maupassant, edited by Denise Brahimi, 11–42. Paris: Le Sycomore, 1982.

Brands, H. W. *The Reckless Decade: America in the 1890s.* Chicago: University of Chicago Press, 2002.

Brennan, Timothy. "Borrowed Light: Nietzsche and the Colonies." In *German Colonialism: Race, the Holocaust, and Postwar Germany*, edited by Volker Langbehn and Mohammad Salama, 3–28. New York: Columbia University Press, 2011.

Brenner, Emmanuel. *"France, prends garde de perdre ton âme . . .": Fracture sociale et antisémitisme dans la République.* Paris: Mille et une nuits, 2004.

Brenner, Neil. "The Limits to Scale? Methodological Reflections on Scalar Structuration." *Progress in Human Geography* 25.4 (2001): 591–614.

Brooks, Peter. *Reading for the Plot: Design and Intention in Narrative.* Cambridge, MA: Harvard University Press, 2006.

Brower, Benjamin Claude. *A Desert Named Peace: The Violence of France's Empire in the Algerian Sahara, 1844–1902.* New York: Columbia University Press, 2009.

Brown, Wendy. "Rights and Identity in Late Modernity: Revisiting the 'Jewish Question.'" In *Identities, Politics, and Rights*, edited by Austin Sarat and Thomas R. Kearns, 85–130. Ann Arbor: University of Michigan Press, 1995.

Bunzl, Matti. "Anti-Semitism and Islamophobia." In *Anti-Semitism and Islamophobia: Hatreds Old and New in Europe*, edited by Matti Bunzl, 1–46. Chicago: Prickly Paradigm Press, 2007.

———, ed. *Anti-Semitism and Islamophobia: Hatreds Old and New in Europe.* Chicago: Prickly Paradigm Press, 2007.

Busi, Frederick. *The Pope of Antisemitism: The Career and Legacy of Edouard-Adolphe Drumont.* Lanham, MD: University Press of America, 1986.

Byrnes, Robert F. *Antisemitism in Modern France.* New Brunswick, NJ: Rutgers University Press, 1950.

Cahen, Émile. "Chronique." *Archives Israélites*, 28 March 1907.

Cancik, Hubert. "'Mongols, Semites and the Pure-Bred Greeks': Nietzsche's Handling of the Racial Doctrines of His Time." In *Nietzsche and Jewish Culture*, edited by Jacob Golomb, 55–75. New York: Routledge, 1997.

Canovan, Margaret. *Hannah Arendt: A Reinterpretation of Her Political Thought.* Cambridge: Cambridge University Press, 1992.

———. *The Political Thought of Hannah Arendt.* New York: Harcourt Brace Jovanovich, 1974.

Carrasco, Odette. *Arthur Meyer, Directeur du "Gaulois": Un patron de presse juif, royaliste et antidreyfusard.* Paris: Imago, 2003.

Carroll, David. "Fascism, Colonialism, and 'Race': The Reality of a Fiction." In *Fascism and Neofascism: Critical Writings on the Radical Right in Europe*, edited by Angelica Fenner and Eric D. Weitz, 141–57. New York: Palgrave Macmillan, 2004.

———. *French Literary Fascism: Nationalism, Anti-Semitism, and the Ideology of Culture.* Princeton: Princeton University Press, 1995.

Césaire, Aimé. *Discourse on Colonialism.* Translated by Joan Pinkham. New York: Monthly Review, 2000.

Chakrabarty, Dipesh. *Provincializing Europe: Postcolonial Thought and Historical Difference.* Princeton: Princeton University Press, 2008.

Chamberlin, J. Edward, ed. *Degeneration: The Dark Side of Progress.* New York: Columbia University Press, 1985.

Chapman, Herrick, and Laura Frader. "Introduction: Race in France." In *Race in France: Interdisciplinary Perspectives on the Politics of Difference*, edited by Herrick Chapman and Laura Frader, 1–19. New York: Berghahn, 2004.

Chesler, Phyllis. *The New Anti-Semitism: The Current Crisis and What We Must Do About It*. San Francisco: Jossey-Bass, 2005.

Cheyette, Bryan. *Constructions of "the Jew" in English Literature and Society: Racial Representations, 1875–1945*. Cambridge: Cambridge University Press, 1993.

———. "Frantz Fanon and the Black-Jewish Imaginary." In *Frantz Fanon's "Black Skin, White Masks": New Interdisciplinary Essays*, edited by Max Silverman, 74–99. Manchester: Manchester University Press, 2005.

Chirac, Auguste. *L'Agiotage de 1870 à 1884*. Paris: La Revue Socialiste, 1886.

———. *Les Rois de la République: Histoire des juiveries*. Paris: Éditions du Trident, 1987. First published 1883 by Arnould.

Chouraqui, André. *Histoire des Juifs en Afrique du Nord, tome 2: Le Retour en Orient*. Paris: Rocher, 1998.

Comte, Auguste. *Système de politique positive, ou, Traité de sociologie instituant la religion de l'humanité*. 4 vols. Paris: Mathias, 1851–54.

Conway, Daniel W. "*Ecce Caesar*: Nietzsche's Imperial Aspirations." In *Nietzsche, Godfather of Fascism?: On the Uses and Abuses of a Philosophy*, edited by Jacob Golomb and Robert S. Wistrich, 173–95. Princeton: Princeton University Press, 2002.

———. *Nietzsche's Dangerous Game: Philosophy in the Twilight of the Idols*. Cambridge: Cambridge University Press, 1997.

Crapez, Marc. *L'Antisémitisme de gauche au XIXe siècle*. Paris: Berg International, 2002.

Cymet, David. *History vs. Apologetics: The Holocaust, the Third Reich, and the Catholic Church*. Plymouth: Lexington, 2010.

Davis, Christian S. *Colonialism, Antisemitism, and Germans of Jewish Descent in Imperial Germany*. Ann Arbor: University of Michigan Press, 2012.

Delahaye, Jules. *Les Assassins et les vengeurs de Morès*. 3 vols. Paris: Retaux, 1905–7.

Deleuze, Gilles. *Nietzsche and Philosophy*. Translated by Hugh Tomlinson. New York: Columbia University Press, 2006.

Dermenjian, Geneviève. *La Crise anti-juive oranaise, 1895–1905*. Paris: L'Harmattan, 1986.

Derrida, Jacques. "Marx & Sons." In *Ghostly Demarcations: A Symposium on Jacques Derrida's "Specters of Marx,"* edited by Michael Sprinker, 213–69. London: Verso, 2008.

———. *Specters of Marx: The State of the Debt, the Work of Mourning and the New International*. Translated by Peggy Kamuf. New York: Routledge, 1994.

Dietz, Mary G. "Feminist Receptions of Hannah Arendt." In *Feminist Interpretations of Hannah Arendt*, edited by Bonnie Honig, 17–50. University Park: Pennsylvania State University Press, 1995.

———. "Hannah Arendt and Feminist Politics." In *Feminist Interpretations and Political Theory*, edited by Mary Lyndon Shanley and Carole Pateman, 232–52. University Park: Pennsylvania State University Press, 1991.

Dobie, Madeleine. *Foreign Bodies: Gender, Language, and Culture in French Orientalism*. Stanford: Stanford University Press, 2004.

Dossa, Shiraz. "Human Status and Politics: Hannah Arendt on the Holocaust." *Canadian Journal of Political Science* 13.2 (1980): 309–23.

Draï, Raphaël. *Sous le signe de Sion: L'Antisémitisme nouveau est arrivé*. Paris: Michalon, 2001.

Drault, Jean. "Morès.—Sa vie.—Son œuvre." *La Libre parole*, 19 July 1896.

Dresden, Donald. *The Marquis de Morès: Emperor of the Badlands*. Norman: University of Oklahoma Press, 1970.

Droulers, Charles. *Le Marquis de Morès, 1858–96*. Paris: Plon, 1932.

Drumont, Édouard. "Anniversaire de Morès—Discours d'Edouard Drumont." *La Libre parole*, 20 July 1899.

———. "Discours d'Édouard Drumont." *La Libre parole*, 20 July 1896.

———. "France et Algérie." *La Libre parole*, 23 September 1898.

———. *La France juive: Essai d'histoire contemporaine*. 2 vols. Paris: Marpon et Flammarion, 1886.

———. *La France juive devant l'opinion*. Marpon et Flammarion, 1886.

———. "Le Général Dodds." *La Libre parole*, 15 May 1893.

———. *Les Héros et les pitres*. Paris: Flammarion, 1900.

———. "Le Monument de Morès." *La Libre parole*, 14 April 1899.

———. "Morès." *La Libre parole*, 22 June 1896.

———. *Le Secret de Fourmies*. Paris: Savine, 1872.

———. "Sem, Cham et Japhet." *La Libre parole*, 21 October 1892.

Du Bois, W. E. B. *Black Reconstruction in America, 1860–1880*. New York: Free Press, 1998.

———. *The World and Africa*. New York: Viking, 1947.

Duffy, Michael F., and Willard Mittelman. "Nietzsche's Attitudes Toward the Jews." *Journal of the History of Ideas* 49.2 (1988): 301–17.

Dunwoodie, Peter. *Writing French Algeria*. Oxford: Clarendon, 1998.

Eiland, Howard. "Nietzsche's Jew." *Salmagundi* 66 (Winter–Spring 1985): 104–17.

Fabian, Johannes. *Time and the Other: How Anthropology Makes Its Object*. New York: Columbia University Press, 2002.

Fanon, Frantz. *Black Skin, White Masks*. Translated by Richard Philcox. New York: Grove, 2008.

Le Figaro. "L'Exemple du mort." 19 June 1896.

Finkelstein, Norman G. *Beyond Chutzpah: On the Misuse of Anti-Semitism and the Abuse of History*. Updated ed. Berkeley: University of California Press, 2008.

Finkielkraut, Alain. *Au nom de l'Autre: Réflexions sur l'antisémitisme qui vient*. Paris: Gallimard, 2003.

Forest, Louis. *La Naturalisation des juifs algériens et l'insurrection de 1871, étude historique*. Paris: Société française d'imprimerie et de librairie, 1897.

Forestier, Louis. Introduction to *Bel-Ami*, by Guy de Maupassant. In *Romans*, edited by Louis Forestier, 1324–41. Bibliothèque de la Pléiade. Paris: Gallimard, 1987.

Foucault, Michel. *"Society Must Be Defended": Lectures at the Collège de France, 1975–76*. Edited by Mauro Bertani and Alessandro Fontana. Translated by David Macey. New York: Picador, 2003.

Foxman, Abraham. *Never Again? The Threat of the New Anti-Semitism*. New York: Harper Collins, 2003.

Frankel, Jonathan. *The Damascus Affair: "Ritual" Murder, Politics, and the Jews in 1840*. Cambridge: Cambridge University Press, 1997.

Frondaie, Pierre. *L'Assassinat du Marquis de Morès*. Paris: Éditions Émile-Paul Frères, 1934.

Gallarotti, Giulio M. "The Scramble for Gold: Monetary Regimes Transformation in the 1870s." In *Monetary Regimes in Transition*, edited by Michael D. Bordo and Forrest Capie, 15–67. Cambridge: Cambridge University Press, 1993.

Ganiage, Jean. *Les Origines du Protectorat français en Tunisie, 1861–1881*. Paris: PUF, 1959.

Garros, Paul de. *La Revanche de l'honneur*. Limoges: Barbou, 1898.

Gautier, Léon. *La Chevalerie*. Paris: Delagrave, 1890.

Geisser, Vincent. *La Nouvelle islamophobie*. Paris: La Découverte, 2003.

Gilman, Sander. *Freud, Race, and Gender*. Princeton: Princeton University Press, 1993.

———. "Heine, Nietzsche and the Idea of the Jew." In *Nietzsche and Jewish Culture*, edited by Jacob Golomb, 76–100. New York: Routledge, 1997.

———. *The Jew's Body*. New York: Routledge, 1991.

Gilroy, Paul. *Postcolonial Melancholia*. New York: Columbia University Press, 2005.

Gines, Kathryn T. "Race Thinking and Racism in Hannah Arendt's *The Origins of Totalitarianism*." In *Hannah Arendt and the Uses of History: Imperialism, Nation, Race, and Genocide*, edited by Richard H. King and Dan Stone, 38–53. New York: Berghahn, 2008.

Girardet, Raoul. *L'Idée coloniale en France, 1871–1962*. Paris: La Table Ronde, 1972.

———. *L'Idée coloniale en France de 1871 à 1962*. Paris: Hachette, 2007.

Gobineau, Arthur de. *The Inequality of the Human Races*. Translated by Adrian Collins. New York: Fertig, 1999.

Graebner, Seth. *History's Place: Nostalgia and the City in French Algerian Literature*. Lanham, MD: Lexington, 2007.

Grant, Richard. "The Jewish Question in Zola's *L'Argent*." *PMLA* 70.5 (December 1955): 955–67.

Grosse, Pascal. "From Colonialism to National Socialism to Postcolonialism: Hannah Arendt's *Origins of Totalitarianism*." *Postcolonial Studies* 9.1 (2006): 35–52.

Guénif-Souilamas, Nacira. "Jews and Arabs in Postcolonial France: A Situated Account of a Long Painful Story of Intimacy." In *Israeli-Palestinian Conflict in the Francophone World*, edited by Nathalie Debrauwere-Miller, 193–206. New York: Routledge, 2010.

———. "Des opprimés se sont mués en oppresseurs de la pire espèce." *Le Monde*, 13 July 2004.

Hacking, Ian. *Historical Ontology*. Cambridge, MA: Harvard University Press, 2002.
Hammerschlag, Sarah. *The Figural Jew: Politics and Identity in Postwar French Thought*. Chicago: University of Chicago Press, 2010.
Harvey, David. *Spaces of Capital: Towards a Critical Geography*. New York: Routledge, 2001.
Herod, Andrew. *Scale*. New York: Routledge, 2011.
Hertzberg, Arthur. *The French Enlightenment and the Jews*. New York: Columbia University Press, 1968.
Heschel, Susannah. *Abraham Geiger and the Jewish Jesus*. Chicago: University of Chicago Press, 1998.
Hess, Jean. "Le Massacre de la mission Morès." *Le Figaro*, 19 June 1896.
Hess, Jonathan M. *Germans, Jews and the Claims of Modernity*. New Haven: Yale University Press, 2002.
Hirshfield, Claire. "The Anglo-Boer War and the Issue of Jewish Culpability." *Journal of Contemporary History* 15.4 (1980): 619–31.
Hobson, J. A. "Capitalism and Imperialism in South Africa." *Contemporary Review* 77 (1900): 1–17.
———. *Imperialism: A Study*. 1905. 2nd ed. New York: Cosimo, 2005.
———. *The War in South Africa: Its Causes and Effects*. London: James Nisbet, 1900.
Holmes, Colin. *Anti-Semitism in British Society, 1876–1939*. New York: Holmes and Meier, 1979.
Holub, Robert C. "Nietzsche and the Jewish Question." *New German Critique* 22.3 (1995): 94–121.
———. "Nietzsche's Colonialist Imagination: Nueva Germania, Good Europeanism, and Great Politics." In *The Imperialist Imagination: German Colonialism and Its Legacy*, edited by Sara Friedrichsmeyer, Sara Lennox, and Susanne Zantop, 33–49. Ann Arbor: University of Michigan Press, 1999.
Horkheimer, Max, and Theodor W. Adorno. *Dialectic of Enlightenment*. Translated by John Cumming. New York: Continuum, 1995.
———. *Dialectic of Enlightenment: Philosophical Fragments*. Translated by Edmund Jephcott. Edited by Gunzelin Schmid Noerr. Stanford: Stanford University Press, 2002.
Hyman, Paula. *The Jews of Modern France*. Berkeley: University of California Press, 1998.
L'Intransigeant. Transcript of Rochefort libel suit. 15 December 1881.
Jameson, Fredric. *The Geopolitical Aesthetic: Cinema and Space in the World System*. Bloomington: Indiana University Press, 1992.
———. "Marx's Purloined Letter." In *Ghostly Demarcations: A Symposium on Jacques Derrida's "Specters of Marx,"* edited by Michael Sprinker, 26–67. London: Verso, 2008.
———. "Modernism and Imperialism." In *Nationalism, Colonialism, and Literature*, by Terry Eagleton, Fredric Jameson, and Edward W. Said, 43–66. Minneapolis: University of Minnesota Press, 1990.
Jennings, Eric. *Vichy in the Tropics: Pétain's National Revolution in*

Madagascar, Guadeloupe, and Indochina, 1940–44. Stanford: Stanford University Press, 2001.

Judaken, Jonathan. "Between Philosemitism and Antisemitism: The Frankfurt School's Anti-Antisemitism." In *Antisemitism and Philosemitism in the Twentieth and Twenty-First Centuries: Representing Jews, Jewishness, and Modern Culture*, edited by Phyllis Lassner and Lara Trubowitz, 23–46. Newark: University of Delaware Press, 2008.

———. *Jean-Paul Sartre and the Jewish Question: Anti-Antisemitism and the Politics of the French Intellectual*. Lincoln: University of Nebraska Press, 2006.

La Justice. "Discours de M. Clemenceau." 9 November 1881.

Kalman, Julie. *Orientalizing the Jew: Religion, Culture and Imperialism in Nineteenth-Century France*. Bloomington: Indiana University Press, 2017.

———. *Rethinking Antisemitism in Nineteenth-Century France*. Cambridge: Cambridge University Press, 2010.

Kalmar, Ivan Davidson, and Derek J. Penslar. "Orientalism and the Jews: An Introduction." In *Orientalism and the Jews*, ed. Ivan Davidson Kalmar and Derek J. Penslar, xiii–xl. Waltham, MA: Brandeis University Press, 2005.

———, eds. *Orientalism and the Jews*. Waltham, MA: Brandeis University Press, 2005.

Karabell, Zachary. *Parting the Desert: The Creation of the Suez Canal*. New York: Vintage, 2003.

Kateb, George. *Hannah Arendt: Politics, Conscience, Evil*. Totowa, NJ: Rowman and Allanheld, 1983.

Katz, Ethan B. *The Burdens of Brotherhood: Jews and Muslims from North Africa to France*. Cambridge, MA: Harvard University Press, 2015.

Katz, Ethan B., Lisa Moses Leff, and Maud S. Mandel, eds. *Colonialism and the Jews*. Bloomington: Indiana University Press, 2017.

Katz, Jacob. *From Prejudice to Destruction: Anti-Semitism, 1700–1933*. Cambridge, MA: Harvard University Press, 1980.

Katz, Jonathan G. "The 1907 Mauchamp Affair and the French Civilizing Mission in Morocco." *Journal of North African Studies* 6.1 (2001): 143–66.

Kauffmann, Grégoire. *Edouard Drumont*. Paris: Perrin, 2008.

Kaufmann, Walter. *Nietzsche: Philosopher, Psychologist, Antichrist*. 4th ed. Princeton: Princeton University Press, 1974.

Kennedy, Ellen. "Carl Schmitt and the Frankfurt School." *Telos* 71 (1987): 37–66.

Kim, Claire Jean. "The Racial Triangulation of Asian Americans." *Politics and Society* 27.1 (1999): 105–38.

King, Richard H., and Dan Stone, eds. *Hannah Arendt and the Uses of History: Imperialism, Nation, Race, and Genocide*. New York: Berghahn, 2008.

———. Introduction to *Hannah Arendt and the Uses of History: Imperialism,*

Nation, Race, and Genocide, edited by Richard H. King and Dan Stone, 1–17. New York: Berghahn, 2008.

Klug, Brian. "A Contradiction in the 'New Europe.'" In *Anti-Semitism and Islamophobia: Hatreds Old and New in Europe*, edited by Matti Bunzl, 54–60. Chicago: Prickly Paradigm Press, 2007.

———. "The Myth of the New Anti-Semitism." *The Nation*, 2 February 2004.

Knight, Diana. "Muslims Are the New Jews." *The Sunday Times*, 15 October 2006.

Knodt, Eva M. "The Janus Face of Decadence: Nietzsche's Genealogy and the Rhetoric of Anti-Semitism." *German Quarterly* 66.2 (1993): 160–75.

Kofman, Sarah. *Le Mépris des Juifs: Nietzsche, les Juifs, l'antisémitisme*. Paris: Galilée, 1994.

Kohn, Jerome. "Arendt's Concept and Description of Totalitarianism." *Social Research* 69.2 (2002): 621–56.

Kristeva, Julia. *Powers of Horror: An Essay on Abjection*. Translated by Leon S. Roudiez. New York: Columbia University Press, 1982.

Lacoue-Labarthe, Philippe. *La Fiction du politique: Heidegger, l'art et la politique*. Paris: Bourgois, 1998.

Langbehn, Volker, and Mohammad Salama. "Introduction: Reconfiguring German Colonialism." In *German Colonialism: Race, the Holocaust, and Postwar Germany*, edited by Volker Langbehn and Mohammad Salama, ix–xxxi. New York: Columbia University Press, 2011.

Lanoux, Armand. *Maupassant le Bel-Ami*. Paris: Grasset, 1979.

Laqueur, Walter. "The Arendt Cult: Hannah Arendt as Political Commentator." *Journal of Contemporary History* 33.4 (1998): 483–96.

———. *The Changing Face of Anti-Semitism: From Ancient Times to the Present Day*. Oxford: Oxford University Press, 2006.

Lebovics, Herman. *Imperialism and the Corruption of Democracies*. Durham: Duke University Press, 2006.

Leff, Lisa Moses. *Sacred Bonds of Solidarity: The Rise of Jewish Internationalism in Nineteenth-Century France*. Stanford: Stanford University Press, 2006.

Lemonnier, Marie. "Juifs et musulmans, frères ennemis?" *Le Nouvel Observateur*, 5 July 2012.

Léoville. "La Mort du Marquis de Morès." *La Libre parole illustrée*, 27 June 1896.

Lewis, Bernard. *Semites and Anti-Semites: An Inquiry into Conflict and Prejudice*. New York: Norton, 1999.

Lewis, David Levering. *The Race to Fashoda: European Colonialism and African Resistance in the Scramble for Africa*. New York: Weidenfeld and Nicholson, 1987.

Libération. "Transcription des conversations entre Mohammed Merah et les négociateurs." 17 July 2012. Web.

La Libre parole. "Les Juifs d'Algérie." 3 January 1896.

Lindemann, Albert S. *Esau's Tears: Modern Anti-Semitism and the Rise of the Jews*. Cambridge: Cambridge University Press, 1997.

Lorcin, Patricia. *Imperial Identities: Stereotyping, Prejudice and Race in Colonial Algeria*. London: I. B. Tauris, 1999.

Loutfi, Martine Astier. *Littérature et colonialisme: L'expansion coloniale vue dans la littérature romanesque française, 1871–1914*. Paris: Mouton, 1971.

Lowe, Lisa. *The Intimacies of Four Continents*. Durham: Duke University Press, 2015.

Lukács, Georg. *Writer and Critic and Other Essays*. Translated by Arthur Kahn. Lincoln: Authors Guild, 2005.

Lyotard, Jean-François. *Heidegger and "the jews."* Translated by Andreas Mitchell and Mark Roberts. Minneapolis: University of Minnesota Press, 1990.

Majid, Anouar. *We Are All Moors: Ending Centuries of Crusades Against Muslims and Other Minorities*. Minneapolis: University of Minnesota Press, 2009.

Mandel, Maud S. *Muslims and Jews in France: History of a Conflict*. Princeton: Princeton University Press, 2014.

Ma'oz, Moshe. Introduction to *Muslim Attitudes to Jews and Israel: The Ambivalences of Rejection, Antagonism, Intolerance, and Cooperation*, edited by Moshe Ma'oz, 1–28. Portland: Sussex Academic Press, 2010.

Marx, Karl. "On the Jewish Question." In *Early Writings*, translated by Rodney Livingstone and Gregor Benton, 211–41. London: Penguin, 1992.

Marx, Karl, and Frederick Engels. *On Colonialism: Articles from the "New York Tribune" and Other Writings*. New York: International Publishers, 1972.

Maupassant, Guy de. *Au soleil*. In *Maupassant au Maghreb*, edited by Denise Brahimi. Paris: Le Sycomore, 1982.

———. *Bel-Ami*. Paris: Gallimard, 1973.

———. *Chroniques*. Edited by Gérard Delaisement. 2 vols. Paris: Rive Droite, 2003.

Maurceley, Baude de. *Amour et gloire, roman franco-saharien*. Paris: Garnier Frères, 1897.

Maurras, Charles. *L'Avenir de l'intelligence*. Paris: Flammarion, 1927.

———. *Kiel et Tanger, 1895–1905: La République française devant l'Europe*. Paris: Nouvelle librairie nationale, 1921.

Mayer, Nonna. "Nouvelle judéophobie ou vieil antisémitisme?" *Raisons politiques* 4.16 (2004): 91–103.

McClintock, Anne. *Imperial Leather: Race, Gender and Sexuality in the Colonial Conquest*. New York: Routledge, 1995.

Mehlman, Jeffrey. "A New Judeocentrism? On a Recent Trend in French Thought." In *Israeli-Palestinian Conflict in the Francophone World*, edited by Nathalie Debrauwere-Miller, 209–21. New York: Routledge, 2010.

Memmi, Albert. *The Colonizer and the Colonized*. Translated by Howard Greenfeld. Boston: Beacon, 1991.

Meynié, Georges. *L'Algérie juive*. Paris: Savine, 1887.

Michel, Marc. *La Mission Marchand, 1895–99*. Paris: Mouton, 1972.

Mignolo, Walter. "Globalization, Civilization Processes, and the Relocation of Languages and Cultures." In *The Cultures of Globalization*, edited by Fredric Jameson and Masao Miyoshi, 32–53. Durham: Duke University Press, 1998.

Milner, Jean-Claude. *Les Penchants criminels de l'Europe démocratique*. Paris: Verdier, 2003.

Mitterand, Henri. Introduction to *L'Argent*, by Émile Zola. In *Les Rougon-Macquart*, edited by Henri Mitterand, 5:1225–89. Bibliothèque de la Pléiade. Paris: Gallimard, 1967.

———. *Zola, tome 3: L'Honneur, 1893–1902*. Paris: Fayard, 2002.

Morès, Marquis de. "Lettre ouverte à M. Casimir-Perier, Président de la République française." *Lettres au peuple*, 11 January 1894.

———. *Rothschild, Ravachol & Cie*. Paris: Hayard, 1892.

Moruzzi, Norma Claire. *Speaking Through the Mask: Hannah Arendt and the Politics of Social Identity*. Ithaca, NY: Cornell University Press, 2000.

Moses, A. Dirk. "Hannah Arendt, Imperialisms, and the Holocaust." In *German Colonialism: Race, the Holocaust, and Postwar Germany*, edited by Volker Langbehn and Mohammad Salama, 72–92. New York: Columbia University Press, 2011.

Mosse, George. *The Crisis of German Ideology: Intellectual Origins of the Third Reich*. New York: Howard Fertig, 1964.

Mufti, Amir. *Enlightenment in the Colony: The Jewish Question and the Crisis of Postcolonial Culture*. Princeton: Princeton University Press, 2007.

Nietzsche, Friedrich. *The Antichrist*, *The Portable Nietzsche*. Edited and translated by Walter Kaufmann. New York: Penguin, 1968.

———. *Beyond Good and Evil*, *Basic Writings of Nietzsche*. Edited and translated by Walter Kaufmann. New York: Modern Library, 2000.

———. *Daybreak: Thoughts on the Prejudices of Morality*. Edited by Maudemarie Clark and Brian Leiter. Translated by R. J. Hollingdale. Cambridge: Cambridge University Press, 1997.

———. *The Gay Science*. Edited and translated by Walter Kaufmann. New York: Vintage, 1974.

———. *On the Genealogy of Morals*, *Basic Writings of Nietzsche*. Edited and translated by Walter Kaufmann. New York: Modern Library, 2000.

———. *Human, All-Too-Human*, *The Portable Nietzsche*. Edited and translated by Walter Kaufmann. New York: Penguin, 1968.

———. *Selected Letters of Friedrich Nietzsche*. Edited and translated by Christopher Middleton. Indianapolis: Hackett, 1996.

———. *Untimely Meditations*. Edited by Daniel Breazale. Translated by R. J. Hollingdale. Cambridge: Cambridge University Press, 1997.

———. *The Will to Power*. Edited by Walter Kaufmann. Translated by Walter Kaufmann and R. J. Hollingdale. New York: Vintage, 1968.

Nirenberg, David. *Anti-Judaism: The Western Tradition*. New York: Norton, 2013.

———. *Communities of Violence: Persecution of Minorities in the Middle Ages*. Princeton: Princeton University Press, 1996.

Noir, Louis. *La Banque juive*. Paris: Ducher, 1888.

———. *Le Massacre de l'expédition du Marquis de Morès*. Paris: Fayard, 1896.

Nolte, Ernst. *Three Faces of Fascism: Action Française, Italian Fascism, National Socialism*. Translated by Leila Vennewitz. New York: Holt, Rinehart and Winston, 1966.

Norton, Anne. "Heart of Darkness: Africa and African Americans in the Writings of Hannah Arendt." In *Feminist Interpretations of Hannah Arendt*, edited by Bonnie Honig, 247–62. University Park: Pennsylvania State University Press, 1995.

Nye, Robert A. *Crime, Madness and Politics in Modern France: The Medical Concept of National Decline*. Princeton: Princeton University Press, 1984.

Olender, Maurice. *The Languages of Paradise: Race, Religion, and Philology in the Nineteenth Century*. Translated by Arthur Goldhammer. Cambridge, MA: Harvard University Press, 2008.

Ory, Pascal, and Jean-François Sirinelli. *Les Intellectuels en France: De l'affaire Dreyfus à nos jours*. Paris: Perrin, 2004.

Owens, Patricia. "The Return of Realism? War and Changing Concepts of the Political." In *The Changing Character of War*, edited by Hew Strachan and Sybille Scheipers, 484–502. Oxford: Oxford University Press, 2011.

Parekh, Bikhu. "Hannah Arendt's Critique of Marx." In *Hannah Arendt: The Recovery of the Public World*, edited by Melvyn A. Hill, 67–100. New York: St. Martin's, 1979.

Parfitt, Tudor. "The Use of the Jew in Colonial Discourse." In *Orientalism and the Jews*, ed. Ivan Davidson Kalmar and Derek J. Penslar, 51–67. Waltham, MA: Brandeis University Press, 2005.

Pascal, Félicien. *L'Assassinat de Morès: Un crime d'état*. Paris: Hardy et Bernard, 1902.

Pavy, Auguste. *L'Expédition de Morès*. Paris: André, 1897.

Pelletan, Camille. "Lettres de Tunis." *La Justice*, 27 October 1881.

———. "La Question tunisienne." *La Justice*, 31 October 1881.

———. "La Question tunisienne." *La Justice*, 2 November 1881.

Pemjean, Lucien. "Supplément illustré." *La Libre parole*, 29 May 1899.

Pick, Daniel. *Faces of Degeneration: A European Disorder c. 1848–1918*. Cambridge: Cambridge University Press, 1989.

Pietz, William. "The 'Post-Colonialism' of Cold War Discourse." *Social Text* 19–20 (1988): 55–75.

Pitkin, Hanna Fenichel. "Conformism, Housekeeping, and the Attack of the Blob: The Origins of Hannah Arendt's Concept of the Social." In *Feminist Interpretations of Hannah Arendt*, edited by Bonnie Honig, 51–81. University Park: Pennsylvania State University Press, 1995.

———. "Justice: On Relating Private and Public." *Political Theory* 9.3 (1981): 327–52.

Le Point. "Nicolas Sarkozy suspend sa participation à la campagne." 19 March 2012. Web.

Poliakov, Léon. "L'antisémitisme est-il un racisme?" In *Racisme et modernité*, edited by Michel Wieviorka, 82–84. Paris: La Découverte, 1993.

———. *La Causalité diabolique.* Paris: Calmann-Lévy, 2006.

———. *Histoire de l'antisémitisme. 2: L'âge de la science.* Paris: Calmann-Lévy, 1981.

———. *The History of Anti-Semitism.* Vol. 4, *Suicidal Europe, 1870–1933.* Translated by George Klin. Philadelphia: University of Pennsylvania Press, 2003.

Polignac, Ludovic de. "A Propos du traité de Ghadamès." *Le Temps*, 16 June 1893.

———. *France et Islam.* Algiers: Remordet, 1893.

Postone, Moishe. "Anti-Semitism and National Socialism: Notes on the German Reaction to 'Holocaust.'" *New German Critique* 19 (1980): 97–115.

Prague, Hippolyte. "La Question du Maroc et les Juifs." *Archives Israélites*, 8 August 1907.

Pratt, Mary Louise. *Imperial Eyes: Travel Writing and Transculturation.* 2nd ed. New York: Routledge, 2008.

Presbey, Gail. "Critic of Boers or Africans? Arendt's Treatment of South Africa in *The Origins of Totalitarianism.*" In *Postcolonial African Philosophy: A Critical Reader*, edited by Emmanuel Chukwudi Eze, 162–80. Oxford: Blackwell, 1997.

Prince, Gerald. "Bel-Ami and Narrative as Antagonist." *French Forum* 11.2 (1986): 217–26.

Rabinbach, Anson. "Why Were the Jews Sacrificed? The Place of Anti-Semitism in *Dialectic of Enlightenment.*" *New German Critique* 81 (2000): 49–64.

Rabinow, Paul. *French Modern: Norms and Forms of the Social Environment.* Chicago: University of Chicago Press, 1995.

Randau, Robert. *Les Colons: Roman de la patrie algérienne.* Paris: Sansot, 1907.

Renan, Ernest. *La Réforme intellectuelle et morale, Oeuvres completes.* 3 vols. Paris: Calmann-Lévy, 1947–61.

Rich, Adrienne. *On Lies, Secrets, and Silence: Selected Prose, 1966–1978.* New York: W. W. Norton, 1979.

Ricoeur, Paul. *Time and Narrative.* Translated by Kathleen McLaughlin and David Pellauer. 3 vols. Chicago: University of Chicago Press, 1984.

Ring, Jennifer. "On Needing Both Marx and Arendt: Alienation and the Flight from Inwardness." *Political Theory* 17.3 (1989): 432–48.

Robinson, Cedric J. *Black Marxism: The Making of the Black Radical Tradition.* Chapel Hill: University of North Carolina Press, 2000.

Rochefort, Henri. "L'Adhésion des puissances." *L'Intransigeant*, 25 April 1881.

———. *Les Aventures de ma vie.* 5 vols. Paris: Dupont, 1896.

———. "Le Dessous des cartes." *L'Intransigeant*, 3 July 1881.

———. "Le Secret de l'affaire tunisienne." *L'Intransigeant*, 27 September 1881.

Rodrigue, Aron. *French Jews, Turkish Jews: The Alliance israélite universelle and the Politics of Jewish Schooling in Turkey, 1860–1925.* Bloomington: Indiana University Press, 1990.

Rothberg, Michael. *Multidirectional Memory: Remembering the Holocaust in the Age of Decolonization.* Stanford: Stanford University Press, 2009.

Rudd, Paul. *La Libre parole illustrée*, 22 August 1896.

Said, Edward. *Orientalism.* New York: Vintage, 1979.

Samuels, Maurice. *The Right to Difference: French Universalism and the Jews.* Chicago: University of Chicago Press, 2016.

Santaniello, Weaver. *Nietzsche, God, and the Jews: His Critique of Judeo-Christianity in Relation to the Nazi Myth.* Albany: State University of New York Press, 1994.

Sartre, Jean-Paul. *Anti-Semite and Jew.* Translated by George J. Becker. New York: Schocken, 1995.

———. *Colonialism and Neocolonialism.* Translated by Azzedine Haddour, Steve Brewer, and Terry McWilliams. New York: Routledge, 2006.

Schivelbusch, Wolfgang. *The Culture of Defeat.* Translated by Jefferson Chase. New York: Picador, 2003.

Schmitt, Carl. *The* Nomos *of the Earth in the International Law of the* Jus Publicum Europaeum. Translated by G. L. Ulmen. New York: Telos, 2006.

———. *Political Theology: Four Chapters on the Concept of Sovereignty.* Translated by George Schwab. Chicago: University of Chicago Press, 2005.

Scholem, Gershom. "*Eichmann in Jerusalem*: An Exchange of Letters Between Gershom Scholem and Hannah Arendt." In *The Jew as Pariah: Jewish Identity and Politics in the Modern Age*, by Hannah Arendt, 240–51. Edited by Ron H. Feldman. New York: Grove, 1978.

Schreier, Joshua. *Arabs of the Jewish Faith: The Civilizing Mission in Colonial Algeria.* New Brunswick, NJ: Rutgers University Press, 2010.

Schwab, Raymond. *La Renaissance orientale.* New York: AMS, 1977.

Segré, Ivan. *La Réaction philosémite, ou, La Trahison des clercs.* Paris: Lignes, 2009.

Serres, Michel. *Feux et signaux de brume, Zola.* Paris: Grasset, 1975.

Shih, Shu-Mei. "Comparative Racialization: An Introduction." *PMLA* 123.5 (2008): 1347–62.

Singer, Barnett, and John Langdon. *Cultured Force: Makers and Defenders of the French Colonial Empire.* Madison: University of Wisconsin Press, 2004.

Smith, Neil. *Uneven Development: Nature, Capital, and the Production of Space.* 3rd ed. Athens: University of Georgia Press, 2008.

Soja, Edward W. *Postmodern Geographies: The Reassertion of Space in Critical Social Theory.* London: Verso, 1989.

Stein, Sarah Abrevaya. *Saharan Jews and the Fate of French Algeria.* Chicago: University of Chicago Press, 2014.

Steins, Martin. "Zola colonialiste." *Revue des langues vivantes* 41 (1975): 15–30.

Sternhell, Zeev. *La Droite révolutionnaire, 1885–1914: Les origines françaises du fascisme.* Paris: Fayard, 2000.

———. *Maurice Barrès et le nationalisme français.* Paris: Fayard, 2000.

Stoetzler, Marcel. "Anti-Semitism, the Bourgeoisie, and the Self-Destruction of the Nation-State." In *Hannah Arendt and the Uses of History: Imperialism, Nation, Race, and Genocide*, edited by Richard H. King and Dan Stone, 130–46. New York: Berghahn, 2008.

Stoler, Ann Laura. *Race and the Education of Desire: Foucault's "History of Sexuality" and the Colonial Order of Things*. Durham: Duke University Press, 1995.

———. "Sexual Affronts and Racial Frontiers: European Identities and the Cultural Politics of Exclusion in Colonial Southeast Asia." In *Tensions of Empire: Colonial Cultures in a Bourgeois World*, edited by Ann Laura Stoler and Frederick Cooper, 198–237. Berkeley: University of California Press, 1997.

Stoler, Ann Laura, and Frederick Cooper. "Between Metropole and Colony: Rethinking a Research Agenda." In *Tensions of Empire: Colonial Cultures in a Bourgeois World*, edited by Ann Laura Stoler and Frederick Cooper, 1–56. Berkeley: University of California Press, 1997.

Sud-Ouest. "Toulouse: Que sait-on du tueur à scooter?" 20 March 2012. Web.

Sutton, Michael. *Nationalism, Positivism and Catholicism: The Politics of Charles Maurras and French Catholics, 1890–1914*. Cambridge: Cambridge University Press, 1982.

Taguieff, Pierre-André. *La Judéophobie des modernes: Des Lumières au Jihad mondial*. Paris: Odile Jacob, 2008.

———. *Rising from the Muck: The New Anti-Semitism in Europe*. Translated by Patrick Camiller. Chicago: Dee, 2004.

Taïeb, Jacques. "Tumulte autour d'un décret: Le décret Crémieux ou la première logique colonial." *Les nouveaux cahiers* 123 (1995/96): 69–79.

Taine, Hippolyte. *Histoire de la littérature anglaise*. 4 vols. Paris: Hachette, 1863–64.

Terdiman, Richard. *Discourse/Counter-discourse: The Theory and Practice of Symbolic Resistance in Nineteenth-Century France*. Ithaca, NY: Cornell University Press, 1985.

Tocqueville, Alexis de. *The Ancien Régime and the Revolution*. 1856. Translated and edited by Gerald Bevan. London: Penguin, 2008.

Todorov, Tzvetan. *On Human Diversity: Nationalism, Racism, and Exoticism in French Thought*. Translated by Catherine Porter. Cambridge, MA: Harvard University Press, 1993.

Toussenel, Alphonse. *Les Juifs, rois de l'époque: Histoire de la féodalité financière*. Paris: Librairie de l'école sociétaire, 1845.

Traverso, Enzo. *The End of Jewish Modernity*. Translated by David Fernbach. London: Pluto, 2016.

———. *The Origins of Nazi Violence*. Translated by Janet Lloyd. New York: The New Press, 2003.

Trigano, Shmuel. *La Démission de la République: Juifs et Musulmans en France*. Paris: Presses Universitaires de France, 2003.

Tvedt, Terje. *The River Nile in the Age of the British: Political Ecology and the Quest for Economic Power*. London: I. B. Taurus, 2004.

Tweton, Jerome. *The Marquis de Morès: Dakota Capitalist, French Nationalist.* Fargo: North Dakota Institute for Regional Studies, 1972.

Vernier, H. "La Capitulation de la France—L'Abandon de Fachoda." *La Libre parole*, 5 November 1898.

Vial, André. *Guy de Maupassant et l'art du roman.* Paris: Nizet, 1954.

Vogüé, Melchior de. *Heures d'histoire.* Paris: Colin, 1893.

———. *Le Maître de la mer.* Paris: Plon-Nourrit, 1903.

———. *Les Morts qui parlent.* Paris: Plon, 1899.

———. Preamble to *Un siècle, mouvement du monde de 1800 à 1900*, edited by Ludovico Péchenard, ix–xxvi. Paris: Oudin, 1900.

———. "Réponse de M. le vicomte de Vogüé au discours de M. Maurice Barrès." Speech. Palais de L'Institut, Paris, 17 January 1907. Available on the website of the Académie Française.

———. *Spectacles contemporains.* Paris: Colin, 1891.

Wasserstein, Bernard. "Blame the Victim—Hannah Arendt Among the Nazis: The Historian and Her Sources." *Times Literary Supplement*, 9 October 2009.

Weill, Nicolas. *La République et les antisémites.* Paris: Grasset, 2004.

Weill-Raynal, Guillaume. *Une haine imaginaire?: Contre-enquête sur le "nouvel antisémitisme."* Paris: Colin, 2005.

Weintraub, Stanley. *Disraeli: A Biography.* New York: Truman Talley, 1993.

Wheatcroft, Geoffrey. *The Randlords: The Exploits and Exploitations of South Africa's Mining Magnates.* New York: Atheneum, 1986.

White, Nicholas. *The Family in Crisis in Late Nineteenth-Century French Fiction.* Cambridge: Cambridge University Press, 2006.

Wieviorka, Michel. *L'Antisémitisme est-il de retour?* Paris: Larousse, 2008.

———. *The Lure of Anti-Semitism: Hatred of Jews in Present-Day France.* Translated by Kristin Couper Lobel and Anna Declerck. Leiden: Brill, 2007.

———. *Le Racisme, une introduction.* Paris: La Découverte, 1998.

Wilson, Stephen. *Ideology and Experience: Antisemitism in France at the Time of the Dreyfus Affair.* Oxford: Littman Library of Jewish Civilization, 2007.

Winock, Michel. *La France et les Juifs de 1789 à nos jours.* Paris: Seuil, 2004.

———. *La France politique, XIXe–XXe siècle.* Paris: Seuil, 2003.

———. *Nationalisme, antisémitisme et fascisme en France.* Paris: Seuil, 2004.

Wistrich, Robert. *Laboratory for World Destruction: Germans and Jews in Central Europe.* Lincoln: University of Nebraska Press, 2007.

Wood, Nancy. *Vectors of Memory: Legacies of Trauma in Postwar Europe.* Oxford: Berg, 1999.

Wright, Gwendolyn. *The Politics of Design in French Colonial Urbanism.* Chicago: University of Chicago Press, 1991.

Wurmser, André. Preface to *L'Argent*, by Émile Zola, 7–37. Paris: Gallimard, 1980.

Young-Bruehl, Elisabeth. *Hannah Arendt: For Love of the World.* New Haven: Yale University Press, 2004.

Yovel, Yirmiyahu. *Dark Riddle: Hegel, Nietzsche, and the Jews*. Cambridge: Polity, 1998.

Zemouri, Aziz, and Jean-Michel Décugis. "Une piste néonazie." *Le Point*, 19 March 2012. Web.

Zimmerer, Jürgen. "The Birth of the *Ostland* out of the Spirit of Colonialism: A Postcolonial Perspective on the Nazi Policy of Conquest and Extermination." In *Colonialism and Genocide*, edited by A. Dirk Moses and Dan Stone, 101–23. London: Routledge, 2007.

———. "Colonialism and the Holocaust: Towards an Archeology of Genocide." In *Genocide and Settler Society: Frontier Violence and Stolen Indigenous Children in Australian History*, edited by A. Dirk Moses, 49–76. New York: Berghahn, 2004.

Žižek, Slavoj. *The Parallax View*. Cambridge, MA: MIT Press, 2009.

Zola, Émile. *L'Argent*. In *Les Rougon-Macquart*, edited by Henri Mitterand, 5:11–398. Bibliothèque de la Pléiade. Paris: Gallimard, 1967.

———. *La Curée*. In *Les Rougon-Macquart*, edited by Henri Mitterand, 1:319–599. Bibliothèque de la Pléiade. Paris: Gallimard, 1960.

———. *La Débâcle*. In *Les Rougon-Macquart*, edited by Henri Mitterand, 5:403–912. Bibliothèque de la Pléiade. Paris: Gallimard, 1967.

———. *Fécondité*. In *Œuvres complètes*, edited by Henri Mitterand, 18:21–396. Paris: Nouveau Monde, 2008.

———. "Lettre à la France." In *Œuvres complètes*, edited by Henri Mitterand, 18:431–37. Paris: Nouveau Monde, 2008.

———. "Lettre à la jeunesse." In *Œuvres complètes*, edited by Henri Mitterand, 18:426–31. Paris: Nouveau Monde, 2008.

———. *Paris*. In *Œuvres complètes*, edited by Henri Mitterand, 17:23–332. Paris: Nouveau Monde, 2008.

———. "Pour *Justice*." In *Œuvres complètes*, edited by Henri Mitterand, 20:397–400. Paris: Nouveau Monde, 2009.

———. "Pour les juifs." In *Œuvres complètes*, edited by Henri Mitterand, 17:427–30. Paris: Nouveau Monde, 2008.

———. "À propos de l'antisémitisme." In *Œuvres complètes*, edited by Henri Mitterand, 18:590–94. Paris: Nouveau Monde, 2008.

———. *Son Excellence Eugène Rougon*. In *Les Rougon-Macquart*, edited by Henri Mitterand, 2:14–369. Bibliothèque de la Pléiade. Paris: Gallimard, 1961.

———. *Vérité*. In *Œuvres complètes*, edited by Henri Mitterand, 20:19–392. Paris: Nouveau Monde, 2009.

Index

FLASHPOINTS

1. *On Pain of Speech: Fantasies of the First Order and the Literary Rant,* Dina Al-Kassim
2. *Moses and Multiculturalism,* Barbara Johnson, with a foreword by Barbara Rietveld
3. *The Cosmic Time of Empire: Modern Britain and World Literature,* Adam Barrows
4. *Poetry in Pieces: César Vallejo and Lyric Modernity,* Michelle Clayton
5. *Disarming Words: Empire and the Seductions of Translation in Egypt,* Shaden M. Tageldin
6. *Wings for Our Courage: Gender, Erudition, and Republican Thought,* Stephanie H. Jed
7. *The Cultural Return,* Susan Hegeman
8. *English Heart, Hindi Heartland: The Political Life of Literature in India,* Rashmi Sadana
9. *The Cylinder: Kinematics of the Nineteenth Century,* Helmut Müller-Sievers
10. *Polymorphous Domesticities: Pets, Bodies, and Desire in Four Modern Writers,* Juliana Schiesari
11. *Flesh and Fish Blood: Postcolonialism, Translation, and the Vernacular,* S. Shankar
12. *The Fear of French Negroes: Transcolonial Collaboration in the Revolutionary Americas,* Sara E. Johnson
13. *Figurative Inquisitions: Conversion, Torture, and Truth in the Luso-Hispanic Atlantic,* Erin Graff Zivin
14. *Cosmopolitan Desires: Global Modernity and World Literature in Latin America,* Mariano Siskind
15. *Fiction Beyond Secularism,* Justin Neuman
16. *Periodizing Jameson: Dialectics, the University, and the Desire for Narrative,* Phillip E. Wegner
17. *The Practical Past,* Hayden White
18. *The Powers of the False: Reading, Writing, Thinking Beyond Truth and Fiction,* Doro Wiese
19. *The Object of the Atlantic: Concrete Aesthetics in Cuba, Brazil, and Spain, 1868–1968,* Rachel Price
20. *Epic and Exile: Novels of the German Popular Front, 1933–1945,* Hunter Bivens
21. *An Innocent Abroad: Lectures in China,* J. Hillis Miller
22. *Form and Instability: East Europe, Literature, Postimperial Difference,* Anita Starosta
23. *Bombay Modern: Arun Kolatkar and Bilingual Literary Culture,* Anjali Nerlekar
24. *Intimate Relations: Social Reform and the Late Nineteenth-Century South Asian Novel,* Krupa Shandilya
25. *Media Laboratories: Late Modernist Authorship in South America,* Sarah Ann Wells

26. *Acoustic Properties: Radio, Narrative, and the New Neighborhood of the Americas*, Tom McEnaney
27. *The New Woman: Literary Modernism, Queer Theory, and the Trans Feminine Allegory*, Emma Heaney
28. *Civilizing War: Imperial Politics and the Poetics of National Rupture*, Nasser Mufti
29. *Late Colonial Sublime: Neo-Epics and the End of Romanticism*, G. S. Sahota
30. *Globalizing Race: Antisemitism and Empire in French and European Culture*, Dorian Bell